PELICAN BOOKS

THE CHURCHES SEARCH
FOR UNITY

Barry Till was born in 1923 and educated at Harrow
and Jesus College, Cambridge, where he read history
and theology. In 1949 he was awarded the Cambridge
University Lightfoot Scholarship in ecclesiastical history with special commendation. During the last war
he served with the Coldstream Guards in Italy. From
1950 to 1953 he was curate of Bury parish church,
Lancashire. From 1953 to 1960 he was Fellow, Dean
and latterly Tutor of Jesus College, Cambridge;
and from 1960 to 1964 he was Dean of St John's
Cathedral, Hong Kong. He was vice-chairman of
the Hong Kong Christian Council and chairman
of many ecumenical committees including those on
church and school planning, broadcasting and tele-
vision, and the joint theological college. From 1964 to
1965 he was temporarily attached to the Missionary
and Ecumenical Council of the Church of England.
Since 1965 he has been Principal of Morley College,
London.

Barry Till is married and has four children. He
lives in Islington and has a cottage in North Norfolk.
He has written *Change and Exchange* (1964), *Changing Frontiers in the Mission of the Church* (1965),
and was a contributor to the *Historic Episcopate*
(1954).

Barry Till

THE CHURCHES SEARCH
FOR UNITY

Penguin Books

Penguin Books Ltd, Harmondsworth, Middlesex, England
Penguin Books Inc, 7110 Ambassador Road, Baltimore, Maryland 21207, U.S.A.
Penguin Books Australia Ltd, Ringwood, Victoria, Australia

—

First published 1972

—

Copyright © Barry Till, 1972

—

Made and printed in Great Britain
by Richard Clay (The Chaucer Press), Ltd,
Bungay, Suffolk
Set in Linotype Baskerville

To Ken Carey
Bishop of Edinburgh
with
Gratitude, Affection and Respect

Contents

Preface

There was another stillness – broken at last by two persons in conversation somewhere without.

'They are talking about us, no doubt!' moaned Sue. 'We are made a spectacle unto the world, and to angels, and to men.'

Jude listened. – 'No – they are not talking about us,' he said. 'They are two clergymen of different views, arguing about the eastward position. Good God – the eastward position, and all creation groaning!'

THERE will be many who, on reading this book, share the feelings of Jude the Obscure when from his lodging window in 'Christminster' after finding the hanging bodies of his three children – 'Done because we are too menny' – he heard the two clergymen arguing about the ritualistic trivium which split the Church of England in the nineteenth century.

On the other hand the book has been written in the hope that not only impatience, but also understanding, will be generated. The issues which dictated the taking or the rejecting of the 'eastward position' were not altogether unimportant, and the issues which have divided the churches and continue to keep them apart cannot be lightly dismissed.

A book on such a subject as the ecumenical movement cannot but be controversial; and however hard its author has attempted to be impartial and fair-minded, it is right that at the beginning he should declare his interest and his own general position.

As an Anglican clergyman from the early 1950s I was always much concerned with the search for the unity of the church. In my last position of major responsibility, as Dean of Hong Kong, I was deeply committed to ecumenical action, as Vice-Chairman of the Hong Kong Christian

9

Council (the equivalent of a national Council of Churches) and as Chairman of the United Theological College and of a number of committees which included Roman Catholics. Returning to England it was difficult not to feel impatient with the conservatism of the churches in this country, not only in matters ecumenical but in many other areas where it seems that ecclesiastical traditionalism is usually the deciding factor, even when the churches are in a state of desperate crisis. Since ceasing (not for these reasons) to operate as an Anglican clergyman, one has become more impatient, as one has seen more clearly from outside the ecclesiastical set-up how ineffective the churches – and especially the divided churches – are in the modern world. I can only hope that this impatience does not unduly colour the pages that follow nor detract from their value as a description of the churches' search for unity.

This book, like many others, has taken longer to write than was originally intended. When it was started in 1965 there were many hopeful signs on the ecumenical scene and the word 'breakthrough' was being constantly used. But increasingly as the book has progressed one has felt as if one were writing not an account of the ecumenical movement so much as its obituary. These have been years when the decline of the churches has accelerated at an alarming rate; when many of the signs which looked encouraging at the beginning of the sixties are now seen to have been only the first swallows of a still-delayed ecumenical summer; and when there have been some specific ecumenical set-backs. All in all at the beginning of the seventies it looks as if the movement for the reunion of the churches as it has developed so far in the twentieth century may have taken so long to come to fruition that in the end it cannot be supported by the rapidly declining churches themselves. Whether this will prove to be true or whether something new will emerge in the place of the movement described in this book remains to be seen.

Preface

I am grateful to many people who have helped with advice on various points. In particular I must thank the following for reading and commenting on individual chapters: The Right Reverend Kenneth Carey, Bishop of Edinburgh, the Reverend Henry Carter, Dr Henry Chadwick, Dean of Christ Church, Dr Owen Chadwick, Master of Selwyn, the Reverend R. M. C. Jeffery, Sir John Lawrence, the Right Reverend Hugh Montefiore, Bishop of Kingston, and Canon David Paton. I am grateful, too, to my wife, who has read and commented on much of the book, and to Miss Barbara Clapham, who has done the same in her guise as the interested but uninformed layman.

BARRY TILL
1 May 1971

Part One

THE BACKGROUND

CHAPTER ONE

The Ecumenical Movement: Causes and Attitudes

This re-union tomfoolery . . .

Letter from a Church of England vicar to The Times,
1960

DEFINITIONS

THE ecumenical movement is the movement among the
Christian churches for the recovery of their visible and
institutional unity. The Greek word *oikoumene* means
'the whole inhabited world'. Its root lies in the word
oikos, meaning a house or dwelling, and *oikoumene* can
therefore have the meaning of 'the civilized world'. The
word appears in the New Testament at Matthew xxiv,
14: 'And this Gospel of the Kingdom will be preached
throughout the whole world' (R.S.V.). It can also be used
to mean the people of the world, as in Acts xix, 27, which
refers to the goddess Artemis, 'she whom all Asia and the
whole world worship'. Here the New English Bible has
the translation 'the civilized world'.

At an early development in Christian vocabulary the
word 'ecumenical' was used of the great doctrinal
councils of the early church before it was split by divisions. The indication was that these councils were those
of the whole church throughout the world – or as far as it
had spread in the world. When a council represented
something less than the whole church it was not dignified
with the title 'ecumenical'. The meaning of the word is
thus beginning to shift from a concentration on the
world to a concentration on the church. Indeed at this
time the word 'ecumenical' could be used to describe

'the church of the whole world', and was therefore virtually synonymous with the other Greek word for the universal church – 'catholic'. When the enthusiasts for the reunion of the church applied the word 'ecumenical' to their movement they were therefore historically justified in claiming that when the church recovered its ecumenicity it would at the same time recover its lost catholicity. To have used the word 'ecumenical' for the church or any part of it during the period of its disunion would obviously have been to deal in a debased coinage – at least in the west. The Eastern Orthodox churches continued to use it of their Councils and hence of their churches; but this underlines the fact that those churches did not recognize the divisions of the church. For them there was only one church – the Orthodox – just as in the west until very recently there was for the Roman Catholics only one church – the Roman.

Early manifestations of the ecumenical spirit were labelled 'eirenical', from the Greek word *eirene*, meaning peace; in the seventeenth and eighteenth centuries several books entitled *Eirenicon* were published, but they urged peace rather than reunion between the churches. When, therefore, the reunion movement proper began in the Protestant churches in the nineteenth century a new word had to be coined to describe it. This word was 'ecumenical'. It entered the general Christian vocabulary after the First World Missionary Council at Edinburgh in 1910. It was not the first time that the church had to coin or change a word to meet its own needs. Not that in taking on the aspect of the recovery of unity the word had altogether lost its original connotation of 'the whole inhabited world'. The delegates to Edinburgh in 1910 were acutely conscious that for the first time in history Christians were meeting from all over the world. And their vision was precisely of a united church which would evangelize the whole world. It was for that that they had come to Edinburgh. From the beginning the Biblical text which was the motto and theme of the movement was St John xvii, 20 and 21, from the so-called high-priestly prayer of Christ on the eve of his death.

I do not pray for these only [that is the disciples], but also for those who are to believe in me through their word, that they may all be one; even as thou, Father, art in me, and I in thee, that they also may be in us, so that the world may believe that thou hast sent me.

In this text, which has formed half-a-century of ecumenical thinking, the unity of the church is bound up with its mission to the world. So the churchly and the worldly meanings of the word 'ecumenical' were brought together in its modern use to describe the Christian unity movement. Although the primary meaning was that of church unity, that unity was seen in a world-wide context.

The early church could not have used the word in any sense to do with the recovery of unity because it was in fact united. That is not to say that there were no threats to unity. Indeed much of the energy of the early church was devoted to evolving ways and means of expressing and maintaining unity in the face of threats to disrupt it (see Chapter 2). It was not until the fifth century that these efforts broke down permanently for the first time and divisions appeared in the church which have remained unhealed to this day. This was in the eastern church; thereafter a worsening rift grew up between the eastern church based on Constantinople and the western based on Rome, a rift which became open and permanent in the eleventh century, and which is in fact to this day still the greatest schism in Christendom. The divisions of the Reformation within the western church are, both numerically and ideologically, less serious than those of the Rome/Constantinople breach – though most western Christians fail to realize this. In any case it is the western divisions, multiplied *ad nauseam* by new splits originating largely in America, which have been exported by the western churches to what used to be called 'the mission field', a term which must be taken to include the western-ized Commonwealth countries as well as the developing nations. (For the history of the divisions of the church see Chapter 3.)

It is necessary to underline the extent and complexity of Christian disunity to British readers because they have inevitably a somewhat simplified picture of the situation. In England people are used to the idea of the predomin-ance of the established Church of England. There are, of course, a number of other churches, but any ecumenical negotiations are bound to be dominated by the C. of E. This is not typical of the ecumenical scene elsewhere. Moreover with the English picture in mind the average Englishman would probably be surprised to be told that the Anglican church is a relatively small one in the world-wide league. The same is true of Scotland. There, the Church of Scotland – a member of the Presbyterian family of churches – is the established church which dominates the scene. The picture in Wales is more typi-cal of the rest of the world in that there is no establish-ment and that churches seeking reunion approach each other roughly speaking on an equal footing, as they would, for instance, in India or the United States. But even in Wales the canvas is not painted with all the range of the ecclesiastical spectrum. Many churches of great significance on the world ecumenical scene are not represented. How many people in Britain would know – far less fully appreciate the significance of – the fact that the Lutheran church is the third largest in the world. It is facts and considerations of this sort which must be under-stood, even by the British, who are notorious for their insularity, if the ecumenical movement is to be seen as a world-wide reality.

Ecclesiastical statistics are very difficult to obtain and to use comparatively, because the different churches apply differing yardsticks of measurement. For Roman Catholics, for instance, membership is reckoned by baptism and at least some Roman Catholic missionary enterprises work by baptizing infants with very little – or no – instruction for the parents. But other churches, such as the Baptist, do not practise infant baptism; their membership figures cannot therefore strictly be compared with those of the Roman Catholics and others. How great can be the difference between baptized and practising adult membership is seen from the fact that in the following list the Methodists give their figures as forty-one and a half million but admit to only just over nineteen million adult members, while for the Congregationalists the equivalent figures are six million and three and a quarter million. However, bearing these limitations in mind, the latest statistics for the major world Christian denominations may be given as follows: [1]

Roman Catholic 58 million
Orthodox (including the Oriental Orthodox Churches – see below pp. 101–6) 122,000,770
Lutheran 77,984,394
Baptist 55–65 million
Presbyterian and Reformed 50–55 million
Methodist 41,500,000
Anglican 40 million
Congregationalist 6 million
Seventh Day Adventists 3,830,000

These figures exclude the Pentecostalists, who are not organized on a world-wide scale, but who, if they were, would certainly come well up in the league – probably between the Lutherans and Baptists; moreover where they are strong they are the fastest (and often the only) growing church. Nor do the statistics include the many millions of Christians all over the world who belong to the hundreds of small, extreme Protestant churches classified as sects.

Using these figures, the Christian cake can be seen diagrammatically to cut up in this shape:

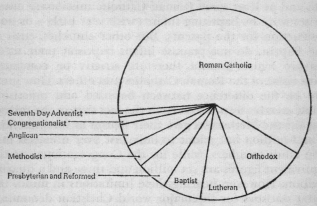

It is especially important for British readers to bear this diagram in mind while reading this book, as it helps to offset the two simplifications of thinking, first, that the divisions of the church spring solely from the Reformation and, second, that they are confined to those western Protestant churches which operate in Great Britain. The size of the Orthodox and Lutheran slices will no doubt surprise most British people. The ecumenical problem is far greater than they realize.

CAUSES: THE SOCIOLOGICAL ANALYSIS

It is natural to ask why the ecumenical drive among the Protestant churches should have been so long delayed after the Reformation, until it took persistent shape as a major factor in church life at the beginning of this century (see Chapter 5). When in 1946 the then Archbishop of Canterbury, Dr Geoffrey Fisher, preached a celebrated 'ecumenical' sermon at Cambridge, inviting the free churches to consider new ways of reaching unity with the Church of England, a friend of the writer's who was 'something in the city' remarked with bluff worldly wisdom that the Archbishop was 'cutting his losses'. In financial terms, in a falling market retrenchment and rationalization were called for. This argument has recently been taken up in a more sophisticated form by the Oxford sociologist Bryan Wilson in his book *Religion in a Secular Society*. His thesis is that the ecumenical movement is the reaction of the churches to secularization in western society. By secularization he means the change in the climate of thought which has led in the west to men's difficulty in accepting Christian belief and in seeing the relevance of the church. Secularization has resulted in a decrease of the power and influence of the church. In England this has led to a steady decline in church membership per head of the population in this century, a decline which recently has become more dramatic. In the United States the same process of secularization has been taking place – indeed society there never had such a firm religious basis as in western Europe (see below, pp. 146–9). However there has not been until recently the same decline in church membership. This, says Dr Wilson, is because churchgoing is accepted as part of the 'American way of life', one of the ways in which people with a great variety of cultural and national backgrounds can express their American identity. As a result of this need for a common Christian allegiance, the argument runs, denominational differences are played down in America and the ecumenical movement finds a well-prepared seed bed.

But the main force of the book is applied to England, with its decaying churches.

Although ecumenicalism has captured the imagination of the leaders of the churches, this process has been in part a growing recognition of the essential weakness of religious life in the increasingly secularized society. The spirit has descended on the waters and brought peace between churchmen of different persuasions only as those churchmen have recognized their essential marginality in modern society.[2]

This is obviously an important argument, with a good deal of truth in it. In particular it must be true that as the climate of opinion turns against the churches their differences will come to seem smaller in the face of a common adversity than they did when most men took a Christian frame of reference for granted and could choose between competing denominations. Dr Wilson puts this from the sociological point of view: 'As the process of secularization has continued, so the differences between denominations have lost their social significance.'[3]

Bryan Wilson's general thesis has been re-argued with greater historical detail by Robert Currie in *Methodism Divided: A Study in the Sociology of Ecumenism*. This book is a study in the divisions of British Methodism in the nineteenth century and the subsequent reunion of Methodism between 1836 and 1932. Mr Currie is able to show that a period of serious decline for all the Methodist denominations set in really 'critically' after 1881 and that 'with one exception only the various unions occurred after that date'. The decade 1911–21 was the worst of all and 'in twelve years Methodism was united'.[4] Mr Currie talks here about Methodist leaders looking for 'sideways growth' by ecclesiastical unions when they found that absolute growth by evangelization was becoming impossible. There does not seem to be much contemporary evidence that this was the way the ecumenical leaders were thinking.

On the other hand there is a good deal of evidence that these leaders thought of union in terms of evangelization: reunion was essential if the Methodist church was once again to start to convert men and women to Christ: 'Only a reunited church can evangelize the world,' wrote Scott Lidgett in 1909; 'we cannot afford in these days the narrowness of outlook, the friction or the isolation which weakens the influence of the Christian Churches.'[5] In 1924 in what they hoped would be a final campaign for reunion – actually delayed until 1932 – the unionists

argued: 'The whole Methodist church will enter upon a
new era of extension which will rival the early days.'[6]
Thus ecumenical plans were linked with missionary
hopes, rather than with fears of decay. This is a pattern
of motivation which is always found in the ecumenical
movement. As Currie says, 'Ecumenicalism is not simply
born of adversity, but of hope in adversity.'[7]

This statement, with its shift of emphasis, is a valuable
corrective to the brutal simplicity of Bryan Wilson's
thesis that the ecumenical movement is simply the reaction of the churches to secularization in the modern
world. None the less the basic premise that the churches
are in a state of drastic decline cannot be denied; it is
clear, too, that whether or not the ecumenical movement
is the result of – or response to – this decline, it must
certainly be seen in that context.

Wilson gives statistics for the Church of England between 1885 and 1960, and these can now be brought
almost up to date with figures for 1968. The following are
the most significant.

Infant baptisms: rates per 1,000 live births in England

1885	623
1900	650
1910	689
1920	678
1930	699
1940	641
1950	672
1960	554
1968	490

Confirmations per 1,000 population aged 12–20 years

1930	35·3
1940	26·8
1950	31·2
1960	34·2
1968	21·4

Numbers of Easter communicants in thousands, and as a proportion per 1,000 population aged 15 years and over

1885	1,384 thousand	84 per thousand
1900	1,902	93
1910	2,212	95
1920	2,194	88
1930	2,285	80
1940	2,018	64
1950	1,867	58
1960	2,159	65
1968	1,795	51

Wilson does not give figures for the other churches in England and seems to ignore the possibility that the fact that the Church of England was declining does not mean that other churches were in a similar state. At the beginning of the nineteenth century, for instance, the Church of England was probably declining while the Methodists were gaining at its expense. In the twentieth century, however, this was not the case. With the limited exception of the Roman Catholics all the churches were declining at about the same rate. Statistics given by the respective church authorities are as follows:

Baptist total membership in the U.K. and Eire and expressed as a percentage of the population

1861	143,000	0·595%
1881	281,000	0·91 %
1901	373,000	0·98 %
1911	419,000	1·1 %
1921	403,000	0·93 %
1931	406,000	0·89 %
1941	382,000	? %
1951	336,000	0·67 %
1961	314,000	0·595%
1969	275,000	? %

Congregationalists' church membership in England and Wales

1930	314,082
1940	297,493
1950	234,150
1960	212,879
1969	168,337

Methodist church membership in England and Wales

1930	499,194
1940	792,192
1950	744,326
1960	728,589
1969	651,139

(The large increase between 1930 and 1940 is accounted for by the uniting in 1932 of the Wesleyan, Primitive and United Methodist churches to form the present Methodist church. The 1930 figure refers to the United Methodist church only.)

Presbyterian Church of England membership

1930	84,146
1940	76,815
1950	69,676
1960	71,329
1969	61,187

The Church of Scotland, which has traditionally been slow to reveal statistics, now confirms heavy losses.

Roman Catholic statistics are the exception to the otherwise general rule that the decline in absolute numbers of institutional Christians set in after reaching a peak somewhere about 1930.

Roman Catholic infant baptisms in England and Wales

1934	65,223
1944	76,811
1954	96,773
1960	118,499
1964	132,435
1969	117,183

The Background

There has been a steady but marked decline in Roman Catholic baptisms every year since the peak year of 1964. Although these statistics are less convincing than those which can be traced further back, it looks as if the general religious decline was delayed, and indeed reversed, in the Roman Catholic church until the mid-sixties, but that it then set in in line with the other churches of England and Wales. Clearly the former advance was dependent partly on high birth-rate figures and also to some extent on gains from other churches. The number of converts, for instance, grew from some 10,000 in 1956 to a peak of over 13,000 in 1962, but had declined in 1969 to 6,598. Similarly mass attendances seem to be on a decline from a peak figure reached in the mid-sixties. In fact R.C. sources have recently reported a fall as great as 8 per cent a year. Thus it seems that even the Roman Catholic church has now joined the others in witnessing a decline in institutional religion, a fact which would probably be both witnessed to and accelerated by the comparatively large numbers of priests who are now leaving their ministry and seeking secular employment.

However Roman Catholic ecumenical interest is a comparatively recent growth; as far as the earlier ecumenical movement is concerned it is the statistics of the other churches which are of most importance. Here the picture for England and Wales seems general. There has been a general absolute decline in outward Christian observance since about 1930. This decline was partially arrested just after the war when some churches entered on a brief period of theological optimism coupled with a small numerical revival. But in the last fifteen years the decline has set in at an increasing rate, and in the last five it could more nearly be called a landslide. These figures become more significant when set against the total population of the country, which has been increasing steadily: in the last 100 years it has more than doubled. Seen in this light the Christian churches in England (other than the

Roman Catholic) were at their strongest, reckoned by percentage of the population, in the first decade of the twentieth century. Thereafter they were declining relative to the population though growing relative to themselves until the 1930s. This probably prevented Christian leaders from recognizing the seriousness of the situation. Recently, however, the churches are declining both relatively and absolutely – at an accelerating rate as the population continues to increase – and now even the Roman Catholics are beginning to feel the blizzard. How serious it is can be shown by the example of the Baptists. In 1861 with a membership of only 143,000 they comprised 0·595 per cent of the population. In 1961 with 314,000 members their percentage rate was exactly the same. Since then the population has increased but their own membership has further shrunk. The same would be true of other churches. The Christian population of England is rapidly becoming a smaller and smaller minority.

Reliable figures for the rest of the world would be more difficult to obtain, but there is little doubt that they would tell much the same tale. In particular the growing point of the churches on the 'mission field' has been dramatically halted since the war with the growth of nationalism and the reaction against Christianity among other things western. Only in the United States, for reasons which have been partially explained by Bryan Wilson, has the general post-war erosion of Christianity not been taking place; but recently even that exception has gone and the churches in America are now also beginning to feel the cold winds of secularization. The sole remaining exception to this general picture of Christian decline is the rapid growth in many parts of the world of left-wing Protestantism and in particular of Pentecostalism (see below, pp. 150–51 and 284–7).

But even granted that the undoubted decline of the churches may of recent years have provided part of the motive for the persistence of the ecumenical drive it can

27

hardly have been the mainspring of the movement at its birth at the beginning of the century. For the church leaders at the beginning of the century did not feel that the church was threatened, that they were in a position of adversity. It was not adversity, or even 'hope in adversity', that inspired the convenors of the Edinburgh Conference of 1910. It was more nearly a state of euphoria. The great cry of the world missionary leaders who called the conference was 'the evangelization of the world in our time'. They were still on the crest of the Victorian and Edwardian wave. The white man was still in the ascendant; he was full of confidence; there was nothing to stop the further advance of his civilization and, with it, of his religion. All this is abundantly clear from the speeches of the Edinburgh Conference (see below, pp. 193–6). What the church leaders did see was that the divisions of the church were a hindrance to the evangelization of the world, which they seriously believed was just round the corner. *This* was the historical mainspring of the movement. The word 'ecumenical' gives a clue to the true motivation of the drive to union. It was to be one church for the whole world. As Kenneth Scott Latourette, perhaps the greatest church historian of this century, has written,

It cannot be said too often or too emphatically that the ecumenical movement arose from the missionary movement and continues to have at its heart world-wide evangelism.[8]

Moreover, as the statistics just quoted have already showed, their mood of optimism was not altogether without justification. It is true that the figures produced by Currie show that Methodism was declining from the 1880s; but Methodism was to some extent an exception in pre-dating the general decline of the churches. With its phenomenal evangelistic successes it had had a period of great growth at the beginning of the nineteenth century, often at the expense of other churches. When the gospel fires burned low a period of decline was bound to set in, and this decline was probably hastened by the divisions within Methodism. But for the other churches decline was to come a generation later. For the moment in 1910 the mood was one of optimism, a mood which even briefly survived the First World War, when the ecumenical cause was – perhaps surprisingly – strongly revived. In short, the period at the beginning of the century which saw the beginning of the modern ecumenical movement was in many ways the high-water mark of the activity of the churches. It would be more true to say that the movement was born of 'optimism in prosperity' than of 'hope in adversity'.

It is true that the first signs of what Wilson calls secularization were there for those who had eyes to see them. For a century at least the western churches had been losing their grip on those power structures and institutions – such as education – through which they had controlled or influenced society. The ways by which this happened had varied according to the type and degree of the establishment of the church in the country in question; but in every case the churches had fought a rearguard action against their loss of power. In this sense secularization was already a threat at the beginning of the ecumenical movement. But it is doubtful, to say the least, whether the position was at that stage seen and rationalized in the way Wilson suggests. Moreover, as the word is now used, secularization means much more now than it did at the beginning of the century, even though the modern form of secularization can be seen by hindsight to have grown out of the earlier tendency in that direction. As the word is now understood it can be said to mean the replacement in society at large of a religious framework for thought and action by an a-religious or atheistic framework. The full force and extent of secularization, understood in this way, has become apparent to churchmen and non-churchmen alike only in the last ten or fifteen years. Therefore once again it must be said that the thesis that the ecumenical movement is the churches' response to secularization is one that hardly stands up to the facts of history – though again it is true that in more recent years some churchmen will have seen the reunion movement in this light.

Lastly, anyone who knows the churches from the inside must feel that Wilson's analysis is open to psychological criticism.

Church leaders are neither as cynical nor as realistic as his thesis suggests. They are in the main devoted, hard-working – even harassed – men. They may be more forward-looking than the majority of their rank and file; but this is not to say much, and they are not on the whole noted for holding very advanced or radical opinions. In common with other churchmen they have not been not-ably quick to respond realistically to the decline of the churches. When they have failed to take many of the more obvious administrative steps which seem called for in the face of this decline, there is no particular reason why they should embark on the more difficult problems of church unity in response to it. Moreover a basic text on the church is that which declares that 'the gates of hell shall not prevail against it'. For many churchmen this is taken to mean that the acceptance of the idea that the church is a sick institution is equivalent to a disastrous lack of confidence in a basic article of faith. Realism is equated with faithlessness. One sees the equation being made in church publications over and over again.

Thus Bryan Wilson's belief that the ecumenical move-ment is the churches' response to their own decline can-not be said to ring psychologically true, any more than it can be seen to stand up to the facts of historical and statistical evidence. Not that it can be altogether dis-missed. Wilson has diagnosed *one* of the motives of *some* of the leaders of the present-day movement. But it still remains necessary to look for a more satisfactory explanation of the rise and persistence of ecumenism.

CAUSES: THEOLOGICAL AND NON-THEOLOGICAL

First, as has already been seen, there is the missionary motive. This was strong at the beginning of the movement before the First World War, and has been strongly revived more recently since the Second World War, when the theme of the unity of the church has been linked with that of its renewal, as both being necessary for its mission. 'One Church Renewed for Mission' was the ecumenical battle-cry of the sixties. Nor must this sense of mission be seen only in terms of the conversion of those outside the church, whether the potential converts were thought of as 'benighted Africans' in 1910 or as 'post-Christian western pagans' in 1960. The mission of the church, for which it needed to find its unity, included its influence in the world in terms of social and political action. This outlook was very much to the fore in the twenties and thirties when 'the social Gospel' was the element in Christianity which was most attractive to many of the most forward-looking church leaders. The situation was clearly summarized at that time by Professor Jaroslav Pelikan in a passage which states the reverse of the Wilson coin.

It would be a misreading [of the development of twentieth-century theology] to interpret the ecumenical movement ... as an expression of the 'ghetto mentality' of Christianity or as a withdrawal from the problems of contemporary life. Such an interpretation is refuted by the careers of many churchmen ... who devoted equal energy and commitment to the three worlds of scholarship, dialogue and ecumenicity.[9]

Another factor in the ecumenical drive and in its persistence has been the purely theological one. It was recognized that, theologically speaking, a divided church was a contradiction in terms. 'I believe in the Holy Catholic Church,' said William Temple, perhaps the greatest of all ecumenical leaders, '... And sincerely regret that it does not at present exist.' This sense of theological scandal was the driving force which converted many to the movement. The church of the apostles, of the Bible and of the early centuries was united; divisions were threatened but were avoided because the idea of them was so unthinkable. As theologians in the twentieth century recovered the idea of the mystical Body of Christ, the church of the Pauline epistles, they began to have a Pauline horror of divisions within the Body (see below, pp. 68–71). This was particularly true of the first Roman Catholic theologians who began to take an interest in the ecumenical movement. It was when, in the fifties, such men as Yves Congar began to discuss the nature of the church, and to recognize that it simply would not do to say that 'the church' was co-terminous with the Roman Catholic church, that they began to urge on their church an interest in the movement; and, as has been remarked, 'it is significant that Roman Catholic ecumenists relatively seldom dealt with the problems of mission'.[10]

On the other hand, obviously theological thinking could act as a brake on ecumenical endeavour. As will be seen later theological conservatives often tended to distrust the champions of the ecumenical cause. The conservative opponents of the current Anglican Methodist scheme in England call themselves 'conservationists' and deplore what they call the Anglican habit of 'doctrinal minimalism': 'the modern concern for church reunion has given it a new lease of life,' they boldly declare.[11] Earlier in the history of the movement this theological opposition was even stronger, though it was of course often mixed with unrecognized non-theological factors. Thus until comparatively recently the doctrines which were seen to be keeping the churches apart were those which centred on the issues of the church, its sacraments and its ministry. Arguing from entrenched (and perhaps often unexamined) traditional and historical positions, the theologians seemed destined to reach deadlock on these questions.

Recently, however, there has been a change in the theological climate which has affected all but the most determined conservatives. This change has been described by Bishop Stephen Neill, perhaps the leading theologian to have been concerned over a period of nearly fifty years with the ecumenical movement. His analysis – in his Bampton Lectures, *The Church and Christian Union* – both adds to and also to some extent corrects the diagnosis of the sociologists Wilson and Currie. He points out that the classical Reformation statements of the Christian faith, to which theologians have ever since turned, were drawn up not with mission to non-Christians but with definition against fellow-Christians in mind. For this reason the doctrine of the church is 'set forth in terms of being and not of function'.

It is taken for granted that the Church is something which exists and is susceptible of observation : all that is required is to give a satisfactory description or definition of that which is known as already existing.

But as soon as one thinks about the church in terms of its mission to the non-Christian world, the frame of reference is changed.

It is borne in upon us that no satisfactory definition of the Church can be arrived at in terms only of its own existence. We have to ask not only 'What is the Church?', but 'What is the Church for?'[12]

This, says Neill, is what has happened to break down some of the long-standing theological barriers to ecumenical advance. It has affected discussions about the sacraments, but perhaps most of all the debate between Christians about the ministry in the church. It will be seen later how the discussion has shifted from being one about ministry *in* the church to being one about the ministry *of* the church. The church is now seen not so much as the Body of Christ in which various people have various functions (which then traditionally become items of dispute) but as the People of God, who are all concerned in the primary ministry common to them all, which is the conversion of the world – whatever that may be taken to mean. When this is understood the various functions and ministries can be seen in perspective – and the issues become much less explosive. Indeed the laity are seen as having the most important ministry (instead of the traditional view of them as second-class Christians or 'pew fodder') because they are the people most in touch with the world.

Perhaps most remarkable of all is the change which has come over the age-old argument about episcopacy and the necessity of bishops in the church. In the ecumenical debate this has been the Anglicans' particular platform. And among Anglicans the traditional argument has been whether bishops are the *esse* or the *bene esse* of the church. That is to say are they essential to the church's *being* (the 'Catholic' position) or are they merely helpful to its well-being (the low-church Anglican view which is obviously more acceptable to Protestant union leaders)? But again this is an argument, as Neill would point out, 'in terms of being and not of function'. Even when a third Anglican view was put forward in the hope of a compromise which was at the same time Biblical and historical in its outlook, it was in terms of the *plene esse* – or fullness – of the church. But Neill, himself a participant, remembers that in the Church of South India unity negotiations, which for the first time brought together episcopal Anglicans and non-episcopal Protestants, it was when episcopacy was talked about in terms of its function

rather than of its theology that the breakthrough came.
The non-episcopal churches

were prepared to say ... it is impossible to have a theology of
that which one has never experienced. We are ready to accept
episcopacy as a fact, a gift and a blessing. But do not expect
us now to have a theory of it.[13]

Bishop Neill is here summarizing the course of negotiations in which he took part some thirty years ago. Since
that time the whole tone of theological discussion on
these matters has changed, so that the acrimonious theological debates on episcopacy of the thirties, forties and
fifties now seem tales of 'old, unhappy, far-off things, and
battles long ago'. This is not, of course, to say that the
old theological outlook was totally misguided, but simply
that the change of emphasis in the new has speeded the
ecumenical plough.

Other theological factors have had the same effect.
Notable here are the common discoveries made by theologians of different churches in the field of Bible studies,
historical reassessment – for instance of Catholic scholars
about Luther – and liturgical scholarship (see below, pp.
224–8).

There are other issues which have tended in the past to
be divisive but in which the churches are now moving
towards a common mind, though more for sociological
and historical than for strictly theological reasons. Foremost among them is the question of church government
or 'polity'. Here the churches have tended to divide between those, such as the Baptists and Congregationalists
and left-wing Protestants generally, where the local congregation is the essential unit, and those where the larger
unit such as the diocese, or (in the Methodist case) the
Conference, is paramount. Historical and ideological
factors have played their part in this debate; for instance
the argument has sometimes been one of 'democracy
versus authority'. Then on these foundations imposing

theological superstructures have been erected. But recently for practical reasons there has been a convergence on matters of polity. The strongest upholders of congregational liberty have found that in modern circumstances some sort of 'connectional', corporate structure becomes a necessity. Some have even found that this is best expressed, not through committees, but through an individual, whether or not he is called a bishop and is in the apostolic succession. On the other hand the more 'authoritarian' churches, even the Roman Catholic, have found that over-centralization can have unhappy results and that, since the strength of the church is largely in its local witness, some expressions of local variety must be allowed for. In the wake of these practical discoveries the work of the earlier theologians to buttress their particular positions has often been stood on its head.

Akin to this is the whole question of the 'establishment' of the churches, which again has proved in the past an explosive ecumenical topic. For instance it caused the break-up of the Church of Scotland in the nineteenth century, and hindered its reunion in the twentieth. Recent developments have largely removed the sting from this particular issue (which in any case is felt in the countries of the ex-Christian west, that is Europe, rather than in the developing countries which have no established churches). Establishment often carried with it automatic privileges. This was, for instance, the case in England from the Reformation until the beginning of the twentieth century. And very hard did the Church of England fight to maintain its privileges throughout the nineteenth century. But it was having to fight not only against the non-conformists but also against the erosion of its privileges by the state – that is against the beginning of secularization. As the process of secularization advanced, the issue of establishment became less and less important between the churches. (Indeed it is strange that Wilson hardly mentions this in his analysis.) This

fact can be seen from the course of the Anglican Methodist negotiations in England. At the beginning of these
negotiations as recently as the fifties it was taken for
granted that the question of the establishment of the
Church of England and of the status of the future united
church would be major issues in the negotiations. But
when the final scheme was published in 1958 the matter
of establishment was shelved for detailed discussion at
the second stage of the union. It was seen that there
would have to be some discussion at that stage, but it was
not seen as a major issue and two things were discounted: 'an establishment of ecclesiastical privilege,
such as the Church of England once enjoyed', and 'formal
disestablishment'.[14] It may be that this is a reflection of
the fact that the Church of England seems to be incapable of making up its own mind what it means or wants
by establishment. But it is also an example of how, in the
changed circumstances of secularization, establishment
has ceased to be an issue which will stand in the way of
reunion.

Other non-theological factors have been grist to the
ecumenical mill. Some of these, such as the simple fact
that ecclesiastical differences do not look as big in the
African bush as they do in an English provincial town,
will be described in later chapters. Similarly war and
hardship have proved to be circumstances which have
impelled men and women to re-examine their traditional
divisions. The desire to be able to share in Holy Communion despite denominational differences in a prisoner-
of-war compound, in a concentration camp or amid the
dangers of persecution or resistance has lowered the walls
of prejudice and ignorance. For instance, a bitter division
had arisen in the nineteenth century between the liberal
and ultra-conservative wings of the tiny French Protestant church. But Bishop Neill records that 'during the
first World War the chaplains of the rival groups had
found themselves brought together into a far closer fel-

lowship ... as they extended their ministrations without question to the members of both churches; they resolved that, after the war, this fellowship should not be allowed to lapse'.[15] The end of what had looked like a particularly bitter quarrel followed within ten years of the end of the war. Similarly it is said of the beginning of ecumenical interest in the Roman Catholic Church:

Representatives of different confessions had shared persecution, made common cause on behalf of the Jews, met in concentration camps and in the resistance movement against National Socialism.... It was certainly no accident that the ecumenical idea gained most ground wherever these experiences had been most deeply felt. When later, at the Second Vatican Council, Dutch, French and German bishops in particular supported the ecumenical movement of the Church, the comment was made, with some justice, that the 'hand of Hitler could be seen here'.[16]

Lastly, in this list of the factors which favoured the rise and persistence of the ecumenical movement, there are undoubtedly social influences to be taken into account. Currie's study of the reunion of Methodism shows this very clearly. Above all there was the impetus given by social mobility and the consequent questioning of established patterns and loyalties. A family which grew up in a village dominated by a Primitive Methodist chapel moves to a city suburb where no such chapel exists, and where they might be somewhat ashamed or embarrassed to fight for one to be built: they are ready to give up their old traditions in the new circumstances and to settle for a larger church or even to campaign for a united one.

The new growth areas, which are largely the most dynamic regions of the denomination, and where the denominational traditions are weak, and the resources of the denomination few, particularly favour the move to the superdenomination. In 1900, 1904 and 1924 areas where Methodism was old and strong ... but either growing slowly or actually declining ...

supported union comparatively weakly; while the new growth areas supported union strongly.[17]

This phenomenon of social mobility is always a factor in the growth of ecumenical feeling. In Europe or America it is the family who move to a new suburb; in Africa it is the native who moves from his tribal area which was evangelized by, say, a Church of Scotland mission to find work in a town hundreds of miles away where the Church of Scotland is not represented and where he is in danger of being unchurched altogether.

Currie also argues that not only geographical but also class mobility favours the ecumenical cause. Our family, moving to their prosperous new suburb from their village or urban back street, may feel somewhat ashamed of their old Primitive Methodist chapel and of its social *mores*.

Ecumenicalism may involve, and institutionalize, upward social mobility. Radical schismatic groups generally have low social status, the parent body a higher status. The doctrine and systems of these low status groups are at a social disadvantage. Members are glad to rid themselves of ... an outlandish denominational label.[18]

This is true. The larger churches tend to be more 're-spectable' both intellectually and in social ethic and customs. It is socially difficult for a successful Methodist to maintain his teetotalism; he is much more comfortable in the C. of E. So younger churchmen on the social up-and-up may tend to favour reunion into a larger church. While on the other hand those who are left behind socially may, as Wilson shows, be those who tend to support, or even to innovate, radical ecclesiastical schisms. It is, says Wilson, these sects which 'represent a continuing and deeply religious alternative to the religious compromise which is often, if not always, involved in ecumenism'.[19] While perhaps it is not possible to accept the pejorative implications of this judgement on the compromise involved in ecumenism, it is certainly true, as later chapters will show, that it is the sects, with their piety, their suspicions and their fanatical and anti-intellectual devotion to vital minor details, which are the most difficult churches to convert to the ecumenical cause (see below, pp. 151–3 and 284–6). But by and large both geographical and social mobility have been factors which have favoured the reunion movement.

DETERRENTS

It may now well be asked why, when there are so many factors – sociological, theological, historical and even accidental – making for church unity, the final results in ecumenical progress over more than half a century have been so small.

The reply must be, in the first place, that they are greater than most people realize. There have been a significant number of unions – though not it may be thought a great number of significant unions (see Chapters 5 and 7). There is a deal of effective inter-church co-operation both through the agency of the World Council of Churches and at a more local level (see Chapters 6 and 9). Both the unions and the co-operation have to be measured against the situation as it was at the beginning of the century. To take an example from England alone: there are people alive today who can remember what it was to live in a village which was divided between church and chapel. The two factions were often not on speaking terms; they might as far as possible deal with different tradesmen. In these circumstances the ignorance and prejudice which existed on both sides was something which the present generation cannot envisage. This fact must be set as a constant reminder to those who are impatient at the slowness of ecumenical progress.

In the second place it must be realized that church divisions were – are – very deep and very long-standing.

Some of them go back to the sixth century; some to the
eleventh; many to the sixteenth; and many more to the
eighteenth and nineteenth. These divisions will be described later (see Chapter 3), because until one has some
picture of their complexity it is impossible to gain a sense
of perspective about the reunion movement. In a word, it
is not surprising that divisions which are centuries old
have taken more than fifty years to mend. Moreover, as
has already been seen, these divisions are compounded of
both theological and what early on in the ecumenical
movement were labelled non-theological factors. Sometimes the schism started for theological reasons, but then
had added to it layers of social or ideological tradition.
Sometimes the original split may have been more on non-
theological grounds, only to be covered with theological
justification. The varying factors will be seen in later
analysis. It may be felt that neither the theological nor
the non-theological factors are sufficient any longer in
this secularized age to maintain the divisions, but it is
none the less important to recognize their existence. It is
one thing to set aside history that is known and recognized, but quite another to discount it out of ignorance.

Having said that there are good and important reasons
why the churches have not moved towards unity as fast as
some might wish in the last fifty years, it must also be
admitted that there are reasons which are less good. Despite the fact that the tide has been running so strongly
in the ecumenical direction, there are not a few Canute
factors which have held it back. For these reasons the
progress towards unity, while being reasonably sure, has
been slower than the optimists, seeing the favourable
omens, might have hoped.

First among the Canute factors has been sheer opposition to the movement as it has developed. There are very
few people who express outright opposition to the idea of
Christian unity – though some examples will be noted
later. Much more common is opposition to the form of

unity which is proposed or to the general character of the movement as it has emerged through the World Council of Churches and other agencies. It has already been noted that this opposition comes mainly from the more conservative forces, both from whole churches of a conservative outlook and from within the life of individual churches. Thus at one end of the ecclesiastical spectrum both the Roman Catholic and Orthodox churches were at first suspicious of the movement and willing to talk about unity only in their own terms – that is that it would be found only by adherence to the organization or the doctrine of the one true church, Catholic or Orthodox. The process by which this hard-line ecumenical thinking was modified will be described in later chapters. For the moment it is enough to note that it represented a highly conservative outlook which had to be modified in a more liberal direction before 'ecumenical dialogue' could take place.

The other ecclesiastical wing is represented by the extreme Protestants of various sects and denominations. Here again the outlook is conservative and authoritarian. It takes its stand on two main tenets, a conservative – or 'fundamentalist' – attitude to the Bible (which, in the face of most modern scholarship, stresses its literal reliability and infallibility) and an insistence on individual conversion experience. Both these evangelical cornerstones have led to conservative evangelicals being suspicious of what they have seen of the ecumenical movement. Their Biblical fundamentalism has caused them to feel that the general ethos of the movement is dangerously liberal, 'unsound' in its attitude to the authority of the Bible, and weak in its presentation of Biblical doctrines, as understood of course by conservative evangelicals. Their insistence on the vital importance of conversion experience has led them to play down the importance of the visible church and of membership of it. In its place they have stressed the reality of the invisible church, and the unity of those who have by their conversion been gathered out of the wicked world, and who therefore share a hidden spiritual unity whatever their denominational allegiance. This means that the insistence of the ecumenical movement since its inception on the necessity of the organic and visible unity of the church has made little appeal to conservative evangelicals – although in the Church of England at least this position has been modified recently as conservative evangelicals have come to terms with the Biblical doctrine of visible church unity, which formerly they had managed to ignore.

The coolness of left-wing Protestantism towards visible church unity has had varying results. In some cases it has meant that whole churches have eschewed the movement: the powerful American Southern Baptist church, for instance, whose best-known member is no doubt Dr Billy Graham, has consistently refused to join the World Council of Churches. In other cases extreme Protestants have left their former denominations to form their own 'sound' sects – and these sects have been notoriously difficult to convert to the ecumenical cause (see below, pp. 284-6). In other cases conservative evangelicals have remained within their own churches but have traditionally been that part of them in which it has been most difficult to generate ecumenical enthusiasm. It was, for instance, an alliance between the conservative evangelicals and the Anglo-Catholics – the two opposite but equally conservative wings of the Church of England – which defeated the Anglican/Methodist proposals in 1969.

Another factor in the Protestant luke-warmness towards the ecumenical movement in general is the fear that there is in it a Romeward drift. Ecumenical leaders have always made it clear that ultimate union must include union with Rome and this has undoubtedly caused Protestant qualms. At the beginning of the twentieth century those who supported Methodist reunion claimed

that a united Methodist church would be a bulwark
against Catholicism (whether of the Anglo or Roman
variety) in England, whereas the opponents of the union
feared that it would take Methodism one step nearer the
Church of England, with its dangerous non-Protestant
propensities. Fifty years later some of the Methodists who
opposed Anglican/Methodist union did so because union
with the Church of England was one step nearer being
'swallowed' by Rome.

Some other 'contra forces' in the ecumenical equation
are most vividly illustrated by a book which constitutes the
most outspoken attack to be launched on the movement
from a 'reputable' source. This book, *Power without
Glory* by Ian Henderson, lately Professor of Systematic
Theology in the University of Glasgow and Moderator of
the Presbytery of Glasgow, reveals some of the other
characteristics of ecumenism which have made it unpopular with its detractors. What made Professor Henderson dislike the movement and all its works is his belief
that the whole operation has been an under-cover movement for the Anglican church to 'take over' the rest of
Protestantism by what is nothing less than a process of
liquidation. The beginnings of the movement after the
Edinburgh Conference are described as 'the diplomatic
activity of the American Anglican body ... to carry out
an extensive programme of church liquidation' and as
'the death warrant of all non-episcopal churches' and 'the
charter of Anglican imperialism'.[20] The Professor sees
the rest of the movement, especially such union schemes
as those of South India and North India which introduce
episcopacy into the united churches, as part of this Anglican imperialistic plot. More particularly 'the present
position is that the Church of Scotland, a body of a
million members, is in danger of being broken in two if it
will not accept *in toto* the nuttiness [*sic*] of 56,000 Scottish Episcopalians'.[21]

The ground which Professor Henderson covers in un-

44

earthing his Anglican imperialistic plot is reviewed in the later chapters of this book, and readers will have a chance to decide for themselves how sinister have been the Anglican machinations. The point at issue here is that a distinguished academic has been impelled into virulent opposition of the whole ecumenical movement because he does not relish the particular form of it in which he has been involved – at top level, it may be said. Undoubtedly this kind of syndrome applies to much of the opposition to the movement. How violent and unbalanced that opposition was in the Professor's case can be seen by a closer examination of some of the details of this book. It contains a number of schoolboy howlers in the historical field, but the Professor is not a historian and this may perhaps be forgiven him. But there are other statements which one is surprised to hear from a Professor of Systematic Theology. The doctrinal proposition that 'God is not a bloody fool'[22] is presumably unexceptionable if perhaps a trifle surprising in its formulation. But one is surprised at an attack on the idea that a Catholic priest 'can turn cheap wine into the blood of Christ'.[23] Would the doctrine of transubstantiation, one wonders, be more acceptable to the Professor if Château Lafitte was invariably used at the mass?

These points have been made to show how deep antiecumenical feeling can run in surprising places when the ecumenical knife cuts near to the bone. During the course of his arguments Professor Henderson does score some more palpable hits. In particular he attacks what he calls 'ecumenical language', by which he believes ecumenical leaders befog the issues and lead their followers astray. In fact for many years the more perspicacious of these leaders have bemoaned the fact that it seems impossible for the World Council of Churches and other ecumenical agencies to produce a document which is not couched in the most hideous theological jargon – known as 'ecumenese'. Far from there being any sinister intent in this failing it has undoubtedly proved a real handicap to the movement, since it has inhibited communication with lay people and given many clergy and laity alike the feeling that ecumenical pundits are not dealing in down-to-earth realities.

Professor Henderson also attacks the movement as being a complicated game of power politics – though with a simple end: ' "Gaiters for the boys" is not a bad description of how the Ecumenical Movement appears to the ambitious Protestant ecclesiastic.'[24] There can be no denying that the movement, like any movement which involves negotiations and ultimately power, is subject to manoeuvring, lobbying and other of the less attractive facets of the political game. Christians, even the ecumenical variety, remain human beings. Anyone wishing to denigrate the movement can seize on this fact. But the more realistic observer will accept it and attempt, as in all analysis and assessment, to separate the chaff from the wheat.

Professor Henderson declares roundly more than once that he does not believe in a united church; his book is dedicated to 'the good Christians in every denomination who do not greatly care whether there is One Church or not'. He attacks ecumenical leaders for identifying their movement with the will of God: 'the point in calling your party policy the will of God is just that it enables you to give hell to the man who opposes it'.[25] It is certainly true that too fanatical an identification of one's own beliefs with the will of God can be dangerous, as Oliver Cromwell had to warn members of Professor Henderson's own church: 'I beseech you in the bowels of Christ, think it possible you may be mistaken.' But to cease to try to know and do the will of God is surely to abnegate the essential element of Christian discipleship. Ecumenical leaders have always made it clear that they believe in the unity of the church of God because they find that that is the example of the New Testament and of the early church (see Chapter 2). Professor Henderson does not attempt to deny this. But he does defend denominationalism within the church.

Denominationalism, the courageous abandonment of the nightmare dogma of the One Church, was an attempt to overcome that basic flaw in Christianity as it had manifested itself in the horrors of the religious wars. It is the conviction that if you cannot agree with your fellow Christians, it is better to live with than to kill them. Denominationalism is a valuable device which enables you honestly and openly to disagree with your fellow Christians on what for them are fundamentals and what for you are over-beliefs and vice versa.[26]

Currie points out that the same argument took place at the time of Methodist unity. Those who were for union believed that it was the will of God. 'Disunity was sinful. Their opponents frequently held, quite sincerely, not only that their own denomination had a purpose, but that denominations in general did so.' Denominationalism gave rein to the valuable principle of competition and was 'held to embody the Protestant principle'. Leading Methodists wrote at the time:

Sects are and have been the very life and salvation of Christianity.... They are a providential and divine appointment to get the whole truth of Christ before the world.
Denominationalism is a very real blessing.[27]

Political observers of this argument may derive some pleasure from the fact that it is the conservatives in it who uphold the merits of competition, whereas the men of the ecclesiastical left are advocating unity and rationalization. Certainly the advocates of unity have always argued that it will increase the effectiveness of the church; that is after all the main point of Bryan Wilson's thesis.

The fear that a united church will have lost some of the advantages of variety and the strengths of small

47

organizations is undoubtedly a point worth taking. Advocates of unity have maintained that unity need not be equivalent to uniformity, but not very much has been done to spell out how this will be achieved. Nevertheless ecumenical supporters invariably fall back on their main argument that unity is the will of God as they believe this to have been revealed. It is perfectly true, to return to Professor Henderson, that at a certain point in western history in the seventeenth century Christians abandoned the idea of the one church, which had led to disastrous wars, in favour of toleration (see below, pp. 162–7). The half-loaf of toleration, said one contemporary, was better than the no-bread of religious war. But even at that time he recognized that it was a 'half-loaf'. Toleration was in the circumstances an advance on persecution in the name of unity; but unity still remained the ideal. Historical religious memories are certainly long, as the events in Ulster show; they can still act as a powerful brake on the ecumenical wheel, as Professor Henderson's books show very clearly. But in the end there is no bridging the gulf between those who are satisfied with the *status quo* of denominationalism and toleration, and those who feel impelled to move forward to unity.

Two Canute factors have now been diagnosed as holding back the strong tide of church unity – the very real complexities of the situation, and the positive antagonism which is usually based on a dislike or rejection of the particular form which the movement has taken. The opposition to ecumenicalism has come from conservative and authoritarian parties within the churches. A third Canute factor can now be analysed – more difficult to pinpoint but in the end without doubt the most powerful delaying force of all. This is the general conservatism in the churches, which has not so much openly opposed the movement as failed to answer to its demands for new thought and consequent change. The movement after all is a *movement* which implies change; and the churches are on the whole conservative institutions which do not respond quickly to change. It is one thing to pay lip-service to the need for unity, but quite another to re-assess and re-order priorities to promote unity at every level. This calls for a more fundamental change of attitude than many churchmen have been able to encompass. This is particularly true when the church is itself in a period of challenge and change. There are numerous reforms and changes before the churches, each with its own claims on budgets and time. This means that priorities have to be weighed and in these circumstances it is not surprising if the most far-reaching and radical reform of all is the one which is relegated to somewhere near the bottom of the league. Lip-service will continue and mild action will be taken, but the fundamental change of attitude needed for real action is slow to come. To take one example at a national level: in the 1950s the top item on the agendas of the Convocations and Assembly of the Church of England was the reform of canon (that is ecclesiastical) law. An immense amount of work was put into this project dear to the heart of a certain type of ecclesiastic. The reform was carried through but many would say that its value has proved negligible. If the same work and effort had been put into matters ecumenical the unity movement would have been much further forward in England today and the Anglican/Methodist negotiators would not have had to admit that in the early seventies the two churches would not be sufficiently educated to be ready to move forward into full union. Or to take a local example: Scunthorpe in Lincolnshire was one of the first urban areas where the churches began to 'think ecumenically'; in the mid-sixties through its local Council of Churches it appointed an Ecumenical Officer, at that time (indeed still) a real move forward for any local church. But at the same time the local Anglicans, the dominant group in the area, were also much concerned with setting up a Group Council for effective corporate

action among themselves and with the rationalization
of their rural deaneries – both admirable and overdue
reforms but hardly so radical or full of potential as
the ecumenical project. In fact the ecumenical experiment never prospered as was hoped and it is the considered opinion of the Ecumenical Officer, himself an
Anglican, that 'if the Council of Churches had received
all the effort and commitment devoted to the Group
Council, the effects might have been remarkable. . . .
"Super church" is a crude phrase, but that is what many of
the more lively local councils of churches have become –
the effective working unit of the whole Church in a
locality – and that is what the Group Council had hoped
to be.'[28] Once again it was a matter of priorities: not of
a choice between good and bad, but of opting for one of
two, or more, desirable courses. In Scunthorpe as in many
other cases it was the most demanding, the ecumenical,
which was the loser.

A point must be made here which explains, though it
does not excuse, the unwillingness of many churchmen to
put their hands to the ecumenical plough in a really
committed way. Ecumenical work is slow and immensely
time-consuming. It is not simply that it requires a positive effort to think in terms of new structures and organizations, outside the well-known denominational ones,
which are necessary to take on some new piece of work. It
is also that, once that effort has been made, it implies the
recognition that ecumenical action will take considerably
longer than unilateral action by one church. The ecumenical movement is – probably unavoidably – committed to action through committees, with all that that
involves – decisions arrived at, referred back to constituent churches, amended, re-debated in committee and so
on. It cannot but be slow. To the reformer who wants to
get something done, it can sometimes be unbearably frus-
trating, especially if (as may often be the case) the reformer is also something of an ecclesiastical prima donna,

who dislikes committees in any case. Quicker by far to go it alone.

Again, the unity movement has roused doubts and suspicions in many a cautious conservative breast precisely because its leaders have so often been associated with other reforming movements in the churches. Between the wars, for instance, the outstanding ecumenical leader was William Temple. But for many people he was suspect because of his social and political views. Even within the movement itself this could lead to trouble and dissension. When the vital decision was made in 1937 to form the World Council of Churches it was opposed by Bishop A. C. Headlam, himself second only to Temple as an Anglican ecumenical leader. In a report to the Archbishop of Canterbury, the cautious Lang, Headlam gave as the prime reason for his opposition and 'extreme suspicion' the fact

that it associates us [i.e. many Anglicans, Orthodox and other opponents of the move in the Faith and Order Movement] too closely with the Life and Work Movement, which has been continually involved in political matters and controversy, and is largely influenced by the passion for identifying Christianity with Socialism.[29]

Headlam's warning was in many ways prophetic. Since the war the World Council of Churches, and indeed many national and local councils of churches, have become more and more committed to the cause of ecclesiastical reform or 'renewal' as part and parcel of the ecumenical movement. A church which was united but not reformed and renewed would in the eyes of many officers of the various ecumenical bodies be a contradiction in terms – something of nothing. In fact it is probably true that many officers of the World Council of Churches and other ecumenical agencies are working in this field precisely because through their radical views they have come to despair of their institutional and denominational

churches. Inevitably left-wing ecclesiastical views and
policies have spilled over into the political field. Thus
the World Council of Churches came under heavy
fire when in 1970 it became known that, through its
Programme to Combat Racism, it was making grants
to various bodies which had declared themselves to be
committed to the use of force to that end. Similarly
the British Council of Churches hardly endeared itself
to country clergymen when it joined the opposition
to the South African cricket tour in 1970. The association
of ecumenical with radical views has certainly prejudiced
the movement with many conservative – or one might
say middle-of-the-road – churchmen.

During the struggle for Methodist union one of its
opponents attacked the reunion party as being based on
'the magnificent ideals of an up-to-date gentleman who
sits in an office and manipulates papers'.[30]

There are two criticisms implicit here, both of which
have often been laid at the door of ecumenical leaders.
The first has already been noticed: it is the condemnation by the conservatives of the 'up-to-date-ness' of the
movement. The second is the feeling of the front-line
clergyman that the movement is directed from an 'office'
and is out of touch with the everyday realities of the
situation. This is a criticism which is often made of the
ecumenical movement, and it is a cap which often fits. It
is particularly true of the World Council of Churches
and of its national and local equivalents, which tend to be
staffed in officers or committees by overlapping personnel.
These bodies have seemed remote from the parish situation and their policies and statements – especially when
couched in hideous jargonistic 'ecumenese' – inappropriate and unhelpful to the parish clergy bearing the
burden and heat of the day. The parish minister who is
worried about money to repair the roof of his church or
opposition to some minor liturgical changes he is propos-
ing receives in his post a Council of Churches document

calling for radical action and talking about 'structures of dialogue' or 'creative tension'. He has heard this jargon from the same source often before and on each occasion his suspicion that it is time 'the man in the office' had a spell of parochial service is reinforced – and the cause of unity suffers. In one way this fact that ecumenical bureaucrats are out of touch with the local situation is, of course, endemic in the bureaucratic situation, but the situation is exaggerated in the ecclesiastical field: the churches have been slow to develop bureaucratic and administrative systems (it has been part of their weakness). Now that they have developed they have been particularly unpopular among conservative churchmen, and the fact that the ecumenical movement has depended so heavily on a bureaucracy has certainly not helped to sell its wares to the parson-in-the-pulpit and the man-in-the-pew. Moreover, as has already been seen, the bureaucrats are often (unlike many bureaucrats) markedly progressive in their thinking and feel they have a prophetic duty to the churches to be pointing the way ahead to the backwoodsmen in the churches. This has exaggerated the gap between the spokesmen of the ecumenical movement and the constituency of the churches to whom their message must get through if their cause is to prosper among many others which are competing for the time and attention of the harassed local vicar or minister.

The example of the harassed minister just cited would be typical of the situation in Britain, where ecumenical bureaucracy has undoubtedly built up resistance to the ecumenical message. How much more must this be true when similar ecumenical exhortations reach churchmen of the non-western nations who cannot easily and naturally deal in either the language or the procedures of the movement. The language is highly technical and/or metaphysical and the procedures centre on the committee, western managerial man's way of conducting business. In neither is the non-westerner at home. This is

the basic reason why despite all the impatience for unity
in the 'younger churches' the ecumenical movement, at
least as represented by the World Council of Churches,
has never taken root among them, with a handful of
exceptions among highly westernized church leaders.
This situation has been realistically appraised as recently
as December 1970 by an official of the World Council
who is particularly concerned with non-western participation.

Up to now the Churches of the Third World have only
made a theological appearance when they have made use of
European-American concepts. Our theological partners from
the Third World, who are different from us, never make themselves heard or else lose interest in this theological debate. It
becomes a luxury which they can only afford when it is sub-
sidized from abroad. The rules of this theological game are
ours even when the game is played in Nairobi or Mexico.[31]

This is a theme which will appear often in the chapters
which follow, but it is important to make the general
point now to set this aspect of the question of resistance to
the ecumenical movement in a world-wide context.

In this discussion of the conservative Canute factors
which hold back the ecumenical tide one element has
appeared by implication a number of times. It is the fact
that the conservatism comes largely from the clergy. This
fact assumes particular significance when it is remembered that the ecumenical movement and the churches
themselves are clergy-dominated. It is true that in the last
five or ten years all the churches, including the Roman
Catholic, have been attempting belatedly to rectify this
state of affairs and to promote the laity from second-class
to first-class ecclesiastical citizenship. This movement
started after the war with a theological re-assessment of
the place of the laity in the church or 'people (*laos*) of
God'. It has now in many cases reached the point of being
reflected in the actual government and organization of

the churches. One recent example has been the synodical movement in the Church of England whereby in 1970 ultimate authority in the government of the church – in doctrinal as well as in administrative matters – passed from the clerical Convocations (which had rejected the Anglican/Methodist unity scheme in 1969) to the new General Synod, with its three constituents of bishops, clergy and laity.

But in spite of these structural alterations it will still be some time before in most congregations clerical domination is replaced by clerical-lay partnership. And the fact remains that during the sixty years of the life of the modern ecumenical movement all the churches have been clergy-dominated organizations. The most frequent form of instruction and communication in the churches is the sermon from the minister to the congregation, with no chance of come-back; on more informal occasions the most regular form would be the talk followed by sporadic questions for a few minutes, a pattern which would be the despair of an adult educationalist and one which allows no real interchange between clergy and laity. In fact it cannot be doubted that in the period of the ecumenical movement the clergy have called the tune for the churches and must therefore be held responsible for whatever for good or ill has happened to them.

On 16 September 1967 Sir Charles Jeffries, a distinguished layman of the Church of England, contributed an article to *The Times* entitled 'A Layman's View of Christian Unity'. He complained of the slow progress being made towards church union and ascribed this to the fact that 'the negotiations and discussions ... are (inevitably) carried on by professional ecclesiastics and theologians, whose point of view is radically different from that of the layman in the pew'. He called for more drastic measures which seemed to him 'very like New Testament Christianity and very like sheer common sense'. And he concluded:

However as far as I can judge they [that is his proposals] are in complete contradiction of the assumption on which the ecclesiastics and specialists approach the question of Christian unity. Is it not time the laity had their say?

As so often happens an article on a religious topic led to a correspondence far more extended than would really be warranted by the proportion of people in the country concerned in the practice of Christianity. Sixteen letters were published which were in sympathy with Sir Charles' point of view; of these seven were from laymen, and nine from clergy. Of the letters published which opposed the original article, two were from laymen and six from clergy. One angry clergyman wrote:

It only goes to confirm the dispiriting experience of many clergy that numbers of their laity just will not take the trouble to inform themselves nor let themselves be informed of the fundamental theological factors behind the disunity of the church. This is surely hardly a cause for the laity to congratulate themselves. . . . Sir Charles Jeffries described himself as an 'untheological layman'. He appeared content to remain so. More's the pity.

The proprietary note in describing the laity as being 'owned' by the clergy – 'their laity' – should be noted. It typifies the fact that the clergy *expect* to dominate the church.

Another of the clergy unfriendly to Sir Charles was well known in ecumenical circles. The Reverend Henry Cooper opened his letter: 'I wonder if Sir Charles Jeffries' article would have been accepted so readily had it been about, say, "a layman's view of medicine", or ". . . of law", or ". . . of military strategy".' Dr Cooper may, of course, have found Sir Charles' cap fitting. However that may be, he concluded in somewhat lofty tones:

The impatience of the layman is natural enough, but somewhat naive. If he would go into the matter more fully, study the doctrine, and assess the consequences in the light of previous history, he would find the matter is far from simple. . . . Some of us have spent many years and hundreds of hours in study and conference trying to find ways forward. It ill becomes those who have not to be self-confident about the answers.[32]

These unhappy letters could be said to be the text for this book. They show how the clergy seem to resent the laity taking a hand in ecumenical affairs. It is true that the issues are complicated; but that is no reason for not trying to tell the laity about them and to involve the laity in the movement. It is true, too, that the laity are becoming impatient. They have good reason to be. They suspect that the dominant clergy are getting their priorities wrong. In the same correspondence Bishop F. A. Cockin wrote that 'the lack of a truly Christian sense of proportion' is the underlying reason for the failure of the ecumenical movement.

This is, one might almost say, the congenital temptation which besets the *clerical* mind. We have a kind of vested ecclesiastical interest in the Church. Its rites and ceremonies, its regulations, its very structure are our special preserve. We are tolerably ready to allow that lay folk have a right to be concerned with the interpretation of Christian faith: but matters of order are the prerogative of the ordained ministry. Because this is so, the 'professionals' in whose hands most of the reunion negotiations rest, tend to make unanimity on these questions, validity of orders, the correct administration of sacraments, even the orthodox interpretation of the nature of a sacrament, the touchstone by which we judge the satisfactoriness of any agreement. Is this the true order of priorities according to the Gospels, according to the mind of Christ? . . . When we face realistically the tasks to which God, being what he is revealed to be in Christ, must be calling his Church, we shall I believe be forced to realize that much of the detail with which these endless debates are concerned is really peripheral. A Church which is setting itself to grapple with Notting Hill or Smethwick, still more a Church which is trying to maintain its witness in East Germany or Peking, will know that unity among Christians needs deeper roots than 'validity' or 'correctness'.[33]

There can be little doubt that the bishop is right: the clergy, who dominate the churches and therefore ecumenical procedures, are unwilling to make changes on those technical matters which most obviously govern these negotiations. Two recent examples from Britain illustrate this fact; no doubt the same type of statistics could be produced for the churches the world over. The circumstances under which members of other churches can be admitted to the sacraments of other churches, especially of the Anglican church, has been a burning question in the ecumenical movement for many years. It is no exaggeration to say that in Britain Anglican slowness on this matter has been *the* most vital single barrier to ecumenical advance (see below, pp. 495–503). In Scotland in 1969 a survey was taken in the Episcopalian church. This showed that, whereas 34·6 per cent of the laity were in favour of relaxing the Anglican rules about intercommunion so as to give unqualified intercommunion to baptized members of all churches, only 12·8 per cent of the 'professionals' – the clergy – were in favour of the same relaxation. What is perhaps more significant is that these percentages obtained throughout the church, despite the fact that the clergy had, no doubt, been teaching 'their' laity to follow their lead in the matter (see below, pp. 468 and 502). This seems to bear out Bishop Cockin's belief that the clergy and the laity have different sets of priorities on the question of reunion. In England, when in February 1971 the Church of England Synod approved some moderate (and one might think long-overdue) changes in the rules governing the admission of members of other churches to Holy Communion, the voting was as follows: bishops 21 for, 10 against; clergy 121 for, 93 against; laity 159 for, 42 against. It is true that the measure was passed, but it is the voting figures which are significant – and typical. In general –

and this does not only apply to the Church of England – church leaders are in favour of cautious and moderate reform, though not as radical as a minority of the clergy. But the majority of the clergy are far more conservative. Especially on these technical matters they are much more cautious than either the leaders or the laity. This, as Bishop Cockin saw, has been the greatest single impediment to ecumenical advance.

And there is no reason to think that this situation is likely to alter in any startling way. It is true that in many churches the laity now have more of a say in the government of ecclesiastical affairs. But often the clergy still have a veto. And the fact is that – at least in the western world – as the churches decline the clergy are increasingly coming to represent the older generations. In these circumstances conservatism is more, rather than less, likely.

In 1922 at the height of the struggle for Methodist reunion, one correspondent wrote to the *Methodist Recorder*, 'It was as if one stood by and watched preparations being made for dismantling the old home in which one had lived as a child, where one's fathers lived and died, and in which one had passed through the most tender and sacred associations of one's life.'[34] How eloquently and sadly those words capture the feeling of rage, hurt and bafflement with which older generations or conservatives watch the changes being brought about by new movements or younger men. But very often in the course of the ecumenical movement, which is in any case a comparatively *new* movement, it is these feelings which have carried the day and held back the tide of change. The conservatives have not been willing to see the houses dismantled. Above all the clergy, whose lives are professionally committed to the old structures, have resisted the process.

In 1967 the British Council of Churches set up a nationwide study course entitled 'The People Next Door'. The object of the course was to educate people in ecumenical action and priorities. A feature of the operation was that clergy were discouraged from joining the ecumenical study groups and above all from leading them. It was hoped in this way to avoid clerical domination and to let the laity have their ecumenical heads. As a result it was known that in many places the clergy actually discouraged the formation of groups, frightened no doubt at what 'their' laity might do off the clerical leading rein. The response was much smaller than was initially hoped for: some 85,000 people took part instead of a predicted two million. But one thing that clearly emerged from the groups was a persistent vein of anti-clericalism on the matter of ecumenical urgency. The following are typical quotations from the group reports.

The chief stumbling block to unity is the clergy and ministers.

All clergy ought to attend courses on Christian unity run by laymen.

The clergy gave birth to us as a body and it is not known whether they wish us to continue as a body – or whether they think they have created a monster and we should now be exterminated.

The laity are more ready to accept ecumenism than the church hierarchies give us credit for.[35]

This anti-clericalism comes, it should be noted, not from unchurched people but from laity who were keen enough to give up several week-day evenings to following the study course. The unearthing of such a mood of dissatisfaction on clerical leadership on matters ecumenical should have showed a red light to the 'church hierarchies' which were being criticized.

In 1954 Bishop Stephen Neill, fresh from his experience as an ecumenical negotiator in South India, wrote

The final and terrible difficulty is that churches cannot unite unless they are willing to die. In a truly united Church there would be no more Anglicans or Lutherans or Baptists or Methodists. But the disappearance from the world of those great and honoured names is the very thing that many loyal churchmen are not prepared to face. . . . Until church union clearly takes shape as a better resurrection on the other side of death, the impulse towards it is likely to be weak and half hearted; and such weak impulses are not strong enough to overcome the tremendous difficulties in the way.[36]

Twelve years later, in 1966, and with very little more outward ecumenical progress made, Bishop Neill concluded his Bampton Lectures, *The Church and Christian Union*, with these words:

When all is said and done, the last and gravest hindrance to unity is simply the deep desire of the denominations to continue their own separate existence. This is frequently rationalized as a concern that there should be no diminution in the body of inherited truth. The tacit assumption is made that this truth can be safeguarded only as long as it remains in the guardianship of this particular denomination organized as it is at present. It is a well-known fact that the majority of the mentally ill are ill because they want to be ill – in some strange way their sickness is of value to them. If the desire to be ill could be replaced by a whole-hearted desire to get well, the patient could arise and walk – but at the price of losing whatever is of value that was represented by the sickness. If the churches really wanted to be one, they could be one within measurable time; what holds them apart is in large measure the deep-seated love of separate existence, and the sense of superiority enjoyed by those who feel themselves to have been endowed with a special portion of the truth. The price to be paid for union is high. It is easy to enjoy fellowship and cooperation. Discussion of plans for union is an interesting and at times enjoyable form of intellectual dissipation. To face the actual plunge into the cold waters of unity is a very different thing.[37]

Bishop Neill adds that in those churches which have found union, 'there the issue of death and life has been frankly faced'. Still more recently a British ecumenical leader commented to the writer, 'I think all the churches are fooling about in this matter of unity, and that none of us are really prepared to die.'

The theme of death and resurrection is central to the Christian religion. It is based on the example of the work of Christ. From the earliest days the church applied the image of death and resurrection to its members. They died and were resurrected in baptism and lived the rest of their lives in this pattern: 'you were buried with him in baptism,' wrote St Paul, 'in which you were also raised with him through faith in the working of God, who raised him from the dead' (Colossians ii, 12). The churches apply this pattern of death and resurrection to their individual members, but they are slow to apply it to themselves. They are unwilling to 'watch the old homes being dismantled'. Death and resurrection in baptism for the individual follows conversion – which, however it happens, is a personal experience. Bishop Oliver Tomkins, one of the leading ecumenists of this generation, has written 'the essence of it is, ecumenicity is something which happens in the souls of Christians'.[38] Perhaps still not enough Christians – and especially clergy – have been converted to ecumenicity to be able to face the consequent death of their separate churches – 'in sure and certain hope', as the Church of England funeral service has it, of the resurrection of Church unity.

There has been ecumenical progress, but its character has been not so much death and resurrection, as too little and too late. It remains to be seen whether the combined effect of all the delaying factors will add up to the final failure of the movement. Later chapters will show that the World Council of Churches, which by the late sixties had become a formidable organization, is now faced with drastic retrenchment because the declining churches can no longer support it; that almost all the movements to unity among the churches the world over are now at a critical stage of breakthrough or failure; that an increas-

ing number of laity are reaching a point of rebellion, or –
perhaps worse – disgust and disillusion. It remains to be
seen whether the churches will find unity along the lines
they have been seeking it for more than fifty years,
whether unity will come too late to be significant – or
whether some altogether new ecumenical pattern will
emerge.

CHAPTER TWO

The Church United:
The First Four Centuries

There is one body, and one spirit, just as you were
called to the one hope that belongs to your call, one
Lord, one faith, one baptism, one God and Father of all.

EPHESIANS iv, 4–6

UNITY IN THE NEW TESTAMENT

THE New Testament has been sorely mistreated by the
divided and competing churches. They have dug into it
as a quarry to extract proof texts. They have then used
these as stones to sling at each other to 'prove' that their
own particular form of church or ministry is Biblical and
right. But the Bible does not lend itself to this kind of
treatment; and in any case (as will be seen later in this
chapter) in the New Testament period no definite form of
ministry had emerged. Almost always, therefore, the
polemical arguments have convinced only the converted.

For instance, from the earliest days of the advancing
claims of the Bishop of Rome the Roman Catholics have
leaned heavily on the 'Petrine text', Matthew xvi, 18–19:
'And I tell you, you are Peter and on this rock [there is a
play on words here for the Greek word for rock is *petra*] I
will build my church, and the powers of death [literally
the gates of Hades] will not prevail against it ...' But
this isolated text, even taken with the general leadership
of Peter among the apostles, is hardly enough to make a
secure foundation for the great weight of the papal
superstructure afterwards erected on it. In the first place
there is nothing to suggest that Peter's leadership and
authority will be transferred to his successors – and in-

deed the presence of Peter in Rome and his foundation of the church there can still not be taken to be proven. Secondly, to rely on this text in support of Peter and his successors is to ignore the more general teaching of the New Testament, and especially of the epistles (which hardly mention Peter) that the church is 'built upon the foundation of the apostles and prophets, Jesus Christ himself being the chief corner-stone' (Ephesians ii, 20; see also Revelation xxi, 14, where the apostles are the twelve foundations of the heavenly city).

Extreme claims for papal authority can therefore call only weak New Testament witnesses and it is perhaps partly in deference to this fact that Roman Catholic scholars have recently been more cautious in what they claim about the pope's position. Father Sebastian Bullough, for instance, in *Roman Catholicism* says: 'The supreme head of the Church's government is therefore the Pope precisely as head of the united episcopate, and with him and under his leadership are all the bishops of the world.'[1] Other Roman Catholics would go even further in backing down from an extreme position on papal authority and this seems to be the general direction in which, since Vatican II, the Roman Church is feeling its way.[2]

High-church Anglicans have also appealed to the New Testament to support their position that only a church with a ministry in the apostolic succession, that is reaching back to the apostles by an unbroken line of episcopal ordinations, can claim an absolute validity for its ministry and thus for its sacraments. But all the learning and ingenuity of the authors of such a book as *The Apostolic Ministry* cannot prove that the New Testament teaches that Christ set up a system by which the power of his apostles would be transferred to their successors in the line of ordination. Once again the case, on New Testament evidence, is not proven.

'The Bible, and the Bible only, is the religion of the

Protestants,' said the seventeenth-century writer William Chillingworth. It was therefore to be expected that the Protestants would appeal to the New Testament in support of the form of ministry they had adopted. The followers of Calvin made great play with Ephesians iv, 11 and 12: 'and his gifts were that some should be apostles, some prophets, some evangelists, some pastors and teachers, for the equipment of the saints, for the work of ministry...' But it was always difficult to see how this list squared with the system of presbyters and elders working within a hierarchy of courts and synods which was developed in the churches which looked to Geneva for their inspiration. Once again the argument appealed to believers but the unconverted remained unconvinced.

The fact is that the New Testament does not contain evidence about the ministry of the church which can be shaped or moulded to guarantee the ministry of any of the historic churches of Christendom, as these later developed. What 'evidence' there is in the New Testament about a ministry is vague and incoherent; this was not a matter to which the church had yet been forced to turn its mind; it must be remembered that the early Christians expected the second coming of Christ to be in their own life-time and therefore the setting up of a permanent and uniform pattern of Christian ministry would hardly have seemed a high priority. The most that can be said is that in the later epistles (I and II Timothy and Titus), whereas formerly stress had been laid on the individual spiritual gifts of the leaders and ministers, now it was 'the office as such in relation to its function in the corporate life' of the church which was seen to be important.[3] Apostles were always the key figures, and their importance lay in the fact that they were the men who had been with Christ in his life-time and were the essential witnesses, not only of his teaching, but also of his death and resurrection. This part of their ministry could not be transferred to any successor; on the other hand certain aspects of their leadership they could and obviously did transfer. But the New Testament is not specific on the details beyond recounting that in the early days in Jerusalem they delegated some of their administrative work to men who were ordained as deacons (servants: Acts vi, 1–6). Ministers who appear later on the scene are elders (*presbuteroi*) and overseers (*episkopoi* = bishops) and, less often, teachers, but the former titles seem to have been used interchangeably and it is not possible to allot specific functions or a definite place in any hierarchical set-up to these first ministers. It is not until the post-New Testament period, that is after the end of the first century, that the definite hierarchy of the three-fold ministry of bishops, priests (or presbyters) and deacons appears, and the steps by which this process took place and became the universal norm are unknown, since there is no evidence which traces them.

It is not possible, therefore, to look to the New Testament for a blueprint of a single agreed and universal ministry on which the unity of the church can be established. Nor is it possible to demand of the New Testament a fully worked-out doctrine of the unity of the church. That again is to ask the wrong question. To complain, as one recent writer, who must be labelled anti-ecumenical, has done, that there is only a 'meagre harvest' of two passages on the unity of the church is to misunderstand the nature of the evidence with which we are dealing. The New Testament is not a theological textbook. It does not set out to argue coherently one Christian doctrine after another. It is a collection of writings recording the life, death, resurrection and ascension of Jesus of Nazareth and describing the results of men and women becoming the disciples of the risen Christ and so creating a new society of Christians or Christ's men.

It is commonly said that Christ 'founded' the church and that its unity springs from this fact. But even this simple statement is not the best way of describing the beginning of the church as we find it in the New Testament. Rather the church was the creation of the Holy Spirit as men and women responded to the apostolic witness and teaching about Jesus Christ and acknowledged him as 'Lord'. This they did in baptism and through baptism they believed they were united with Christ in his death and resurrection. Both the teaching and the symbolism of the act expressed this: 'you were buried with him in baptism, in which you were also raised with him through faith in the working of God, who raised him from the dead' (Colossians ii, 12; see also Romans vi, 3–5, and Galatians iii, 27, which speaks of being 'baptized into Christ'). In baptism men 'put on' Christ; they became his followers; they received his spirit; they entered his church. The unity of the church was the unity which men found in the common experience of baptism; it was a unity which bound them first to Christ and then to one another. When he saw this unity threatened the writer to the Ephesians exhorted his readers to 'maintain the unity of the spirit in the bond of peace', giving as his all-inclusive reason, 'there is one body and one spirit, just as you were called to the one hope that belongs to your call, one Lord, one faith, one baptism, one God and Father of us all' (Ephesians iv, 3–6).

It is not certain whether or not St Paul was the author of the epistle to the Ephesians, but the thought is certainly 'Pauline', and the passage quoted contains his favourite metaphor for the church – that of the 'body'. St Paul was the earliest of the New Testmant writers and his thought was essential to the formation of Christian doctrine. He uses a number of metaphors about the church, all of them strongly suggesting its unity. These were: 'the Body of Christ' (I Corinthians xii, 17–20, and Ephesians iv, 11–15); 'the household of God' (Ephesians ii, 19); 'the temple of God' (Ephesians ii, 21, and I Corinthians iii, 16 and 17); 'God's building' (rather vaguer references connected with the foregoing passages); and 'the

Bride of Christ' (Ephesians v, 22–32; the actual phrase is not used but the whole passage speaks of it and the metaphor itself occurs in Revelation xxi, 9). This last idea, that of the Bride of Christ, is different from the others, and may be considered first. It has behind it the idea of the unity between Christ and his church, which can be compared to the unity of marriage – and for St Paul the unity of marriage is the unity of 'one flesh'. In this passage the metaphors of the bride and the body are actually mixed, for he says that 'the husband is the head of the wife as Christ is the head of the Church, his body' (Ephesians v, 23). Returning in the same passage to the idea of the bride he says that the church must be 'presented before him [Christ] in splendour without spot or wrinkle or any such thing' (v, 27). Clearly this virginal, bridal purity must include the unity of the church. Unless St Paul had badly lost control of his metaphor it would be unthinkable for Christ to have more than one bride – and the very fact that St Paul's teaching about marriage dwelt so much on the idea of the fleshly union is a pointer to the 'tangible' nature of his thought about the church.

The same is true of the other metaphors he uses. The temple, the building, the body – with the possible exception of the household, they are all very tangible ideas. They suggest visible entities. Those who think of the unity of the church only or primarily in terms of an invisible church created by the unseen bonds between 'true believers' have failed to reckon with this 'outward and visible' – or concrete – element in Paul's thought. Moreover the metaphors have another thing in common: they are all collective nouns. They describe a whole which is made up of various parts – people in the household, stones in the temple, limbs and organs in the body – but in which the whole is greater than the mere aggregate of the sum of the parts; it is, as it were, 'prior' to them. This is most clearly seen in the image of the body, which ex-

presses a unity in the church which overrides the individuality of its members. Indeed the individuality of
each single member gains significance only when it acts as
a part of the whole: 'if the whole body were an eye,
where would be the hearing? ... If all were a single
organ, where would the body be? As it is there are many
parts, yet one body' (I Corinthians xii, 17–20). In fact
Paul put forward his image of the body to the Corinthians precisely because their individualism was running
riot and wrecking the unity of the church. He had to
show that their individuality only made sense *within* the
wider unity of the body of the church into which they
had been baptized: 'by one Spirit we were all baptized
into one body ... you are the body of Christ and individually members of it' (I Corinthians xii, 13 and 27).

When the image of the body occurs again in Ephesians
it is once again with reference to the variety of gifts of the
individual members (Ephesians iv, 11–16). But here the
emphasis is subtly different. In I Corinthians Christ is the
whole body and all the members are parts of him. In
Ephesians he is the head of the body, and the members
'are to grow up in every way into him who is the head, into
Christ' (Ephesians iv, 15). In other words Ephesians allows
for the growth or 'building up' of the body, 'until we all
attain to the unity of the faith and of the knowledge of
the Son of God, to mature manhood, to the measure of
the stature of the fulness of Christ' (iv, 13). There is, in
fact, in this body room for imperfection: 'unity in Christ
does not eliminate growth, nor dangers hostile to the
growth of the Body. . . . The unity of the body is divinely
grounded and furnished. Yet constant vigilance is required to secure it.'[4] The idea that Christians have in
one sense still to become what, in another sense, in Christ
they already are – the tension between being and becoming – is not uncommon in the New Testament. It can be
seen in the belief about baptism, and it is seen here in
what was believed about the church. Broadly speaking it

can be said that these two aspects of the Pauline meta-phor of the body, that of Corinthians and that of Ephe-sians, are mirrored later in 'Catholic' and 'Protestant' teaching about the church respectively. Catholics have tended to see Christ as the whole body; they have em-phasized the perfection of the church, its indefectibility and infallibility; for them the church is often 'the exten-sion of the Incarnation of Christ'; the idea of the second coming and of judgement is played down. In reply Protes-tants tend to stress the headship of Christ over his body, the church; it has still to achieve perfection; it is liable always to corruption, and hence open always to reform; Christ the Head remains always the Judge.[5] The original metaphor of the body speaks clearly of a unity which is tangible, outward and concrete, yet within this unity both aspects of the body idea must be retained if justice is to be done to the full New Testament teaching.

An earlier reference to Christ as the head of the body comes in Colossians: 'he is the head of the body, the church; he is the beginning, the first-born from the dead' (Colossians i, 18). This introduces a new Pauline thought, and one which again stresses the unity of the church. Christ was the first-born from the dead through his resur-rection. As such he was the head, not only of the church, but of a new race or a new creation; he was the 'second Adam' (I Corinthians xv, 20–48). 'The old has passed away, behold the new has come' (II Corinthians v, 17). The beginning of this new dispensation had one marked and visible result in the life of the church: in the church the old fixed barriers of the ancient world were removed – 'here there cannot be Greek and Jew, circumcised and uncircumcised, barbarian, Scythian, slave, free man, but Christ is all and in all' (Colossians iii, 11). There was in fact a new unity in the church and for all mankind the divisions of race, class and culture no longer existed.

But it was a unity which was not to be the sole pre-rogative of the church. The church holds it in trust for the world. In time the whole world will find the unity already discovered in the church as a result of its faith in the risen Christ. Indeed this thought explains the significance of the very word St Paul used for the church. *Ekklesia* means literally 'called out' and was the word used in the Septuagint (the Greek version of the Old Testament) for the congregation or assembly of Israel. Clearly Paul had in mind the parallel between the church and Israel, the chosen people of God's old covenant. From this idea it was no far cry to telling Christians 'you are a chosen race, a royal priesthood, a holy nation, God's own people' (I Peter ii, 9). They would have known what this meant. For each of these phrases – and again they are all collective nouns – had a special Old Testament significance and was heavy with overtones. The Jews saw themselves as God's chosen people, elected from among all the nations of the world. But they always knew that this election was not for any special privilege, but in order that they might bring their own gifts to the rest of the world. 'I will make you a great nation,' Jehovah had said to Abraham, 'and in you all the families of the earth will be blessed' (Genesis xii, 2). This belief was particularly strong in the prophets. They had to fight the debased notion that Israel had been elected for her own glorification and for the defeat and humiliation of her enemies. The true vision was otherwise: God intended the unity of the human race, and Israel's function was to be 'the instrument of peace, of the divine purpose of healing for all mankind'. The nations would flock to Jerusalem; but they would do so, not to be humiliated, but to share in the light and life of Israel and in the knowledge of the Lord. Israel was to be 'the magnetic centre of unity'.[6]

The prophets were therefore passionately concerned about the unity of Israel. After the divisions between the north and south kingdoms, and the differences between those who had gone into exile and those who had re-

mained in the home country, they felt that the unity
which Israel held in trust for the world had been lost. 'I
will make one nation in the land,' was the cry of Ezekiel
from exile (Ezekiel xxxvii, 22). 'It cannot be over-empha-
sized that, in the profoundest passages in the Old Testament, unity is essential for the discharge of the functions
of the servant of the Lord.'[7] St Paul believed that the
church had inherited the election of Israel, as by grafting
a new branch into the original stem of an olive tree
(Romans xi). The function of the church was the same as
had been that of Israel – 'riches for the world' (Romans
xi, 12). And the method would be the same. The prophets
had come to see that Israel would fulfil her calling in the
role of the 'suffering servant' in the world. For St Paul,
too, Christians and the church were bound to suffer for
they had been united with Christ by 'baptism into his
death'. In that baptism, and in the suffering which it implied, they found their unity, and the unity was a foretaste of the unity of the world: 'for as many of you as
were baptized into Christ have put on Christ. There is
neither Jew nor Greek, there is neither slave nor free,
there is neither male nor female: for you are all one in
Christ Jesus' (Galatians iii, 27 and 28). But St Paul also
believed that, if the old Israel could be cut off for its
disobedience, so could the new: 'for if God did not spare
the natural branches neither will he spare you' (Romans
xi, 21). As much as the prophets he would have deplored
any disunity in Israel, as making impossible the fundamental task of reconciling the world to God, and in that
process of reconciliation re-creating the world's peace and
unity in Christ: 'for he is our peace, who has made us
both one and has broken down the dividing wall of
hostility ... that he might create in himself one new man
... so making peace, and might reconcile us both [that is
Jews and Gentiles] to God in one body through the
Cross' (Ephesians ii, 14–16). Once the church had lost its
own peace it could hardly bring peace to the world, and

must therefore be in danger of the same judgement which befell the old Israel.

For St Paul the unity of the church was based on its unity with Christ, and both in turn were based on the unity – or reconciliation – which by his death Christ had made between the world and God. This attitude could very well be called mystical – and St John took the mystical basis of the unity of the church a step further. His image for the unity between the believer and Christ is that of the vine: 'I am the vine, and you are the branches: he who abides in me and I in him, he it is that bears much fruit' (John xv, 5). The parallel between the image of the vine and that of the body of Christ is obvious; in each Christ is the whole and individual Christians are parts; in each there is an organic cohesion of the parts within the whole. Where St John takes his image a step further is that the vine is not self-sufficient within itself. There is a vine-dresser. 'I am the true vine and my Father is the vine-dresser. . . . As the Father has loved me, so have I loved you; abide in my love' (John xv, 1 and 9). The unity between the believer and Christ is of the same nature as that between Christ and his Father. It is the unity of love – a love which springs in the first place from the love of God the Father.

This idea is further developed in John xvii, the chapter known as the high priestly prayer. Jesus recognizes that the hour of his death has come. He has done all he can for his disciples; now he prays for them as he leaves the world.

Now I am no more in the world, but they are in the world, and I am coming to thee. Holy Father keep them in thy name, which thou hast given me, that they may be one, even as we are one. . . . Sanctify them in the truth; thy word is truth. As thou hast sent me into the world, so I have sent them into the world. . . . I do not pray for these only, but also for those who are to believe in me through their word, that they may all be one: even as thou, Father are in me, and I in thee, that they

may also be in us, that the world may believe that thou hast
sent me. The glory which thou hast given to me I have given
to them, that they may be one even as we are one, I in them
and thou in me, that they may become perfectly one, so that
the world may know that thou hast sent me. (John xvii,
11–23)

This passage, which has become the greatest single scriptural text for the ecumenical movement, speaks for itself.
The marks of the church are holiness, truth, unity and
apostolicity. It is sent to the world – the meaning of
apostolicity – to convert the world to the same unity of
love which it has with Christ, and Christ has with the
Father. It is primarily through seeing the unity of the
church in this love that the world will be converted. The
teaching of the Fourth Gospel is the same as that of St
Paul: unity is essential to the church if it is to fulfil its
task in and for the world.

The evidence of the New Testament teaching on the
unity of the church is, therefore, very strong. That the
teaching is not explicit should not cause any surprise. In
the first place, as has already been said, the New Testament writers were not out to write a theological textbook.
In the second place the church *was* united and there was
in fact no reason to spell out in theological terms that
unity, which was taken for granted as a datum. On the
other hand all that was said about the church made it
clear that nothing less than full unity, inward and outward, would match up to the picture presented. Inwardly
the unity must be complete and without discord, or the
mystical element in the teaching of St Paul and St John
would hardly be satisfied and outward unity would become a mockery. Outwardly the unity must be complete,
not only because of the very concrete and tangible images
used to describe the church, but also because it was
through the tangible agency of the sacraments that the
believer entered the church and maintained his membership of it. In baptism he found a unity with Christ and

his fellow believers which was strengthened and maintained by the Lord's Supper – a sacrament to which St Paul applied the word *koinonia*, or communion, which also he used to describe the unity of the church.

This same word *koinonia* is employed in the historical passages of the New Testament to describe the unity of the church. The unity of the early days in Jerusalem is set out as follows: 'they devoted themselves to the apostles' teaching and fellowship [*koinonia*], to the breaking of bread and the prayers' (Acts ii, 42). That fellowship, or communion, with the apostles was thought to be essential is seen in another passage where Paul and Barnabas, after a long period of independent missionary activity among the Gentiles, returned to report to the apostles in Jerusalem and received from them 'the right hand of fellowship' (Galatians ii, 9). This, of course, is a Pauline passage and it was in fact Paul who had come to use the word *koinonia* as typifying the quality of the unity of the church. Most typically and surprisingly of all he used it for the great collection which he made among the Gentile churches for the mother church in Jerusalem, which had fallen on bad days. St Paul set great store by this collection – even risking his life for it – because it was a symbol of the new unity between the Jews and Gentiles, and it is this episode which shows most clearly the fact that even in those early days the church had a sense of its universal, or, as we should now say, catholic, existence. It might have been expected that the small and scattered Christian communities would feel and be self-contained. But this was not the case. The sense of the unity of these scattered churches seems to have been paramount, and Christians could move from one to another and be welcomed into the same universal 'fellowship'. Indeed as P. T. Forsyth – himself a Congregationalist and therefore not likely to under-emphasize the importance and independence of the local congregation – puts it, 'the total church was not made up by adding the local churches together, but the local church was a church through representing then and there the total church'.[8]

But here again in these historical passages the unity of the church in the New Testament is more implicit than explicit. In fact, within the overall unity, it is the dissensions and disagreements which come more to the surface of the Acts of the Apostles and the various epistles. There was the difficult position of Paul *vis-à-vis* the Twelve, as an apostle 'born out of due time' who yet claimed the same authority as those who had known Jesus in his life and at his resurrection. There was the great controversy, which all but split the church, over preaching to the Gentiles and the terms on which they could be admitted to the church. There was the personal squabble on missionary tactics between Paul and Barnabas which brought to an end their collaboration. There is all the evidence of trouble in the local churches – doctrinal and disciplinary – which led to so much fevered letter-writing by St Paul. Indeed, as we have seen, it was precisely against the party disputes which were threatening to split the church in Corinth that Paul produced his great metaphor of the body in which the individuality of the various parts could be made to serve the unity of the whole.

This is in fact the picture which emerges from the New Testament; it is important not to over-idealize it. There were great scandals and divisions; there was constant controversy. How could it have been otherwise when there was so much to be hammered out? But over all there was a sense of unity. The greater the tensions the more store the early Christians set by the unity of their church.

UNITY AND DISSENSION IN THE FIRST FIVE CENTURIES

The same basic pattern emerges from the history of the church during the first five centuries of its life. As it grew in size and also moved away from the honeymoon period of the days of the apostles, the doctrinal disputes became more complex and the disciplinary and personal ones less edifying; they are also better documented. But over all, the pattern – and the demands – of unity remained. Moreover as divisions became more common and blatant, though not until the fifth century permanent, there developed a corresponding horror at the sinfulness of the situation. 'Nothing angers God so much,' said St John Chrysostom, Bishop of Constantinople at the end of the fourth century, 'as the division of the church. Even if we have done ten thousand good deeds, those of us who cut up the fullness of the church will be punished no less than those who cut his body' (that is literally at the crucifixion).[9]

The two words which were used of divisions and false teaching were schism and heresy respectively. St Paul used both words and detected both tendencies already in I Corinthians (i, 10; xi, 18–19; xii, 24–25). In the early church it was usual to distinguish heresy, which was doctrinal error, from schism, which was orthodox dissent, or, as St Augustine put it in 400, 'while holding the same opinions and worshipping with the same rites as the rest, to delight simply in the division of the congregation'.[10] As a matter of fact the division between heresy and schism was never so clear-cut as this makes it sound, either in the early church or in the divisions which have come more recently. For instance many doctrinal disputes have led to divisions which continued and were perpetuated long after the original doctrinal issue was settled or became of no importance. Similarly most schisms start from a disagreement on some matter of church government or discipline; but it is not very difficult for an argument on a practical matter, such as the rebaptism of a reformed heretic or the terms of re-admission to the church of someone who has lapsed under the pressure of persecution, to become a theological controversy about

78

the authority, and indeed the very nature, of the church. Nevertheless the broad distinction between heresy and schism is useful in analysing the divisions of the church.

During the first five centuries there were three main sorts of heresy. The first was that which has been called 'enthusiasm'[11] or perfectionism. When the expected second coming of Christ did not take place within the lifetime of his earliest disciples the church had to settle down into a routine pattern of life. There were some who resented this: they tried to revive the early spirit; they continued to look for the second coming, usually in the form of the setting-up of a visible kingdom of Christ; they often resisted the regular ministry and ministrations of the church, believing in a more exclusive body of separated believers. They tended, in fact, to excess. Such were the Montanists in the second century, the Novationists in the third and the Donatists in the fourth. Such, too, in succeeding centuries from the Middle Ages to our own day have been many small non-conformist sects. In dealing with these enthusiasts the church had to tread very warily, not least because, enthusiasm apart, they were orthodox, often fiercely so. It is here that the dividing line between heresy and schism is at its thinnest. Moreover it is never easy to answer the argument of 'holier-than-thou'. In fact many more dishonest – and equally ineffective – answers have been given than that of the great Bishop Butler of Durham to John Wesley: 'Sir, the pretending to extraordinary revelation and gifts is a horrid thing, a very horrid thing.'[12] For the early church the enthusiasts condemned themselves by the very fact of their separation. The natural answer to them was to stress the necessity of conformity to the outward life and machinery of the church. Even the great St Augustine, spiritual giant though he was, in the end had to fall back on this argument against the Donatists. Not surprisingly the usual result of this policy was to make the perfectionists go even further in their idealistic and exclusive teach-

ing, an early example of the fact that at a moment of
crisis in church controversy each side tends to exaggerate
its own position at the expense of the balanced truth
which lies between (or across) the extremes.

The second main type of heresy was that known as
Gnosticism. This was the temptation to water down
Christianity by incorporating into it philosophical or
magical 'knowledge' (Greek *gnosis* = knowledge) from
other religions current in the ancient world. Since all
these other systems, except Judaism, believed in mixed,
or syncretistic, systems, it was not easy for Christianity to
reject Gnosticism. But in the end the early church came
to realize that in the Greek world it must be the religious
odd man out. Similarly in the politics of the Roman empire the early Christians came to see that they must stand
out against the current and almost meaningless practice
of emperor worship (another form of syncretism or poly-
theism) – even at the expense of persecution. This double
sense of being religiously and politically unique in the
ancient world must have done a great deal to strengthen
the church's feeling of its unity. It was literally *contra
mundum* – against the world – and could not afford the
luxury of internal divisions. It is perhaps no coincidence
that the era of lasting divisions was also the first era of
'success' for the church; while in more recent times it is
hardly surprising that as the church has seen itself becoming again a minority institution in the world it has redis-
covered the necessity of its unity.

The third group of heresies was that in which the early
church struggled to work out its belief first about the
relationship between God the Father and God the Son
(the Arian controversy), and then, having established the
divinity of Christ, about the relationship of the divine
and human elements in his nature (the Monophysite and
Nestorian controversies). It was these arguments which
were the most agonizing and divisive for Christian believers. This was not a controversy with the world (as the

Gnostic had partly been), but within the church. The
New Testament evidence was inconclusive and the very
language of the beliefs had to be fashioned as the debate
proceeded. Many devout and sincerely thoughtful men
found that their speculations turned out to be heretical,
which they had never meant them to be, and that as a
result they were beyond the pale; on the other hand
many less scrupulous operators were not slow to muddy
the waters. The controversies took place mainly in the
east, for it was the eastern, or Greek, theologians who
had the interest and skill, and also the language and
philosophic terms, to carry it on. Westerns for the most
part proved to be more interested in practical matters,
and when they intervened in the eastern imbroglio their
solutions, though often decisive, tended to be over-simple,
hampered as they were by the fact that Latin is not a
language which lends itself to subtle speculation. The
Greeks indeed became passionately involved, as Gregory
of Nyssa found when he came to Constantinople for a
council in 381:

The whole city is full of it, the squares, the market places,
the cross-roads, the alleyways; old-clothes men, money changers,
food sellers: they are all busy arguing. If you ask someone to
give you change, he philosophizes about the Begotten and the
Unbegotten; if you enquire about the price of a loaf, you are
told by way of reply that the Father is greater and the Son
inferior; if you ask 'Is my bath ready?' the attendant answers
that the Son was made out of nothing.[13]

It was obviously a sign of great vitality in the church that
lay people were involved in this way. If it is also true that
the fact that the debate had spilled over into the market
place could lead to unseemly riots, it has to be remembered that in Constantinople, the new and Christian
Rome, circuses had been banned, so it is hardly surprising that some of the old manners were transferred to this
new form of entertainment.

The fourth and fifth centuries of the church's life were,

then, occupied with these great controversies; the means of settling them were the General, or Oecumenical, Councils. Councils of bishops, called to discuss important questions, had become common in the third century, especially in Africa. But these General Councils were the first at which the whole church was represented. This at least was the theory, though in fact, since the councils took place in the east and discussed matters which excited easterns rather than westerns, the vast majority of the bishops came from the lands round the eastern end of the Mediterranean, the patriarchates of Alexandria, Jerusalem, Antioch and Constantinople. Nevertheless here was an impressive outward display of the unity and extent of the church which had so recently been persecuted and despised. Moreover, although the councils were called to settle the various doctrinal questions which were so vexing the life of the church, the opportunity of having so many different churches represented was also taken to compare notes on government and discipline. These and other disputed questions were settled by a series of rules, or canons, which were accepted as having supreme authority. Sometimes the emperor himself presided over the assembly (though he did not take an active part in the debate) and this too would add lustre to its authority. Indeed the very possibility of holding such large councils representative of the whole civilized world depended on the newly won interest and support of the Roman state. One aggrieved – and admittedly pagan – commentator was quick to complain that the imperial postal service was being diverted from its proper use in the cause of church administration. But the Emperor Constantine, at least, would have considered this arrangemen more than justified. He had hoped, no doubt, to gain a new spiritual force in the politics of the empire as a result of his alliance with the church, and he was dismayed to find it in such disarray because of its doctrinal disputes. He lost no time in lecturing the bishops on the folly of this state of affairs and it was, in fact, he who called the first General Council, at Nicaea in 325. This concerned the Arian controversy and produced the formula known since as the Nicene creed. The second General Council at Constantinople marked the end of the Arian dispute and saw the beginning of the Christological debates – about the human and divine elements in the person of Christ. Next came the Council of Ephesus in 431, which made a somewhat abortive attempt to damp the fires at that time raging round the person and teaching of Nestorius. Lastly in the series the Council of Chalcedon in 451 drew up a statement of faith on the two natures of Christ which has since been accepted as orthodox.

These councils were undoubtedly impressive achievements and the modern church rightly looks back to them as such. The doctrinal questions they debated were extremely difficult and were of vital importance to the belief of the church at that time and since – though how far the actual Greek formulas they produced are immediately relevant today is a matter which can be disputed. The councils symbolized and made effective the unity as well as the strength of the church; indeed the Council of Chalcedon was the last occasion on which representatives of the whole church met to debate its great issues. After that the lasting schisms in the unity of the church meant that a truly oecumenical, or world-wide, council could not be convened. The eastern and western branches of the church went on holding councils and claiming ecumenicity for them, but as far as any real attempt at representation was concerned the parting of the ways came after Chalcedon. Not that the actual activities of the councils must be over-idealized. In detail they were often far from edifying: the councils were the scenes of ecclesiastical infighting and the tactics used by opposing sides left much to be desired. There were scenes of violence and slander: the Patriarch of Alexandria, for instance, was not above trying to intimidate the opposition with the threat of the

fierce and unruly monks who came in his train; attacks
on personal morals were used to re-inforce accusations of
heretical opinions. Yet all this was in a way a reflection of
the fact that the questions being fought out were still
open and that the answers mattered desperately to the
protagonists.

Nor must it be thought that, authoritative as they
were, the councils produced their results as by a divine
thunder-clap. Clearly their formal deliberations were
only the tip of the iceberg of the debate current in the
church. Nor, once they had produced a solution, was all
opposition silenced. It took over fifty years for the formula hatched at Nicaea to find general acceptance, while
that produced at Chalcedon was not so much a definite
solution to the problem as a compromise which designated the area outside which speculation could not be
permitted – certainly a wise tactic on such a thorny question and one which later ecumenical formula-makers
would do well to follow. Nor, again, did a council decision immediately heal the divisions of the church. For
instance the Arian controversy had led to a schism in the
see of Antioch which began in 325 and continued for
nearly a hundred years – long after the original doctrinal
issues had been settled. Because of the importance of the
see of Antioch as one of the four great patriarchates of
the east, the rest of the church, including Rome, became
involved in this schism and it was a matter of vital and
divisive importance which bishop the other churches or
dioceses recognized and supported. But one important
principle emerges from the confused history of this controversy: it was perfectly possible for Diocese A (for
example the Bishop of Constantinople) to be in communion with B and C (for example Rome and Alexandria) even though B and C were actually out of communion with each other. There were other examples, and
many permutations, of this principle, but the fact is that
in the early church communion was not such an absolute

and legalistic matter as it has become in later history. There were many cases of schism within a bishopric or between sees, but one broken link did not destroy the whole chain of unity.

Nor must it be supposed that once a heresy had been condemned by a council, it came to a sudden end, though the textbooks are apt to imply this by not following the movements any further. Heresies usually had founders, often great and devout men, and these founders created loyalties and started traditions. So their churches continued – and no doubt did good Christian work – for decades and even centuries after the founder had been condemned. The most important example of this in the so-called undivided church was that of the Arians – an example which is evident to all those who go to Ravenna and see the Arian and Orthodox baptisteries standing side by side in the same town. The Goths were converted by one of their compatriots, Ulphilas, who had been consecrated a bishop by the then Arian Bishop of Constantinople. The Goths in turn converted other tribes on the boundaries of the empire and these first overran and then were assimilated by the empire, making their capital in Ravenna in the sixth century. But their triumph was shortlived and during the same century by a dual process of conquest and pursuasion the Arians disappeared. It was later heresies which founded churches which became permanent and remain with us to this day.

Schism in the early church, as distinct from heretical division over some doctrinal matter, could start for many reasons and be continued for one or more of many others. A schism became formal, or open, when rival contenders claimed the same see. At this moment the controversy ceased to be local; other churches had to take sides and decide who was the true (or 'catholic') bishop. Questions of church discipline or government were frequent sources of schism. How, for instance, were those who had lapsed or foresworn the faith under persecution to be

treated? or notorious sinners, murderers or adulterers?
Were they to be rebaptized or not? And what of lapsed
priests? Were they to be re-admitted to their ministry or
revert to lay status? These were some of the questions
which could divide to the point of schism a church which
had still to make up its mind whether it was a company of
saints or a school for sinners.

Obviously, too, disputed episcopal elections could lead
to schism. According to one contemporary historian the
riots in Rome in 366, after the governor and the mob had
taken over on one such occasion, 'killed 160 of the people,
men and women, and wounded a very large number, of
whom many died'.[14] Personal rivalry and jealousy, in
fact, played a large part in the promotion of many a
schism. Sometimes, too, the interference of meddling and
ambitious women stirred waters that were already
muddy. 'Nothing will so avail to divide the church as
love of power,' said St John Chrysostom, who from his
vantage point at Constantinople was in a position to
know.

It was not a far cry from personal rivalry within a diocese to power politics between sees or patriarchates. As
the church grew and became more fully organized local
self-sufficiency gave way to regional or 'national' self-consciousness. Theological rivalry and misunderstanding between Alexandria and Antioch, and jurisdictional rivalry
between Alexandria and Constantinople, the 'upstart'
patriarchate created by the fiat of Constantine – these
factors entered into and prolonged and exacerbated
many of the doctrinal disputes of the fourth and fifth
centuries. In these matters Rome tended to back Alexandria not only for doctrinal reasons, but also for political
ones, for Rome had no more reason to love the new and
rival 'Rome' – Constantinople – than had Alexandria.
These are only the chief examples of the divisive effects of
church politics.

Liturgical differences constituted another factor which

could cause disputes and embitter or prolong schisms. Then as now differences in church services would be more real to the average layman than the niceties of theological controversy. The most notorious example of this kind in the early church was the Quartodeciman controversy in the second century when the east and west fell out over the thorny question of the way of calculating the date of Easter. The dispute was sharp and led to one of the earliest attempts by Rome to exert its authority in the east. It was also an early illustration of the fact that it is all too easy to demand uniformity in the cause of unity – a lesson which the church has still hardly learned. But on the whole the early church avoided this pitfall and managed to combine its consciousness of its fundamental unity with a recognition and tolerance of considerable divergences in practical matters. While unity was the fundamental premise this was possible; but once unity was lost, liturgical and other differences loomed larger and uniformity came to be seen as a more desirable goal.

Last of these causes of disputes in the early church are the social and political issues. Many of the heresies and schisms of the first five centuries arose from the adoption of an extremist position on one subject or another. Not infrequently such movements began in country areas which were economically and educationally more backward than the great centres of Roman urban civilization in which the church had its earliest roots. For instance, the greatest schism-cum-heresy of the early church was perhaps Donatism, which laid waste the church in North Africa in the fifth century. The Donatists were for the most part country people, poor, fierce and untamed, who resented the less harsh and puritanical attitudes of their more sophisticated urban Christian neighbours. They took no more kindly to Roman rule than they did to Roman civilization. So when the case between Donatists and Catholics was submitted to a Roman court they were not likely to be impressed when the judgement went against them. *Quid imperatori cum ecclesia* – What has the Emperor to do with the church? – they asked for the first but not the last time in Christian history. Thus social and political suspicions prolonged the bitter struggle which terribly weakened the church when later in the century it had to face attack from the Vandals.

The church had begun to be affected by nationalism; the baneful influence of politics was to be still more serious to the eastern church at the end of the fifth century and was to play an even larger part in the schisms which led to the first permanent breaks in church unity.

THE STRUCTURE OF UNITY IN THE EARLY CHURCH

The church of the first five centuries was, then, divided in many ways and for many reasons. Some of the divisions had at their roots differences which were doctrinal, or intellectual, or temperamental. Some were caused, or at least contributed to, by what are now called 'non-theological factors'. The quarrels which sprang from these various causes were far from edifying and give one to question how rose-tinted are the spectacles worn by those who hold up 'the early and undivided church' as the great pattern and example to the later church and particularly to those who are seeking unity today. Yet in spite of everything the church *was* undivided in the early centuries. Divisions were protracted and bitter, but they were not permanent; they could be – and were – mended. The *fact* from which Christians started was still the unity of the church.

During this time the church developed a life and an organization which both expressed and safeguarded this unity. The New Testament set forth the principle of visible unity, but the embodiment of the principle came later. Organization was in any case bound to come as the church grew; but there is no doubt that the form of the organization was to some extent influenced by the need to express unity and – conversely – to combat heresy and schism. To try to decide which came first, the positive expression or the negative defence, is a somewhat chicken-and-egg argument which need not concern us here.

Fundamentally the problem was that the apostolic witness had to be preserved and handed down to succeeding generations. But this was essential not only, or even primarily, for the sake of the church itself, but so that the church could preach the apostolic Gospel to the world. Any organization which persists with a corporate life is bound to develop a tradition. But the Christian tradition was more than a set of rules or propositions; it was rooted in historical events, in the life, death and resurrection of Jesus Christ, and in the witness of the apostles to the meaning of those events. Though St Paul set high store by his own apostolic authority, he knew that it was more important that he stood within the already formed Christian tradition:

> For I delivered to you as of first importance what I also received, that Christ died for our sins in accordance with the scriptures, that he was buried, that he was raised on the third day in accordance with the scriptures, and that he appeared to Cephas, then to the twelve. (I Corinthians xv, 3–5; see also xi, 23–25)

The word here translated 'delivered' is the verb from which is derived the Greek word for tradition – *paradosis*, literally a giving over or across. In the language of the early church, therefore, tradition was not simply something inherited from the past, something passive; essentially it was an activity, the delivery of the Gospel to the world in each new generation. What was delivered was the apostolic witness to Christ and how essential was the apostolic element in the tradition can be seen from the words of Papias about A.D. 130 – a key time in the formation of the tradition immediately after the end of the apostolic period.

But I will not hesitate to set down for your benefit ... all that ever I carefully learned and carefully recorded from the elders, guaranteeing its truth. For I did not take delight, as most men do, in those who have much to say, but in those who teach what is true.... And if anyone chanced to come who had actually been a follower of the elders, I would enquire as to the discourses of the elders, what Andrew or what Peter said or what Philip, or what Thomas or James, or what John or Matthew or any other of the Lord's disciples.... For I did not suppose I could get such profit from the contents of books as from the words of a living and abiding voice.[15]

The preservation and preaching of this 'living and abiding voice' of the apostles was 'traditioned' by the early church through four channels.

In the first place there were the scriptures. When St Paul spoke of the scriptures he meant the Jewish writings of the Old Testament. Soon however there grew up in the church a corpus of Christian writings which were seen to be essential to the apostolic witness as the apostles themselves died. The Gospels were attempts to commit to writing the oral tradition of the apostles, and it should be noted that any conflict, such as is now often supposed, between scripture and tradition would have been unthinkable to the early Christians. The oral tradition was in fact prior to the written, and the written was a conscious attempt to preserve the oral – that which was, as St Paul said, 'received'. At first there was no clear distinction between earlier and later writings. Later, however, certain heretical sects, especially the Gnostics, claimed to have discovered new books, and added them to the general corpus, setting great store by them. The result was either to add to, or fundamentally to distort, regular Christian teaching. (This is a process, it can be noted, which has been repeated by certain heretical sects of the last hundred years, such as the Mormons and the Christadelphians.) It became necessary, therefore, for the church to define which *were* its scriptures and to declare them to be authoritative. Thus the canon of the New Testament was formed alongside that of the Old. This was done in rather a haphazard way, but the principle of selection is clear. The canonical books of the New Testament were those which were thought to have apostolic authority. They were what Gregory of Nyssa called in the fourth century 'the evangelic and apostolic traditions'.

During the struggle in the second century against the Gnostics, with their appeal to a hidden underground tradition, Irenaeus claimed that even if the apostles had not committed any writings to the church, Christians would have been able to follow 'the rule of faith which they delivered to the leaders of the church'; this was the creed, the second line in the transmission of the apostolic tradition. Irenaeus recognized that there were local differences in the credal summaries of the faith, but claimed that essentially the faith was one, an expression and symbol of the unity of the church.

For the church believes these points of doctrine just as if she had but one soul and one and the same heart, and she proclaims them, and teaches them, and hands them down with perfect harmony as if she possessed only one mouth. For, although the languages of the world are dissimilar, yet the import of the tradition is one and the same. For the churches which have been planted in Germany have not believed or handed down anything different, nor do those in Spain, nor those in Gaul, nor those in the east, nor those in Egypt, nor those in Libya, nor those which have been established in the central regions of the world.[16]

So closely was the rule of faith connected with the apostles that by the end of the fourth century it was being recounted how the Apostles Creed had been composed by the apostles on the day of Pentecost at the direct inspiration of the Holy Spirit, each of the Twelve having contributed a clause!

It must also be realized that the creeds were not originally tests of orthodoxy; this was a character they only
assumed in the great doctrinal disputes of the fourth and
fifth centuries. Originally the creeds were the basis of the
summary of faith which was taught privately to catechu-
mens before their baptism and which was then publicly
declared by the new Christians at the solemn sacramental
ceremony. Thus they were an essential part of the 'delivery' of the Gospel to each new generation of believers.

Mention of baptism brings us to the third strand in the
traditioning of the apostolic witness in the church. This
was its sacramental and liturgical life. Baptism was essentially a sacrament of unity, for through it, as we have seen,
the new believer was united both to Christ and to his
fellow believers in the church. This was especially felt
when schism threatened the unity of the church and
when there was as a result any controversy over the rights
and wrongs of heretical baptism. St Cyprian of Carthage
in the third century returned constantly to the theme
that there was only one church and that therefore there
could only be one baptism. The true church alone possessed the gift of the Holy Spirit, and therefore baptism
outside the church was automatically invalid.

But it is [impossible] to approve the baptism of heretics and
schismatics, to admit that they have been truly baptized. . . .
He cannot give the Holy Spirit, because he that is appointed
without [the church] is not endowed with the Holy Spirit, he
cannot baptize those who come; since both baptism is one and
the Holy Spirit is one, and the church founded by Christ the
Lord upon Peter by a source and principle of unity, is one
also.[17]

Those, therefore, who joined the catholic church from a
heretical or schismatic body must be rebaptized.

The other essential sacramental element in the apostolic tradition was the eucharist or breaking of bread. St
Paul himself made this plain: 'for I received from the

Lord what I also delivered [traditioned] to you, that the Lord Jesus on the night when he was betrayed took bread . . .' (I Corinthians xi, 23). From the beginning the eucharist was the central act of Christian worship, and other, non-eucharistic, services were only added later as optional extras for the specially pious. And again the eucharist was essentially a sacrament of unity. The very symbolism of the bread and wine made this clear, for bread and wine each consist of a number of small original units – grains of wheat and grapes – which after an organic change have been made into a new whole which transcends the sum of the original units. St Augustine therefore was able to teach that in the eucharist the same sort of change took place and individual Christians were transformed into a united church: 'we being many are one bread, one body. . . . Christ willed that we should belong to him, and consecrated the mystery of our peace and of our unity on his table.'[18]

Beside baptism and the mass the word 'tradition' was also applied by some writers to various other liturgical practices, such as the making of the sign of the cross. But it was clearly recognized that there was a difference in importance between those parts of liturgical tradition which were apostolic and scriptural, and those which were not. A church leader like Cyprian taught that liturgical practices could be added to scripture as long as they did not run contrary to the apostolic teaching of scripture, but that it must be recognized that these were the traditions of men which would and could vary from church to church. What could not vary, except in detail, were the apostolic essentials of the tradition – baptism and the eucharist. Thus again it was clear to the early church that essential unity in the apostolic tradition did not imply uniformity throughout the church.

The fourth strand in the delivery of the apostolic witness to Jesus Christ was that of the ministry of the church.

We have seen that by the end of the New Testament period the form of the Christian ministry was still un-settled; but by the second quarter of the second century the threefold ministry of bishop, priests and deacons was more or less universal throughout the church. Unfor-tunately the period during which this happened is a blank, so we cannot tell how the historical process took place. All that can be said with any certainty is that the standardization of the ministry must have arisen from the need of the church to organize itself in the new circum-stances of its – probably unexpected – survival into the post-apostolic age, and in view of the various threats and pressures with which it was faced.

The first evidence of the acceptance of a threefold ministry comes in the writings of Ignatius, Bishop of Antioch at about the end of the first century. There is no attempt to explain the ministry; it is accepted and its authority constantly reiterated. Above all the bishop is held up as the symbol and guarantee of unity in the church, both in doctrine and practice.

Shun divisions.... Do you all follow your bishop as Jesus Christ followed the Father, and the presbytery as the Apostles.... Let no man do aught of things pertaining to the church apart from the bishop.... Wheresoever the bishop shall appear, there let the people be; even as where Jesus may be, there is the universal church ... that everything which you do may be sure and valid.[19]

In this and many similar passages Ignatius 'pressed home the out-and-out divine authority of the bishop as the spiritual monarch of the individual church'.[20]

At about the same time as Ignatius was writing of the threefold ministry Clement was writing from Rome to the Corinthian church which was – not for the first time – troubled by divisions. It cannot be said with certainty that Clement was Bishop of Rome and in his letter he still speaks of bishops and presbyters without any clear distinction, but he does produce an important test of the authority of the ministry which was absent from the teaching of Ignatius. This was the principle of continuity.

> Our apostles knew through our Lord Jesus Christ that there would be strife over the name of the bishop's office. For this cause therefore . . . they appointed the aforesaid persons, and afterwards they provided a continuance, that if these should fall asleep, other approved men should succeed to their ministration.[21]

It was, therefore, wrong for the Corinthians to turn to other ministers than those in the regular succession.

The same principle was taken a step further by Irenaeus in his writings against the Gnostics. The danger of this heresy was that its followers claimed to have a hidden source of teaching which had flowed – as it were underground – from the earliest days to themselves. This was nonsense, said Irenaeus.

> The tradition of the apostles . . . manifested in the entire world, it is possible for all, who wish to see the truth, to contemplate clearly in every church; and we are in a position to enumerate those who were by the apostles instituted in the churches, and the successions of these men to our own times; those who neither taught nor knew anything like the ravings of the heretics.[22]

Here then is the origin of the idea of the apostolic succession as guaranteeing the continuity and purity of the apostolic tradition. But it should be noticed that this was not a mechanical or 'tactile' continuity by succession or ordination; indeed in the church of these times the probability is that bishops were consecrated at the hands of the local presbytery. The succession is that of open and continuous teaching: the bishops were the 'deliverers' of the apostolic tradition to their own generation.

Another early writer who developed the idea of the apostolic authority of the ministry was Cyprian, Bishop

of Carthage in the middle of the third century. Faced
with rebellion in his own church and conflict with no less
powerful a neighbour than Rome, he stressed the fact
that the unity of the church was its essential characteristic and that this unity was based on the unity of the
episcopate, which in turn sprang from a single apostolic
root.

There is one church, divided by Christ throughout the
whole world into many members, and also one episcopate
diffused through a harmonious multitude of many bishops.[23]

The episcopate is one, each part of which is held by each one
for the whole. The church also is one, which is spread abroad
far and wide into a multitude by an increase of fruitfulness.
As there are many rays of the sun, but one light; and many
branches of a tree, but one strength based in its tenacious root;
and since from one spring flow many streams ... yet the unity
is preserved in the source. Separate a ray of sun from its body
of light, its unity does not allow a division of light ... cut off
the stream from its fountain, and that which is cut off dries
up.[24]

Thus anyone who separates from the church and from
the episcopate condemns himself; for the visible church is
the only possessor of the sacraments and outside the
church there is no salvation. 'It is impossible to have God
as a Father without having the church as a mother.'[25]

In practice the unity of the church and of the episcopate on which Cyprian dwelt was embodied in the
councils of bishops over which he presided, those of the
North African church being the precursors of more
general councils which have already been discussed.
Clearly such a body would have great authority; yet
Cyprian insisted that, though a decision of the majority
of bishops would carry the authority of the episcopate –
what he called the 'cement' of the unity of the church – it
could in no way diminish the authority of any particular
bishop. If a single bishop dissented from the majority, his
own opinion and practice was absolute in his own dio-

cese, and he was not thereby cut off from the rest of the church.

Much of the development of the early church, therefore – in Bible, creeds, sacraments and ministry, which together traditioned the apostolic witness to Christ – took place against a background of schism and heresy. Yet the church retained a basic unity, expressed in some diversity. But the position arrived at by the time of Cyprian left two problems which were going to be central to the debate on unity, not only at that time but ever since.

Cyprian's teaching about the validity of heretical sacraments – baptism, eucharist and ordination – had been tough. The Catholic church alone possessed true sacraments, therefore outside the church there was no salvation. Those who were in were in and those who were out were out. This at least had the logic of simplicity. But the situation was not often as simple as this logic demanded. Heresy and schism tended not to be clear-cut, and it was not always possible to tell who was in and who was out. In any case it was not the fault of the hapless convert that he had been converted by and baptized into the wrong church. Charity demanded some change in Cyprian's position. So too did expediency: it was obviously going to be far more difficult to get a schismatic to join the Catholic church if his rebaptism was insisted on. Cyprian's position was, therefore, modified during the period of the early church – and by another African, St Augustine. In his work as a bishop Augustine leaned over backwards to make it possible for Donatists to return to the fold. He taught that baptism is not invalidated by the wrong views of the minister; therefore Donatists did not need to be rebaptized. Cyprian's position had also been open to a third, theological criticism. It had implied that the sacraments were the exclusive property of the church. But the later position was that they belong to God and the church: it is Christ who is the real minister of baptism, the true celebrant of the Lord's Supper, the giver of holy orders. Baptism, therefore, is still Christian baptism even if it is administered outside the church. To maintain this position, and yet to continue to insist that there is still *some* difference between Catholic and non-Catholic baptisms, Augustine had to think a step further. He introduced the distinction between validity and efficacy. Baptism outside the church was valid and did not have to be repeated. But it was not efficacious; it did not do what baptism should do. It only became efficacious when the convert entered the Catholic church. When this happened he was received by the laying-on of hands and admitted to the full benefits of Christian baptism which had been hitherto withheld. This principle was extended by Augustine to the other sacraments. It rested on the double argument, not only that Christ was the true minister of all sacraments, but also that the Holy Spirit operates only within the Catholic church and therefore the sacraments work only within the fold. By coining the concepts of validity and efficacy Augustine had set up a theology which recognized, and tried to cope with, the fact that the church could be divided. These ideas have, therefore, played a great part in all subsequent debates on unity. No one could say that they are perfect or foolproof. Augustine would have been the first to admit that they were only an attempt to meet an impossible and intolerable situation. They had improved the situation but not solved it. The position of the Donatists had been eased, but in reality the eggs were still left in the Catholic basket. Cyprian's position had been modified, but the fundamental question of authority in – and the authority of – a divided church, that question had still not been tackled.

The second problem that Cyprian left was more practical. He had based the unity of the church on the unity of the episcopate and had developed the idea of the moral authority of councils of bishops. But though he had repudiated the idea of a 'bishop of bishops', this was in fact a not illogical next step in the development of the government and organization of the church. It is no coincidence that it was possible for later writers to take his treatise *On the Unity of the Church* and, without too obviously mutilating the text, to insert into it a number of passages which made the unity of the church stem back to the Petrine commission and Peter's foundation of the church in Rome.

From the beginning of the second century the bishops of Rome exercised a certain moral authority in the church at large. This was partly because of the prestige of the double apostolic foundation of the Roman church – Petrine and Pauline; it was also partly due to the fact that authority would naturally accrue to the church of the capital of the world, especially as, since all roads led to Rome, the church there acquired the experience of dealing with so many of the problems which arose. Nevertheless if Rome became too interfering other churches were quick to resent it and resist. Cyprian himself in the third century refused to toe the Roman line on rebaptism. But a century later a council of western bishops held at Sardica in 343 to discuss the Arian question agreed that in certain circumstances the bishop of Rome should act as a court of appeal in church disputes. A hundred years later Rome advanced theological arguments to buttress this position. The great Pope Leo ruled from 440 to 461. He pressed his claims to jurisdiction in Africa, Spain and Gaul, basing them explicitly on the divine and scriptural authority of the Roman supremacy, and in the same spirit he intervened decisively (though perhaps not altogether comprehendingly) at the Council of Chalcedon. In all this he was much helped by the practical fact that, whereas in the east power was divided between the great patriarchates, in the west there was no church which could seriously and continuously challenge the power of Rome. Moreover, in the east the Patriarch of Constantinople was inevitably overshadowed by the

Emperor, but in the west once the seat of government was removed from Rome the pope became increasingly the political leader. It was, indeed, Leo who persuaded the Huns to withdraw beyond the Danube, thus gaining a breathing space in the decline of the western empire.

So the authority of the bishop of Rome continued to grow in the west. But in the east his authority was never accepted. There the doctrine and practice of the church on this matter has remained much where Cyprian left it – though Cyprian himself was an African and a Latin: practical authority lies with the individual bishop in his diocese; moral authority on matters of faith and government lies with the bishops in Council.[26] It was the widening divergence between these two views about the seat of authority – the Roman and the Cyprian/eastern – which was to lead to the greatest of all the breaches of the unity of the church – and which remains unresolved to this day.

CHAPTER THREE

The Church Divided:
The Last Fifteen Centuries

I believe in the Holy Catholic Church, and sincerely
regret that it does not at present exist.

ARCHBISHOP WILLIAM TEMPLE

THE EARLIEST DIVISIONS IN THE EAST:
NESTORIANS AND MONOPHYSITES

THE earliest breaks in the unity of the church to have
remained unhealed to this day took place in the eastern
church in the fifth century. Technically they were divisions on doctrinal matters and those who left the fold of
the Catholic church were heretics; but in fact the underlying causes of division were political and cultural as
much as doctrinal.

The first lasting heresy which led to the foundation of
a separate church was Nestorianism. In the controversy
about the person of Christ, which occupied the eastern
church in the fifth century, Nestorius was a supporter of
the Antiochene school. That is to say he tended to stress
the humanity of the redeemer, 'in every respect tempted
as we are' (Hebrews iv, 15, a passage often quoted by
Nestorius), against the Alexandrine emphasis on his
divinity. In 428 he became Bishop of Constantinople –
and walked into a hornets' nest. He was accused of heresy
and of belittling the divinity of Christ. The attack was
led by Cyril, Bishop of Alexandria, and thus to the doctrinal dispute was added the church politics of the jealousy of Alexandria for Constantinople. Nestorius was
condemned at the Council of Ephesus and deposed.
Whether he was really a heretic is an open question. The

whole business was extremely complex; later he himself
claimed that his position was that adopted by the orthodox party in upholding the two natures in Christ, human
and divine, against the Monophysites.

However that may be Nestorius disappeared from the
scene and died in obscurity. Here the matter might have
ended but for the fact that there was a disaffected section
of the eastern church which was ready to espouse his
cause. This was the Persian church. Persia was a separate
state on the boundary of the Roman Empire and a thorn
in its flesh. Christianity was persecuted as a threat to
national unity and a potential Roman fifth column. The
church in Persia, therefore, became strongly nationalistic
in order to proclaim its political loyalty; in 424 it declared itself independent of the church in general and in
particular of the patriarchate of Antioch; it was not represented at the Council of Ephesus, which condemned
Nestorius, and in any case its theology tended to be
Antiochene: little by little, the division between Persian
Nestorians and Imperial Orthodox became complete. It
was the first lasting breach in the unity of Christendom.
'And how much heresy was there? Very little we are
tempted to say. The formal (Nestorian) confession of 486
was little different from the definition of Chalcedon, and
if – which I do not assert – worse heresy intervened, that
was due to the isolation and not its cause. Certainly there
must have been a failure to comprehend western Christology, but that could have been cured by fellowship. It was
the politics and the nationalism and the personal disputes and the name of Nestorius which determined in
very large part the separation of the churches.'[1]

The Nestorians were great missionaries. Spreading east
in the sixth century they founded Christian settlements
in Arabia, south-west India and Turkestan. Most interesting of all, in 635 a Nestorian missionary, Olopan,
arrived in Sigan-Fu in north-west China, then the capital
of the Tang dynasty. He became a leading figure in the

Chinese Empire and founded a Nestorian church there which survived for at least 150 years. What its chances of longer survival and wider influence would have been had it had behind it the strength of the Catholic church itself is one of the most fascinating, albeit fruitless, 'ifs' of history. In the event the Nestorians, like the other churches of the east, came under Moslem political rule in the seventh century. Though not subject to regular persecution they slowly declined until finally a remnant fled from the great Mongol Timur (Tamerlane) to the mountains of Kurdestan. There they survived, virtually unknown, devoid of learning but very tenacious of their traditions, until contact was made with them by the Anglican church in the nineteenth century. Known now as the Assyrian Christians, they were caught up in the political aftermath of the First World War and have now been placed under the rule of Iraq.

Other Nestorian survivors are to be found in South India and are known as Malabar Christians. They too have been astonishingly tenacious of their Syriac liturgical tradition. They were recognized as 'orthodox' by the Portuguese Roman Catholic missionaries who arrived in South India in the sixteenth century. They therefore allied themselves with Rome, but later found that their customs were being interfered with. Some broke away and joined the Jacobite church of South India. These were the descendants of their old enemies the Monophysites, showing that in some circumstances liturgical bonds can be stronger than doctrinal. But again in time this union did not work out and in 1930 a body of the old Malabar Christians allied themselves with Rome. There are now, therefore, two churches in South India descended from the Nestorian division, each in a separate 'uniat', that is semi-independent, communion with Rome.

The history of the Monophysite and Coptic churches is in many ways similar to that of the Nestorian, though the doctrinal point of departure was at precisely the opposite end of the theological scale. The Nestorians were said to impugn the divinity of Christ; the Monophysites so stressed his divinity as to end up with a single nature in which the divine element had swallowed up the human (Greek: *monos* = one, *phusis* = nature). This was Alexandrine-type teaching and Eutyches, its sponsor, claimed only to be following St Cyril of Alexandria, the hammer of the Nestorians. Nevertheless he was condemned at the Council of Chalcedon in 451. The Egyptian church refused to accept the Chalcedonian definition and became formally Monophysite, though for some time there were lively and unedifying disputes in Alexandria between the majority body and the orthodox. In all this isolationism, nationalism and the Coptic language and culture played their part.

More significant in the long run was the Armenian schism, and here again politics played a large part in the founding of a separate church. Armenia was a small tribal state on the imperial border, a buffer between the Empire and Persia. It was the first kingdom to be converted *en masse* to Christianity – with the baptism of its king at the end of the third century. In 374 the Armenian church rejected their ecclesiastical dependence on Caesarea and a little later the monarchy disappeared and the kingdom was divided between the Roman and Persian Empires. So began the continuing history of the Armenian people, never their own masters, subjugated to a succession of foreign rulers, but maintaining their national identity by the bonds of race, language, culture and religion. The church was not represented at Chalcedon and soon came under Monophysite influence; they were certainly not likely to favour the Nestorian tendency of their Persian masters.

A substantial part of the Syrian church also became Monophysite at the beginning of the sixth century when Constantinople itself was, for political reasons, showing

signs of sympathy for that cause. The Syrian Monophysites are known as 'Jacobites' after their leader Jacob
Baradaeus, who was consecrated Bishop of Edessa in
542.

Thus by the sixth century the churches of Alexandria
and Syria, as well as those of Armenia and Persia, were
split from the orthodox and imperial capital of Constantinople – and even more so from the west. As a result the
church was less able to withstand the expansion of Islam
in the seventh century. Mohammed had been born (*c.*
570) at a critical moment when it looked as if the old
Arabian heathen civilization was, even in the south, giving way before Christian culture and religion. Mecca was
one of the last of its strongholds. But the Christian impetus slackened, and from Mecca came the counter-attack
of the 'fighting puritanism' of Islam, committed to unifying Arab society and giving it a strong moral basis.[2] Its
success was phenomenal. During his brief rule (634–43)
the Caliph Omar extended his empire through Syria,
Persia and Egypt, as well as the Arabian peninsula. It is
perhaps the most dramatic evidence in history of the way
in which the church can be disastrously weakened by its
divisions.

The pattern of the subsequent history of the Coptic,
Armenian, Jacobite and Nestorian churches is very similar. The general policy of Islam was one of tolerance
towards subject religions, so long as they minded their
own business. But from time to time they could be subject to fierce persecution, a fear which continued, and
indeed reached its culmination, in the terrible Armenian
massacres of 1893, 1896, and 1915, which so horrified
England. The various churches could therefore be
weakened by apostasy, as well as by the less dramatic
erosion caused by intermarriage and psychological and
social pressures. The wonder is that these tiny communities survived at all. But survive they did in their
ghettoes, jealously guarding their traditions and cut off

to a large extent from their surroundings and, until modern times, from each other. As a result there is in these churches an extraordinary sense of timelessness. There are thought to be about three million Armenians today, of whom about 100,000 are in communion with Rome; another 100,000 are to be found in North America and there are Armenian churches in London and Manchester. The Copts remain unique to Egypt, where they number about three and a half million out of a total population of over twelve million. There are said to be about 200,000 Syrian Jacobite Christians centred on Antioch. Nestorians survive in pockets in the Middle East as well as in South India.[3]

The British public is hardly aware of these ancient churches, except when one of their representatives appears in exotic costume in some ceremony in Jerusalem, perhaps connected with the continuing scandal of the squabble over the Church of the Holy Sepulchre. Yet with their strong and continuous traditions, embalmed in unchanging liturgical practice, they cannot be left out of the ecumenical picture.

THE EAST/WEST SCHISM

These struggles and divisions in the eastern church were as nothing compared to the great struggle between the east and west, Constantinople and Rome, which was to occupy the church for the next six hundred years or more, and lead to the greatest of all its schisms – beside which even the break at the Reformation comes only a sad second.

Constantine had made a history-shaping move when he founded his new capital in the east, his own city Constantinople. It is said that he wished to have a new – and Christian – Rome; we cannot be sure that this is true, but certainly he chose a superbly defensible site which was to resist invasion, other than that of the fifth column, for over a thousand years. Throughout all the time known in the west as the Dark Ages, and on to the end of the Middle Ages, Constantinople survived, the glittering capital of a great Christian Empire, and at its centre the Church of the Holy Wisdom – St Sophia – symbol of the continuity and power of the orthodox faith.

Not that Rome liked the rising of the new star. When the Council of Constantinople in 381 declared that 'the Bishop of Constantinople shall have the prerogative of honour after the Bishop of Rome, because Constantinople is New Rome' (Canon 111) Rome protested – and continued to do so for centuries. The popes did not like the idea, accepted universally in the east, that the importance of a diocese was measured by its standing in the imperial governmental scheme of things: it made too close an alliance between church and state. So from the fourth century Rome more and more emphasized the fact that her authority rested on her apostolic foundation: 'It was during the reign of Pope Damasus (366–84) that the expression *sedes apostolica* became synonymous with the See of Rome or of Peter.'[4] A century later another great pope, Gelasius (492–6), produced the classic definition, from the Roman point of view, of the relationship between church and state: 'There are two things by which this world is governed, the sacred authority of the pontiffs and the royal power. Of these, priests carry a weight all the greater, as they must render an account to the Lord even of kings before the Divine Judgement.' (Typically enough he had been challenging the right of the eastern emperor Anastasius to intervene in religious affairs.) But the eastern emperors would not have seen it thus. They believed in the harmonious collaboration between state and church – *imperium* and *sacerdotium*. Here is how the great Emperor Justinian saw the ideal in the sixth century:

God's greatest gifts to men derive from his infinite goodness – the *sacerdotium* and the *imperium*, the first serving divine

interests, the second human interests, and watching over them.
Both come from the same principle, and perfect human
life. . . . If the priesthood is sound and trusts completely in God
and if the Emperor rules the polity entrusted to him with
justice and honour, mutual harmony will arise which can only
prove useful to the human race. God's true dogmas and the
priests' honour are therefore our first care.[5]

This was the perfect expression of the Christian society as
the Byzantine Emperors understood it. Moreover Justinian in his time, and the Orthodox church ever since, was
willing to admit the primacy of the Roman church; but it
was a primacy of honour; the Bishop of Rome was to be
the first among equals with his four fellow patriarchs;
together they, with their bishops, constituted the Pen-
tarchy covering the jurisdiction of the whole church.
Justinian even admitted that in doctrinal matters the
pope should have the last word; but all the same 'he had
no intention of prejudicing the Emperor's right in the
Christian Commonwealth. He remained the supreme
master, the representative of God on earth, taking care of
the material and spiritual needs of his subjects.'[6]

But once again it must be understood that this was not
simply a matter of the powers of church and state. More
fundamentally it was a question of authority, the nature
and the seat of authority in the world. It was not politics;
it was theology. Matters were indeed finely balanced;
nevertheless all might have been well and the tightrope
stretched by Justinian might have held, had the political
situation created by him continued. But it did not. The
Roman Mediterranean Empire was a united reality for
the last time under that great ruler. After him came the
deluge: barbarian invasions in the west and Muslim
power in the east. The Romans had called the Mediterranean 'our sea' – *mare nostrum* – but from the seventh
century it became increasingly an Arabian sea. This
meant that communications between Rome and Constantinople were a great deal more difficult, for the over-

land route was also at risk. The paths were already divergent, and had been on many different matters from as far back as the second century. Now misunderstanding and misinformation magnified differences which earlier could be held within one common understanding. The process of growing apart was accelerated.

Not, even so, that it was sudden. Indeed all things considered the wonder, perhaps, is that it took so long for the breach to come. That it was delayed so long is one more proof of the strength of the belief in unity and in the impossibility of disunity. But in the end the divisive factors were too strong. In the eighth century the popes were threatened by the Lombard invasions and appealed to Constantinople, but in vain. They felt betrayed and turned to the rising power of the Franks in the west. In 800 Leo III crowned Charlemagne as the Holy Roman Emperor: 'The open breach between Constantinople and Rome should therefore be dated from the reign of Pope Leo III.'[7] It is significant that it was at this time that the question of the *filioque* – the traditional doctrinal bone of contention between the eastern and western churches – came into prominence. The Orthodox began to complain that the western church was introducing into the Nicene Creed the idea that the Holy Ghost proceeds not from the Father alone, but from the Father *and the Son* (Latin *filioque*). The Greeks felt that in saying this the Latins were upsetting the balance of the doctrine of the Trinity which had been so carefully worked out in the first five centuries. They were undermining the idea that the believer comes to the Son through the Spirit and so to the Father through the Son. It would be an exaggeration, no doubt, to say that they suspected that the Latins preferred to think that the believer comes to the Son through the church – but that at least shows something of the meaning of the debate. Not that all Greeks took this aspect of the addition of the *filioque* clause as seriously as this: to this day there are some Orthodox theologians who do not consider that the clause is in fact heretical. But what all did – and do – agree on, was that the addition was unjustified – and to that extent intolerable. The Creed could be altered only by an Ecumenical Council, and the Latins had made the addition without any such backing. Once again it was a question of authority.

Another source of friction was the rivalry between east and west in the missionary field. In the ninth century Orthodox and Catholics found themselves competing to convert the Bulgarians – to a different creed, differing liturgies and rival claims of authority. As a result of this controversy in 867 the Patriarch Photius went so far as to declare Pope Nicholas deposed, an unusual direction for the assertion of power. Then again there was a continuing political confrontation in southern Italy where the Greeks maintained the last bridgehead of their power in the west. The destruction of this bridgehead in the eleventh century by the Norman conquest of Sicily and southern Italy (aided and abetted by Rome, as the Byzantines believed) 'was therefore a major turning point in the relationship between east and west, and contributed considerably to the rupture between Rome and Constantinople'.[8]

Meanwhile all the time the stronger popes were advancing their own claims and establishing their own freedom. This was largely in the context of the politics of the west, but what the papacy claimed could be interpreted by Constantinople as a direct attack on the idea of authority as it was understood in the east. For instance, when in the eleventh century the western church, intent on reform, fought to rid itself of lay domination, this could be seen in the east as overturning the traditional alliance between church and state; thus the widening gap between east and west resulted in repeated failures of communication. In fact reading the story of this thousand years of growing estrangement is like watching a

Greek tragedy. Time after time it seems that there is a hope of reconciliation, but time after time fate intervenes and once again the paths are set on their divergent courses.

In the ninth century the formidable Patriarch Photius was handicapped by a disputed election. His contemporary, the no-less-formidable Pope Nicholas, listened to his enemies, against the on-the-spot reports of his legates in Constantinople, and backed the opposition to Photius. There were recurrent massacres of Latins in Constantinople, not least of Venetian traders whose commercial successes maddened the Byzantines. At the beginning of the eleventh century the names of the popes were removed from the diptychs in Constantinople; these were the prayer lists of those with whom the eastern patriarchate was in communion. Matters came to a head in the middle of the eleventh century when once again a great pope, Leo IX, faced a formidable patriarch, Michael Cerularius, a member of the Byzantine imperial family. Cardinal Humbert was sent as a legate to Constantinople in 1054. High-handedly he raised all the old contentious arguments. When he found the easterns in no mood to climb down, he entered St Sophia and placed on the altar a papal bull excommunicating the patriarch. Returning home he represented his action as a great victory for Rome and for her supremacy. But in fact the wording of the bull 'shows better than any document how the western church had recently developed on its own lines under the influence of the reformers, and how little understanding the latter had of the customs and usages of the eastern church'.[9]

The year 1054, then, is the official date of the breach between the east and west. But it was not seen at the time as definite, and matters might have been patched up once again had it not been for a new explosive factor – the crusades. 'It was the crusades which made the schism

definitive: they introduced a new spirit of hatred and
bitterness; and they brought the whole issue down to the
popular level.'[10]

The intention, of course, was exactly the opposite and
at first the western crusaders reinstated imperial rule and
orthodox religion in the lands they reconquered. But this
did not last. Co-operation became more and more uneasy; the westerns thought the easterns were hopeless, and
the easterns thought the westerns were barbaric. Finally
in 1204, despite threats of excommunication from Innocent III, the most powerful of all the medieval popes, the
crusaders entered and sacked Constantinople. It was the
richest prize in the world, and they reaped the traditional
fruits of war – and did so in the traditional way of
soldiers. There were three days of appalling pillage; the
altar and the icon screen of St Sophia were torn in pieces
and prostitutes installed on the patriarch's throne. 'Even
the Saracens are merciful and kind compared with these
men who bear the cross of Christ on their shoulders,' was
the comment of one outraged citizen.[11] Small wonder
that for many generations, and even centuries, the
Orthodox were unable to see western Christians as fellow-
believers. To religious misunderstanding and distrust
there was now added intense and remembered national
hatred. 'The Crusaders brought not peace but a sword;
and the sword was to sever Christendom.'[12]

The rest is epilogue. There were talks of reunion and
even of a further crusade which would right the wrongs
of 1204. When in 1274 the Emperor Michael Palaeo-
logus for political reasons patched up a union, he was
treated as an apostate and denied Christian burial in his
own capital. 'Better my brother's empire should perish,
than the purity of the orthodox faith,' said his sister.[13] At
the end of the Middle Ages politics led to another
reunion. The Council of Ferrara-Florence (1438–9)
reached uniformity of doctrine but an agreement to
differ on traditional matters of liturgy and practice; the

Greeks – or all but one of them – accepted the *filioque* and an ambiguous statement on papal supremacy. It was a statesmanlike solution, but the people would not accept their leaders' formula – not for the last time in ecumenical diplomacy. The union was never ratified in Constantinople. This time it was an imperial Grand Duke who voiced popular opinion: 'I would rather see the Moslem turban in the midst of the city than the Latin mitre.'[14]

He did not have long to wait. In 1453 the Turks were at the walls which Constantine had built for the Christian Rome. The last Christian service took place in the great church of the Holy Wisdom on 29 May; for once crisis had submerged the differences and it was a united service for Orthodox and Catholics. It was too late. The emperor received communion and went out to die fighting on the walls. The unhappy struggle between old and new Rome was over . . . for the new Rome was no more.

Orthodoxy since the Schism with Rome

But there was a third Rome waiting in the wings of history – Moscow. From Constantinople Christianity had spread northwards to areas which had been beyond the pale in the days of the original Roman Empire. In the ninth century Moravia was the mission field, and in the tenth Bulgaria: in 945 Constantinople recognized an independent patriarchate of Bulgaria; it was the first national church of the Slavs and a logical extension of the idea of a fellowship of autocephalous (that is: self-governing under a patriarch) orthodox churches. Further north and east, Serbia was converted at about the same time; for many years its allegiance was undecided between west and east, but in the fourteenth century it became another independent patriarchate in the eastern family. Further north still Romania followed the same pattern though its people were not Slav but Latin, in

race and language. As a result 'the second largest Orthodox Church today is predominantly Latin in character'.[15]

It was, however, the Slavs of Russia who were the most
important converts to Orthodoxy. At the end of the tenth
century the Tsar Vladimir was converted and set to work
to Christianize his realm with astonishing success and
rapidity. Like the Byzantines the Russians at one moment preferred the domination of heathens – in this case
the Tartars – to submission to Roman domination; but
eventually the Tartars were both defeated and converted
and by the end of the Middle Ages the great land of
Russia was established as a Christian nation with its
capital at Moscow. In 1510 the monk Philotheus of Pskov
(typically enough a Russian with a Greek name) wrote to
the Tsar Basil II:

> I wish to add a few words on the present Orthodox Empire
> of our ruler: he is on earth the sole Emperor [Tsar] of the
> Christians, the leader of the Apostolic Church which stands
> no longer in Rome or in Constantinople, but in the blessed
> city of Moscow. She alone shines in the whole world brighter
> than the sun. . . . All Christian Empires are fallen and in their
> stead stands alone the Empire of our ruler. . . . Two Romes
> have fallen but the third stands, and a fourth there will not
> be.[16]

It was the old vision in a new setting. Nothing could
more perfectly illustrate the feeling of continuity which
is the chief characteristic of the Orthodox church.

Not, of course, that there were no changes at all. The
Russians contributed their own type of spirituality, a
very simple mysticism, and that emphasis on the redemp-
tive nature of human suffering which is best known in
the west through the novels of Dostoevsky. Indeed the
one schism in the Russian church came from an attempt
in the seventeenth century to root out all later Russian
additions to the Greek central tradition. Those who
wanted to hold to the Russian ritualistic ways split off

and were known as the Old Believers. They were a rallying point for malcontents for over two hundred years and
were finally recognized by the state in 1881. Old Believers
had been fleeing from Russia since the seventeenth century, and after the Revolution colonies of them left the
homeland to settle in China; since the communist regime
was established there in 1949 they have been finding their
way in considerable numbers to the western world via
Hong Kong. They make a pathetic addition to the
twentieth century role of refugees.

Again, in the Russian Empire, after the time of Peter
the Great, the state played a larger part in the affairs of
the church than in the Byzantine. The church, in fact,
grew accustomed to being unable to regulate its own
affairs and this no doubt was later to affect its attitude to
a regime which was fundamentally hostile to its existence. On 4 November 1917 Tikhon, the Archbishop of
Moscow, was chosen Patriarch of all Russia. Two days
later Lenin and the Bolsheviks gained control of Moscow.
Persecution of the church followed and Tikhon at first
led the opposition to the new regime; later however after
a period of imprisonment he recanted and withdrew his
former anathemas. His successor in 1927 went further
and virtually identified orthodox churchmanship with
Soviet citizenship. But a number of bishops, priests and
laymen refused to follow suit; they broke away and formed
a 'catacomb' or underground church. Once again, therefore, as in the early church, persecution has led to schism,
and hence to problems of recognition. Other Orthodox
churches, including the Patriarch of Constantinople,
recognize the church in Russia rather than the underground opposition. On the other hand – by the principle
already described as typical of the eastern church, and
known as 'economy' – they also recognize the Russian
Church in Exile which is bitterly against the Soviet government and also against the established church in the homeland. The church in exile, itself split into three or more

factions, now has its main base in America, which presumably makes any question of a *rapprochement* between it and the Russian government and church even more difficult.

Orthodox churches are, of course, not unused to living under the shadow of unfriendly governments. All through the long period of the Ottoman Empire, until its break-up in the nineteenth century, this was their lot. In fact the church became the natural rallying point of nationalistic opposition to Moslem rule, and its leaders often the leaders of revolt – a fact which explains why it is quite natural to Orthodox eyes for Archbishop Makarios to have played the part he has in the troubled affairs of Cyprus. With the decline of the Ottoman Empire it was possible for structures and patriarchates to emerge, notably in Greece and Romania, both of which had formerly remained under Constantinople. The Orthodox patriarchates of self-governing churches other than Russia are now Constantinople (which has under its wing various small cut-off Orthodox communities); Alexandria, where there are a few Christians who are not Copts; Antioch, now decimated by the years of Moslem rule; Jerusalem, in much the same position; Greece, the only 'established' Orthodox church, with seven million members; and Cyprus, the last of the churches tracing its history back to the four patriarchates of the ancient church of the east. Behind the Iron Curtain there are independent churches in Serbia, Bulgaria and Romania, each in a somewhat differing relationship with the respective governments of their country. Then there are fringe churches, more closely bound up with Moscow, in Georgia, Poland and Czechoslovakia. Lastly there are a number of churches which have sprung from the activities of (mainly Russian) Orthodox living in various parts of the world; these include Britain, Australia, China, Korea, Japan, France and Latin America, but more significant

churches exist in Canada and the United States which have
been fed by successive waves of European immigration.
Most surprising of all there is a not inconsiderable Orthodox church in Kenya and Uganda; this is a break-away,
partly inspired by nationalistic motives, from the western-
based churches in those countries, but it seems that African
soil is not unfriendly to Orthodox growth.

The Orthodox church is, in fact, spread more widely
throughout the world than is generally realized. It lives
its life against a great variety of backgrounds, political
and social. Political difficulties stand in the way of the
calling of an Orthodox conference or council, such as ex-
presses the unity of other world-wide churches. In the
1930s there was some talk of a synod, but the idea never
materialized. After the war it was revived by Athenagoras, the present Patriarch of Constantinople. A conference met at Rhodes in 1961 to plan an agenda, but
once again the plan proved still-born. It is therefore important to realize that the various Orthodox churches
must be treated in church politics and ecumenical negotiations as the separate entities which in fact they are.

Nevertheless they are members of the same ecclesiastical family, with family characteristics which set them
apart from all the churches of the west, Catholic or
Protestant. Chief among these characteristics is a sense of
tradition, of continuity with the past, expressed in a rich
and unchanging liturgy. The great English Byzantine
historian, Steven Runciman, says of the typical member
of the Empire: 'The divine liturgy was to the Byzantine
the great experience of his regular life, and his loyalty to it
was unbounded.'[17] The delegation which the Russian
Emperor Vladimir sent to Constantinople in the tenth
century found that this was true.

The Greeks led us to the edifices where they worship their
God and we knew not whether we were in heaven or on earth.
For on earth there is no such splendour or such beauty, and

we are at a loss how to describe it. We only know that God
dwells there among men and their service is fairer than the
ceremonies of other nations. For we cannot forget that beauty.[18]

The same point is made today by Paul Verghese, an
Orthodox who has lived enough in the west to know how
his church looks through western eyes:

> The distinctness of the Orthodox Church cannot be located
> in the differing theological formularies. It is to be seen more
> in the ethos of spirituality that stems from the Eucharist. It is
> a spirituality which does not minimize the value of truth, but
> refuses to maximize intellectual formulations as vehicles of
> truth. If the notion of original sin, and therefore of the forgive-
> ness of sins, occupies the centre of western spirituality, it is the
> vocation to transfigure the body, as well as material creation,
> in order to express the glory of God, which is at the heart of
> Orthodox spirituality. In the west there has been a strong
> emphasis on the great gulf between God and man, which
> continues to exist even after the Incarnation. . . . In the east
> the assumption is that because God became man, man can now
> live in unity with the God-man. To oversimplify, *encounter* is
> the western word; *union* is the eastern norm. . . . Union with
> Christ is not totally absent from the western tradition . . . but
> quite often this union with Christ is seen in a much too
> individualistic way, and without the possibility of affirming the
> goodness of all creation. In the Eucharistic encounter the
> Church takes the whole of history with it into the presence of
> God.[19]

A western Christian – Roman Catholic or Protestant –
might say that this description over-simplifies to the point
of caricature. Yet it is certainly true that the parting of the
ways between east and west, in differing spiritual, doctrinal and liturgical emphases, came very early in the history of the church: as early perhaps as the second century.
The controversies of the early church were fought out in
terms of Greek philosophy and its ideas, and the Latins,
or westerns, took very little interest in them. It would not
be true to say that the Greeks had no doctrinal disputes
after the sixth century, but they had none to rival those

of the first five centuries; by then the tradition was formed, and in much the same terms as those used by Paul Verghese. On the other hand the only doctrinal dispute of the early church which stirred the Latins passed the Greeks by. This was the Pelagian heresy and its refutation by St Augustine in the fifth century. It concerned human depravity, sin, free will and the means by which a man reached salvation – the same themes which were to lead to the crisis of the Reformation. So it comes about that, although a Protestant and a Catholic may be on different sides of the fence when they are talking about salvation, grace or the sacraments, the fence is a western one which does not exist in the east; they at least know what they are talking about – but the eastern would not.

Again, the western would say in reply to Verghese that his description shows all too clearly that the Orthodox remain Greek rather than Jewish (and hence Biblical) in religious outlook, with their emphasis on the spiritual and mystical rather than the concrete and historical. This is a case which can obviously be argued, but the argument did not split the early church, which knew 'no distinction between Jew and Greek ... but Christ is all and in all' (Romans x, 12, and Colossians iii, 11). Christian teaching, in its real catholicity or universality, was bound to be impoverished when it no longer included both the eastern and the western outlooks. No one with any knowledge of the history outlined in this section has been surprised that the whole character of the debate in the World Council of Churches has changed since the admission of the Russian Orthodox church to full membership of the Council in 1961. No plan for the union of the church which thinks only in terms of the reunion of the west and leaves the east out of account can be called ecumenical.

THE SCHISM OF THE WEST: THE REFORMATION

The Unity of Medieval Christendom

The unity – and uniformity – of the western church, and of the culture which it created, was developing steadily at least from the time of the great Pope Leo in the fifth century. With the collapse of the imperial power in the west the pope became a focus of unity and the church a symbol of continuity. When government failed in the so-called Dark Ages the church continued its work and especially its work of evangelization. Thus when new political and national groupings emerged at the end of that period they had to come to terms with the church and all that it stood for, including its unity. The greatest single example of this process, and one which was to have an immense influence throughout the Middle Ages and beyond, was the crowning of Charlemagne as Holy Roman Emperor by Leo III on Christmas Day, 800.

There followed the centuries which are known in the west as the era of 'Christendom'. In this period there were three main factors which made for unity and three counter-acting forces which pulled in the opposite direction. In the first place there was the great character and abilities of successive popes and the spiritual and creative forces, largely in the monastic orders, on which they could call; against this was recurrent corruption in the church 'in head and members', to use a fifteenth-century phrase to describe the corruption of the papacy itself and of other parts of the far-flung organization. Secondly there was the policy of political and administrative centralization on Rome, the impetus of which continued even when the papacy itself fell on evil days; opposed to this policy of centralization were the forces of nationalism both in church and state. (Perhaps the most famous of all the examples of this conflict coming to a head was the murder of Thomas à Becket, Archbishop of Canterbury, in his own cathedral by the knights of Henry II.) Thirdly there was the homogeneity of the religious, philosophical and cultural climate of western Europe, created under the aegis and patronage of the church and expressed in the common language of Latin; against this remarkable expression of intellectual unity there were the forces of heresy and the intellectual ferment which was generated by philosophical debates within Christendom itself.

The positive factors making for unity were at their strongest in the eleventh and twelfth centuries and this accordingly was the period of greatest unity in western Christendom. The tenth century had been a low period, with Rome ruled by women, the mistresses and mothers of the popes, and the church outside Rome largely under the control of feudal lay power. After fifty nadir years, however, Leo IX set about a vigorous policy of reform inside the church, and Gregory VII (1073–85) followed this up with an attack on the system of lay investiture through which lay magnates had been able to appoint their own candidates to great as well as small ecclesiastical offices. In the two centuries which followed, papal efficiency increased, the monastic orders were at their most effective, and the intellectual life of the church was at its most vigorous, reaching its zenith in the great philosophical and religious edifice of the scholasticism of which Thomas Aquinas (1225–74) was the greatest exponent. Innocent III (pope 1198–1216) was the greatest of the medieval popes in terms of the exercise of ecclesiastical power to impose spiritual and political unity in Europe. 'In making the right of the papacy to interfere in secular affairs depend on its duty to control the moral conduct of rulers and upon the theory of papal feudal overlordship, he was enabled by the circumstances of his age and his own will power and personality to make theory and practice correspond to an extent without parallel either before or afterwards.'[20] Thus he made a reality of the papal claim of *plenitudo potestatis*, or universal rule. He was able to arbitrate in imperial elections and to substantiate his claim to approve or veto the chosen candidate; he successfully interfered in the dynastic affairs of the King of France; he imposed his candidate for the archbishopric of Canterbury on King John and was able to make that monarch acknowledge his feudal overlordship; his political writ ran from Scandinavia to the Balkans. Not for nothing did he compare himself to Melchisedech, the priest-king, and for the first time proclaim the pope vicar of Christ, describing his office as 'set in the midst between God and man, below God but above man'. The next step came in 1302 when in the Bull *Unam Sanctam* Boniface VIII claimed for the papacy not only the spiritual but also the temporal sword of government. The claim of the church confident of its own unity to impose unity on the world could go no further.

But it was in vain. Within a year of *Unam Sanctam* Boniface VIII was the prisoner of the King of France at Anagni, his birthplace near Rome. It was the resurgence of nationalism; the papacy was to be involved in the crosscurrents of this very strong tide for centuries to come. Immediately Boniface's successors from 1307 to 1377 had to transfer their seat of authority to Avignon, where in political matters they were virtually under the control of the kings of France. The bid for world unity through political-spiritual unity had failed.

Worse was to come. In 1378, after the return to Rome, the papacy itself became divided over an election disputed on nationalistic grounds. This situation persisted for some forty years and at one time there were in fact three rival popes. It raised in an acute form the question of authority in the church. If the papacy itself, which had claimed to be the unifying centre of all power, was divided, where did final authority and where did true unity lie? The answer to this question was evolved during the councils which were called to try to sort out the papal crisis. The conciliar movement produced a doctrine of the final location of power within the church. By the 'Articles of Constance' (1415) it was agreed that a General Council derived its authority directly from God, and that all Christians, including the pope himself, were subject to its decrees. This theory, which played down the papal emphasis on centralization and gave a chance of more local autonomy, was naturally popular with the national churches. It found its chief supporters in the French church and therefore became known as Gallicanism. In the nineteenth century at the time of Vatican I and the decree of the infallibility of the pope, the issues were once again raised and the Gallicans, French and others, fought an unsuccessful rear-guard action. With Vatican II the matter of the location of authority within the church has again been opened, though in a somewhat different form, and the debate continues.

Underlying all this was the fact that at the end of the Middle Ages the church was in need of reform and this time no real sources of re-invigoration were tapped. The councils and various individuals tried but in vain. The intellectual unity of western Europe was breaking up; the old taunt that the schoolmen spent their time arguing how many angels could be accommodated on the head of a pin was partly true; and the new, more sceptical, learning of the Renaissance was attracting the best minds. Reformation, in one form or another, was at the door.

Luther and Lutheranism

'At the beginning of the sixteenth century everyone that mattered in the Western Church was crying out for reformation.... [But] when churchmen spoke of reformation, they were almost always thinking of administrative, legal or moral reformation; hardly ever of doctrinal reformation. They did not suppose the pope's doctrine to be erroneous. They supposed the legal system and the bureaucracy to breed inefficiency, graft, injustice, worldliness and immorality.'[21] The fact that when reformation came it was primarily doctrinal was due to Luther.

Not that the other factors which traditionally threatened the unity of the church were absent. Certainly Luther's teaching would never have spread like a forest fire if it had not sparked the tinder of German nationalism. But there was more to the movement than a skirmish against abuses or the rousing of nationalism. There was Luther's new theological teaching based on his personal spiritual experience. It was this in the end which gave the movement its particular strength and stamped it with a doctrinal emphasis which is characteristic of Lutheranism to this day.

Luther was not simply the belching peasant of much popular legend. He was a monk and a theologian, a professor at a very young age, trained in the subtleties of late scholastic thought. But he found that neither his training nor his monastic exercises could satisfy his conscience, laden with a burden of guilt. He turned to the Bible and to St Augustine. In particular he found a new outlook in St Paul and in the text in Romans, 'The just shall live by faith.' He found that he could cast himself on the mercy of God and on the righteousness of Christ. To him this represented a new theology, a new idea of God, and he began to incorporate his new insight in his lectures. Six months before his famous Ninety-Five Theses of 31 October 1517, which set the Reformation alight, he wrote:

My theology, which is St Augustine's, is getting on, and is dominant in the university. God has done it. Aristotle is going down hill and perhaps he will go all the way down to hell. . . . Nobody will go to hear a lecture unless the lecturer is teaching my theology – which is the theology of the Bible, of St Augustine, and of all the true theologians of the church. I am quite sure the church will never be reformed unless we get rid of canon law, scholastic theology, philosophy and logic as they are studied today, and put something else in their place.[22]

Here the doctrinal basis which Luther gave to his reformation can be clearly seen. It was all very well, but unfortunately his teaching did not remain in the university and did not work from there as a leaven in the lump. Caught by the winds of nationalism the movement spread and grew. There were two results. In becoming popular the teaching was inevitably simplified. Luther's well-based theology (which Roman Catholic theologians now admit was not heretical) was changed into popular slogans. 'Justification by faith alone' – *sola fideism* – became the watchword of the Reformation. Secondly this sudden success precipitated a head-on clash with Rome. At the diet of Worms in 1521 Luther found himself forced into the position of no return. Probably he did not actually say, 'Here I stand; I can no other.' What he did say was the theological equivalent. Asked to recant he replied, 'Unless I am proved wrong by scriptures or by evident reason, then I am a prisoner in conscience to the Word of God. I cannot retract and I will not retract. . . . God help me. Amen.'[23] It was again a question of authority. In the face of the assertion of the authority of the church, Luther appealed to scripture, the Word of God, evident reason and his conscience – and by the Word of God he did not simply mean the bare scripturalism of later popular Protestantism. Later he was forced into the position of saying that even General Councils could err. In sum, he was asking whether the pope or the church had the right or the power to define a doctrine not found in scripture. It was here that the break came. It was a tragedy, and he knew it; there is much evidence of the interior struggles he suffered in the face of the revolution which, almost unwittingly, he had set on foot. A further tragedy was that the rival positions became set so quickly that there was no chance of compromise. Rome delayed calling the reforming council which so many people were demanding, and by the time it did meet its mood was to destroy Protestantism root and branch. There had been a more conciliatory party led by Cardinal Contarini and under his influence a conference at Ratisbon in 1541 'attained the astonishing success of agreement upon the doctrine of justification by faith'.[24] But the discussions bore no fruit; Luther himself would have none of them and Contarini on his return to Italy found himself suspected of heresy and his moderation discredited, so that the way was open to the intransigence of the Council of Trent. 'Moderate men who engage in ecumenical conferences,' comments Professor Owen Chadwick of the incident, 'need to remember that not all the members of their respective churches are moderate men.'[24] It was not the first, nor the last, time that this painful lesson had to be learned.

Meanwhile Luther found himself with a new church on his hands. The first essential was to draw up a confession of faith by which Lutheran teaching could be explained to the world. This was done in the Augsburg Confession of 1530, which has ever since been the basic document of Lutheranism. It was the work of the studious and peaceable Melancthon and set the fashion whereby Protestant churches declared their position through a set of doctrinal articles. Luther and Melancthon continued to claim that they were purifying the old church rather than founding a new one, but their articles, like all the later ones, showed where they believed the essential Christian emphases to lie. Justification – that is, man's standing with God, and therefore ultimately his salvation – is by faith in Christ alone and therefore cannot be won by works – though faith results in good works. The church is defined as the congregation of the faithful in which the Gospel is rightly preached and the sacraments duly administered. (Luther, like all other main-stream reformers, accepted the creeds, and when pressed on the article about the church fell back on saying that it referred to the invisible church of faithful believers throughout the world.) Instead of the traditional seven sacraments, Lutheranism maintained there were three – baptism, the eucharist and auricular confession. The Lutheran liturgy for the eucharist, though in the vernacular, was rich and not anti-ritualistic and reflected the fact that Luther continued to believe in the 'real presence' of Christ in the bread and wine, while rejecting as a medieval addition without warrant in scripture the doctrine of transubstantiation, which had been accepted as authoritative since the Fourth Lateran Council of 1215.

In the phenomenal years of its early growth Lutheranism depended much on the support of the German princes. Traditionally, therefore, Lutheranism became associated with the power of the state and especially with that of the 'godly prince', whose authority meant so much to the church. In any case the authority of the bishops was ended. Some of their administrative functions were taken over by the princes, but Luther always intended that spiritual powers should remain with the church. Sometimes this resulted in a 'bishop' figure – a superintendent – and sometimes a committee – the consistory; the pattern varied as it was set up in the various German states.

Lutheranism was not confined to Germany, however. It spread north to Scandinavia; and here matters were simpler. As early as 1519 the Danish bishops had broken away from Roman jurisdiction, and when the monarchy became Lutheran the result was a national episcopal Lutheran church, but one in which the bishops had lost the continuity of bishops in the apostolic succession. In Sweden this continuity was maintained; the house of Vasa, rebelling against the Danes, gained the support of the church, and in the end adopted for Sweden a

Lutheran church in the apostolic succession, but very much under the control of the state.

The piecemeal development of Lutheranism and the character of Luther himself – more a prophet than an organizer – meant that there were many loose ends in the movement. It was inevitable too that, once the breach in the unity of the church had been made and the floodgates opened, it would be impossible to control the forces set free. In many places Luther's moderation gave way to extremism.

At the same time as Lutheranism was sweeping northern Germany a separate form of Protestantism was gaining control of the cities of Switzerland. The earliest leader here was Zwingli. He was a man of the Renaissance and an attacker of abuses, less of a traditionalist than Luther, and more of a simplifier. Above all he was not satisfied to stop where Luther did on the doctrine of the eucharist. For him Christ's words 'this is my body' and 'this is my blood' were to be taken not literally but figuratively. Christ was not *really*, in the sense of substantially or corporeally, present in the bread and wine; the communion was a memorial the faithful made of his death, and their thanksgiving for it. This radical teaching horrified Luther, who with characteristic outspokenness insisted that 'the Body of Christ is truly broken, eaten and torn with the teeth'. Thus began the first bitter controversies within Protestantism, which did not stop even when Calvin produced a compromise doctrine on the eucharist. Zwingli himself died, in battle, in 1531 but his influence was not at an end. His teaching had a great effect on the English Reformation – and on English Protestants to this day – while in Zurich and other Swiss towns his influence remained predominant. There was, therefore, a third form of 'mainline' continental Protestantism besides Lutheranism and the Calvinism which was soon to develop.

But the radicalism of Zwingli the humanist was as

nothing to the extremist fringe which was soon to develop from the Protestant revolt. The open Bible had become the symbol of the Reformation and once men – many of them barely literate – began reading the Bible without the tramline guidance of the traditional teaching of the church, trouble was bound to come. The Bible is full of apocalyptic images which have a strange fascination for the simple, as is shown by the history of many modern sects, such as the Jehovah's Witnesses. Early in the Reformation a group came to believe that they were the agents of the New Zion, with the duty of exterminating the ungodly. In 1533 they seized the government of Münster in Westphalia and two years later tried to repeat their coup in Amsterdam and other Dutch cities. Luther and Melancthon gave them no support and they were soon put down. But the fear of anarchic extremism did not disappear: 'For a hundred years and more the ill-omened name of Münster was enough to destroy the arguments in favour of religious toleration, enough to prove that Anabaptists, however law-abiding, were better suppressed.'[24] The word Anabaptist became in fact a blanket term of abuse applied to all Protestant extremists, a bogey word, a stick with which to beat anyone who refused to toe the line of the local Protestant conformity. Anabaptists were to be feared as much as Roman Catholics.

This was a pity, because most of them were law-abiding, even if some were faintly comic. Believing that only true believers would be saved, they rejected infant baptism and also the attempt to make all society conform within an established form of religion. They tended therefore to withdraw from society into their own communities. Such were the Hutterites who flourished in Moravia. Whole families lived a common life in communal buildings, abhorring private property – an amazing resurrection in a family context of the old monastic ideal, which still survives in South Dakota and makes one of the more picturesque elements of the American ecumenical scene. Such too were the Mennonites, whose centre was in Holland and who still survive there and in America, where also are to be found the followers of Caspar Schenkfeld. Such, lastly, were those Protestant extremists who denied the doctrine of the Trinity on the grounds that its formulation was not to be found in the Bible. These men were not sceptics but radicals, genuine religious seekers who were nevertheless regarded with equal horror by orthodox Protestant and Catholic alike.

Calvin and Calvinism

This outburst of extremist activity shows that the Reformation period was one of great religious vitality. But at the same time, of course, the splinter movements were destroying the last vestiges of the idea of the unity of the church. They were also fatally weakening Protestantism in face of Roman Catholicism – and the fact was that now rivalry between the churches was the great religious issue of the time. On top of this the Roman Catholics had closed their ranks and were counter-attacking. The hawks had beaten the doves; a soft policy towards Protestantism was discredited and the harsh tactics of the Counter-Reformation were beginning to pay off.

This was the background to the life and work of John Calvin. He was a reformer of the second generation: 'The problem now was not the overthrow of papacy, but the construction of new modes of power.'[25] The secret of his success was that he established a perfect example of what a reformed church and community should be. By concentrating his efforts he was able after a long hard struggle to produce a model which could with suitable modifications be reproduced in other European situations. This was at Geneva, called by John Knox, one of the many who came to learn there, 'the most perfect school of Christ which hath been since the apostles'.[26] After Calvin Lutheranism spread no more; the new pattern, for Holland, Scotland and elsewhere, was the 'reformed' one.

There were three essential characteristics of this reformed, or Presbyterian, system, which have marked it from that day to this. The first was its highly dogmatic content. Calvin wrote the textbook of Protestant theology, a thing which Luther had never done. This meant that inevitably he had to follow through on some questions which Luther had left in the air. The most significant of these was predestination. Luther had taught that men were justified by faith, and that faith was the gift of God. Why some men received the gift of faith and others did not was a question he never pursued. Calvin did. He had to admit that since all men did not receive the gift, therefore Christ did not die for all men, but only for the elect. The rest were predestined to damnation. Calvin admitted that this decree was *quidem horribile* – somewhat horrible, or awesome – but he insisted that God's sense of justice could not be judged by man's. In any case he was more concerned with the positive and pastoral aspects of the matter, to give the elect the 'assurance' of their salvation, whatever the circumstances in which they found themselves. Once again, as in Luther's case, it was the later and lesser followers who tended to fasten on the doctrine and caricature it, so that in the end it was a struggle on the finer logical points of predestination which split Calvinism. But for Calvin himself, it was his insistence on the majesty of the will of God, both in individual and cosmic terms, which gave to the religion of his followers its typical sense of austerity and high seriousness.

Calvin's second great achievement for Protestantism was to remodel the ministry of the church. Luther's doctrine of the ministry had tended to be pragmatic and even opportunist, according to the circumstances in which his followers found themselves. Often this meant in practice the dependence of the church on the state. Calvin believed that there was an essential Biblical form for the ministry, through which he would 'reassert the independence of the church and the divine authority of its ministers'.[27] The ministry consisted of pastors, teachers and elders. Real authority lay with the pastors, who had the final power of interpretation and therefore of policy. But Calvin's most typical contribution to the idea of the Christian ministry was that of the elder; these were specially commissioned (and in that sense ordained) laymen and it was they who with the presbyters formed the consistory, which effectively governed the local congregation. It is the stress on the importance of elders which Presbyterians are always anxious to bring to ecumenical discussions of the doctrine of the ministry.

The consistory was the vital tool in the third element in Calvin's new-look Protestantism – the establishment of theocracy. The consistory applied religious discipline. In Geneva its weekly meetings examined the details of the lives of individual members of the congregation – their clothes, hair-style and so on – and also pronounced on wider questions such as the bank rate and the cost of living. Those who did not conform were excommunicated and then handed over to the city council for secular punishment. In many ways this was like the old system which the bishops' courts had tried so unpopularly to enforce; but in the case of Geneva and other reformed communities the discipline was a great deal harsher – and it worked. Together with the dogmatic austerity of Calvinistic theology, this was the practical basis of that Puritanism which is the best-known characteristic of the way of life of a reformed or Presbyterian community. It is an outlook which cannot be discounted to this day.

The Counter-Reformation

The tragedy of the Counter-Reformation, alike for Protestant and Catholic, was precisely the fact that it was the *Counter*-Reformation. Indeed one distinguished Roman Catholic theologian has recently labelled it the 'Counter-Protest'. It was a protest against the Protestant protest. That is not to say that the need of reform, agreed by all to be necessary, was ignored, but that the main character of the movement was negative, defensive and polemical. Before the Reformation broke there was some chance that liberal and 'progressive' thought would trigger off a reforming movement within the church. Erasmus, the greatest and most typical of the humanist scholars of the Renaissance, had thought of himself primarily as a theologian and of his work as having some influence on the church: he believed that through his kind of learning – radical in the sense of going back to the roots – the simplicity of the Gospel could be recaptured: 'Nothing is simpler nor truer than Christ,' he said. 'I should wish that this simple and pure Christ might be impressed upon the mind of men.' Other humanists thought like him – but reform was not to follow this pattern. Erasmus influenced both those who were to become Protestants and those who were to remain Catholics, but when the battle was joined neither movement could afford the luxury of slow reform through education and enlightenment. The reformers proved to be too radical, too contentious and in the end too illiberal for Erasmus, and the Catholics in their reaction to Protestantism rejected his liberalizing influence. In England Sir Thomas More was another man of the Renaissance whose work could not bear fruit in the harsh climate of the times. As a young man he had hoped for reform within the church – even somewhat utopian reform – but when the crunch came he was one of the few who refused to recognize the king's supremacy over the church in England and died upholding the authority of the pope.

Typical of the churchmen who were influenced by the Renaissance, and who might, in less stern times, have led a moderate reformation from within the church, was the Italian cardinal, Contarini. He it was who led the Catholic side in 1541 at Ratisbon when such a surprising amount of common ground with the Lutherans was found. But when he returned from the conference he was suspected of heresy and died the following year. In Rome the tone was set by men like Cardinal Caraffa (later Pope Paul IV) who denounced Ratisbon as a theological betrayal. The year Contarini died Caraffa persuaded the pope to refound the Inquisition and to give it greater powers. In 1540 the Jesuits had been formally recognized; with their quasi-military discipline and their zealous obedience to the pope, they were to become the storm-troops of the Counter-Reformation. In 1545 the long-awaited Council was at last convened at Trent. On the main practical issues between Catholics and Protestants it re-affirmed dogmatically the Catholic position. On some of the more fundamental doctrinal matters its definitions were such as to allow for some liberty of opinion and even for future re-assessment. The fact that these definitions came to be seen as erecting insuperable obstacles between the two sides was more the result of their polemical treatment by the parties in question than of the original wording of the Council. The climate was not such as to allow any scope for the exercise of moderation.

An outstanding example of this process was on the all-important question of the authority of the church. The Protestants looked on the Bible as the basis of Christian doctrine: Article VI of the English Thirty-Nine Articles – 'Holy Scripture containeth all things necessary to salvation' – was a typical Protestant approach. The Council of Trent wished to uphold the authority of Catholic tradition. Some of the bishops wanted all the traditions of the Roman Catholic church to be declared sacred. But in the end more cautious counsels prevailed and a very vague phrase was used. Similarly the relationship between scripture and tradition was left vague. It had been intended that the Council should say that Catholic truth was to be found 'partly in scripture' and 'partly in tradition', which would have set up tradition as an independent authority which could add to scripture. But again the text was modified and the more neutral word 'and' (*et*) was used; this did not necessarily imply that tradition was independent of scripture; it could mean that tradition interpreted scripture. 'With this *et* the Council avoided a decision. . . . One cannot emphasize enough that nothing, absolutely nothing, was decided at the Council concerning the relation of scripture and tradition.'[28] Yet from the time of the Council Roman Catholic teaching on this matter was along the lines of 'partly . . . partly', that is that there are two sources of authority. And Protestants were not slow to pick this up, and to make polemical hay of it. This is a typical example of the way in which the Counter-Reformation widened the gulf between the two sides. It is only recently that tempers have cooled enough for scholars to take a new look at the Council and see that it was not altogether the extremist body it had seemed in the past.

The Reformation and the Counter-Reformation divided not only the church but also Europe. Religious marching and counter-marching was added to political, and undoubtedly made it more bitter, for sometimes the religious allegiance of a whole nation was at stake. The men of that age could not conceive that a state could be religiously divided. They could not fail to recognize that the church was divided but they felt that within the state unity must still prevail. Religious toleration was a concept that had to wait for a new and, in many ways, a less religious age. So it came about that after nearly a hundred and fifty years of war and uneasy truce, and of much terrible suffering, a peace of exhaustion was reached:

By 1648 the religious map of Western Europe, as it would persist for 300 years, had taken shape. In the north Protestants were in control – Lutheran churches in Sweden, Norway, Denmark, Iceland, the northern and central states of Germany; Calvinist or Reformed churches in Scotland, the Netherlands, Hesse, the Palatinate, and a few of the western German states. In the south the Catholics were in control – Spain, Italy, Austria, Bavaria and elsewhere in southern Germany. And across Europe ran a belt of disputed states in which victory was not yet clear: Ireland ... England ... France ... Switzerland ... and some of the middle states of central Germany.[29]

The concept of a united Christendom of the western church was shattered.

ANGLO-SAXON PROTESTANTISM

The occasion of the Reformation in England was the desire of Henry VIII to get his marriage to Catharine of Aragon annulled so that he could marry Anne Boleyn and, hopefully, secure a male heir to the throne. He had some reason to think that the papacy would find itself able to fall in with these plans, but in the event after much procrastination it became clear that this would not prove to be the case. So Henry decided to break with Rome. Among a number of acts of parliament to sever the links, the most decisive was the Act in Restraint of Appeals in 1533. By it ecclesiastical appeals could no longer go from the English archiepiscopal courts to Rome, a method by which the papacy had often in the past interfered with English ecclesiastical jurisdiction. In one sense therefore Henry was acting very much along the same lines as many strong and nationalistic English kings before him – though of course proceeding to the logical conclusion of the policy. The next year, 1534, came the Act of Supremacy declaring the king 'supreme head of the Church of England'. Despite the fact that this formula omitted a face-saving clause – 'so far as the law of Christ allows' – formerly inserted by Convocation, the clergy with a few honourable exceptions gave way remarkably easily. The breach was complete.

No doubt one of the reasons why the change from Roman to royal jurisdiction was effected so easily was that Henry's policy was to maintain the outward life of the church much as before. It was to be non-papal Catholicism. This policy swung around a little, according to the circumstances in which he found himself, but there was no doubt that its course was dictated by Henry. Not that there were no genuinely Protestant stirrings in England. Before Henry's roving eye fell on Anne Boleyn there had been meetings at a Cambridge inn, which got it the name of 'little Germany', and it was one of these decided Protestants, Thomas Cranmer, whom Henry made his Archbishop of Canterbury, though he gave him no scope in his own life-time. But non-papal Catholicism was too subtle and difficult a policy to survive in those religiously explosive times. The tiller was bound to swing one way or the other, and as soon as Henry's hand was removed it swung hard – towards Zurich and Geneva. The short reign of Edward VI was the high-water mark of Protestantism in the Church of England. But, typically enough, this was based not so much on doctrinal articles as on Cranmer's second Prayer Book of 1552. This was markedly Protestant, though not as much so as people like John Knox could have wished. Also the fact that it set up an ordered liturgy which included translations of many of the medieval prayers meant that, whatever the underlying theology, there was still in England a feeling of continuity and tradition which had been largely lost on the continent.

Not that the Prayer Book of 1552 had very long to take root. Mary succeeded to the throne in 1553 and England returned to the papal jurisdiction. In time the fires of

Smithfield were lit and Cranmer was one of those to meet his death. These executions caused a breach between Protestants and Roman Catholics in England deeper than any arising from the previous political church manoeuvring – especially when the memory of the persecution was kept alive in succeeding generations by a book as vivid as Foxe's *Book of Martyrs*. But when Mary died it was Anne Boleyn's daughter, Elizabeth, who succeeded her and the Protestant succession was established.

Elizabeth negotiated a cautious religious settlement, hoping by avoiding extremes to erect a framework of religious unity for the country. England was to be Protestant, though not as Protestant as the Protestants hoped. The church was still to retain much of its traditional government, including episcopacy, and the apostolic succession was preserved – though only just. Thus the character of the Church of England was finally settled. It was to be an established religion, and has remained so, with the consequence that it has also tended to be a religion of the establishment. Within a broad spectrum of conformity on a few basic essentials (the royal supremacy, the Thirty-Nine Articles, the Prayer Book and the Ordinal, which sets up without defining the threefold ministry of bishops, priests and deacons) considerable latitude of action and interpretation is allowed.

Within this framework there is always the chance that one party or another will claim to be the 'true' and 'essential' Church of England at the expense of its comprehensiveness, and the various parties can look back to some favourable high-water mark in history to substantiate their claims: already for instance in the thirty years before Elizabeth's succession the pendulum had swung within the field of the royal supremacy from non-papal Catholicism to Swiss-type Protestantism. Elizabeth herself was to find that it was not possible to halt the swing of the pendulum. Many of the extreme Protestants, returning from Switzerland and known as the 'wolves of Zurich', became bishops in the new settlement. They saw the set-up as one of what they called 'leaden mediocrity' and they were determined to do away with 'the dregs of popery'. They gave Elizabeth and her moderate archbishop, Parker, a rough ride. It was the first of many occasions on which conflicts between the parties within the Church of England, even between its leaders, were all too obvious – a phenomenon which has baffled many outside onlookers from that day to this, and which makes many ecumenical negotiators suspicious of Anglican delegations – for which faction do they represent?

The Protestant attack turned into a full-scale attempt to capture the establishment and to complete the Reformation by making the Church of England Presbyterian. The attempt failed and the idea was buried until it was resurrected nearly a hundred years later, when Presbyterianism was briefly established in England at the end of the Civil War. In Scotland, on the other hand, the Presbyterians won a long-drawn battle. There the crown pursued with greater or less vigour a policy of establishing a church roughly along Church of England lines; this attempt, which led at one time to the English Civil War, was resisted steadily by the Presbyterians, with the Covenants to defend their religion and preserve it for the nation. The Covenanting cause finally triumphed with the arrival of William of Orange in 1688.

Thomas Cartwright, the first great English Presbyterian leader, had had to flee the country, and at one time in the 1580s was minister of a congregation of English merchants at Middelburg in Holland. Here he encountered two other ministers in exile, Robert Browne, and Robert Harrison; and here began the schism between Presbyterianism and Congregationalism. The Brownists, as they were at first called, were like the continental extremists already described. They believed in a 'gathered' church of believers, not in an established

church. There was no question therefore of capturing the
establishment; they wished to push on to a complete
reformation 'without tarrying for any': 'the kingdom of
God was not to be begun by whole parishes, but rather of
the worthiest, were there never so few . . . indeed if any of
you [the Presbyterians] could show a church planted,
although it were but of ten Christians, it were worth
more than the half, yea than the whole that you have all
yet done.'[30]

This principle of separation, of the gathered church or
congregation, which had its own entity and was not
necessarily allied to any other Christian body, now became another option in the Protestant world. It had its
difficulties. It was not easy to be sure that a church was
really composed of the elect and was therefore a true congregation. There was therefore a continuous tendency to
schism. Moreover the separatists were bound to encounter the problems of all first-generation extremists.
What happened when the second generation came along
and were not quite so convinced as their fathers? Could a
church be continuously sloughing off its skin?

The Congregationalist ideal was hard indeed to maintain. Furthermore there were other extremists waiting in
the wings. The first English Baptist church dates from a
London congregation of 1612. They too were believers in
a gathered church, and they logically enough made believers' (rather than infant) baptism an essential part of
their programme; but unlike other Protestants of the
time they resisted Calvinism in theology. A man *chose*,
they said, to be baptized into the true church. These were
the 'General Baptists'. But in 1633 the adoption of believers' baptism by another London congregation of Calvinist separatists led to the rise of 'Particular Baptist'
churches in many parts of the country. These were the
most permanent among the hundreds of extremist
Protestant sects which flourished in England during the
seventeenth century.

Within this context of the seventeenth-century proliferation of sects there arose yet another Christian variation which was, in a way, a reaction against the exclusiveness and Calvinistic intolerance of the sectarian movement. This was Quakerism, the foundation of which by George Fox may be said to date from 1668. Fox's fundamental conviction was that 'every man was enlightened by the divine light of Christ'.[31] He rejected the teachings and traditions of all churches as being man-made and threw himself on the 'inner light' of Christ: 'This I saw in the pure openings of the light, without the help of any man; neither did I then know where to find it in the scriptures, though afterwards, searching the scriptures, I found it.'[31] For Fox, unlike the Calvinistic Puritans, the Holy Spirit dwells in some sense in all men, but perfectly in the believer, who is therefore particularly open to his guidance, especially in practical matters. From this belief, put into practice in the famous silent sessions of 'waiting on the Spirit', sprang many of the charitable activities which characterized the Friends and gave them an influence weighty beyond their small numbers in both England and America.

The last date given in this melancholy catalogue of increasing disunity in England was 1668. Thus within a century of the Elizabethan settlement the ideal of a country united religiously within a loose conformity to the Church of England had proved hopeless. Toleration of disunity was the only logical solution. In fact it took some further time yet, and a renewal of attempts at union, before the logic of events was recognized, so strong was the underlying belief that religious unity was an essential foundation of the life of a nation.

The Evangelical Revival

But by the eighteenth century the fact that the nation was no longer a religious unity was recognized. So, too, was the fact that it could no longer be called a Christian nation in the sense that the whole population had a religious allegiance to one church or another. Large numbers of people were out of the reach of any church. Here was the background to the next great religious movement after the Reformation, a movement which in its turn led to further schisms in the non-Roman churches. This was the Evangelical Revival, or, as it was known in America, the Great Awakening. The chief characteristics of this movement were powerful preaching to large or small groups on the assumption that they were non-Christian, the threat of damnation and the appeal for personal conversion and allegiance to Christ. The two greatest exponents of this type of preaching in Britain, both of whom also had large followings in America, were George Whitefield and John Wesley. Whitefield's followers remained on the whole loyal to the Church of England, but those of Wesley became 'the people called Methodists'. The difference was partly doctrinal, for Whitefield unlike Wesley was strongly Calvinist and his followers felt at home within the evangelical wing of the Church of England – except for a few who seceded and formed the Countess of Huntingdon's Connection, whose chapels are still to be seen to this day.

But it was more a matter of organization, for which Wesley had a genius. He did not mean his followers to leave the Church of England, but in order to maintain their fervour after their conversion he organized them in small groups which sprang up everywhere in the wake of the preaching journeys which he made to the tune of an average of 8,000 miles a year. Inevitably the allegiance of these people was to their Methodist groups and 'class meetings' more than to the – often supine or discouraging – parish church. In 1774 the first Methodist Annual Conference was held and in 1784 there was a more radical break when Wesley ordained Dr Thomas Coke to act as bishop to the Wesleyans in America and commissioned

Coke to ordain Francis Asbury, an American, to similar work there. The supervision from London by the Church of England of its work in America was deplorable and amounted in fact to almost total neglect; Wesley believed that as a priest of the Church of England he had the power to ordain. He himself maintained his determination 'to live and die a member of the Church of England'. But in fact this step was decisive. It created immediate schism in America, where in 1791, the year of Wesley's death, there were nearly 50,000 Methodists. Four years later the break came in England, when the Methodist Conference took the decision to administer the sacraments in Methodist chapels and went on to declare that all ministers 'in full connection with the Conference' were automatically ministers without any formal ordination. Thus, though the Methodist ministry in America was episcopal (though outside the apostolic succession), in England it was non-episcopal – though the laying-on of hands at ordination was later introduced.

In 1795, the year of the formal break, there were some 75,000 Methodists in England. The movement spread very rapidly but it did not avoid its own divisions: the New Connexion in 1797, the Independent Methodists in 1806, the Bible Christians in 1819, the Primitive Methodists in 1820, the Tent Methodists in 1822, the Protestant Methodists in 1829, the Arminian Methodists in 1833, the Wesleyan Methodists in 1836, and the Wesleyan Reformers in 1850. The underlying reason for this succession of schisms was the religious ferment of the time. Matters of doctrine were not in dispute; it was much more a matter of ethos and enthusiasm – and of rebellion against settling down into respectability with a highly organized, bureaucratic and clergy-centred church. But the cumulative effect of these divisions within Methodism was disastrously to weaken a movement which otherwise had seemed likely to become the strongest church in nineteenth-century urban and industrial England.

The ferment of the Evangelical Revival led to other schisms. The Plymouth Brethren were founded by an ex-Anglican priest, J. N. Darby (1800–1882), who travelled widely not only in Britain, but in America and on the Continent. Wherever he went disunity followed in his wake and schisms from existing churches took place. In time under his leadership the 'Closed' Brethren split off from the 'Open'. The latter stress the unity of the church and welcome fellowship with other Christians; but the former stress the separation of Christians from the world; they closely control the activities of their members and, for example, forbid them to sit down to table with 'non-believers' even in the same family. This stern and un-lovely sect is now the major branch of the Plymouth Brethren, particularly in America, and is very active in overseas missionary work. Another movement which sprang from the Evangelical Revival and is now world-wide in its ramifications is the Salvation Army. Its founder, William Booth, was originally a Methodist and an itinerant preacher. Like Wesley before him he claimed that he never meant to found a separate church; but he left the Methodists to start his own mission in 1861, and since then his followers have led their entire Christian life within the Army, which has its own rules and hierarchical organizations – though it dispenses with the sacraments – and makes demands of absolute obedi-ence. Booth cared not only for the souls but, unlike some evangelicals, also for the bodies of the poor; it is this which has given his movement its most marked and admired characteristic.

Nor did the longer-established churches avoid further schism in the eighteenth and nineteenth centuries. The (Presbyterian) Church of Scotland was rent by small secessions throughout the eighteenth century and finally by the events known as the Disruption, which took place in 1843, when 474 ministers out of a total of 1,203 seceded from the established church, taking their congregations

with them. Here again the issue was not strictly one of
doctrine, but of discipline or government: the rebellious
presbyteries were demanding a voice – or at least a veto –
in the choice of ministers; it was another revolt of the
local churches against a centralized and clergy-dominated
bureaucracy. But such disputes did raise fundamental
questions about the nature of the church. In Scotland the
new church was rapidly and efficiently organized and
maintained its independence until 1929; nor are the results of the Disruption eradicated to this day, for a section of the Free Church – the 'Wee Free' – has not felt
able to take part in the general union.

These struggles were not without their side effects in
England. In the eighteenth century English Presbyterianism had moved towards Unitarianism: as a result 'there
are probably no chapels, there is certainly no organized
society, called Presbyterian and claiming a continuous and
orthodox succession from the original English Presbyterians: the "English Presbyterian Church" of the present
day is a Scottish colony, organized within the nineteenth
century, whose whole antecedents lie beyond the border.'[32]
This being so, the troubles of the Scottish Presbyterians
could not fail to have their repercussions on the English.

Wales was in no better sort. Here further breakaways
came as a result of the Evangelical Revival. The church
in Wales – Anglican and established, in fact part of the
Church of England – was in particularly low water in
the eighteenth century. Evangelical preachers therefore
found many followers among the Welsh and this in turn
led to a multiplicity of chapels and sects, as every reader
of English cartoons knows. So strong, even in its disunity,
was non-conformity in Wales that in 1920 the Anglican
church there was finally shamed into disestablishment.
But deplorable as was the scene in Great Britain by the
end of the nineteenth century, it was as nothing compared with that in America.

The Background

AMERICAN CHRISTIAN PROLIFERATION

On 16 September 1620 the Pilgrim Fathers set sail from Plymouth. They were Separatists, or Congregationalists, and they were seeking in the New World that religious freedom which they had not found in the Old. Sad to say they did not apply in their colony of Plymouth, Massachusetts, the principles they had looked for in Europe. 'Having become a church, they harried the sects.'[33] Baptists and Quakers looked in vain for toleration; the so-called congregationalist churches were supported by a universal tax and very soon an attempt was made to set up a theocracy along Genevan lines. What did remain of separatism was the feeling that the various churches were independent units with no over-riding sense of the unity of the whole church. In fact this outlook can be said to apply to all the churches in America and is the historical basis for the remark by one Church of England bishop with wide experience of ecumenical dealings with Americans: 'All churches in America, whatever their polity, are congregational.'[34] The same thing was said in another way by a more recent visitor to America: 'What surprises and shocks me is your apparent blindness to the flat contradiction between a collection or even a federation of sects and the fundamental idea of Christ's Church ... standing forth and bearing witness that the work of Christ in every land is to bind men together in one universal family.'[35]

This congregational idea of local churches as separate units was undoubtedly one of the factors which has contributed to the extraordinary divisiveness of the churches in America. Another was the fact that when the Constitution of the United States came to be drawn up there was no established religion; instead the principle was laid down of the division between church and state. Not all the states had followed the theocratic path of Massachusetts: in 1785 Virginia set the example later followed

146

in the Federal Constitution. A preamble to a statute which may have been drafted by Thomas Jefferson contained these words:

Whereas Almighty God hath created the mind free; that all attempts to influence it by temporal punishments or burdens, or by civil incapacitations, tend only to beget habits of hypocrisy or meanness, and are a departure from the plan of the holy author of our religion . . . that therefore the proscribing of any citizen as unworthy of public confidence by laying upon him an incapacity of being called to offices of trust or emolument, unless he profess or renounce this or that religious opinion, is depriving him injuriously of those privileges or advantages to which . . . he has a natural right.

The effect of this argument was to renounce any idea of an established religion, and the statute ended with the words 'Truth is great and will prevail; if left to herself . . . she is a proper and sufficient antagonist to error.'[36] These were the sentiments which led to the vital principle in the Federal Constitution of 1791: 'Congress shall make no law respecting an establishment of religion, or prohibiting the free exercise thereof.'[37]

This was a religious revolution. Since the conversion of Constantine in the fourth century it had been taken for granted in the countries which assumed a Christian civilization that church and state must be tied together in the same bundle. A natural outcome had been that the state could not recognize religious disunity; in Britain for instance this had led to the anomaly of the Anglican Church being established on one side of the border and the Presbyterian on the other, with the same monarch as head of each. Though religious toleration had been reluctantly conceded at the end of the seventeenth century non-conformists still suffered many political and social disabilities of a kind which the American constitution found intolerable. Not that the Americans were renouncing Christianity; that is quite clear from the words quoted. But faced already with a multitude of churches with none dominant, and influenced no doubt by the philosophy of 'enlightenment' current at the time, they established a pattern of religious neutrality which has since been accepted not only by western-type states where Christianity is the dominant religion but also by those, such as India, where it is not. This pattern, by removing the necessity of unity, can make further church divisions more easy; but on the other hand it can act as a spur and a challenge to the churches to assert their unity in the neutral nation.

In America so far the former has been the result. The churches have proliferated: 'The religious history of the United States is that of an ecclesiastical fecundity and fertility carried to a point which must distress any theologically minded Malthus.'[38] In the first place all the divisions of the Old World have been transplanted to the New. As wave after wave of European immigrants reached the United States they brought their religious allegiance with them. Moreover expatriates tend to be conservative in matters of religion for obvious psychological reasons: their faith and its observance is for them a surviving link with the home country, a symbol of continuity and security. They are therefore loath to see changes in the religious practices in which they have been reared even when these practices are inappropriate. For example second-generation immigrants who are perfectly at home in the language of the new country often still prefer to worship in that of the old. Thus in one town or even district there could be separate Lutheran churches for Germans, Swedes, Norwegians and Danes. Add to this divisions produced within America itself and the result was that in 1924, although with four million followers the Lutheran was third largest Protestant church in America, it was divided into twenty denominations. The more closely knit Presbyterian church had ten denominations. Similarly with the Orthodox: 'In North America there are between two and three million Ortho-

dox, subdivided into at least fifteen national and jurisdictional groups.... The chief problem which confronts
American Orthodoxy is that of nationalism and its place
in the life of the church.'[39] Even the Roman Catholics
did not escape these divisions between French and Irish
there were serious divisions between French and Irish
Catholics which all but led to permanent schism.

In the nineteenth century, too, American political
and social disputes led to divisions within churches which
had been established in the country for generations. The
Baptist, Methodist and Presbyterian churches were all
split on the great issue of slavery. In the 1840s each of
these churches found themselves involved with test cases
about the ownership of slaves. The southern portions of
the churches seceded and two of the rifts remain unhealed
to this day. The issue of slavery has passed, but that of
segregration remains and in general the churches of the
south maintain that theological and social illiberalism
which is typical of the 'Bible Belt'. Thus the very strong
Southern Baptists refuse to join the World Council of
Churches and keep themselves rigidly apart from ecumenical activities in the mission field.

America has also produced its own schisms and consequent denominations. Since the separate existence of
the Methodist church was really caused by its strength
and success in America, Methodism could almost be
called an American division of Christianity. Similarly in
America the Baptist church was not so much a European
importation as 'the result of local circumstances'.[40] Its
founder, Roger Williams, searching for religious freedom, settled in Providence, later named Rhode Island,
where from 1639 he insisted on complete religious toleration. From there the Baptist church spread. It was much
strengthened by the revivalism of the eighteenth century
– the Great Awakening – and in the nineteenth it and
the other great evangelical church, the Methodist, were
better able to minister to the changing needs of the

'frontier' than were the more established and less mobile churches such as the Congregationalist and Presbyterian. As a result of this the Baptists and Methodists are now the two largest non-Roman Catholic churches in America: the Baptist family of churches numbers some $11\frac{1}{2}$ million, though it is split into nineteen separate denominations; the Methodist $8\frac{1}{2}$ million with nineteen denominations, the Methodists having been as self-divisive in America in the nineteenth century as they were in Britain.

Another important church whose foundation is wholly American is the Disciples of Christ, now the sixth largest Protestant denomination in the United States, with a membership of some two million. This church was founded by Thomas Campbell in 1827. 'Sick and tired', as he said, 'of the bitter jarrings and janglings of a party spirit', he had tried to heal the European divisions in Presbyterianism which he felt to be meaningless in Pennsylvania. The only result was that he was ejected from his church, and he founded the Disciples in an attempt to establish a church which would be a centre of Christian unity. His cry was 'back to the Bible', and in an attempt to return to a primitive church round which men of goodwill could unite he was determined to sweep away manmade creeds and organizations which he saw as 'stumbling blocks – the rubbish of ages'. But the only result was to found another Protestant church – though one which has remained always devoted to the cause of Christian unity.

A more recent development of American Protestantism has been the Pentecostal movement. To revivalism, with its stress on conversion, the Pentecostalists add the idea of a second conversion – or baptism with the Holy Spirit – with a stress on holiness. This baptism tends to take the form of 'speaking with tongues', a phenomenon which not uncommonly follows strongly emotional preaching, though most nineteenth-century evangelists – like St Paul, who also encountered it (I Corinthians xiv) – tended to discourage it. In 1906 at some meetings in Los Angeles there were particularly striking cases of speaking with tongues, which were not discouraged, and from there Pentecostalism spread rapidly both in America and Great Britain. The movement is congregational in character and its churches are known as Assemblies of God, though a central organization in Britain, the Elim Four Square Gospel Alliance, is well known for its huge meetings in the Albert Hall. In 1942 there were nearly five thousand Pentecostalist congregations in the United States, with a quarter of a million members. Yet at that time Dean Sperry was able to write his book *Religion in America* without any specific mention of the Pentecostalist movement. Such a thing would not be possible now. From and in North America the Pentecostalists have spread so that 'the emergence of the Pentecostalist churches and their missions has been among the most startling phenomena of the church history of the twentieth century'.[41] This has been particularly the case in Latin America. In Brazil and Chile the Pentecostalists are the fastest-growing churches in the world. In the rapidly changing social conditions of Latin America, where traditional Roman Catholicism is to a large extent failing to hold the people, it is Pentecostalism which is filling the religious vacuum. Similarly though not so strikingly, Pentecostalist membership in Kenya, Uganda and Tanganyika increased between 1957 and 1961 from 55,000 to 90,000.

Nor must it be thought that Pentecostalism is necessarily a movement which takes place *outside* the traditional churches. In the United States it is thought that there are some 20,000 Roman Catholic Pentecostals, and there are similar movements in other churches.

The Sects

The picture of religion in America is still not complete. There are the sects, 'the bodies which inherit the Reformation passion for a church purged of worldliness and purified after the primitive pattern'.[42] These extreme Protestant groups, sometimes schisms of schisms, all trace back to revivalism and are fed by it. They tend to pick on one aspect of Biblical belief or imagery and to fasten on it: the Book of Revelation is their happy hunting ground. Their names are as exotic as their beliefs: 'The Church of the Living God and Pillar and Ground of Truth', 'The National David Spiritual Temple of Christ Church Union', 'The Latter House of the Lord, Apostolic Faith', and so on. Their leaders often make Messianic claims and sometimes wield an obviously sinister power on their followers. In America many are, of course, Negro communities, and it must be remembered that these sects are an aspect of under-privilege. Often the poor and uneducated do not feel at home in the established churches, with their middle-class customs and leadership. The sects provide a spiritual home for such people, and often a sect loses its attraction when it becomes itself relatively successful and respectable.

Individually, or even collectively, the sects are not of very great importance, reckoned simply in terms of their membership. In the American census of 1942 two hundred sects listed contributed between them only three per cent of the total church membership of the country. It is of the nature of the sects that they are small and exclusive. Yet for all their small numbers they must not be discounted in the total picture of the church. For they are now no longer an American phenomenon. Wherever evangelistic Protestantism is preached against a background of poverty and poor education, sects are likely to spring up. The back streets of Hong Kong sprout churches with names and activities similar to those in the back streets of Chicago. Above all the sects are growing in Africa, partly no doubt as a result of the revolt against the traditional western-dominated 'missionary' churches.

An analysis of the sects in America is therefore of wider interest than simply American, for the same sect types can be found in many places in the world. They can be classified according to the emphasis of their main characteristic. The list runs as follows:

(1) the pessimistic sects which despair of social progress and look for a catastrophic ending of the present world order; (2) the perfectionist sects which seek to realize the elusive ideal of holiness through freedom from desires of the flesh; (3) the charismatic sects, which rest their case on spiritual gifts, such as tongues, trances, visions and 'jerks' in general; (4) the communistic sects, which require the renunciation of all personal property, and occasionally hazard the secret practice of free love; (5) the legalistic sects which stress the observance of rules and distinctive manners, such as the substitution of hooks and eyes for buttons, or the antipathy to musical instruments in church; (6) the egocentric sects, with whom religion is a device for escaping pain and disease, and a means of promoting physical comfort; (7) the esoteric sects, which guard a mystery only known to the initiated.[43]

Many of these categories apply also to the last class of religion thrown up by American Protestantism. These are the 'Christian Deviations'. Their beliefs are so eccentric and far from what might be described as 'normal' Christianity that they would hardly merit inclusion in this chapter at all, were it not for the fact that they have sprung from within Protestant Christianity and that in their missionary work they still claim to be the only true interpreters of the Bible. All started in America and all have spread to Great Britain and, through their missionary work, to many 'non-western' countries. They tend to dramatize and take literally the apocalyptic imagery of the Bible, with their tales of horsemen, plagues and the rest. Since they claim their teaching can be understood only by the 'elect', they tend to appeal to simple and uncritical people. Many of them too bring in a special and extra source of revelation either in written form or through the inspired teaching of their founder.

These 'Christian Deviations' are, in order of founda-

tion: the Seventh Day Adventists (founded 1831), with
their strong – though frequently postponed – emphasis
on the second coming of Christ and the millennium: the
Christadelphians (founded 1848), with a similar emphasis
and an insistence that only those within the sect will rule
in the theocracy based on Jerusalem and escape annihila-
tion; the Jehovah's Witnesses, founded by C. T. Russell
in 1872 and again proclaiming, though often postponing,
the end of the world and the founding of a militant
theocratic kingdom; their teaching goes so far and gains
such a hold on their adherents that it is often held to be
politically subversive; the Latter Day Saints, or Mormons, who were founded in 1830 when Joseph Smith
claimed to have discovered the Book of Mormon, and
added it to the Biblical writings; after their astonishing
trek westwards in the 1840s the Mormons founded their
model theocracy at Salt Lake City; from this headquarters they preach their exclusive faith in many parts of the
world and their young male missionaries knocking on
doors two by two are a familiar sight in many cities;
lastly, the Christian Scientists, founded in the 1870s by
Mrs Mary Baker Eddy, and appealing in this case usually
to the better-off members of society; here a somewhat
expurgated Bible, together with the writings of Mrs
Eddy, are claimed as the true teaching of Christ, Scientist,
to a neurotic age: suffering and death are unreal and the
effect of false teaching about the reality of matter; illness
is to be cured, not by medicine, but by opposing right
thinking to the illusions of the patient about his state.
Lastly there is the Oxford Group, founded in the 1920s
by Frank Buchman, an American Lutheran minister who
had experienced an evangelical conversion in England.
This movement was at first supported by many individual Christian leaders but as its claims have become
more exclusive and far-reaching its links with Christianity have become more tenuous.

It is in the United States that the, literally, fantastic

divisiveness or Protestantism is seen most clearly. Yet America remains basically a 'religious' country – indeed as Dr Alec Vidler commented, 'appallingly' so. In many ways, therefore, and especially financially, America is the Christian headquarters of the world. Having received as imports the divisions of western Christendom, America now exports these divisions with many additions of her own. So, though reunion is more difficult in American than in other western churches, it is at the same time more urgent. But even after union has been achieved among the older and younger churches, there will probably still be sects which started in America and which have stood aside from the general movement to union.

Part Two

THE BEGINNINGS

CHAPTER FOUR

The Stirrings of Conscience

> For I do from my heart forgive all those that seek my life, as I desire to be forgiven in the day of strict account; praying for them as for mine own soul. That although upon earth we cannot accord, we yet meet in heaven, unto our eternal comfort and unity, where all controversies shall be at an end.
>
> JOHN PENRY, *on the eve of his execution for non-conformity, 1593*

ECUMENICAL SUCCESS AND FAILURE AT THE TIME OF THE REFORMATION

THE traditional church machinery for maintaining or repairing unity was that of the Ecumenical Council. As has been seen the great Ecumenical Councils of the early church had been more or less successful. But the last council which is agreed by both western and eastern churches to be oecumenical – or world-wide, representing the whole church – is that held at Nicaea in 787, the second at Nicaea and the seventh Oecumenical Council. After that the growing apart of the two branches of the church meant that, though each continued to hold its separate councils, they were not truly oecumenical and neither side recognized those of the other. The two churches came together briefly in an attempt to heal their differences at the Council of Ferrara-Florence in 1438–9, but as we have seen their solution was rejected in the east. After that the fall of Constantinople and the pre-occupation of the western church with its own schisms meant that there were no formal reunion negotiations between the two churches.

But the idea of a council as the machinery of reconciliation persisted in the west. At the Reformation the calling of a council was the great hope of those who wished to reform the church before it was too late. Had it not been too late the promising, but in the end abortive, meeting at Ratisbon might have led to a more general council for reunion and reform. As it was, Trent, and the way it was interpreted, closed the door to such hopes. Meanwhile the Protestants had their own divisions, and once again they turned to the machinery of a council to heal them. Their worst quarrels were over the doctrine of the Holy Communion – the 'apple of discord' as they themselves called it. Their most persistent ecumenist was the Strassburg reformer Martin Bucer (1491–1551). It was he who stage-managed the meeting in 1529 at Marburg, which was the most determined attempt to reconcile the Lutheran view of the eucharist with the extreme Protestant position of Zwingli. The attempt failed, but Bucer continued with his efforts to get the leading continental reformers together to what he called 'a free Christian Council'. A little later, too, Cranmer in England was writing to his continental colleagues urging a council on them.

In fact there were a number of councils which drew up agreed articles or 'formulas of concord' as they were known. After Wittenberg in 1536 the German and Swiss Protestants were able to recognize each other as fellow-Christians, but no steps were taken to cement the unity. At Zurich in 1549 in the *Consensus Tigurinus* articles were drawn up on the sacraments which became the common doctrine of Swiss Protestantism; but they were unacceptable to the Lutherans and in any case after Calvin's death the various Swiss churches settled back into the channels they had previously carved for themselves. Poland was a melting pot of the Reformation with many churches represented. In 1570 at the Consensus of Sendomir an agreement was reached between the Lutheran, Reformed and Bohemian traditions of Protestantism which was all the more remarkable in that the

Lutherans were for once willing to abandon the Augsburg Confession as the basis of their belief. Some years later, driven by the logic of events, Poland became the first country to adopt an official policy of religious toleration. In France, after bitter wars of religion against the Catholics, the Protestants narrowly failed to carry the day. Finding themselves beleaguered they looked for allies outside their own country. At a synod at Tonniens in 1614 they evolved the idea that it was possible to make a distinction between essentials and non-essentials of belief. On the former agreement was essential but on the latter it was possible to agree to differ.

This was in theory a great step forward, but in practice it was not a step which led anywhere, for the articles were not taken up. The spirit of the time was against such peace-making. There were two main reasons why positions were being hardened rather than the reverse. In the first place not many theologians would have agreed with the French idea that it was possible to differentiate between essentials and non-essentials in religion. Most of them in every church took it for granted that there was such a thing as the original and essential Christianity – the *depositum fidei* – which it was their job either to preserve or to recover, depending on whether they were on the Catholic or Protestant side of the fence. This deposit, which had been left to the church by Christ and his apostles, was unchangeable; if in the great Reformation debate it could be proved that any church had altered it, either by addition or subtraction, then that side had lost the argument. This point is well illustrated by a story from seventeenth-century England.

Sir Henry Wotton [we are told by Izaak Walton] visited the church of a friendly priest in Rome to hear the vesper music. And the priest, 'seeing Sir Henry stand obscurely in a corner' sent to him a choirboy with a small piece of paper on which he had written 'Where was your religion to be found before Luther?' And presently Sir Henry wrote underneath 'My religion was to be found then, where yours is not to be found now, in the written word of God.'[1]

While this idea of an essential, package-deal, Christianity prevailed it was inevitable that each church should claim to possess the package and should consequently refuse to bargain or negotiate about it.

Secondly the geographical factor was anti-ecumenical. Even after the break-up of the Reformation the idea persisted that church and state must be tied together and that there must therefore be religious unity within any given state. This long-held belief delayed the growth of ideas of religious toleration, for a refusal to toe the religious line could always be taken as a sign of political disaffection. It also made genuine ecumenical encounter more difficult; for while the various churches were confined to their own areas there was no spur to reunion. Each tended to cultivate its own garden, to regard itself as self-sufficient and to avoid the risks and uncertainties of ecumenical endeavour.

EARLY PROPHETS OF TOLERATION AND ECUMENISM

It was therefore not surprising that the first great prophets of ecumenism after the Reformation were for the most part laymen, men who were not too closely involved in the hierarchies and power-structures of their churches. Nor is it surprising that they were almost all men who had travelled a good deal and, having experience of life in more than one communion, had come to see the folly of the exclusive claims officially put forward by each separate church. Thus Jacob Acontius was born in Italy and came to England by way of Switzerland; Isaac Casaubon, perhaps the greatest scholar of all these liberally-minded churchmen, was born and educated in Geneva but lived most of his life in Paris; Johannes

Comenius (1592–1670) was a Bohemian and a member of the Moravian church, but studied in Germany, worked in Poland and travelled in many other countries; Leibniz worked in a number of German states and had wide contacts on both sides of the religious fence in France. Finally two men who influenced the Church of England had the same experience of travel: John Dury (1596–1680) was born a Scotsman and worked as a Presbyterian minister in Germany before being ordained in the Church of England; Daniel Ernst Jablonski (1660–1741) was born in Poland, but had a Bohemian background and was educated first in Germany and then at Oxford.

The thought of these men was on three main lines each of which ran contrary to the prevailing ideas of the time. In the first place they attacked the evils of religious persecution and advocated toleration. In his book *The Stratagems of Satan*, which was dedicated to Queen Elizabeth, Jacob Acontius attacked many of the presuppositions of her religious settlement. He saw that persecution was ineffectual and tended usually to have precisely the opposite effect to that intended. He even saw that it had a psychologically harmful effect on those who practised it. It was therefore one of the 'strategems of Satan'. Church and state should be separated so that the church no longer had the power to persecute. The church would be strengthened by having to stand on its own feet, for truth is its own safeguard and will prevail. Tension and controversy are in fact healthy for the church, and doubt should be seen as 'a stage on the road to truth'.

Parallel to Acontius's advocacy of toleration, and complementary to it, went his attack on doctrinal overemphasis. Confessions were 'the cackle of men';[2] he wished to simplify Christian doctrine and find a common meeting ground between the churches on a few essentials. This idea of simplifying Christian doctrine and distinguishing between essentials and non-essentials was 'the authentic note ... and the root principle of the ecumenical minds of [this] age'.[3] It is the second theme which they had in common.

One position is laid as the ground work of all this negotiation, which is that the only means to re-unite divided Protestants, and knit their churches together in a bond of brotherly love, is to bring them to a public confession of one and the same Confession of Faith in respect to Fundamentals. For I find it agreed upon and yielded on all sides, that if the fundamental truthes of faith and practice be acknowledged and confessed by two churches, that those two churches ought for this cause to profess sisterly love one towards another, and they ought not for some difference in things not fundamental to break the unity of the spirit through unprofitable debatements.[4]

This was the belief of John Dury as a result of his geographical and spiritual pilgrimage from country to country and church to church. Similarly Grotius, the Dutch philosopher and international lawyer, emphasized the common ground between all the churches and refused to admit the credibility of the claim of any church to a monopoly of truth – or even to have within it the capacity to develop the full potential of Christian teaching. To demonstrate this Grotius examined each church in turn and found it wanting – the Roman because of its insistence on papal primacy, the Calvinist because of its doctrine of predestination, and so on. In this test he applied the yardstick of what he called 'the Golden Centuries', that is the apostolic tradition as it was developed and maintained in the ancient church.

This appeal for agreement on the basis of a return to the early and undivided church was typical of the thought of the ecumenical prophets of the seventeenth century. It was known as the *consensus quinquesaecularis* (the agreement of the first five centuries) and it appears in the work of Casaubon, Calixtus (1586–1656) and others besides Grotius. The Protestant cry of 'the Bible and the Bible only' had resulted in a war of confessions, each claiming unique Biblical authority, and in this age of patristic scholarship an appeal to the wider basis of early church history seemed no doubt more promising. In the eighteenth century theological fashions changed; the early church was thought to be ignorant and benighted and no guide for intelligent Christians in an enlightened age. Later prophets of unity pleaded for a return to simplicity and to what they called 'reasonable orthodoxy' – but in any case the eighteenth century, with its emphasis on reason and moderation, did not produce men with the fire in the belly to make their ecumenical protest at a time of general indifference to the state of the church.

For the third thing which the seventeenth-century advocates of unity had in common was a vision of what a united church could achieve. It was this vision which gave them the courage to make their protest; unity was not an end in itself but a means of achieving good in the world which would not otherwise be achieved. Grotius saw that the church was handicapped in its missionary work by its divisions; his principal theological work was indeed a handbook for missionaries. Leibniz considered himself the disciple of Grotius; seeing the current political divisions of the western nations he worked for the construction of a unified Europe and a united church. His plan was for the reconstitution in modern terms of the medieval *corpus Christianum*, which was to be the spiritual centre of mankind, the mainspring of a great crusade which would convert the world. In his vision of an ideal society acknowledging the sovereignty of God through the worship of a united church Leibniz came near to the modern theologians' idea of the Coming Great Church. Another thinker with a world-wide vision was John Comenius. Disgusted with the disunity of the church, he produced a great scheme for world education which he saw as the surest means of propagating charity in the world. World government, with its headquarters in England, was to be achieved through three agencies, a universal educational council, a world peace court as the supreme political arbiter, and an Ecumenical Ecclesiastical Council which would have supervision over the religious life of mankind.

Clearly such a plan was centuries ahead of its time. Even less ambitious hopes were doomed to failure. The early ecumenical prophets, being for the most part laymen, had very little influence on the actual workings of their churches. Those churches themselves continued in their disunity and developed their own traditions in separation. Nor were the politicians favourable to ecumenical enterprise – and their support would have been essential if any real progress were to be made. An example of one exception to this rule will illustrate the ecumenical climate of the time. It comes from the beginning of the nineteenth century, but it is in the spirit of the eighteenth. Political changes in the map of Europe had resulted in the fact that the enlarged kingdom of Prussia was no longer a religious unity. Parts of the state were Lutheran and parts Reformed, the church to which the ruling family belonged. In 1817 the King of Prussia decreed the unity of the Protestant churches in his dominions; differences between Lutherans and Reformed were to be treated as non-existent. In fact this administrative arrangement made little difference to the life of the church until the government tried to cap it with a new united liturgy. Then there was immediate opposition, especially from Lutherans, many of whom founded a break-away church. The union was in its inception an administrative convenience, supported by some enlightened laymen, including the king himself, but not by the church leadership of rank and file; it led to further large schisms and it was many years before the new church acquired a life of its own. The unexpected intervention of powerful laymen to cut the Gordian knot had found the church in Prussia unready for the challenge of unity. There can be little doubt that the same would have been true of other countries of fragmented Christendom. The message of the ecumenical prophets had fallen on deaf ears.

THE ECUMENICAL POSITION OF THE CHURCH OF ENGLAND

The Church of England was conceived as a religious and political compromise. By her ecclesiastical settlement Elizabeth had hoped to establish a church which would embrace all but the extremists of the sixteenth-century religious spectrum. She was over-optimistic and her settlement immediately came under fire from the Protestants. At first its position was maintained only by stern political action which drove the Protestants first underground and then into schisms. Later the Church of England developed a theological line of its own by which it was able to defend itself against Protestant charges of half-heartedness with the reply that a church could be reformed without having to go the whole Protestant hog, and that the fact that a doctrine or practice had been abused by the Roman Catholics was no reason for abandoning it altogether: in other words it was a question of the baby and the bath-water.

The first Anglican unashamedly to take up this position was Richard Hooker. He countered the Presbyterians, not by claiming that the Anglican position was as scriptural as that of the more thorough-going reformers, but by maintaining that there were other sources of authority in the life of the church than simply the Bible. Certainly on many matters the authority of the Bible was paramount; but even then the Bible had to be interpreted by reason; and there were other areas where it could not or did not legislate; here the tradition of the church, again understood and applied with reason, was the best guide. Thus Hooker saw that the crucial problem of the Reformation

– and indeed of the church itself in controversial questions – was that of authority; and he brought his mind to bear to analyse the sources and types of authority in the church. He himself was primarily a philosopher and drew heavily on the medieval Thomist tradition. Those who followed him were more theologically inclined. In particular men like Launcelot Andrewes were great patristic scholars and firmly established the Anglican appeal to the tradition of the church of the first five centuries; they also drew more deeply on Catholic wells, especially in devotion, worship and the sacraments.

This was the beginning of the 'high-church' party in the Church of England. But soon there was very nearly no church at all. In the Commonwealth period the church was dispossessed at home and only a handful of her leaders continued her life in exile. Wooed by Roman Catholics and Presbyterians, it must have been tempting for them to throw in their hands and collaborate with what looked like the logic of history – that there was only room for Catholic and Reformed versions of the church and not for a *via media*. Yet it was these men who most clearly stated the Anglican position as Catholic yet reformed – Catholic in its essential continuity in belief and devotion with the church of the past (and especially with the undivided church of the Fathers) but reformed in having purged the accretions and abuses of the late-medieval church, which had been the underlying cause of the Reformation and had had the effect of driving the English church out of communion with the Roman. John Bramhall, one of the exiles and later Archbishop of Armagh, had a picturesque metaphor for the Anglican standpoint:

We do not arrogate to ourselves either a new Church, or a new religion, or new Holy Orders. . . . Our religion is the same as it was, our Church the same as it was, our Holy Orders the same as they were, in substance : differing only from what they were formerly, as a garden weeded from a garden unweeded.[5]

It could be objected that in theory, as well as in practice, it was not only this metaphor for the Church of England which was picturesque, but that the very idea itself was far-fetched. Nevertheless we see here something which was to become typical of the Anglican outlook and which still determines the Anglican approach to all matters of church unity.

Bramhall had picked on 'Holy Orders' as a key question – and so indeed they were, especially for Anglicans of a more 'catholic' outlook. Were Anglican orders 'new' or 'old'? And what were Anglicans to think about the orders – and hence the sacraments – of other churches? The earlier, more Protestant, defenders of the Anglican settlement were willing to uphold the practice of episcopal government, which had been retained in the Church of England; but they had not been willing to deduce from the practice any theory of the church in general or of orders in particular. In fact in discussing the question with continental Protestant colleagues they had tended to play down the fact that the Church of England had retained the apostolic succession. They knew that some Protestants would accept the fact that episcopacy was an allowable form of church government; against those who attacked it as 'the dregs of popery' they themselves might say that it was a good form of church government, and one which should be used as the Church of England happened to have retained it. But beyond that they would not go. Hooker's theory of the church, however, gave it the power to create its own ministry and endow it with high authority. From the days of the apostles 'a thousand five hundred years and upward the Church of Christ hath now continued under the sacred regiment of bishops. Neither for so long hath Christianity been ever planted in any kingdom throughout the world, but under this kind of government alone.' For him the authority of this tradition was paramount: 'If anything in the Church's government, surely the first institution of bishops was from heaven, was even of God.'[6] The church would, therefore, have to have very good reasons for dispensing with episcopacy and Hooker could not see any such reasons, though he does allow that it would be within the church's power to do so.

Some later writers of the school known as the Caroline divines were not so careful to cover their tracks and even said that it was not possible to dispense with episcopacy in the apostolic succession and that a church which had done so was no church and had no valid sacraments. But this was not the position taken by most seventeenth-century high-churchmen. Launcelot Andrewes, for instance, admitted that 'some part of the divine law is missing' from non-episcopal churches, but would not go on to unchurch them: 'Nevertheless if our form [that is episcopacy] be of divine right, it doth not follow from thence that there is no salvation without it. He is blind who does not see churches consisting without it; he is hard-hearted who denies them salvation.'[7] Once again Bramhall put it in a nutshell. Quoting Andrewes he added a note explaining the importance of 'distinguishing between the true nature and essence of a church, which we do readily grant [the foreign reformed churches], and the integrity or perfection of a church, which we cannot grant them without swerving from the judgement of the Catholic Church.'[8] Here was a typical example of the working out of the Anglican position of a church which was Catholic and reformed.

The Caroline divines applied these principles in their dealings with foreign Protestants. They felt that the continental reformed churches were real churches which had been forced to abandon episcopacy because of the crisis of the Reformation. On these grounds foreign Protestants were allowed communion in England and many high-churchmen would communicate with Protestant churches abroad. On these grounds, too, it seems that many if not all of the foreign Protestant ministers who sought to enter the ministry of the Church of England were allowed to do so without re-ordination, a privilege which was extended also to Scottish Presbyterians. Thus individual exceptions could be made in the case of foreign Protestants on the grounds of charity and 'economy' (that is the principle that in a divided church perfect rules cannot be made) but at the same time the high-church Anglicans in insisting on episcopacy as an absolute rule for the Church of England were aware that nothing must be done which would endanger the eventual reunion of the whole church (including Rome) on the basis of a united episcopal ministry.

It was in this spirit that a batch of negotiations took place at the end of the seventeenth century between representatives of the Church of England and certain foreign churches. In the first place a German, Daniel Ernst Jablonski, who had been educated at Oxford, worked for the drawing together of the Prussian and English churches. He realized that doctrinal agreement was not a very promising starting point for union, so he proposed instead first the introduction of episcopacy on English lines into the Prussian church and then the adoption in Prussia of a translation of the English liturgy. These ideas were taken up with enthusiasm by Archbishop Sharpe of York and by Convocation, but in the end nothing came of them. Some years later an even more distinguished churchman began ecumenical negotiations. This was Archbishop William Wake of Canterbury. He approached the Swiss churches with a suggestion that they should adopt episcopacy; but nothing came of the idea; despite the patristic learning with which Anglican ideals of episcopacy were put forward it was too early by far for the foreign reformed churches to go back on the history of the Reformation.

Even more interesting is Wake's correspondence with the French Catholic theologian Du Pin. This came at a particularly vital time, since in 1718 there seemed to be a possibility of a break between the French church and Rome. It was in fact Du Pin who first approached Wake to sound him out on the possibility of a union between the English and Gallican churches. During the course of a long correspondence Du Pin went very far to 'bend' Catholic doctrine to make it acceptable to the Church of England. Wake on his side clearly felt the attraction of an alliance between two non-Roman but Catholic churches. But once again no conclusion was reached; it was essentially a correspondence between individuals; Du Pin himself was suspect even among the Gallicans and in the eighteenth century it would have taken more than archiepiscopal influence to have moved the Church of England in a 'Catholic' direction.

Some years later another Archbishop of Canterbury was in correspondence with another continental Roman Catholic. In 1752 Thomas Herring was asked by the King of Sardinia if he would part with the bones (as relics) of his medieval predecessor, Archbishop Anselm. He replied that he would certainly have 'no great scruples' in the matter:

> But if I had I would get rid of them all if the parting with the rotten remains of a Rebel to his King, a Slave to the Popedom and an Enemy to the Married Clergy (all this Anselm was) would purchase Ease and Indulgence to one living Protestant. . . . Really for this end, I would make no conscience of palming on the Simpletons any other old Bishop with the name of Anselm.[9]

It was perhaps a promising reply as far as the King was concerned (actually the bones were not transferred), but it could hardly be said to have been ecumenical – or, as they would then have said, 'irenical' – in tone. In the eighteenth century – that age which 'tried to be more reasonable than it was reasonable to try to be' – some ecclesiastical temperatures cooled; but there was no corresponding rise in ecumenical fire.

The Church of England was prepared to be charitable towards foreign Protestants on the grounds that they could not be blamed for having lost episcopal government and the apostolic succession. No such charity could be extended to English dissenters, for they had purposely turned their back on episcopacy and rebelled against the government of bishops. This at least was the theological argument, but clearly there were other factors, not least the feeling that to leave the established church was to break the desirable unity of church and state, and to take a political as well as a religious step. The most drastic example of the policy of insistence on episcopal government came at the Restoration in 1660. Before his return to England Charles II had made vague promises to dissenters about 'a liberty to tender consciences' and had sketched a policy which gave some hope of a modified national church which should be able to include men of good will. But the restored Church of England determined on a very different policy. The outcome of this was the 'Great Ejection' when, on St Bartholomew's Day 1662, some 1,760 of the sitting incumbents of parishes all over the country were ousted from their benefices for nonconformity in general, and in many cases in particular for the non-possession of episcopal orders. Moreover there followed a series of statutes aimed at penalizing nonconformity.

This was not a good background against which to try to put into effect the policy of a broadly based national church in which moderate non-conformists could find a place – the policy of comprehension as it was called. Nevertheless negotiations to this end continued on and off for another generation, a fact which is one more proof of the tenacity of the idea of the necessity of a united church and state. Scheme after scheme was discussed. These centred not so much on the doctrinal formula of the Thirty-Nine Articles as on the need to revise the Prayer Book, the Ordinal and ecclesiastical administration generally. Above all there was the question of ordination and the stumbling block of re-ordination. Richard Baxter, the dissenting leader at the early negotiations, observed:

The grand stop in our treaty was about Reordination; and Dr Wilkins still insisted on this, that those consciences must be accommodated who took them for no ministers who were ordained without bishops.[10]

Wilkins, the bishop of Chester, was the leading Church of England exponent of comprehension. He was not the last moderate Anglican negotiator to have to look over his shoulder and remember the importance of carrying the high-church wing along with him. So the idea of Protestant religious unity in England petered out. Even at a time when the Protestant cause itself was threatened by the policies of the Roman Catholic King James II, the church authorities gave a thumbs down to a Bill for Comprehension. It was the end of the ideal. In its place the Revolution Settlement of 1688 brought toleration, that other ideal which had had so long to wait in the wings. Orthodox (that is Trinitarian) Protestant dissenters were to be allowed freedom of worship under regulated conditions. It was toleration of a sort, but the civil disabilities remained, and with them much of the rancour. Dissenters could take no part in the public life of the nation. Above all education in schools and at the universities remained closed to them. They were to remain second-class citizens.

This situation continued throughout the eighteenth century with only minor concessions: for example by the practice of 'occasional conformity', that is occasionally receiving communion at the hands of the Church of England, dissenters who showed themselves thus well-disposed were allowed to hold certain public offices. It was not until 1828 that the Test and Corporation Acts were formally repealed so that dissenters, who now of course included the Methodists, could enter public life. A year later by the act for Roman Catholic Emancipation the same rights were given to Roman Catholics and for the first time it became possible for the Roman Catholic church to organize itself in the country on a regular basis.

The rest of the century saw a steady opening of doors hitherto closed to non-conformists of all sorts. One by one they acquired rights now taken for granted but formerly denied to them. These included the right to legal registration of the births and deaths of non-conformists, the right to hold their own wedding and burial services and, above all, the right to enter the universities of Oxford and Cambridge. Each of these 'concessions' meant an erosion of Anglican privilege and a further step towards a neutral and hence a secular society, and each was to a greater or lesser extent resisted by some sections of the Church of England. Open animosity continued, therefore, between the established church and the various non-conformist bodies throughout the century and as each issue was raised the wounds were re-opened. But the surgery was necessary. There could be no real hope of moving forward to union until grudging toleration was replaced by something like genuine equality and the old memories of Anglican privilege had had a chance to die away. By the beginning of the twentieth century this position was at last reached.

CHAPTER FIVE

The Modern Ecumenical Movement

The great new fact of our era.

ARCHBISHOP WILLIAM TEMPLE *on the ecumenical movement in his Enthronement Sermon, Canterbury 1942*

NINETEENTH-CENTURY ROOTS

THE modern ecumenical movement has its roots in the nineteenth century. Three main aspects of nineteenth-century history, each with its origins outside religious life, profoundly affected the churches and in time precipitated the movement to reunion.

The first was the expansion of western civilization and technology in the undeveloped countries and especially in Africa and Asia. In the secular field this resulted in colonization, in the religious in missionary expansion. The Gospel followed the flag, or even in some cases preceded it; once again it was often a case of the connection of church and state; Christianity was an essential part of western civilization and the spread of one implied the spread of the other. Thus the nineteenth century was the era of the greatest expansion of the church since its foundation. Or rather of the churches, for as in the case of America, so in Africa and Asia it was the divisions of the church which were exported along with its Gospel. To some extent, it is true, areas of missionary work were allotted or accepted according to areas of political influence and certain churches were therefore particularly influential in certain areas, but this was by no means always the case and very soon western missionaries found themselves rubbing shoulders with members of churches which they had managed to avoid or ignore 'at home'.

Naturally enough their feelings of kinship and common enterprise in these remote areas overcame the prejudices and animosities which they had acquired in the west. Moreover there were two additional factors which tended further to confuse the missionary scene: in the first place Roman Catholic missions were active everywhere, even in areas where otherwise political considerations had given the predominance to a single Protestant denomination; in the second, the very coming of western ways and civilization broke up the static tribal pattern and made society more fluid and mobile than it had ever been before. The result was that natives who had been converted and lived at first in one church found themselves moved suddenly into the area of another; at best they were completely baffled by customs and rituals which seemed to bear no resemblance to their former religious practices, at worst they were unchurched.

Missionaries, therefore, found that the divisions of the church not only gravely handicapped them in the preaching of the original gospel, but also complicated the on-going Christian life of their converts. Very often the all-too-obvious effect of conversion was to take an Asian or an African out of his unified tribal and cultural background into a divided and even a warring church. The claim that the Christian Gospel made men 'all one in Christ Jesus' became a mockery which was much more glaring in the new circumstances than it had been in the west, which had become accustomed and adjusted to the divisions of the church. Not surprisingly the missionary situation threw the scandal of Christian disunity into bold relief.

One possible solution was to meet the problem at home by ignoring it, and to undertake missionary work on a non-denominational basis. This was a solution particularly welcome to those who were influenced by the evangelical revival, with their emphasis on conversion and individual Christianity rather than on the corporate life of the church. In England it led to the foundation in 1795 of the London Missionary Society, which aimed at converting men to Christ without influencing which church they should join. But in practice the ideal was impossible, as missionaries of the L.M.S. were soon to discover; in the mission field the idea was tacitly dropped and L.M.S. converts became to all intents and purposes Congregationalists. Similarly other non-denominational missionary societies, Swiss and American, have resulted in the event in one more denomination in the church overseas.

A more promising line of advance lay in co-operation between missionaries and missionary societies at home and abroad. As early as 1819 there was a committee of mission boards in London, and other countries followed suit. Similarly national conferences of missionaries started to take place in the overseas countries from the middle of the century; a little later there were international conferences. These meetings were undoubtedly worth-while, not least for the Christian fellowship which they generated in these early days of ecumenical meetings. But they could get so far and no further. In the first place their efforts were mainly directed to arranging agreements of 'comity', that is bargains about areas of influence and promises not to 'sheep steal' – but we have already seen that such arrangements were bound to break down as society became more and more mobile. Secondly these conferences were by and large meetings of individuals – and of like-minded individuals at that; they were not meetings of delegates whose decisions would bind their churches. Thirdly they were meetings of *westerners*; it was the missionaries who at this stage were most scandalized by the situation; their converts were at first more willing to accept it. In other words something was necessary which was at once more radical and more far-reaching than these early efforts if the nettle were really to be grasped.

As early as 1805 William Carey, a Baptist cobbler and an outstanding missionary in Bengal, had proposed the holding of a great world missionary conference at the Cape of Good Hope in 1810 – and had seen further that such conferences would have to be held every ten years. The idea was shrugged off at the time as 'Carey's pleasing dream'.[1] Exactly one hundred years later the dream became a reality at the World Missionary Conference at Edinburgh in 1910 – 'that crucial event in the history of the ecumenical movement'.[2] This conference did not suffer from the three disadvantages of its predecessors. It was able, therefore, to accomplish much more in missionary co-operation. But more than that it marked the true beginning of the modern ecumenical movement.

The second change in western history which was decisive both for the churches in general and in particular for the ecumenical movement was the social change of the industrial revolution which created modern technological urban society as we now know it. The word 'revolution' is not too strong, though it happened at different times in different places and indeed is still continuing. The movement need not be described here except in so far as it affected the churches. The churches were – and to a large extent still are – geared to working in a rural society or in small well-defined communities such as market towns. They have hardly yet got the measure of the new urban communities, with their huge sprawling populations, their lack of a single centre or focus of interest and their stratification of activities and complexes of power. In fact the churches have signally failed to cope with the consequence of industrialization and urbanization. The 1851 Census showed that only about 35 per cent of the population of England were church-going. Yet this was at the height of what would be thought of as the Victorian 'religious era'; after that date it seems that the proportion of church members to the total population decreased steadily, while just after the turn of the century the actual membership figures of the churches began to decline (see above, pp. 23–6).

For other reasons also than mere numbers the churches were losing influence. In the new society, with its increased complexity, the state was being forced to take an ever-increasing part in the regulation of affairs. Where before so much had been left to voluntary effort, and particularly to the charitable activities of the churches, now the interference and power of the state grew, while that of the churches declined. The most obvious example of this tendency is in the field of education, where the church once had a virtual monopoly; as this monopoly was eroded there followed a tug-of-war between church and state which was – and is – even more bitter in France, for instance, than it is in Great Britain. The details of this steady decline in the influence of the churches need not detain us. The fact is that by the end of the nineteenth century, when the overseas commitments of the churches were greater than ever before, their influence at home was waning. The realities of the situation could be disguised or ignored for some time, but sooner or later they would have to be recognized: it was no longer realistic to think of western countries as 'Christian', and non-western as the 'mission field'. The traditional Christian countries of the west were what the French came to call *'pays de mission'*. With their long Christian traditions it would be an exaggeration to say that they were pagan in the sense that parts of Africa are pagan; but they were – and are – definitely 'post-Christian'.

There was a third factor which affected the churches, and contributed to their weakening in this period. This was the intellectual crisis which hit them from about the middle of the century. Everyone knows how the publication of Darwin's *Origin of Species* in 1859 (and a number of similar but less well-known books) put the cat among the theological pigeons by raising doubts about the Biblical account of the creation of the world and the evolution of man. What is less well known is that there were other intellectual movements and discoveries at the time the digestion of which was an even more traumatic experience for the churches. The application of new techniques of historical scholarship to the Bible led to serious doubts about its trustworthiness and about the miraculous element not only in the Old but also in the New Testament. What was worse, the fact that Christ is recorded as having accepted such Old Testament miracles as Jonah in the whale's belly seemed to raise questions about his omniscience and hence, so it was thought, about his divinity. The whole basis of traditional Christian belief was thus being challenged.

The different churches reacted in different ways to this crisis and the nature of the reaction tended also to influence – if not to govern – their reactions to each other and to the ecumenical movement as it developed. The Roman Catholic church rejected any idea of coming to terms with the various new intellectual and social movements of the time – and its attitude to the ecumenical movement until quite recent years can be understo only in terms of this rejection, and of the dogmatic and psychological position to which it led. During his very long reign (1846–78) Pope Pius IX set the face of the church firmly against any forms of liberalism. This policy came to its climax in 1864 with the Syllabus against 'the principal errors of our time', which contained the famous and all-inclusive condemnation of the idea that 'the Roman Pontiff can and should reconcile himself with progress, with liberalism, and with recent civilization'. Forty years later the same policy was adopted with more subtlety but with equal effect by Pius X when he condemned the so-called Modernist Movement, the writings on Biblical, historical and doctrinal subjects of a number of Roman Catholic theologians who were urging the church to take seriously the methods and some of the findings of modern scholars. Pius X made it clear that in condemning the intellectuals he was seeking to protect the great mass of simple people from having their faith undermined, and this paternalistic approach to authority and its problems remains the typical Roman Catholic attitude to this day, though it is of course now being strongly challenged within the church itself. Moreover it was not only a negative policy; it had its positive side. In 1854 Pius IX defined the doctrine of the Immaculate Conception of the Blessed Virgin Mary. This doctrine, which further encouraged the cult of the Mother of Christ, was particularly popular in backward Roman Catholic areas and was anathema in Protestant circles. Nearly a century later, in 1950, Pius XII again defined as required universal belief a doctrine which had been latent in popular practice and worship for centuries, the Assumption of the body and soul of the Virgin Mary into heaven at the end of her earthly life. Once again Protestants could only see this as Mariolatry, while for those who were concerned with the future of the whole ecumenical movement the step could not but be seen as one which deliberately put further obstacles in the way of progress.

Between these two events came the definition of Papal Infallibility in 1870. This again was a response to a long-standing popular demand in the church. In particular the Jesuit leaders of the Counter-Reformation in the seventeenth century had advanced the authority of the pope virtually to the point of infallibility. But it had never been defined. Indeed in the nineteenth century there was still an opposition party to be overcome; these were mainly French and German liberal theologians who maintained the ideas of the medieval Conciliar movement that supreme authority in the church lies not with the pope but with a General Council. At the General Council of 1870, Vatican I, this party was defeated. The question of infallibility was brought to the fore, advanced in the agenda and the decree passed. The council was meeting under the shadow of the Franco-Prussian dispute and when war broke out it had to disband hurriedly without finishing its business; in particular the doctrine of the church was not discussed and so the question of the relationship between the infallible pope and the church was left hanging in the air. The pope was declared to be infallible when defining doctrine in matters of faith and morals on his own authority and without the consent of the church. But the occasions of such definitions were uncertain and no one knows how many infallible decrees there have been since 1870. The extreme supporters of papal authority were therefore dissatisfied: the influential English Roman Catholic journalist W. G. Ward, who had said he would like an infallible decree every morning on his breakfast table with *The Times*, was disappointed. Moreover there is always the question, as theologians soon saw, of who is to interpret the decrees once they have been pronounced. Logically only an infallible pope can interpret his own infallible decrees, but the process cannot go on *ad infinitum*. The doctrine therefore left many loose ends. But for the moment papal spiritual authority had been boosted, just at the time when papal temporal authority as a head of state came to an end. And a further chasm had opened not only between Roman Catholics and Protestants, but also between the Roman and Orthodox churches.

At the other end of the theological spectrum the extreme Protestants – those who had been affected by or had grown out of the evangelical Great Awakening – also reacted to the new intellectual climate in an authoritarian way. They clung to the Bible and its verbal infallibility or 'inerrancy' against all the evidence which was building up to make such a position impossible. The Bible was the inspired Word of God on which the Protestant position was built and therefore any shaking of the foundations must endanger the whole edifice. Those who adopted such a position came to be known as 'fundamentalists', because (as they said) they stood by the fundamentals of their faith. Some churches, such as the Southern Baptist in America, the Plymouth Brethren and most of the smaller sects, adopted this position *in toto*. In other Protestant churches and in the Church of England an evangelical wing clung to fundamentalism and were the main opponents of the introduction of 'liberal' ideas.

But in the main-line churches of Protestantism these ideas gradually gained ground – though not without bitter struggles – as theologians came to see that it was possible to reconcile new intellectual methods and insights with the essentials of traditional belief. Clearly much depended on what was meant by 'essentials', and here on the whole it was the German Protestant theologians who went furthest in stripping down the faith, until little more was left than Christ the great human teacher and example, the founder of the 'Protestant ethic'. There can be no doubt that the theological struggles which took place on these critical issues consumed much of the energy of leaders and thinkers who were the very men who might otherwise have given the ecumenical movement an earlier start. But weakening though in some ways they were, the struggles were necessary if the church was to survive into the modern world; in going through this intellectual crisis the various churches and their theologians found that they were now working on common ground; the old denominational differences were becoming less important than thought on new issues and in this field scholarship became increasingly international and interdenominational. In the end, therefore, the intellectual ferment of the nineteenth century was one of the factors which led directly to the ecumenical movement of the twentieth. And the attitudes taken up by the churches to the theological crisis largely governed the attitudes they were going to adopt to the ecumenical challenge, at least in its early years.

NINETEENTH-CENTURY ECUMENISM

Not that the nineteenth century was devoid of ecumenical activity. The Evangelical Revival, with its resultant wave of individualistic Protestantism, led to many further schisms in the church. But there was some progress in the opposite direction especially among the older denominations. There were no less than eight reunions between separate branches of the Presbyterian church in Canada between 1818 and 1875. In 1900 two of the free Presbyterian churches in Scotland came together in a union which affected over a thousand congregations. The Methodists had started the century with evangelical ferment and multiple divisions. But before mid-century the tide began to flow the other way and there were Methodist reunions in 1836, 1857 and 1907. There was a Methodist union in Canada in 1884 and in Australia in 1902.

These acts of union, and others like them, were all within the same branches of the church. In that sense they were relatively easy and it can be said that they were rationalizations in view of hard economic or organizational facts; it can also be said that they followed on the realization that by the mid-century church membership was already beginning to dwindle, or that some of the unions of Methodists had at their heart a desire to form a common front against the Church of England and its dangerous high-church teaching and practices. All this may be part of the truth, but it is not the whole truth. These unions took place before the scandal of disunion was generally recognized as it was in the twentieth century. Though they were within a single denomination they usually took place only after a hard struggle. The smaller the church, the stronger, often, was the sense of loyalty to it and the sadness at its passing: 'We shall lose the family feeling that belongs to a small denomination,' wrote a layman of the Methodist New Connexion.[3] These early acts of union may have been belated and unambitious, but at least some of the protagonists were genuine pioneers of the modern ecumenical movement.

There were, however, very few attempts at unions which crossed the denominational boundaries. In America the missionary situation on the westward-moving frontier led to the Plan of Union (1801–52) 'which for over half a century united for the purposes of evangelism the Presbyterians and the Congregationalists'.[4] But it did not lead to plans for closer unity, and similarly discussions in America between the Reformed and Lutheran churches foundered on the rocks of conservatism. These and other American schemes were based on the idea of a loose federal unity between the churches in which they would be bound together, as one of their leaders said, 'like sticks in a faggot'. The main eventual outcome of this movement saw the foundation in 1908 of the Federal Council of Churches. The Council was joined by many Protestant churches and provided an important forum for ecumenical discussion; but it made little or no progress at the local level and its aims were always for federal rather than organic unity.

It was natural that the American melting pot should be the scene of the first important discussions between different churches. The European situation was more static and there were fewer such experiments in the nineteenth century. One famous and ill-fated scheme was the foundation of the Jerusalem Bishopric in 1841. This was a joint scheme between the Prussians and the English whereby the bishopric in Jerusalem was to be held alternatively by a Lutheran and an Anglican. The motives were at least as political as they were religious and hardly any attention seems to have been paid to the existence of the Orthodox church in Jerusalem. The first English bishop was transported to Palestine by the navy: 'They offered the frigate *Infernal*. Alexander refused to travel in a warship of this name, but did not object when they substituted the frigate *Devastation*.'[5] The entire enterprise had this Gilbert and Sullivan flavour (as did many other nineteenth-century missionary efforts); it came to an end in 1881.

The ecumenical position of the Church of England as it developed in the nineteenth century must be understood, since it is an essential clue to the subsequent history of the ecumenical movement. The century saw the church divided within itself as never before. Anglicans tend to boast that they are a comprehensive church holding together various forms or aspects of Christian belief and practice which in other churches have become separated. There are, as has been seen, historical reasons for this; but very often what outsiders see in the Church of England is not union but something like internecine war, and this was particularly true in the nineteenth century.

On the one hand there were the evangelicals, much strengthened by the Great Awakening and very often feeling strong bonds with like-minded Christians in other churches. They emphasized personal conversion and piety and the unity of the invisible church which was composed of the truly converted. On the other hand there were the high-churchmen, who received a new lease of life from the Tractarian Movement which started at Oxford in the 1830s. They stressed the importance of the visible church: the fact that the Church of England possessed the apostolic succession, not its establishment or its position in the country, gave it its spiritual and true authority. Having the apostolic succession it was a branch of the Catholic church, together with the Roman and Orthodox churches. Having the apostolic succession it had true sacraments and true ministers and was therefore a true ark of salvation, which unhappily the Protestant churches, without the apostolic succession, were not. This was a clear-cut position which attracted many of the best men in the Church of England, though it failed to hold John Henry Newman, who had first formulated it. By

isolating the apostolic succession as the only touchstone it
went further than the teaching of the seventeenth-century high-churchmen, and strengthened and simplified
their position. The new high-churchmen were not necessarily anti-ecumenical, because they saw clearly the necessity of the unity of the visible church. Talk of invisible
unity would not satisfy them, nor would federal unity
suffice. Nothing less than the organic unity of the church,
with a visibly unified ministry, would do. In one sense,
therefore, the new teaching gave impetus to the ecumenical movement and safeguarded it from being primarily a
pan-Protestant affair. But the impetus tended to be in
one direction. Many Tractarians were only really interested in eventual union with Rome, though some of them
for virtually the first time saw the importance of drawing
near to the Orthodox church. In any case they were at
first, and long remained, highly suspicious of any friendly
approaches to the churches of the Reformation or the
Evangelical Revival: for instance they passionately
fought the scheme for the Jerusalem Bishopric.

Between these two parties in the Church of England –
and often opposed by both of them – were the men
known for want of a better word as 'broad-churchmen'.
As has been seen their main energies went into the intellectual controversies of the time, but on them fell also the
task of defining an ecumenical position which would not
only satisfy but also represent all opinion in the Anglican
church. Anglican it had to be because the Church of England was now waking up to the fact that as it spread
throughout the world there were certain aspects of its
life, such as the establishment, which it could not always
take with it. In 1867 the first Lambeth Conference of
bishops in communion with the Archbishop of Canterbury took place. As they looked at themselves and the
church the bishops saw at once, and deplored, the fact of
its disunity. But it was not until the Conference of 1888
that they recognized that they must adopt an attitude, or

a policy, towards the search for reunion. Then they defined what they considered to be 'the principles of unity exemplified by the undivided Catholic Church during the first ages of its existence'. These principles they took over from a meeting of the American Episcopal church in Chicago in 1886.

As inherent parts of this sacred deposit, and therefore as essential to the restoration of unity among the divided branches of Christendom, we account the following, to wit:

1. The Holy Scriptures ... as 'containing all things necessary to salvation', and as being the rule and ultimate standard of faith.

2. The Apostles Creed, as the Baptismal Symbol; and the Nicene Creed, as the sufficient statement of the Christian Faith.

3. The two sacraments ordained by Christ himself – Baptism and the Supper of the Lord. . . .

4. The Historic Episcopate, locally adapted in the methods of its administration to the varying needs of the nations and peoples called of God into the unity of his Church.[6]

These four points are the 'Lambeth Quadrilateral' on which ever since Anglican ecumenical policy has been based.

The Anglican Lambeth was not the only world denominational conference which resulted from the missionary expansion of the churches in the nineteenth century, though it was the first. There followed, in order of foundation, the Presbyterian Alliance of Reformed Churches (1875), the Methodist Ecumenical Conference (1881), the Old Catholic Churches Union (1889), the International Congregational Council (1891) and the Baptist World Congress (1905). These conferences were ecumenical in the sense that they were world-wide and in one way they enabled the churches to understand and organize themselves in the context of the whole world and ultimately of the ecumenical movement. But of course they were not ecumenical in the sense of inter-church, and it can be argued that by building up the sense of world denominational allegiances they have weakened or impeded the growth of the feeling of the necessity of local church unity.

The twentieth century is the age of conferences, but they began in the nineteenth. There was another type of Christian conference which was organized for people of differing denominations. These were mainly for evangelicals, with their sense of unity among themselves whatever their denominational alliance. Such were the undenominational conferences held at Keswick in the 1870s to follow up Protestant evangelistic missions – for this was the great age of Moody and Sankey and other mass evangelists. The idea of these conferences soon spread to other countries. Such too were the meetings organized by the Methodist minister and travel agent, Henry Lunn, at Grindelwald in the 1890s, though Lunn managed to get to these meetings men whose outlook was other than his own evangelicalism; such meetings did much to dispel prejudice and ignorance at a personal level among those who attended them, for the bitter disputes which had taken place with the rise of the Oxford Movement and its 'ritualistic' practices had led to many exaggerated and unfounded fears. Another agency where Christians of different churches learned to work together was the Young Men's Christian Association which (with the Y.W.C.A.) provided the first vital ecumenical experience of many young men and women. This was particularly true of the Asian countries, where the movement was very strong: the 'Y's for instance in India and Japan attracted in the 1890s young nationals, such as V. S. Azariah, who were later to become both local church leaders and world ecumenical figures.

Another movement which sprang from the evangelical wing of the churches but soon acquired a wider ecumenical outlook was the Student Christian Movement, with its missionary branch the Student Volunteer Movement for Foreign Missions. The origins of this movement, which was the ecumenical cradle of so many later leaders, were in America and Britain and in the student missions of D. L. Moody. But in 1895 the World Student Christian Federation was founded in Sweden and the movement thus became a more than Anglo-Saxon affair. Its motto could be summed up in the telegram sent from Japanese to American Y.M.C.A. students: 'Kyoto, July 5th, 1889. Make Jesus King. Signed Five Hundred Japanese Students.'[7] Its aim was 'the evangelization of the world in our time' and its leaders early realized that such a programme could be carried out only by a united church. This was above all the message of the American Methodist John R. Mott, an ex-student secretary of the Y.M.C.A. and the first general secretary of the W.S.C.F. By his world-wide travels with this message in those pre-aeroplane days Mott became for many people 'the ecumenical movement incarnate'.[8] It may seem an exaggeration to talk about the work of one man in this way, but these were the early days and it needed the evangelistic zeal of a few men to convert others to the ecumenical ideal so that from them the ripples in the pond could spread outwards. Before the ideal could become a movement it had to convert and fire individuals: 'The essence of ... ecumenicity is something which happens in the souls of Christians. It is a new understanding of the Body of Christ,' in the words of Bishop Oliver Tomkins, a second-generation convert of the ideal.[9] This was the reason for the crucial importance of a few individuals such as John R. Mott.

But the S.C.M. and the W.S.C.F. did more than this at the beginning of the modern ecumenical movement. They evolved the principle by which it was possible for Christians of widely differing views to take part in ecumenical conferences without feeling that they were being disloyal to the special truths cherished and upheld by their own

particular churches. Previous conferences, such as those
held at Grindelwald, had been meetings of individuals
who represented only themselves and not their churches
or any specific Christian organizations. In fact they had
been *un*-denominational; they had disregarded denominational differences and had not tried to tackle them in a
search for unity between the churches. The basis of the
S.C.M. was *inter*-denominational: 'it recognizes [its members'] allegiance to any of the various Christian Bodies
into which the Body of Christ is divided. It believes that
loyalty to their own denomination is the first duty of
Christian students and welcomes them into the fellowship of the Movement as those whose privilege it is to
bring into it, as their contribution, all that they as members of their own religious body have discovered ... of
Christian truth.'[10] In other words the underlying principle of co-operation within the S.C.M. was not that of
the lowest common denominator but that of the highest
common factor. The ideal of the movement was that the
churches 'would give their riches, not give them up;
would share their heritage, not surrender it'.[11] On the
old principle of undenominationalism the high-church
wing of the Church of England had steered clear of ecumenical meetings, seeing in them only 'pan-Protestant'
get-togethers where 'Catholic' principles would have to
be abandoned. Now at the beginning of the twentieth
century after ten years of discussion the S.C.M. sold the
idea of interdenominationalism to the key high-church
leaders. And just in time.

TOWARDS THE WORLD COUNCIL OF CHURCHES,
1910–38

*The Edinburgh Conference of 1910 and the
International Missionary Council to 1938*

In 1910 the official missionary societies of the main western non-Catholic churches called the first World Missionary Conference at Edinburgh. It was the greatest single breakthrough towards ultimate reunion since the Reformation, 'the crucial event in the history of the ecumenical movement'.[12] It was crucial not only for what it directly accomplished and set on foot, but also because of the precedents and patterns it established which have moulded the subsequent history of the ecumenical movement.

In the first place the conference started on an interdenominational basis which thus became the principle of the twentieth-century ecumenical movement. At first the Society for the Propagation of the Gospel, the high-church Anglican missionary society, had turned down the invitation to be officially represented. Later its Secretary, Bishop Montgomery, became convinced that 'for the first time, so far as I am aware, the undenominational platform has been forsaken' – and consented to join the Conference: it was, as he said, 'an immense advance towards the yet far distant reunion of the future'.[13] The conference thus included high-church Anglican representation and the infant ecumenical movement was saved from a 'pan-Protestant' image.

Secondly, the fact that this was a world missionary conference set the ecumenical movement firmly within the context of the mission of the church, where it has remained ever since. The reasons why the urge to unity was first felt in the mission field have already been seen. The Conference accepted the validity of these reasons and pointed the way forward for the future. Its report was based on the premise that 'the aim of all missionary work is to plant in each non-Christian nation one un-divided Church of Christ'.[14] The mission and the unity of the church are two sides of the same coin. It was from this time that the key text of John xvii, 20, became the watchword of the ecumenical movement:

Neither for these only do I pray, but for them also that be-lieve on me through their word; that they may all be one ... that the world may believe that thou didst send me.

Thirdly, before it broke up the Conference established machinery to continue its work. The existence of such means of continuing pressure and debate has been essential to the whole movement, ultimately leading to and continuing in the World Council of Churches. Without such continuity the movement would have flagged between its conferences; with it it has steadily gathered momentum. As the Chairman said in his closing address: 'The end of the Conference was the beginning of the conquest. The end of the planning is the beginning of the doing.'[15] The Continuation Committee was charged among other things with the task of conferring with the missionary societies on the best way of setting up a permanent International Missionary Council – which in the end it was itself to become. It was not for nothing that the Con-ference had always been seen as a consultative body with responsible delegates planning for the future. The first officers of the Committee were John R. Mott and J. H. Oldham, another Y.M.C.A. and S.C.M. man. This too was significant. From its earliest days the ecumenical move-ment was able to attract to its service men of outstanding vision and ability.

One consequence of this, and another feature of Edin-burgh in particular and of the movement in general, was that ecumenical conferences and committees were always willing to be critical of the established attitudes of the churches and often proved to have been prophetic in their criticisms. For instance, the Edinburgh Conference consisted of over 1,200 delegates from 159 missionary societies, itself an impressive achievement. But of the 1,200 only eighteen were 'nationals' or 'non-Europeans'. Most people in 1910 would have thought nothing of this. It was taken for granted that the westerners would dominate the churches as they had dominated the world since the beginning of the era of discovery at the end of the fifteenth century. It needed a prophetic eye to see the writing on the wall even after the staggering defeat of Russia by the Japanese in 1905. It needed courage to criticize the effortless, but presumably un-Christian, superiority of westerners over 'natives'. The best-remembered speech of the conference was by the Indian V. S. Azariah. It started with the words

My personal observation ... has revealed to me the fact that the relationship between the European missionaries and the Indian workers is far from what it ought to be. ...

It ended with the words

Through all the ages to come the Indian Church will rise up in gratitude to attest the heroism and self-denying labours of the missionary body. You have given us your goods to feed the poor. You have given us your bodies to be burned. We also ask for *love*. Give us *friends*.[16]

Azariah was not one of those elected to the Continuation Committee, but another outstanding Indian was elected together with a Japanese and a Chinese. The proportion of non-westerns was thus amazingly high, an example of the fact that the ecumenical movement tended to think ahead of its time – and of its constituent church members.

Lastly the conference was typical in that it attracted outstanding young men and so threw up future ecumenical leaders. Its Chairman was John R. Mott, still a young man. The twenty-eight-year-old William Temple was there as a steward appointed by the S.C.M.; he often said in later years that it was at Edinburgh that he had his first vision of the unity of the world-wide church for which he was to work so hard and of which he was at the time of his death the leading advocate. Also present as a young man was the outstanding Church of Scotland theologian, John Baillie, who was later to become one of the original Presidents of the World Council of Churches. Again, one of the delegates was the American Charles Henry Brent, the Anglican Bishop of the Philippines.

The conference in its terms of reference had specifically excluded discussion of 'the questions affecting the differences of Doctrine and Order between the Churches'. This was probably wise at the time, if the meeting was to take place at all, but Bishop Brent saw it would not do. These questions could not be ignored if the movement was to have a healthy future. As soon as Brent got back to America he proposed to his church a movement which would set on foot a conference beteween the churches which would be devoted to 'questions touching Faith and Order'. But before the proposal could be followed up the First World War intervened, and further ecumenical progress was impossible.

After the war the Continuation Committee and then the International Missionary Council were at once in action – and in a way which clearly established their usefulness. This was the question of the administration and eventual return of German missionary property in their former African colonies, and also of the freedom of German missions to restart their work. There was much bitterness over this issue, which for some time kept the Germans out of international missionary co-operation, but in the end the single-handed efforts of Oldham on their behalf overcame the trouble long before other war wounds had healed. The I.M.C. had proved its worth. Another activity of the post-war years was the setting-up of branches of the I.M.C. all over the world. These

National Missionary Councils were the result largely of Mott's travels and of his determination that the I.M.C. should not be a central body merely but should have a life of its own in the countries which it served. It was the first round in a long struggle by international ecumenical agencies to make sure that the vision was transferred to, and the work carried out at, lower levels. Later the word 'grassroots' was used to describe the effort necessary to stir nations and parishes into individual activity.

One event was particularly significant. In 1922 the National Missionary Council of India was transformed into the National Christian Council. This was more than just a change of name. It was a recognition that the proper ecumenical agency for India was no longer a committee of the western-based missionary societies but one of the churches which they had planted and which were beginning to come to an independent life. This was probably the first National Christian Council to be founded. It was a pioneer step of immense importance; since then national Christian councils in almost every country in the world have come into being and have been able to speak, especially in grave crises such as the withdrawal of western government, in the name of all the churches – except of course until recently the Roman Catholic. In line with this policy of 'indigenization' the Indian council insisted from its beginning that half its members should be nationals. It was a bold step to take for those days; again ecumenical thought was ahead of its time. But one member who sat on both councils said that, though man for man the old one was the stronger, as a council the new was more effective. The secretary however was a westerner, the Presbyterian William Paton, soon to return to England to become Secretary of the I.M.C.

Paton's first task on transferring to London in 1927 was to organize the follow-up conference to Edinburgh 1910. This took place at Jerusalem in 1928. It was a much smaller conference than Edinburgh had been, and it ran into great difficulties. It was the heyday of theological liberalism and some of the delegates 'put forward certain ideas which, if accepted, would have meant a revolution in the whole conception of Christian missions; the task of the missionary would have been understood, not as trying to turn believers of other faiths into Christians, but as co-operating with them in the discovery of the riches of their own faiths.'[16] This drastic liberalism provoked a violent reaction from the conservatives and the conference nearly ended in deadlock. From this it was saved by William Temple doing what he described in a letter home to his wife as 'my parlour trick', and producing a statement which all parties would accept.[17]

Theological debates also dominated the next world conference of the I.M.C. held at Tambaram, near Madras, in 1938. By this time the conservatives were in the ascendant. This, however, was not the old fundamentalism but the new conservatism which had sprung from the theological revolution set on foot by the Swiss theologian Karl Barth. Instead of the usual pile of preparatory papers for the conference, the delegates all read one book, Hendrik Kraemer's *The Christian Message in a Non-Christian World*. This sweeping affirmation of the finality and absoluteness of the Christian faith in the face of any of its rivals, and as the only hope for the world, carried the day.

It could be asked what good came of mounting these expensive conferences to debate 'academic' theological issues. The leaders would presumably have said that the academic issues have to be translated into practice and therefore discussed at the conference table. The ecumenical movement has not escaped the criticism that it gives too much of its time to being a theological sounding board removed from the immediate concerns of parishes and missions on the ground. But however that may be the fact remains that since it is a part of the world Chris-

tian movement it cannot escape being caught up in the
general Christian debate of the time, and furthermore it
has been shown over and again that in the greatest basic
theological questions the divisions of opinion are not
between churches but within the churches and between
individuals across the denominational boundaries.

Not, however, that the conferences did nothing practical. The very fact that a major conference was held for
the first time in Asia was significant; it enabled many
more non-westerners to be present, and it was generally
agreed that the most impressive delegation was the Chinese. Seeing the number of people of all races as well as
creeds, one delegate said 'This *is* the Holy Catholic
Church', while it has been said of another, Cyril Garbett,
later Archbishop of York, who was receiving his ecumenical baptism, that the experience altered his whole ministry and turned him from a typical 'C. of E. parson' into
the world Christian statesman that he became. The two
conferences also set on foot important pioneering projects. Jerusalem had seen the importance of the economic
changes which were coming to what are now known as
the developing nations and had set up a committee to
look into this; Tambaram saw the importance of increasing world-wide literacy and of having Christian literature
to meet the new need. Once again ecumenical agencies
were looking ahead of the time; but not for the first or
last time their pleas fell on deaf ears in the churches. In
any case within months of Tambaram war once again
intervened.

The Life and Work Movement, 1925–37

In 1914 the King of Sweden appointed the comparatively
youthful Nathan Söderblom to the Archbishopric of
Uppsala. For the next four years Söderblom watched
from the side lines the First World War. This experience
of Christian impotence in face of world tragedy, com-

bined with an international and ecumenical training, inspired Söderblom to found the Life and Work Movement, the second strand in the thread which ultimately became the World Council of Churches. The title Life and Work was translated in German by the phrase 'practical Christianity', and this gives a rough idea of the scope of the movement. A somewhat fuller description, and one which shows that the movement was in any case part of the post-war Christian climate, comes from the title of the conference called by English church leaders in 1921 – the Conference on Christian Politics, Economics and Citizenship (C.O.P.E.C.). The preparatory studies of Life and Work covered such subjects as the church and economic, industrial, social and international problems. In 1925 the first Life and Work Conference met in Stockholm.

In many ways this conference was an ecumenical advance on Edinburgh 1910. In the first place the 600 delegates were full representatives of their churches, not of agencies of the churches. Moreover for the first time the Orthodox churches were represented at a major ecumenical gathering – and by such men as the Patriarch of Alexandria and Archbishop Germanos, who was the great Orthodox ecumenical leader of the time; their presence and their contributions created a deep effect.

The motto of the conference was 'communion in ecumenical worship and service'. It was often said at the time that while doctrine divides, service unites and once again questions of Faith and Order were excluded from the agenda. But very soon it was discovered that practical questions could not be discussed without reference to theology. The opening sermon had talked about 'setting up the kingdom of God in this complicated civilization of the twentieth century', but this was immediately met with a counterblast from a German bishop: 'Nothing could be more mistaken or more disastrous than to suppose that we mortal men have to build up God's kingdom in this world.' The theme of this theological struggle was to run right through the Life and Work movement which had set out by eschewing theology. It was going to prove impossible to divorce service from doctrine.

For the moment the Life and Work movement continued with the Germans supporting what they considered a Biblical view against what they called the optimism of the Anglo-Saxons, and particularly of the Americans. Continuation committees were set up, in which George Bell (later Bishop of Chichester) emerged as an outstanding leader and in which the leading questions of the day were debated. Through them, as was said at the time, 'the movement became a laboratory of fertile ideas and projects'.[18] But the questions were changing. After the war it was 'war guilt', and then for a honeymoon period the League of Nations and pacifism. But by the thirties the clouds were again gathering; the German churches were having to struggle for their existence under a totalitarian regime, and when the next great Life and Work conference met at Oxford in 1937 the German delegates were at the last moment forbidden to attend it. Under the guidance of J. H. Oldham this conference had excelled in that careful preparation which was coming to be a marked feature of ecumenical work. Papers and books were written by a very distinguished body of men, lay as well as clergy and including among them individual Roman Catholics. But when the delegates actually met, they found as at Tambaram that the trend was overwhelmingly away from the liberal optimism of the twenties. In the new climate many of the old leaders confessed that they felt 'complete strangers'; but there was no putting the clock back. The great cry at Oxford, and for many years afterwards, was 'Let the church be the church'. The motto may seem somewhat meaningless, though no doubt it sounded like an Old Testament prophecy to the beleaguered German Christians. What in fact it meant was that the Life and Work ecumenical leaders were now seeing that they could not escape from the problem of the nature of the church: 'our endeavours must be rooted in the whole doctrinal, educational and sacramental life of the Church,' said one of them.[19]

Nevertheless the Life and Work movement had by 1937 done enough to show that the churches could think together about the world's problems, and that in so doing they could grow together. After the war, when more resources were available in the World Council of Churches, thought was to be translated into action on a very considerable scale.

When the Oxford Conference broke up the delegates were joined at a great service at St Paul's Cathedral by those who were about to go to the second World Conference of Faith and Order at Edinburgh. For many of them it was a matter of breaking the train journey between Oxford and Edinburgh; Life and Work and Faith and Order could hardly stay apart much longer.

The Faith and Order Movement, 1910–37

Bishop Brent had returned from Edinburgh in 1910 determined that Faith and Order must be the next item on the ecumenical agenda. He had got the American Episcopalian church to back him and another Anglican, J. Pierpoint Morgan, put up the money to get the movement under way. As soon as the war was over a delegation from the Protestant Episcopal Church of the U.S.A. undertook an ecumenical pilgrimage in Europe to sell the idea of Faith and Order to church leaders there. They had a surprisingly warm response in Constantinople and were not unsuccessful in France and Scandinavia, but in postwar conditions they did not gain access to Germany; this was unfortunate, since German Protestant leaders were unwilling to be taken for granted and looked somewhat suspiciously on this strongly American and Anglican movement.

The delegation also visited Rome in the hope of enlisting the interest of the pope in the nascent movement. They had an audience with Benedict XV, but found that

the contrast between the Pope's personal attitude towards us and his official attitude towards the Conference was very sharp. One was irresistibly benevolent, the other irresistibly rigid.

As they left the audience a written statement was handed to them. It contained these words, summarizing the preceding meeting:

His Holiness added that the teaching and practice of the Roman Catholic Church regarding the unity of the visible Church of Christ was well-known to everybody and therefore it would not be possible for the Catholic Church to take part in such a congress as the one proposed. However His Holiness ... earnestly desires and prays that, if the congress is practicable, those who take part in it may, by the Grace of God, see the light and become reunited to the visible Head of the Church, by whom they will be received with open arms.[20]

This made abundantly clear the attitude of the Roman Catholic church to the ecumenical movement.

In some ways therefore the start made by the Faith and Order enthusiasts had not been too propitious. But at least a start had been made – and that very quickly after the war. In 1920 a meeting was held at Geneva to plan a World Conference, and this set up the usual continuation and consultative committees. Obviously on questions of Faith and Order the ice was thinner and the need to tread warily greater, especially as the Orthodox were involved and it was highly desirable that they should continue to be. In all this a great deal of the essential work of organizing and establishing trust and contact was done by Bishop Brent's right-hand man, the American Anglican layman Robert Gardiner. Unhappily he died before the first World Conference on Faith and Order which was held in Lausanne in 1927.

It was not an easy meeting. Bishop Brent, the chairman, had said, 'it is not a conference which aims at complete agreement', but one at which 'both agreements and disagreements were to be carefully noted'. But even so differences were sharp and it proved difficult to reach agreed formulas. In discussing 'The Church's Common Confession of Faith', for instance, the Orthodox and the Anglo-Catholics took it for granted that this must mean the Nicene Creed, but one Congregationalist replied: 'Well, I think we should clear all that old lumber out of the way', while another delegate asked an Anglican colleague: 'Can you tell me of any volume in which I could read one of these old creeds they have been talking about?'[21] He was relieved to find that the 'volume' was as easily come by as an Anglican prayer book. No story from the early ecumenical movement illustrates more clearly than this the depth of the chasms which had grown up over the centuries between the divided churches. In the end the Conference managed to produce only one report which all, including the Orthodox, could sign. The Germans, too, felt unhappy about the Anglo-Saxon methods, an unhappiness which was not helped by the language barrier. But still a start had been made. Bishop Brent did not live to carry on the work he had begun; when he died it was said that he had more friends to mourn him than any man of his time. When the inevitable, but essential, Continuation Committee was set up its chairman was another Anglican, Archbishop William Temple.

The Continuation Committee formed influential ecumenical study groups which was an essential step if the suspicions and misunderstandings of Lausanne were to be overcome. It also prepared for the second World Conference at Edinburgh in 1937. There the theological preparation of the intervening years bore fruit. The conference agreed on a report on the meaning of 'the Grace of our Lord Jesus Christ', and found that on this subject there was 'no ground for maintaining division

which was adopted by a standing vote at the Edinburgh Faith and Order Conference of 1937.

We are one in faith in our Lord Jesus Christ, the incarnate Word of God. We are one in allegiance to Him as Head of the Church, and as King of Kings and Lord of Lords. We are one in acknowledging that this allegiance takes precedence over any other allegiance that may make claims upon us.

This unity does not consist in the agreement of our minds or the consent of our wills. It is founded in Jesus Christ Himself, who lived, died and rose again to bring us to the Father, and who through his Holy Spirit dwells in His Church. We are one because we are all the objects of the love and grace of God, and called by Him to witness in all the world to His glorious Gospel.

Our unity is of heart and spirit. We are divided in the outward forms of our life in Christ, because we understand differently His will for His Church. We believe, however, that a deeper understanding will lead us towards a united apprehension of the truth as it is in Jesus.

We humbly acknowledge that our divisions are contrary to the will of Christ, and we pray God in his mercy to shorten the days of our separation and to guide us by His Spirit into fulness of unity.

We are thankful that during recent years we have been drawn together; prejudices have been overcome, misunderstandings removed, and real, if limited, progress has been made towards our goal of a common mind.[25]

The question was, how would the churches respond to the prophetic lead? We have seen the rebuff which the Faith and Order pioneers received from the pope in 1920. In 1928 the position of the Roman Catholic church towards the ecumenical movement was defined and explained in the papal encyclical *Mortalium Animos*; to take part in ecumenical conferences is to acknowledge the implication at their foundation, that there is some good in all religions. It is thus to start on the slippery path to 'naturalism and atheism' and is 'tantamount to abandoning the religion revealed by God'. Roman Catholics on the other hand must hold with equal certainty all dogma defined by Rome; it is a matter of all or nothing.

Thus it is clear why this Apostolic See has never allowed its subjects to take part in the assemblies of non-Catholics. There is but one way in which the unity of Christians may be fostered, and that is by furthering the return to the one true Church of Christ of those who are separated from it; for from that one true Church they have in the past fallen away.[26]

Officially Roman Catholics were not so much as allowed to join in the Lord's Prayer with non-Catholics. There were, too, other Roman Catholic rulings which exacerbated the situation: for instance the very strict Roman Catholic rules in relation to 'mixed' marriages (that is, between Roman and non-Roman partners) have always been a source of grievance (see below, pp. 420–24); again, while the Roman Catholic church claimed the full benefits of religious toleration in countries where it was not dominant, in many of those where it was, it denied religious freedom to non-Catholics on the grounds that to allow toleration was to permit the teaching of error. This unhappy state of affairs was resolved at Vatican II (see below, pp. 399–401).

The Roman Catholic church had, therefore, to be counted out of the ecumenical movement as it was developing in the first half of the twentieth century. On the other hand the Orthodox in 1920 took a somewhat surprising initiative. From Constantinople came an Encyclical Letter 'Unto all the Churches of Christ wheresoever they be'. It called for 'Closer intercourse and ... understanding' as a step on the road to eventual unity, and went so far as to suggest exchanges of students and relationships between theological colleges. This augured well for Orthodox interest in ecumenical affairs and indeed the impression made by the Orthodox delegations at the early conferences, after so many centuries cut off from the western churches, was very great. But there were difficulties. At Lausanne in 1927 the Orthodox found that they could not subscribe to most of the resolutions of the Conference, because their only conception of the basis for a united church was an entire acceptance of the Orthodox position – though it is said that when Archbishop Germanos, the leader of the Orthodox delegation and the probable inspirer of the 1920 Encyclical, returned to his seat after making the Orthodox position plain, the tears were streaming down his face. Moreover the Orthodox were divided among themselves. Their constitutional and political divisions have already been noted; on top of this there were the different attitudes diagnosed by a knowledgeable observer, Bishop Headlam, as being between 'the rigidly Orthodox and those with a more moderate and critical outlook ... those who simply adhere to their inherited Orthodoxy and those who are trying to adjust it to the facts of the modern world'.[27] These were problems the Orthodox themselves had to solve, and the solution was made no easier by political differences. Meanwhile the fact that the Greek-based churches were involved in the ecumenical movement was of the utmost importance, though there was no question as yet of any Orthodox church being concerned in union negotiations. With the Orthodox, above all, it was a matter of making haste slowly and here such contacts as, for instance, the repeated visits of Bishop Headlam to the churches of the Balkans were very important.

The year 1920 saw another striking act of ecumenical initiative. This was the 'Appeal to All Christian People' issued by the Anglican bishops at the Lambeth Conference. It was perhaps remarkable that ecumenical matters should have come to the fore everywhere immediately after the First World War, but it is probably true that these ecumenical stirrings were the outcome both of the shock administered by the war and of the optimism prevailing in the post-war aftermath. The opening words of the encyclical letter from the 1920 Lambeth Conference show this:

The weakness of the church in the world today is not surprising when we consider how that bands of its own fellowship are loosened and broken. . . . But the war and its horrors, waged as it was between so-called Christian nations, drove home the truth with the shock of a sudden awakening. Men in all Communions begin to think of the reunion of Christendom not as a laudable ambition or a beautiful dream, but as an imperative necessity.

The letter went on to acknowledge those who believe in Jesus Christ and are baptized in the name of the Trinity as 'sharing in the universal church of Christ which is His Body'. Calling for reunion the bishops quoted the Lambeth Quadrilateral as the Anglican basis for negotiations; but as far as the historic episcopate was concerned they softened the somewhat bleak way of presenting its necessity hitherto adopted. A united Church must have

a ministry acknowledged by every part of the Church as possessing not only the inward call of the Spirit, but also the commission of Christ and the authority of the whole body. May we not reasonably claim that the Episcopate is the one means of providing such a ministry? It is not that we call in question for a moment the spiritual realities of the ministries of those Communions which do not possess the Episcopate. On the contrary we thankfully acknowledge that these ministries have been manifestly blessed and owned by the Holy Spirit as effective means of grace. But we submit that considerations alike of history and of present experience justify the claim which we make on behalf of the Episcopate.[28]

This acknowledgement of the 'reality' of other ministries was of great psychological importance as a basis for discussions on this thorny subject between Anglicans and non-episcopal churches. This was especially so when the letter went on to say that 'the office of a bishop should be everywhere exercised in a representative and constitu-

tional manner' – thus offsetting the bogy of 'prelacy'
which was such a potential stumbling block to, for instance, English non-conformists. Furthermore the bishops
undertook that if it came to reunion Anglican bishops
and clergy would accept from other churches 'a form of
commission or recognition' which would commend them
to the non-episcopal congregations while hoping that non-
episcopal ministers would accept 'a commission through
episcopal ordination'. The Appeal ended with another
re-assuring note: 'We do not ask that any one Communion should consent to be absorbed in another.' All
this represented a high-water mark of Anglican ecumenical spirit – and one from which in some ways and on
some occasions the tide of Anglican feeling seems to have
receded.

UNION NEGOTIATIONS IN BRITAIN, 1920–50

The optimism engendered by the Lambeth Appeal led at
once to a series of meetings between representatives of
the Church of England and of the Federal Council of
Evangelical Churches. These being the first meetings of
this sort since the seventeenth century, there was a great
deal of ground to be covered. One of the practical matters discussed was the interchange of pulpits, that is
Church of England clergy preaching at Free Church services and *vice versa* – a practice then hardly thought of.
On doctrinal matters the debate turned on the matter of
orders and after some years the two Church of England
Archbishops wrote a memorandum in which they
acknowledged in the spirit of Lambeth 1920 that Free
Church ministries were 'real ministries of Christ's Word
and Sacraments in the Universal Church'. This was very
hopeful – but the gilt was to some extent removed from
the gingerbread by the words which follows: 'Yet ministries, even when so regarded, may be in varying degrees
irregular or defective.' A lot depended on what was

meant by 'irregular' and 'defective', and free churchmen hoped that the Lambeth Conference of 1930 would take a further step forward. When it failed to do so they were very disappointed, and, though the meetings continued, the spirit of optimism has gone out of them and enthusiasm waned. A similar thing happened to a series of meetings between the Church of England and the Church of Scotland.

The fact was that while a few leaders were enthusiastic about the possibility of closer church relations in Britain the great mass of clergy and laity were either indifferent or actively hostile. The ecumenical fire had not yet caught.

There might be, within a stone's throw of each other in a town or a village, a parish church and what used to be called a dissenting chapel, but of fellowship and understanding between them there was usually none. If ever the High Church servers of St Gregory Thaumaturgus, who had received much 'definite Church teaching', contemplated the future state of the Saints in Lantern Yard, they could only hope, even in their most generous moments, that there might be something in certain 'uncovenanted mercies' (occasionally mentioned by the charitable vicar) to mitigate the unpleasantness of their lot : the Saints in Lantern Yard, on the other hand, were almost ecstatically unanimous in being under no shadow of doubt that the entire congregation of St Gregory's – with its 'goings-on' that were for a hissing and a reproach to Israel – would burn for all eternity in Hell. But this mattered less than the blind indifference of both to the shame and disgrace of disunion. Each was perfectly happy in its own corner of the Lord's vineyard.[29]

And prejudice was even worse each way between Roman Catholics and the rest.

Thus, after a hopeful post-war start in Britain, relationships between the different churches did not greatly improve in the inter-war years. During the Second World War negotiations began between the Congregational and

Presbyterian churches in England which aimed at inter-communion and mutual counsel. This form of federal union was achieved in 1951, but after that the two churches did not in fact move forward to any closer union, until recently staying virtually separate and autonomous. Nor was it until after the beginning of the Second World War that the British Council of Churches was formed. In 1942 sixteen denominations founded the B.C.C. on the same basis as the newly emerging World Council of Churches, with which it has maintained the closest contacts. Compared with the 'non-western' countries the foundation of a Council of Churches in Britain came deplorably late: it will be remembered that the Council of Churches in the United States was founded as long ago as 1908.

There were only two major ecumenical events in Britain in the inter-war years, other than the conferences already described. Both were unions within a single denomination. In 1900 the Free Churches of Scotland had united, leaving only two churches, the Church of Scotland and the United Free Church, which between them accounted for 90 per cent of the Presbyterians in Scotland, and in any case the vast majority of the country. Some of the leaders immediately began to look for a further union of these two churches. True to its name and its history the Free Church was suspicious of the Established, and indeed of the very idea of establishment. Before the 1914 war it was agreed that the establishment did not imply any control of the church by the state – far less indeed than in England – but was in fact the way of publicly expressing the recognition of the Christian religion by the state. But still the deep-rooted hesitations and suspicions of the Free churchmen continued and it was not in fact until 1929 that a full union between the churches was achieved. Even then a small minority of the United Free Church could not be satisfied and had to be left behind; but after the union of 1929 Presbyterianism in Scotland was more united than it had been for centuries.

The other major British act of union within a confession was the foundation of the united British Methodist Church in 1932. The last Methodist union, in 1907, had brought together three of the important dissenting Methodist churches into the United Methodist Church. The major Methodist denominations were now that church, the Primitive Methodists, and the Wesleyan Methodist church, with the last, the parent body, larger than the other two put together. Discussions for the next phase of union started before the First World War but were not consummated for over twenty years. It had all along been taken that the three churches must be involved and there were great difficulties which led to one scheme after another being rejected. The main issues were that the 'free' churches felt that the Wesleyan Methodists were clergy-dominated; they wanted more room for lay initiative at all levels, and especially at Conference, the central governing body; they disliked what they called 'the ministerial aristocracy' and felt that the Wesleyans were not far removed from Anglicans: they had 'recently shaken hands with a bishop'.[30] The Wesleyan Methodists, on their side, were suspicious of the free churches' claim to be the true followers of Wesley and felt that they were more 'Protestant' than Wesleyan; in particular the Wesleyan Methodists disliked the free church insistence on the right of the laity to administer the sacraments.

On both sides there were those in favour of union and those against, and those in favour tended to be closer to each other than to the dissentient members of their own churches. Their chief argument was the need for rationalization, the folly of keeping huge chapels and tiny congregations struggling on independently of each other and side by side in towns and villages. In the end it was decided that a 75 per cent vote for union should carry the day and the vital vote of ministers in the Wesleyan

Methodist Conference was exactly 75 per cent. Those who believed in union rejoiced and were convinced that 'the whole Methodist Church will enter upon a new era of extension which will rival the early days'; others sounded a more cautious note: 'There is nothing in the union of churches, considered in itself, that inevitably or even probably leads to the new birth of the spirit.'[31] The latter proved to be the truer prophets. The decline of Methodism was not halted, and above all the much needed rationalization did not take place (see below, pp. 381–2).

ACTS OF UNION OUTSIDE BRITAIN, 1920–45

The pace of the movement for reunion was agonizingly slow – for those who had the cause at heart – in Britain in the first half of the twentieth century. In other parts of the world things were a little better. Without detailing all the acts of union which took place a few of the more important must be mentioned. In Britain the Methodists had moved slowly to union in 1932. In America they followed suit in 1939. In the United States the Methodists were split three ways, first between episcopal and non-episcopal Methodists, and then (on the slavery issue) between north and south. From 1910 to 1939 reunion was hammered out, first on a federal and then on a more organic basis. The resulting church is episcopal – though the bishops are in the 'Wesleyan' rather than the 'apostolic' succession – and at the same time democratic; it united the largest number of Christians ever to come together into one church, with a membership according to the latest figures of over nine million. Considering the position of American Methodism within world Methodism, and indeed world Christianity, this union was and is of very great importance.

Previous to the American Methodist union the largest united church to come into being had been the United

Church of Canada in 1925. This was a union bringing
together four distinct churches and it came itself as the
last in a line of smaller acts of reunion; indeed it was
reckoned that there were forty churches and nineteen
acts of union in the background of the 1925 agreement.
In the event the uniting churches were the Presbyterian,
the Congregational, the Methodist and a church known as
the Local Union. Once again the negotiations were long
drawn-out, having started in 1902, and once again, as in
Scotland, there was a substantial minority which could
not, despite these long delays, be reconciled to the scheme.
These were, on the whole, the large, rich, conservative
Presbyterian congregations and in the end about a third
of the Presbyterian church decided to remain outside the
union. During the – sometimes bitter – course of this controversy the questions of the rights of minorities and constitutional and legal position of the church had been
raised in an acute form. Nevertheless the union finally
took place and when it did so it was on the basis of the
highest common factor – each denomination bringing to
the new church its own particular strength and witness.
This was expressed in the union service by the representatives of the respective churches in the following
formulas:

Presbyterian: In vigilance for Christ's kirk and covenant,
in care for the spread of education and devotion to sacred
learning.
Congregational: In the liberty of prophesying, the love of
spiritual freedom and the enforcement of civic justice.
Methodist: In evangelical zeal and human redemption, the
testimony of spiritual experience, and the ministry of
sacred song.
Local Union: In the furtherance of community life within
the Kingdom of God.[32]

The wording may seem anachronistic and even somewhat
jejune; but the intention of a common treasury, where
before there was division, is made plain.

There were other unions between churches which were basically Presbyterian and Congregational in background. In 1924 a number of missionary agencies in India, representing 'home' missions from all over the world, came together to form the United Church of Northern India – a belated shedding of the western apron strings, but one which was hardly yet taking place in Africa. In 1927 the main churches at work in China, with the exception of the Roman Catholic, the Anglican and the Lutheran, came together to form the Church of Christ in China. The basis of this union was very simple – an acceptance of Jesus Christ as 'Redeemer and Lord', of the Bible as the 'supreme authority in matters of faith and duty', and of the Apostles Creed as expressing the 'fundamental Christian doctrine'. But it also allowed the uniting churches to retain their own 'original standards of faith'. The union was, therefore, a loose one which had been arrived at without the painful hammering-out which had gone into other schemes. It was indeed more of a federation of churches than an organic union, but such an arrangement was perhaps the only practicable one in a vast country such as China, where the congregations were so few and so scattered.

During the 1939 war a united church was founded in Japan under government pressure. A law was passed saying that no religious body with less than 5,000 members would secure recognition and registration to legalize its activities. As the various Protestant churches were all very small this forced them to come together, and those which refused to join the Kyodan, the new united church, were in fact persecuted. Once again it was a loose federal union; in fact at first it amounted to little more than giving the National Christian Council the name of a united church in order to satisfy the legal requirements. After the war the legislation was repealed and a number of the uniting churches, notably the Anglican, Lutheran, Baptist and certain Holiness groups, withdrew from the shotgun marriage. The remaining churches, which again comprised the Presbyterian, Congregational and Methodist elements, had to set about turning the marriage of convenience into a genuine union. This involved recognition by their supporting missions, the acceptance of a common doctrinal basis and the creation of central and united administrative machinery. This took some time and the Kyodan in a sense found itself going through the same processes of debate and self-understanding as the World Council of Churches, but the church now exists as a strong and united body representing central mainstream Protestantism.

Another place where such a union took place was the Philippines. In 1929 the Presbyterians and Congregationalists came together, with an American imported Protestant body, and in 1944, again under Japanese pressure, they were joined by the Disciples of Christ and the Methodists; but after the war this union broke up, only to be reformed with somewhat different ingredients in 1948. The situation in the Philippines is, of course, very different from that in, say, China or India. The vast majority of the population is Roman Catholic and the background of union is therefore not so much a missionary situation as one of continuous Catholic social and nationalist pressure.

In all these union schemes, and in others which have not been mentioned, two areas and churches are conspicuous by their absence. In the first place there were, with one minor exception, no acts of church union in Africa. The non-Roman Catholic churches in Africa were almost entirely of British parentage and had not proceeded far in the direction of indigenization. While the ecumenical fire burned low in Britain, the Africans were unlikely to lead the way and the continent which was slow in waking did not in fact produce ecumenical leaders as Asia had done.

Secondly no Anglican church had as yet been involved

in a consummated union scheme. The Reformation divide between episcopal and non-episcopal reformed churches had yet to be bridged. In fact negotiations to do just this had been going on in South India since 1919, but the actual union did not finally take place until 1947. (It will be described in a later chapter as being part of the post-war breakthrough.)

One important arrangement involving the Anglicans must however be mentioned. This was the Bonn Agreement of 1930 between the Church of England and the Old Catholic church. The Old Catholics are a group of small national churches which have at various times separated from Rome and repudiated papal supremacy and infallibility, while retaining in other ways essential Catholic belief and practice. The first split came in Holland in the eighteenth century when three bishops in Utrecht refused to follow the Roman line on a doctrinal and jurisdictional matter. This small church was enlarged in the 1870s when a number of Roman Catholics could not accept the Infallibility decree and Old Catholic churches were formed in Germany, Austria and Switzerland. The Old Catholic churches retain the apostolic succession and in 1925 they recognized the validity of Anglican orders. Closer relations followed. The Old Catholics were somewhat worried about the position and beliefs of the evangelicals in the Church of England – as well they might have been because an extreme evangelical would certainly be very different from an Old Catholic – and the evangelicals in the Church of England reciprocated with doubts about the Old Catholics. But in the end a concordat was drawn up establishing intercommunion between the two churches on the following basis:

1. Each communion recognizes the catholicity and independence of the other, and maintains its own.
2. Each communion agrees to admit members of the other communion to participate in the sacraments.
3. Intercommunion does not require from either communion

the acceptance of all doctrinal opinion, sacramental devotion, or liturgical practice characteristic of the other, but implies that each believes the other to hold all the essentials of the Christian Faith.[33]

This was in fact a practical arrangement, based more on the acceptance of ministries and sacraments than of doctrine, between two churches whose spheres of influence did not overlap. Clearly a closer union between two churches coming together in one place would have to be based on slightly more than an implicit agreement to differ. The Old Catholic church is a small one and in terms of the numbers involved the intercommunion arrangement was not very significant. But in terms of a formula for intercommunion between neighbouring churches the arrangement was potentially an important precedent. It allows for churches to recognize that for historical and cultural reasons there can be considerable differences between them and yet they can be in communion.

The Bonn concordat has been repeated in a post-war agreement between various branches of the Anglican Communion and the Philippine Independent Church; the latter is a sizable body which broke from Rome, largely on nationalistic grounds, at the beginning of the twentieth century, and which, again, maintained 'Catholic' belief and practices and a ministry in the apostolic succession. There is every reason to expect that this sort of pattern will be followed as churches in different parts of the world and with differing cultural backgrounds seek to establish relationships with each other.

Part Three

THE CONTEMPORARY
ECUMENICAL SCENE

CHAPTER SIX

The World Council of Churches

Here at Amsterdam we have committed ourselves afresh
to Him, and have convenanted with one another in
constituting this World Council of Churches. We intend
to stay together.

Message from the First Assembly of the W.C.C., 1948

THE BACKGROUND

THE contemporary ecumenical scene is dominated by
three movements all of which have come to the fore since
the end of the Second World War. The first is the foundation of the World Council of Churches and the subsequent history of that movement. The second is the
quickening pace of unity negotiations between the
churches all over the world which stand in the tradition
of the Reformation. The mainspring of this movement
was the foundation of the Church of South India on
27 September 1947. This event was so momentous as
to justify the use of the current jargon word 'breakthrough'. Quite literally, for the first time since the
Reformation the divisions between non-episcopal
churches in the reformed tradition and episcopal
churches in the 'apostolic succession' had been broken
through. It was possible now to conceive that branches of
the Anglican church could unite with the successors of
other churches of the Reformation. In fact major unity
negotiations which did *not* include the Anglican church
were to become the exception rather than the rule.

Both these movements took place independently of
Rome. The Roman Catholic church was still officially
standing outside the ecumenical movement, though there
were signs after the war that individual Roman Catholics

were taking a greater interest in what was going on. This picture changed with the accession of Pope John XXIII in 1958 and his summoning of the second Vatican Council. The Roman Catholic church now began to take an official interest in the ecumenical movement. Although its first approaches have inevitably been tentative compared with the much more experienced ecumenical operations of other churches, they cannot be ignored even by the most die-hard Protestants in the movement. There are those who think that the new factor of the interest of Rome will slow up or even radically change the unity movement as it has been developing among the non-Roman churches. There is no evidence that Rome itself would wish this – rather the opposite. There are others who believe that it would be a disaster if the fact of the warmer front from Rome were made an excuse for any slackening of ecumenical initiative as this has so far developed. But there is no denying that the advent of Rome on the ecumenical scene has complicated the issues, though the new turn in events must be welcomed by all who realize that it is folly to talk of a united church and to be excluding from the ultimate calculations the largest, most widespread and yet also most highly centralized church in the world.

There were several factors, common to the life of all the churches, which had the effect of providing a tide favourable to the move towards reunion. The first was the movement known as Biblical Theology. After the war Protestant and Anglican Biblical scholars ceased to be so negative and destructive in their attitude to the Bible and began instead to see the necessity of taking the thought-world of the Old and New Testaments seriously and seeking to understand the great themes of Biblical teaching. This represented a great recovery of confidence for the church, and one which was common to all the churches. Whether in the end of the day a restatement of Biblical themes as they arose from the world in which they were written was particularly helpful to the church in teaching its message to the twentieth century is a question which need not concern us here. For our purposes the point is that this common rediscovery of the Bible was a movement which cut across all the churches and made some of the old debated questions look small in comparison. The effect of such a trend on the ecumenical movement would in most cases be implicit rather than explicit, but when the Anglican and Presbyterian leaders in Great Britain reported unanimous agreement at the end of their Conversations in 1957, they said:

It has been of primary importance for the present series of Conversations that all four churches represented in them have been associated with one another within the Ecumenical Movement and have also shared in the revival of interest in Biblical Theology which has been a notable feature of the last few decades. This meant that the Conversations could be held from the beginning in an atmosphere of assured friendship and that on many matters germane to them a common outlook and commonly held convictions could be taken for granted.[1]

Alas the commonly held convictions applied to the leaders but not to the rank and file of the churches.

Biblical Theology was originally the creation of Protestant and Anglican scholars but it came to be extremely important for Roman Catholics. It meant that at this stage they could join in the stream of modern Biblical scholarship at a positive and constructive moment, having as it were by-passed the years in which the Protestant approach to the Bible tended to be negative and destructive. Thus Roman Catholics came to share in and contribute to the movement, and little by little without any dramatic pronouncements or sudden *volte-face* the attitude of Rome towards modern Biblical scholarship was modified; instead of the fulminations against the 'Modernist Movement' and the repetition of Biblical teaching which no Protestant theologian could take seriously, some of the 'assured findings' and insights of nearly a hundred years of Biblical scholarship began to appear in Roman Catholic textbooks and commentaries. The importance of this movement which had slowly but surely gathered force was seen most dramatically at the Vatican Council, when the original highly conservative document on 'Revelation', prepared and presented by the arch-conservative Cardinal Ottaviani, was rejected by the Council and a new drafting commission set up which included Cardinal Bea, head of the Ecumenical Secretariat and himself a leading Biblical scholar, who had not been a member of the previous commission. This was a single dramatic example of the way in which new insights stemming from Biblical Theology influenced the work of the Council – and also in general are now influencing Roman Catholic thought in an ecumenical direction.

Another branch of scholarship which had had a common influence on the churches in the ecumenical movement has been the revived interest in the early fathers of the church. This has again been particularly important for the Roman Catholic church, since an interest in the patristic period has had the effect of undermining an approach to theological questions which has in the past been based on medieval theology, and particularly on St Thomas Aquinas. (A striking moment at the Vatican Council came when the influential liberal Cardinal Léger of Montreal objected to the phrase *'philosophia perennis'* for the scholastic theologians of the thirteenth century, as giving them a position which amounted almost to infallibility.) Such a revival of patristic interest will be particularly important in the relationship between the Roman Catholic and the Orthodox churches.

In the general field of historical studies, also, scholarship has become more balanced and irenic. It is now possible, for instance, for a Roman Catholic to write an appreciative book about Luther's theological views or for an Anglican to write with sympathy about Bossuet or Newman. In general, therefore, the finding of common ground in various fields of study has had an important ecumenical influence.

Another seminal common interest has been the Liturgical Movement, which started among Roman Catholics in Germany before the war and has aimed at giving lay people a greater part to play in church services, so that they become active participants instead of passive observers. As part of the movement the liturgies themselves have, where necessary, been pruned and modernized. The most spectacular example of these reforms has been the adoption of the vernacular in the Roman Catholic mass and the radical rearrangement of churches to bring the priest and his actions nearer to the people. The same sort of thing has been happening in many Church of England churches, while following the original and successful example of the Church of South India, many branches of the Anglican Communion have dropped their sacred-cow attitude to the Prayer Book and have embarked on far-reaching re-writings of the Communion and of other services. All this has had its effect on the Protestant churches also. For some time many of them had been feeling their way towards a richer expression of worship in liturgical forms, even if this meant adopting a fixed liturgy. The fact that much typical Protestant worship centred on the minister as he preached and offered extempore prayer, and that the new trends of the liturgical movement focused more on the whole worshipping community, further encouraged many Protestant churches and congregations to embark on liturgical experiment. Here again, therefore, there was a gradual convergence of the churches on to common ground.

As it affected the Roman and Anglican Communions the Liturgical Movement resulted in an emphasis on the part of the man-in-the-pew, and this enhancement of the importance of the laity touched other parts of the life and thought of the churches. The whole church was coming to be seen as the *laos* – that is people – of God, and this *laos* was made up of clergy and people together, with 'the laity' playing an equal, though different, and not a minimal role. This fact was being emphasized by many leading Roman Catholic theologians, and was of course especially welcome to many Protestants, with their historic emphasis on 'the priesthood of all believers'. But conversely – and ironically – this very battle-cry was beginning to lose its force among Protestants. Presbyterians had in fact always given due weight to the importance of the ministry, but other Protestant churches have been coming to share this view and the Congregationalists in particular have been moving towards the idea that the church is more than a lay-dominated federation of congregations. Here again, then, the churches were moving out of their old entrenched positions and beginning to find themselves occupying common ground.

There has been one more post-war movement which has generally affected the ecumenical climate in all the churches. This is the Week of Prayer for Christian Unity. For some time the churches had been setting aside certain seasons to pray for the unity of the church. But the seasons varied and the forms of prayer differed: in the Roman Catholic church, for instance, the season for prayer for Christian unity was the Feast of the Chair of St Peter, while the prayers were for the return of non-Catholics to the fold of St Peter. Such prayers were not likely to spread a general spirit of good will, and similarly much Protestant praying stuck to its own limited terms of reference. It was the Abbé Paul Couturier who more than anyone else was responsible for ending this unhappy state of affairs. When he started his movement for the Week of Prayer for Christian Unity he was an obscure parish priest in Lyons. By the time that he died, still in Lyons, the week (strictly speaking an octave of eight days annually, ending with the feast of the Conversion of St Paul on 25 January) was being widely observed in the Roman Communion and in at least those churches which are members of the World Council; Couturier himself was one of the great pioneering figures of the ecumenical movement. The secret of his prayer was simple: it was prayer 'without strings', which made it universally acceptable. It was prayer 'for the unity of the Church of Jesus Christ, as He wills and when He wills'.

By the very nature of the belief to which they are committed Christians will clearly attach great importance and efficacy to the power of such prayer being offered in thousands of churches throughout the world. But quite apart from any question of the spiritual effect of successive Weeks of Prayer, the psychological effect was bound to be considerable. Many congregations found themselves praying for unity for the first time. Up to then it had simply not been on their agenda, but now, with the churches giving their official backing to the Week of Prayer, the issue could not be avoided. Moreover the week became the occasion for joint services and for the exchange of pulpits between ministers of differing denominations – though at first Roman Catholics could not enter so fully into these activities. Thus ecumenism was beginning at last to work through to 'the grassroots', as so many ecumenical leaders had urged for so long. It may seem pathetic that this happened really widely only after the end of the last war – and happened at first in such a limited way – but it is a fact none the less. And it is a fact without which all the working and planning of church leaders are doomed to failure.

THE COUNCIL 'IN PROCESS OF FORMATION'

The decision to form the World Council of Churches, by combining the Faith and Order and Life and Work movements, was reached in 1937. It was quickly acted on. At a meeting in Utrecht in 1938 the provisional committee of the World Council of Churches 'in process of formation' was set up. The first Chairman was to be

Archbishop William Temple, and the first General Secretary Willem Visser 't Hooft, a thirty-seven-year-old Dutch minister and the General Secretary of the World Student Christian Federation. The first General Assembly of the World Council was planned for 1941 – but by that time Europe was at war.

It might have been expected that the war would end co-operation between the churches, let alone the growth of the World Council. But this did not happen. In 1939 there were fifty-five potential member churches of the World Council, by 1945 there were ninety. Moreover the way the work developed during the war under the small staff based on Geneva was in a sense to determine the subsequent character of the Council. Visser 't Hooft himself wrote later:

> At first it seemed as if it would at least mean that the clock of ecumenical history would be definitely set back. ... But right in the midst of war the tide turned. New and even larger tasks presented themselves. And what the contacts between the churches lost in frequency, they gained in intensity and depth. ... Never before in ecumenical history had it become so very clear that there are urgent tasks which no church alone can perform and that there must be a body, however small and weak, which by its very existence demonstrates the ultimate cohesion of the churches. ... The ecumenical task was spiritually easy and simple, because in spite of the enormous technical difficulties, the marching orders were so very clear and the basic unity of the defenders of the faith was so deeply felt.[2]

Right from the beginning in 1938 Visser 't Hooft had insisted that the World Council should be a source of action as well as discussion. During the war the refugee problem raised its terrible head and an Ecumenical Refugee Commission was established in Geneva. Among other things it financed the work of rescuing thousands of Jews from camps in southern France after the Laval government had handed them over to the German regime. Another task which was organized ecumenically was a chaplaincy service to prisoners of war, which included the distribution of nearly two million Bibles, prayer and hymn books and pamphlets in numerous languages. At the end of the war this type of activity was stepped up and a Department of Reconstruction and Inter-Church Aid was created to mobilize help for the most needy churches. Temporary wooden churches were erected all over Europe, pastors' salaries were implemented where there was a crying need, such as in cities which had been destroyed by bombing, provision was made for theological literature, for clerical retraining, and so on. When the refugee work already mentioned was combined with all this there was formed the embryo of the Department of Inter-Church Aid and Service to Refugees which was to play such a vital part in the future life of the World Council of Churches, especially as in the post-war period the problems increased rather than diminished.

The provisional committee held its first post-war meeting at Geneva in 1946. German church leaders were there, but one who might have been expected to lead the post-war ecumenical movement was absent. Dietrich Bonhoeffer, perhaps the most influential theological thinker of his time, had been executed by the Nazis in 1945 for his part in the resistance movement; as late as 1942 he had managed to meet George Bell, the Bishop of Chichester and a great Life and Work leader, in Stockholm, to tell him something of the opposition to Hitler and to urge some modification to British policy in the light of it. Other great leaders had passed during the war. Archbishop William Temple had died, a comparatively young man, in 1944. The Provisional Committee minuted that his death

constitutes an irreparable loss for the whole ecumenical movement. It is felt by all of us that no one can take his place in representing the Council and in mastering all the obligations involved.[3]

Indeed no one did take his place, for after that the World Council had, not a single President, but a Praesidium of five members. Another grave loss had been the passing of the Presbyterian William Paton, the Secretary of the International Missionary Council and an Associate Secretary of the Provisional Committee. The other Associate Secretary had also died; he was Dr Henry Smith Leiper, an American Congregationalist who had done a great deal to champion the cause in his own country. The new movement was going to be launched by new leaders.

FOUNDATION, NATURE AND CONSTITUTION

The first Assembly of the World Council of Churches met at Amsterdam on 23 August 1948. One hundred and forty-seven churches became its members.

Christ has made us his own, and he is not divided. Here at Amsterdam we have committed ourselves afresh to Him, and have covenanted with one another in constituting this World Council of Churches. We intend to stay together.[4]

This intention has been largely fulfilled. The only churches to withdraw have been: the Chinese churches at the time of the Korean war; the Baptist churches of Scotland and the Netherlands (the latter because of 'the imperialism of the national churches, *rapprochement* with the Catholic church, the danger of Marxist infiltration, ecumenical impatience and a theology of relativism'[5]); and three Dutch Reformed churches in South Africa which withdrew in 1961 after a World Council Consultation at Cottesloe, Johannesburg, had condemned the theory and practice of apartheid. On the other hand, of course, since the original foundation many more churches have joined the W.C.C. In 1970 the total number of member churches was 239.

The original basis of the W.C.C. was very simple:

The World Council of Churches is a fellowship of Churches which accept our Lord Jesus Christ as God and Saviour.

In the early days such simplicity was clearly desirable but it was increasingly felt by many – especially the Orthodox members – that, although the basis was in no sense meant to act as a confession of faith, the absence of any reference to the Trinity was a weakness. Accordingly in 1961 at the New Delhi Assembly the basis was expanded to its present form:

The World Council of Churches is a fellowship of churches which confess the Lord Jesus Christ as God and Saviour according to the Scriptures and therefore seek to fufil their common calling to the glory of the one God, Father, Son and Holy Spirit.[6]

The World Council does not test churches for membership against this basis: it is the responsibility of each church to weigh its own acceptance of the formula. The only tests of membership applied by the Council itself are those of size and stability: clearly if the meetings are not to be swamped very small churches cannot be admitted to full membership, and therefore a status of associate membership has been evolved for churches with a membership of less than 10,000; similarly the Council needs to be assured that a church has a reasonably stable existence.

The governing body of the W.C.C. is the General Assembly composed of delegates appointed by the member churches. These assemblies have met every six or seven years since Amsterdam, at Evanston, Illinois, in 1954, at New Delhi in 1961 and at Uppsala, Sweden, in 1968. Between assemblies the general direction of the movement is in the hands of the Central Committee, which until Uppsala consisted of one hundred members.

This committee usually meets annually, and with such numbers of members, staff and observers its gatherings are themselves considerable affairs; they are therefore given a theme, much along the lines of a General Assembly, so that each meeting becomes a theological thinking point about the aims and work of the Council. Below this there is a small Executive Committee which meets twice a year. The ongoing work of the Council is done by its various Departments and Commissions, each of which has a Secretariat and a committee which is at the same time both expert and representative of the member churches. At first the Central Committee and the Executive Committee were composed equally of the Faith and Order stream and the Life and Work stream, but this differentiation died out; since the development of the work during the war had tended to throw the emphasis on the Life and Work side, the Faith and Order Commission has rather kept itself to itself.

So in 1948 the Council was constituted and so, with minor modifications, it worked until the New Delhi Assembly in 1961. The first Chairman of the Central Committee was Bishop George Bell, and his Vice-Chairman and successor was Franklin Clark Fry, who remained Chairman of the Central Committee until his sudden death just before the Uppsala Assembly. Dr Fry was President of the United Lutheran Church in America, and this itself is significant; the leadership was passing away from the early prophetic individual figures and into the hands of many of the official church leaders. To that extent the movement was becoming institutionalized; but the fact was that the leaders of the major churches were by now in any case ecumenically-minded and the Council was fortunate in obtaining the services of such men as Dr Fry and of a succession of very able staff members.

Lastly there was the all-important question of finance. The World Council is financed from the contributions of

member churches and of individuals. These latter vary
from generous single gifts such as that from John D.
Rockefeller at the end of the war which set up the Ecumenical Institute at the Château de Bossey a few miles
from Geneva (which has been the vital centre of much
regular ecumenical study) to the collections from individuals and congregations such as the well-organized and
publicized Christian Aid Weeks held annually for Inter-
Church Aid in Britain. Income and expenditure has risen
steadily and impressively, but one fact has remained
constant since the first post-war accounts: over half the
income of the W.C.C. has come from the United States.

One question which has continuously exercised the
W.C.C. and its members and staff is the basic one of
nature and function, 'What is the World Council?' It is a
council of churches and not of individuals or committees
of churches. It therefore has some official status, but in
fact all its actions need to be ratified by the churches in
their own life; and therein has been its chief weakness.
Many of its conclusions and resolutions have proved to
be only pious hopes for want of practical implementation by and in the churches. William Temple had said in
the early days that its pronouncements would only have
the weight of their own moral authority, and the writ of
this authority often failed to run in the churches, let
alone in the world. The Amsterdam Assembly attempted
a fuller definition:

The fact must be recognized that the Assembly possesses no
authority to speak on behalf of the churches. And in no manner can it claim ... to be an authoritative ecclesiastical mouthpiece of the Una Sancta, such as is assumed in the Papal *ex
cathedra* utterances.[7]

The World Council is not, in short, in its own often
repeated words a 'super-church'. It has always seen itself
as the servant of the churches. As late as 1963, when
attempting a redefinition, it still produced the formula:

'The Council is not the Church; it is not seeking to be a Church or *the* Church. . . . It offers itself as a servant of the churches and of the Church.'[8] Its particular service has been to bring the churches out of their isolation, to enable them to meet each other, to discuss common problems and, where possible, to formulate common policies and take corporate action. But specific plans and negotiations for unity are not within its brief. Yet it was natural that as the Council grew and began to wield more resources, it began to question this limited status, though more implicitly than explicitly. In particular the officers and committees of the Council came to be conscious of a corporate entity and felt that this should be recognized. The year 1963, which produced the self-limiting definition just quoted, produced also a speech from the General Secretary, Dr Visser 't Hooft, pointing out that the definition had been criticized 'because its concept of the W.C.C. was static rather than dynamic'.

It had not ascribed ecclesiological quality . . . to the W.C.C. But had the churches in the Council not learned something as they lived together? Was there not a growth in fellowship which should express itself in a deeper and richer self-understanding of the Council and did that experience not force us to admit that the nature of the Council should be described in ecclesiological categories?[9]

There is a tension here which has never been fully resolved. The issue has been further complicated by recent self-doubts in the World Council which will be described later.

DEBATE: AMSTERDAM, 1948, AND
EVANSTON, 1954

The provisional committee before Amsterdam had hoped that the Assembly would be 'something else, and more, than a world conference for common consultation. In certain circumstances and under certain conditions it will be expected to speak and act on behalf of the co-operating churches.' This was said in the context of a feeling that in this respect the pre-war conferences had been somewhat disappointing. It has been seen that the Council had to eschew the role of being an authoritative mouthpiece, even of the churches it represented. It was, nevertheless, left with the role of 'a world conference for common consultation'. To the cynical, indeed, the W.C.C. can all too often look like a body engaged in endless consultations which are hardly ever implemented by the member churches. There is, as will be seen, a good deal of truth in this view. On the other hand consultation cannot be avoided. It is a way of bringing the churches out of their isolation, and it repeatedly proves the fact the main theological differences on major world issues do not follow – but cross – the lines of denominational boundaries.

The theme of the Amsterdam Assembly was 'Man's Disorder and God's Design'. Clearly this theme was related to the war and the post-war world. In fact it was too soon after the war to reach much agreement, and in any case the setting-up of the Council itself and of the guidelines for its work consumed most of the energies of the delegates. But from one of the sections there did emerge the watchword of 'the responsible society' as an alternative to capitalism on the one hand or communism on the other – a theme not without relevance in the post-war world, and belatedly exhumed as the Conservative watchword for the seventies.

The second General Assembly took place at Evanston, Illinois, in 1954. The theme was 'Jesus Christ, the Hope of the World'. 'The time has come,' said the Central Committee in setting up this subject, 'when the World Council of Churches should make a serious attempt to declare, in relation to the modern world, the faith and hope which are affirmed in its own basis and by which the churches live.' But in fact, as so often, the Council was speaking, not only to the world, but to itself. The subject was central to the continuing debate in the W.C.C. on how far the churches should be involved in the world and its plans with the object of advancing the kingdom of God on earth, or how far that kingdom would be reserved for some dramatic intervention by God 'at the End'. In Christian theology the theme of 'Hope' is what is known as an eschatological subject, that is it concerns the objective of history and the end of the world. It was, as has been seen, a basic question underlying the whole Life and Work movement and having a long history of debate from Stockholm onwards. As was only to be expected the Assembly found it hard to come to any satisfactory conclusion. In fact it had to be admitted that 'Evanston 1954' was something of a disappointment. There were nearly fifteen hundred participants and the whole affair was mounted with magnificent American organization, but after Amsterdam there was a slight, perhaps inevitable, feeling of disappointment. In the words of one well-known delegate, the 'ecumenical honeymoon is over'. At Amsterdam the press and radio coverage had been very extensive; at Evanston it was by no means so good, and the best publicized statement was a speech by the Bishop of London to the effect that the World Council was a mixture of American money, Dutch bureaucracy and German theology. There was too much truth in this attack to make it a laughing matter.

GROWTH AND WORK, 1954–61

Nevertheless the period between the second Assembly at Evanston in 1954 and the third at New Delhi in 1961 was one of very great growth and activity in the W.C.C., underlining the fact that the real strength of the movement lies not so much in its occasional full-scale Assemblies as in the regular work of its staff and the smaller specialized consultations and study groups through which the various departments are organized. In fact the General Secretary admitted that in these years the work grew faster than the officers would have wished, partly through the general 'acceleration of history' particularly with the speed of change in Africa and Asia, and partly because the churches were making more and more demands on the Council and its resources.

At Evanston the work of the Council had been organized into three main divisions: Studies; Ecumenical Action; and Inter-Church Aid and Service to Refugees.

The first department of the Division of Studies was that of Faith and Order. The Faith and Order movement had held its third world conference – Lausanne and Edinburgh being the two earlier ones – at Lund in 1952. This conference followed the same method as its predecessors, which was the comparative study of the various theological questions which are the traditional issues between the churches. But the method proved stultifying. 'One of the veterans plaintively asked his compatriots at Lund: "Can we go on for ever and ever, round and round in the same circle, explaining ourselves to one another?" Another delegate wrote subsequently of the "dead end which Faith and Order found in its old procedure at Lund", and a British journal published an article on the subject titled "The Ecumenical Dead-End Kids" – the point was the same: the old comparative approach had led to a *cul-de-sac*.'[10]

The pattern changed therefore after Lund. Instead of comparative study it was decided to take certain subjects and to try to study them ecumenically from first principles in a way which one optimistic delegate hoped 'may well correspond eventually to the development of ecumenical theology in the fourth and fifth centuries'.[11] The subjects chosen were: Christ and the Church, the importance of which is that theologians recognize that what they think about the church will and should spring from what they think about Christ, and therefore 'if the churches learn to understand one another from the centre, from Christ, then also the problems between the churches will gradually find solution';[12] Worship, which was obviously important in the light of the Liturgical Movement; Tradition and Traditions, which was to be an attempt to draw distinctions between the necessary general tradition of the church by which the Gospel is handed on and the various (and often unrecognized) man-made traditions of the individual churches; and finally Institutionalism, a sociological survey of the way that churches become 'institutions' and these institutions provide one of the 'non-theological factors' which keep the denominations apart. Study groups on these subjects were set up in America and Europe, and in some cases in Asia.

These subjects were all very well. They were intelligent and interesting, and well worth consideration, even if somewhat donnish. They were a genuine attempt to get away from the dead end of comparative debates. But it has been pointed out that 'direct study of the ministry ceased, really, between Edinburgh in 1937 and Montreal in 1963, at the very time when church union negotiations were increasing'.[13] If Faith and Order had continued their debate on the ministry at this time they might have been able to add perspective to some of the discussions in union negotiations. This is an example of the thought of the World Council getting ahead of that of its constituent churches, and so being of less use than might have been hoped.

Not that Lund was altogether a disappointment. The 'message' from the Conference was one of the most forceful in a long series of such documents which too often bear the stamp of last-minute drafting by an over-worked and over-tired committee and end up in that jargon known as 'ecumenese' of which the movement became belatedly aware and ashamed at about this time. (At Evanston an Information Service was created, to try to offset the fact that 'the World Council of Churches is known everywhere for the length and incomprehensibility of its publications'.[14])

We have now reached a crucial point in our ecumenical discussions. As we have come to know one another better our eyes have been opened to the depth and pain of our separations and also to our fundamental unity. The measure of unity which it has been given to the churches to experience together must now find clearer manifestation. A faith in the one Church of Christ which is not implemented by acts of obedience is dead. There are truths about the nature of God and his Church which will remain for ever closed to us unless we act together in obedience to the unity which is already ours. We would, therefore, earnestly request our Churches to consider whether they are doing all they ought to do to manifest the oneness of the people of God. Should not our Churches ask themselves whether they are showing sufficient eagerness to enter into conversation with other Churches and whether they should not act together in all matters except those in which deep differences of conviction compel them to act separately?[15]

This call to the churches to act together unless there was good reason for not doing so was to be repeated many times in the coming years. It was indeed the logic of the situation, as the message said, but it was a logic which the churches were not ready to respond to. This was one of the many occasions when the World Council appealed to deaf ears in its constituent churches and congregations.

The second department in the Division of Studies was that of Church and Society. This undertook a number of studies, the most important of which had the title 'Our Common Christian Responsibility towards Areas of Rapid Social Change'. It was realized that the result of the impact of western technology on many hitherto backward areas of the world would be to bring devastating changes at an unprecedented speed, and that this would create political, social and ethical problems of a similar nature all over the world. Between 1955 and 1960 a major study was mounted and sociological research was undertaken all over the world. This was seen as typical of the World Council's role in speaking not only *for* but *to* the churches. It was felt that the study had the effect in many places of alerting the churches to problems which they might otherwise have overlooked or shied away from. At the same time it was felt that the study had shown that the churches were often not ready to meet the challenge of rapid social change: 'The study had raised serious questions about the structure of the Church and its capacity to respond to the challenge of change. Most churches and Christian Councils are not yet organized to carry out effective study and action in regard to these problems of social change. . . . There is a great sociological gap between the churches and the world in which they live.'[16] This criticism by the W.C.C. of the out-of-date structures and activities of the churches was coming to be typical of many of its pronouncements, and was a further indication of the danger of a gap opening up between the Council and its constituent churches.

Other departments in the Divisions of Studies were those of evangelism and missionary studies, which undertook a series of studies on such subjects as the theology and methods of the missionary work of the church. As the churches moved away from the feeling of religious and cultural superiority in 'non-Christian' countries and of established religion in 'ex-Christian' countries such studies were coming to be seen to be important. But here again the World Council's thinking was in advance of that of its individual member churches.

The second division was that of 'Ecumenical Action', which conceived its function as the evolving of 'creative and valid ideas which would by their momentum slowly penetrate the life of the churches'. At the same time the Division knew that it had to strive 'to escape from the limitations of a "North Atlantic oulook" '.[17]

Its most significant department was that 'on the Laity', which was beginning to preach in season out of season the fact that 'the whole church shares Christ's ministry in the world and the effective exercise of this ministry must largely be by church members, when they are dispersed in the life of the world'.[18] This point may seem so obvious as hardly to be worth making, let alone devoting a great deal of ecumenical and international effort to. But in discussions on church unity the problem of the nature and functions of the ordained ministry *within* the church had loomed so large that it had tended to swamp the prior question of the ministry of the whole church. This new emphasis undoubtedly helped in a number of specific negotiations to put matters into perspective and to take the heat out of such emotionally and historically charged questions as the historic episcopate and the apostolic succession. In this way the Division of ecumenical action had known that its work had important overtones for that of Faith and Order – an example of the constant overlapping between various branches of the W.C.C. At the same time the Division wanted the implications of its work to be practical as well as theoretical and it pursued these interests in Departments on 'The Co-operation of Men and Women in Church and Society' and on Youth. Besides the usual – and by now inevitable – round of conferences and consultations, the best-known and most worth-while work here was that of the Ecumenical Youth Camps: year by year young people were brought together on an ecumenical basis to do practical works of service, pipe-laying, road-building and the like. Between 1955 and 1960, 262 such camps were held involving 5,650 workers.

The third Division at this time was that of Inter-Church Aid and Service to Refugees, the work of which continued along the lines already described. Calling upon growing resources this Division had become the chief agent of ecumenical action.

NEW ISSUES BEFORE NEW DELHI

During the whole period leading up to the New Delhi Assembly in 1961 the World Council and its officers had various other interests besides the regular work just summarized. In the first place they were much concerned about the development of so-called 'world confessionalism'. We have already seen that for some time the various churches had been creating international structures for denominational self-consciousness and co-operation.

The fear of the W.C.C. was that these powerful international bodies might divert the attention of their local churches from the prior necessity of local union. In particular it was felt that some churches might hesitate to go ahead into local unity for fear of losing the powerful financial backing of their world confessional organization; it was also pointed out that psychologically these great international juggernauts with their band-wagon of world conferences and the like gave delegates from some small minority churches a feeling of spurious power and international fellowship and prevented them from getting to know Christians from other churches on their own doorstep. The leaders of the confessional organizations have always replied with indignant and hurt denials that these things are neither the purpose or the outcome of their work ... and the debate continues (see below, pp. 277-9).

A development at this time which gave the World Council more satisfaction was a movement running in precisely the opposite direction. This was the establishment of regional Christian conferences. The East Asia Christian Conference held its first meeting in 1957 at Prapat in Sumatra under the chairmanship of Bishop Sobrepena of the United Church of the Philippines. This conference was organized by and for Asians and it was said that for the first time they did not feel guests in their own country; it was the westerners who for once were the

guests. The conference affiliated itself to the W.C.C. and
organized its own leadership, which it very largely shared
with the W.C.C., men such as the dynamic Methodist
from Ceylon, D. T. Niles, who with J. R. Mott had been
one of the two preachers at the opening service at
Amsterdam. The E.A.C.C. held its second meeting in 1959
in Kuala Lumpur and a further succession of conferences
to assess the situation and mission of the churches in its
various areas in 1963. In many ways the E.A.C.C. is the
W.C.C. on a smaller and local scale. It is to be hoped that
it will increasingly have the work of the W.C.C. devolved
upon it and so be able to work out ecumenical possibilities away from the 'North Atlantic' atmosphere of the
parent body.

It was not surprising that the first signs of a regional
ecumenical movement came in Asia, for Asia has always
thrown up the ablest non-western Christian leaders, and
indeed much of the earlier ecumenical inspiration came
from there.[19] But Africa was not slow to follow suit. In
1958 the first All Africa Christian Conference met in
Nigeria. Africa south of the Sahara was thereby launched
on a programme of establishing itself as a regional ecumenical body, an event which took place in 1963 at a
second conference at Kampala. At these conferences the
strong indigenous – to avoid the word anti-western – feeling of African Christians made itself felt, a feeling which
received its most telling platform at New Delhi when Sir
Francis Ibiam, the Governor of Eastern Nigeria, delivered a speech strongly critical of western and missionary church policy. Such plain speaking from a man who
had worked all his life as a distinguished doctor alongside Europeans in a Scottish medical mission, and might
be thought to be 'thoroughly westernized', came as an eye-
opener, and points the importance of the freedom of
regional ecumenical conferences to develop away from
western dominance. (To complete this particular section, though running ahead of the dates set in it: a con-

ference of churches in the Pacific area was established in 1966, while Latin America is moving in the same direction. Not to be outdone a similar movement among the European churches has developed since 1959!)

The other main concern of the W.C.C. in the years leading up to New Delhi was integration with the International Missionary Council. This was in a way an obvious move, and one which had been foreseen by such people as Temple and Paton. But there had been reasons for delay especially on the side of the I.M.C. In the first place the I.M.C. had for long feared that in an amalgamation of the two bodies its own strong missionary emphasis would be lost in the 'talking shop' atmosphere of the W.C.C. In this respect the growing emphasis being given in the W.C.C. to the renewal of the church and the strengthening of its missionary outreach tended to allay a lot of fears and suspicions. The second hesitation from the I.M.C. side concerned the general tone of the W.C.C. The I.M.C. was constituted not of churches but of National Christian Councils and of Missionary Societies. Many of these were of a conservative evangelical – or fundamentalist – tradition, and as such they were suspicious of the W.C.C., regarding it as 'unsound' on questions of the authority and inerrancy of the Bible and generally speaking unscriptural and 'liberal' in its theology. A spokesman for this point of view wrote in 1959:

There are prominent elements in the W.C.C. which do not really want to make the movement all-embracing.... We are dealing with an active hostility on the part of a small but influential secion of W.C.C. leadership.... It is doubtless unfair, but is it too unfair, if I suggest that the motto of many in the Ecumenical Movement would seem to be not 'That they may all be one', but 'That all the more respectable of them may be one'?[20]

There was some truth in this and there may certainly have been more common ground between all the W.C.C. member churches (especially the 'club' of its officers) than between them and conservative envangelical churchmen; but the W.C.C. side would say that fundamentalist fears and suspicions were vastly exaggerated, especially since the recovery of theological confidence since the war, and that in fact unfriendliness and non-cooperation invariably stems from fundamentalist initiative.

This particular debate continues. In the case of the I.M.C. the integration went ahead because the great majority of I.M.C. members desired it and voted for it; but it did result in the withdrawal of a number of former I.M.C. members from the new joint body notably the Congo Protestant Council which, working in a predominantly Roman Catholic missionary area, had been dominated by fundamentalist and evangelical missionaries, anxious to make converts even in the Roman Catholic native population.

For these reasons, the seemingly obvious step of uniting the W.C.C. and the I.M.C. had been delayed. But there had been co-operation between the two for many years. From the earliest days of the World Council of Churches in process of formation there had been a joint committee with the I.M.C. and the two bodies had together sponsored the Churches Commission for International Affairs – of which more later. The individual leaders had known each other and worked together and were themselves convinced that each party would gain by the amalgamation which would 'quicken the missionary consciousness of the churches and the church consciousness of missions'.[21] So the plans for unification were finally laid before the New Delhi Assembly in 1961.

THE INTERNATIONAL MISSIONARY CONFERENCE, 1947–61

Meanwhile the I.M.C. had since the war been proceeding with its own work mainly through three major meetings – at Whitby, Ontario, in 1947, at Willingen,

Germany, in 1952 and in Ghana in 1957. The background of all these meetings was the movement for nationalism and independence which was sweeping through the countries of the 'younger churches' and the parallel need in the churches to shed the old dominance of the west and to develop an indigenous Christian and church life, so that the younger churches, firmly rooted in their own soil, could become independent and could continue their own missionary work under their own direction. Again the moral seems obvious but it was not an easy one for missionaries to learn. On the other hand it is perhaps remarkable that the more enlightened missionary thinkers were not stampeded into a feeling that there was no further use at all for the western missionary working overseas. That this was not so was seen in the thought of the Whitby Conference. The conference returned to the urgency of the feeling abroad at the time of the first I.M.C. Conference at Edinburgh in 1910.

The task of world evangelism starts today from the vantage ground of a church which, as never before, is really world-wide. This universal fellowship is, in the oft-quoted words of William Temple, the great new fact of our era. It is working itself out today in a real partnership between older and younger churches.... When we consider the present extension of the Church, and the divine and human resources available, we dare to believe it possible that, before the present generation has passed away, the Gospel should be preached to almost all the inhabitants of the world....[22]

This was a task which could be achieved only by the pooling of all the resources of all the churches, and hence the key phrase – or catch phrase – which emerged from Whitby was 'partnership in obedience'. At Willingen this thinking went further and 'mission in unity' became the cry.

The delegates at Willingen also heard one of the strongest and most impatient calls for unity from the representatives of the younger churches. They told the rest of the conference:

We believe that the unity of the churches is an essential condition of effective witness and advance. In the lands of the younger churches divided witness is a crippling handicap. We of the younger churches feel this very keenly. While unity may be desirable in the lands of the older churches it is imperative in those of the younger churches.

Suitably transmuted into the official message of the conference this read:

The love of God in Christ calls for the threefold response of worship, unity and mission. These three aspects of the Church's response are interdependent; they become corrupted when isolated from each other. Division in the Church distorts its witness, frustrates its mission, and contradicts its own nature. If the Church is to demonstrate the Gospel in its life as well as in its preaching, it must manifest to the world the power of God to break down all barriers and to establish the Church's unity in Christ. Christ is not divided.[23]

So on its side the I.M.C. was ready to move forward to the uniting of the two movements.

THE THIRD GENERAL ASSEMBLY, NEW DELHI, 1961

When the Third General Assembly met at New Delhi in November 1961 the bringing together of the World Council and of the International Missionary Committee was the first item on its agenda. This involved a new structure for the W.C.C., which will be considered later.

Two other important changes had to be considered. The first was the elaboration of the basis of the Council, a move already referred to and one which did something to allay the fears of liberalism held by some of the more conservative members, especially the Orthodox. The second was the ratification of a statement on 'The

Nature of the Unity We Seek', which had been prepared
by the Faith and Order Commission. This was in fact not
so much a change as a clarification and a definition for
the Council and for the world, and since it is the latest
and fullest statement of the aims of the ecumenical
movement in the W.C.C. it may be quoted in full:

We believe that the unity which is both God's will and his
gift to his Church is being made visible as all in each place who
are baptized into Jesus Christ and confess him as Lord and
Saviour are brought by the Holy Spirit into *one* fully committed fellowship, holding the one apostolic faith, preaching
the one Gospel, breaking the one bread, joining in common
prayer, and having a corporate life reaching out in witness and
service to all, and who at the same time are united with the
whole Christian fellowship in all places and all ages in such
wise that ministry and members are accepted by all, and that
all can act and speak together as occasion requires for the
tasks to which God calls his people.[24]

'All in each place' was the key phrase and became the
catch slogan, emphasizing that unity must be local so that
it can be seen everywhere – or it is nothing.

The fourth event for which New Delhi was significant
was the application and reception of new member
churches. Above all, the Russian Orthodox church joined
the world Council, bringing in its wake the Orthodox
churches of Bulgaria, Romania and Poland.

In 1948 strenuous efforts had been made to bring the
Russian church into the W.C.C. at its inception, but
these efforts had been rebuffed in no uncertain terms,
both theological and political; nor later had the Council
been afraid to speak in a way which would be unwelcome
to the communist bloc, condemning, for instance, the
Korean 'act of aggression' and coming down firmly on
the side of the United Nations' intervention. This new
accession to the ranks of the member churches was therefore immensely significant, not only for the numbers
involved, but for the political and theological break-

through which it represented. And when the nine days of the political wonder had passed it was found that the theological factor was the most important of all. For the Russians, once in, entered most fully into the World Council discussion – or to use its own jargon, the continuing dialogue. It is true that the Orthodox churches of the eastern Mediterranean had long been valued members, but they had tended to be voices crying in a North Atlantic Protestant wilderness. This new move was fundamentally to shift the balance of theological power in the W.C.C.

Among the various other new member churches there were two which were of particular interest to ecumenical pundits. These were small churches from Chile, but the significant thing about them was that they were Pentecostalist, the first representatives of this rapidly growing new family of Christian churches (see above, pp. 150–51): indeed it could be said that these were the first 'fringe' churches to join the movement. Another significant fact was pointed out by Dr Visser 't Hooft; with the latest additions there were now twice as many member churches from Asia, Africa and Latin America as there had been at the inception of the World Council – a witness to the growing independence of the churches in the 'developing nations'.

One more change – or 'ecumenical first' – must be noted at New Delhi. It was the first Assembly to which the Roman Catholic church sent official observers. Hitherto those who had attended World Council meetings or conferences of any sort had done so in a private capacity; indeed at Evanston the local Roman Catholic Archbishop of Chicago had strictly forbidden attendance – and it was noticed that a surprising number of journalists had suddenly taken to carrying breviaries! But the years between Evanston and New Delhi, 1954 to 1961, had seen Pope John and the beginning of Vatican II; the thaw was beginning to set in.

The actual theme of the New Delhi Assembly was 'Jesus Christ the Light of the World', a subject chosen appropriately for a meeting in Asia. This theme was perhaps somewhat lost in the important events which took place at the Assembly, but one thing was clear to delegates whose ecumenical memory stretched back to meetings before the war and especially to the last great meeting in India, that at Tambaram in 1938. The fiercely negative attitude to other world religions, associated with the 1938 conference and with the name of Hendrik Kraemer, had been replaced by a much more all-embracing view in which Christ was indeed seen as *The* Light of the World but in which the other great world religions were not denied their measure of illumination; the Christian approach, therefore, to them and to their adherents was to be based on sympathy and understanding. For the rest the main stress was laid on the renewal of the churches so that they and their members should be better able to serve the world with all its changing needs. This was to be the key-note of the work of the W.C.C. in the period after New Delhi.

NEW STRUCTURES AND NEW LOOK, 1961–8

The integration of the I.M.C. into the W.C.C. meant the creation of new structures for the working of the reformed World Council. There were now to be four main Divisions. These were the Division of World Mission and Evangelism, the Division of Studies, the Division of Ecumenical Action and the Division of Inter-Church Aid, Refugee and World Service. The divisions are divided for working purposes into Departments, though in fact many of the Departments overlap, not only with the work of other Departments in the same division, but also with that going on in other divisions. Thus the Division of Studies has a Department of Missionary Studies, which is clearly much concerned with what is going on in the Department of World Mission and Evangelism. (Later, in fact, this Department was incorporated into the D.W.M.E.) Another complication is that two branches are also constituted as Commissions. These are the D.W.M.E. and the Faith and Order Department of the Division of Studies. The purpose of this is to give the ex-independent operations of the I.M.C. and Faith and Order a somewhat enhanced status and a measure of continuing independence. It is also possible for a Commission to have member churches and organizations which are not full members of the World Council itself. In this way it was hoped that it would be possible for the D.W.M.E. to keep the co-operation and interest of conservative evangelicals; this has not in the event been altogether the case though recently the situation has been improving. Similarly, it has enabled the Faith and Order Commission to involve Roman Catholics in their work to a greater extent than is possible with the full World Council.

W.C.C. structure since New Delhi is shown overleaf.

The Division of World Mission and Evangelism was charged at New Delhi with the responsibility of 'bringing into all parts of the World Council an awareness of the missionary dimension of the Church's life and to deepen the concern for evangelism in the whole thinking and work of the Council'. It was seen that this was not simply a continuation of the work of the old I.M.C.

Our temptation will be to think of the Division simply as a continuation of the interests of the I.M.C. with emphasis on Asia, Africa and South America. We must resist this temptation.... We are concerned not with three continents but six.[25]

The recognition that it is not only the old 'missionary' countries but the whole world which is the concern of the mission of the church was to become the dominant theme of the work of the D.W.M.E. It was more fully spelled out at the first world conference of the new

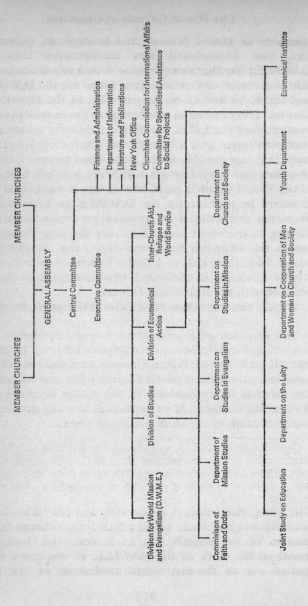

MEMBER CHURCHES

MEMBER CHURCHES

GENERAL ASSEMBLY

Central Committee

Executive Committee

Division for World Mission and Evangelism (D.W.M.E.)

Division of Studies

Division of Ecumenical Action

Inter-Church Aid, Refugee and World Service

Finance and Administration
Department of Information
Literature and Publications
New York Office
Churches Commission for International Affairs
Committee for Specialised Assistance to Social Projects

Commission of Faith and Order

Department of Mission Studies

Department on Studies in Evangelism

Department on Studies in Mission

Department on Church and Society

Joint Study on Education

Department on the Laity

Department on Cooperation of Men and Women in Church and Society

Youth Department

Ecumenical Institute

Commission held in New Mexico in 1963. Here the theme was 'Mission on Six Continents'. It was recognized at last that the old idea of 'home base' and 'foreign mission' was dead for ever. In the first place the old home base in the 'west' is now as much a 'mission field' as the former mission countries. In the second with the technological revolution the world is increasingly becoming a 'global village', so that the church is faced with the same problems in its mission in every one of the six continents. Thus the interdependence of missionary work was recognized: it is more and more possible for the churches to pool and share experience and manpower. Missionaries are no longer clergymen only; they include lay experts such as journalists, agriculturalists and engineers who may be drafted for short service advisory posts to any part of the world.

All this was a fuller understanding of another idea that was thrown up at New Delhi, that of 'joint action for mission'. Practical examples of such joint action were seen in the establishment of experimental urban and industrial church centres on an ecumenical basis in Port Harcourt, the new oil, industrial and shipping complex in Nigeria, and Durgapur, one of the boom steel towns north-west of Calcutta (see below, pp. 470–72). But despite a lot of talk and some planning the Joint Action for Mission programme was slow to get off the ground, and is still – nine years later – in the process of implementation.

The Division of Studies has as its main Department the Commission of Faith and Order, which was responsible for the fourth World Conference on Faith and Order, held in Montreal in 1963. Here 'some participants received the impression of chaos' – though professional ecumenists were quick to pronounce it 'promising chaos'.[26] The chaos was perhaps inevitable. This was the first occasion on which the full effect of Orthodox participation in a theological discussion was felt. As the

General Secretary noted, 'after a long period of separation it is not easy to engage in real dialogue'. But at least that was what was attempted. In the past at Faith and Order meetings the Orthodox had tended to sit back while the western delegates drew up their formulas and then to register Orthodox dissent; at Montreal they joined fully in the discussion from the outset so that nothing could be taken for granted. Add to this the fact that Roman Catholic observers also played their full part and it could truly be claimed that 'for the first time it was possible to perceive the ecumenical problem in all its aspects'.[27]

Further to confound confusion 'we had attempted too much too quickly'.[28] None the less, some useful and lasting work was done. The study on the theme 'Tradition and Traditions', an explosive subject especially with the Orthodox in the discussion, led to some remarkable conclusions being accepted by the conference: it even went so far as to acknowledge that 'we can say that we exist as Christians *sola traditione*, by tradition alone'. This was a donnish reference to the old Reformation war-cries that the Christian life could be lived *sola fide*, by faith alone, or that Christian truth is to be found *sola scriptura*, in the Bible alone; in either case it was an admission that it is absurd to think that the church can or should believe that there is such a thing as 'pure' faith in which tradition plays no part; it was also a significant move towards the Orthodox conception that the life of the church *is* the living tradition of Christ and the Apostles.

Another thorny question was tackled by the conference, that of the ministry. It was in fact twenty-five years since this had been the subject of a Faith and Order conference and it was immediately apparent that much water had passed under the bridges since Edinburgh 1937. In particular, as has been seen, there was the recognition that the whole church is the people of God and that it is the whole church which has a missionary responsibility. In fact some delegates showed themselves suspicious of the 'new line' being developed about the laity in the World Council and elsewhere, whereas some of the 'new liners' showed 'considerable reluctance ... to say anything very positive at all about the ordained ministry'.[29] So in the end no real progress was made and this was perhaps what the officers of the conference had in mind when in their final statement they said: 'It is increasingly clear that many of our long-defended positions are irrelevant to God's purpose' – a lesson which needs to be learned by many an ecumenical negotiator.[30] Working on this basis the Faith and Order Commission decided that in future it should study not only questions which have been at issue between the churches but also some of the great basic Christian themes. This is the present policy and it 'means that it has been recognized at last that working for unity involves more than merely dealing with the past. The old differences between the churches are also seen in a fresh light when they are examined within the context of the great questions of today.'[31] 'At last', indeed, it is!

Another department in the Division of Studies, that of Church and Society, also mounted a World Conference in this period. The 1966 Geneva conference on 'Christian Response to the Technical and Social Revolutions of Our Time' was seen in fact in line as the third World Conference of the Life and Work movement. It was a conference not of member churches but of selected specialist delegates who would speak *to* their churches on their return rather than *for* their churches at the conference; in the process of selection a special effort was made to find laymen and non-westerners, especially in view of the fact that one of the subjects of debate would be the rift between the have and have-not nations, or, as it was coming to be known, the problem of the 'third world'. The conference also discussed the difficulties involved in rapid social change and the issues raised for Christians by the need for 'nation-building' in many of the newly independent countries. But one question became unexpectedly critical: that of Church and Revolution. How far should Christians welcome and even encourage and take part in change which is not brought about by the slower methods of evolution, but is accomplished by revolution? It is a question which touches many aspects of life today and the debate revealed deep differences of opinion between the radicals and the conservatives; some thought that such an explosive issue should never have been brought before the conference, while others praised the leaders for facing up to a basic issue. The debate continues.

Next, the Department of Missionary Studies was, and is, engaged on a study ('The Missionary Structure of the Congregation') arising from the finding of the rapid social change project that the churches are too inflexible to be able to meet the challenges of a changing world. Here the purpose was to find out how far congregations are tied down by out-dated structures, such as the regional parish system, so that they become inward-looking and interested only in self-perpetuation, rather than in missionary work and in service to the world around them. Research was undertaken throughout the world, but its directors had to admit that they had not in fact cut much ice with the churches. It was the old story of the back-room boys from the Council being out of touch with the life of the churches by being too far ahead of it. But the point was made for those who had eyes to see that a united church would be severely handicapped if it accepted without questioning patterns of structure and ministry based on outdated social concepts.

The Division of Ecumenical Action is concerned, as has been seen, with men and women in church, family, and society, with the laity and with youth. This work it continued in the usual ways, while also pooling all its interests in a study for the Uppsala General Assembly entitled 'Towards a New Style of Living'.

'*The Division of Inter-Church Aid, Refugee and World Service* was created by the churches to convey ecumenical help to those in distress.' Despite various changes its name is still too cumbrous and hardly describes its true work. Partly it functions as the agent of aid between the churches; thus if one church is in distress and needs help it can look to the Division. This aspect of the work has been of very great significance where the Orthodox are concerned, since it has made the Orthodox churches in various parts of the world feel in a practical way the strength of the fellowship to which they belong. This more than anything else has made the World Council real for the Orthodox after so many centuries cut off from the western churches; it has been particularly important in allaying Orthodox fears and suspicions based on the memory of past proselytization in Orthodox countries by Protestant missions. Inter-Church Aid has also worked to finance the projects for Christian aid and service where the less rich churches have appealed for the help of their better placed fellows. Such work has been organized through an elaborate check-list of projects and priorities and where necessary the Division and the local churches have had the advice of a special Committee for Specialised Assistance to Social Projects.

But besides this work, rightly described as Inter-Church Aid, the Division undertakes work in which all the churches jointly act for the relief of human suffering or the improvement of social conditions. Continuing work among refugees has been typical of this side of its activities and between 1961 and 1965 the Division added to its other refugee work a service in Bengal to help to meet the plight of the thousands of refugees in West Bengal after the partition of India and Pakistan. The Division is also quick to come to the support of areas stricken by natural disasters. The Skopje earthquake was one such typical emergency: the World Council built 124 houses in the new township. Again the Division seeks to bring Christian aid to areas in need as a result of political disturbances. It has been able through Polish church channels to work in North Vietnam and has also had a substantial operation in South Vietnam in conjunction with the East Asia Christian Council. Its work in Algeria has also been typical. After the withdrawal of the French from that country it was seen that there would be an acute shortage of skilled workers, technicians and administrators and a Christian Committee for service in Algeria was set up; at one time this had as many as 250 workers, of whom half were Algerians. Farm- and trade-training schools were set up and clinics started; above all a huge project of afforestation was undertaken: to save the Sahara encroaching from the south no less than twenty-two million timber and fruit trees were planted to replace those lost in the war. This was a five-year plan which was then run down though help continued to be given to the Algerian government in other ways.

Such was the work of the Division in the years between New Delhi and Uppsala. As it looks ahead the Division can hardly expect that there will be less calls on its services from the world, whatever other sections of the World Council have to be cut back. The tasks are legion; the most important work is that of establishing priorities. It is now thought that in the next ten years priority will have to be given to work which can genuinely said to be 'development'.

THE COMMISSION OF THE CHURCHES ON INTERNATIONAL AFFAIRS

There is another agency of the World Council which has so far not been described – the Commission of the Churches on International Affairs, originally a joint project of the W.C.C. and the I.M.C. The Membership of this Commission has been mainly lay, the Chairman being Sir Kenneth Grubb, and its primary concerns have been political and diplomatic rather than social or economic. As such its approach has been pragmatic and cautious – 'possibly over-cautious' it has said in self-criticism – rather than prophetic. It has worked closely with such international bodies as the United Nations, the Food and Agriculture Organisation and the International Labour Office, and for this reason has been largely based on New York.

After the war the first concern of the Commission was human rights. Spelling out the U.N. Charter on this subject, it worked mainly on religious liberty. An important Declaration on Religious Liberty was accepted by the Amsterdam General Assembly in 1948 and had the effect of strengthening the hitherto somewhat milkwarm U.N. article on that subject, so that it included the right to change one's belief and the right of religious self-expression in teaching, preaching and practice as well as in worship. The Commission went on to make a survey of the conditions of religious freedom throughout the world, which included the treatment of Protestants in such Catholic dominated countries as Spain, Italy and Colombia. It is possible, indeed probable, that this survey had some influence on the astonishing reversal in Roman Catholic teaching on religious liberty which took place at Vatican II (see below, pp. 399–401); it is certain that progressive forces in Rome had been in touch with members of the Commission.

Another field of interest for the Commission was that of economic and social development. Here their work was rather more prophetic than cautious. As long ago as 1958 the Commission had advised the World Council that 'the picture would be brighter if [developed] countries would contribute at least one per cent of national income to international development'.[32] This idea of a percent-

261

age 'tax' from the developed to the developing nations was later adopted by the U.N. and became a feature (admittedly minor) of western political life.

THE FOURTH ASSEMBLY, UPPSALA, 1968

So stood the world Council of Churches on the eve of the Fourth General Assembly at Uppsala, Sweden, in July 1968. The theme of the Assembly was 'Behold, I make all things new'. This was in line with the thinking of every branch of the World Council during the past five years.

Not that it was a completely new idea. As long ago as the Amsterdam Assembly Bishop Bell had said, 'Our first and deepest need is not new organization, but the renewal, or rather the rebirth of the actual churches.'[33] But the idea of renewal had come to the fore in the sixties. 'One Church Renewed for Mission' had been the theme of a British Council of Churches Conference at Nottingham in 1963, but it could well have applied to many W.C.C. conferences which had been prodding the churches to thought and action on the concerns of renewal and mission as well as on that of unity. The movement for the rediscovery of the unity of the churches was now seen as only one item on their agenda; if they were to meet the needs of the time, unity was not enough, renewal was equally urgent. Hence the text, 'Behold I make all things new'.

In fact in the various sections of the Uppsala Assembly the renewal theme did not come through with the strength which some no doubt had hoped for. There were two reasons for this, both lessons which might have been learned from Montreal. The first was the actual method of procedure, which led as usual to drafting and re-drafting against time, and in the end, as one delegate put it, to 'a kind of theology-by-show-of-hands'.[34] The second was the rift that appeared in almost all the sections between the radicals and the conservatives. On the one hand there were the western theologians faced with a 'post-Christian' situation and the secularization of society and willing to respond if need be with the most radical solutions, such as the so-called 'death of God' theology and the questioning of the very need of a visible institutional church; on the other hand there were the conservatives, mainly the Orthodox, some of whom could at least claim to be the world's experts at being Christians in a secular society! It was noticeable that the Roman Catholic observers who took an active part were willing to be on the radical side; so 'the discussion illustrated (not for the first time) how much nearer in some respects the Christians of the West (whether Roman, Anglican or Protestant) are to one another than to their brothers of the Orthodox East'.[35] It was a question of 'wave-length', as one reporter observed. So Uppsala reiterated what had been noticed already since New Delhi, that there had been 'a slowing up of the progress towards deeper consensus'. It was inevitable with the advent in force of the Orthodox, because the World Council had to maintain its ideal of being 'a place of dialogue for all convictions held in its member churches'.[36]

What did come out of Uppsala, it was generally agreed, 'was its preoccupation – at times, almost its obsession – with the revolutionary ferment of our time, with questions of social and international responsibility, of war and peace and economic justice, with the pressing, agonizing, physical needs of men, with the plight of the underprivileged, the homeless and starving, and with the most radical contemporary rebellions against all "establishments", civil and religious'.[37] As the Division of Studies had been urging on congregations, the Assembly recognized that 'the world was writing the agenda for the meeting; the right of the world to do this was largely taken for granted and Uppsala tried to read the writing, understand it and respond to it with a willingness to accept the necessity for changes as tumultuous for the

Church itself as for the rapidly changing world'.[38] Obviously this was particularly difficult for the Orthodox, with their belief in the unchanging nature of the church's life and teaching and their self-protection from the winds of changing western contemporary thought; so in the end nothing very positive or striking was achieved, except, it was felt, 'that the main importance of this Assembly has been its affirmation of Christian solidarity with mankind'.[39]

The Assembly was noteworthy for one other thing. This was the restiveness – to put it at its mildest – of the youth participants. Already it had been noted that young people 'see little sense in the investment of more time in the creation of ecumenical plans and ideas if the cheques the fathers signed in the past are not cashed first'.[40] At Uppsala these feelings came to the boil – most dramatically, in the course of the closing service, with a silent procession of placard-bearing youth participants who had kept an all-night prayer vigil in the Cathedral and whose placards reminded the worshippers of some of the starkest issues on the world's 'agenda'; but also throughout the detailed discussions when the youth delegates constantly demanded that the drafting of statements should be more urgent and more practical – until one exasperated delegate complained that young people seemed to think that no one over thirty could cope with the problems of the world and that the church had never faced them before, an attitude he might well have observed without undertaking the journey to Uppsala.

It is not necessary to report the debates in the various sections of the Assembly in detail. More important are the underlying themes which emerged, especially as these affected the future strategy and plans of the W.C.C. In each of the themes which will be mentioned the radical/ conservative split was clearly felt.

The first fundamental debate was on the subject which has come to be known as 'secular ecumenism'. This is no less than a radical questioning of the whole basis of the ecumenical movement as it has developed in the twentieth century. Is a concern with the organizational and institutional unity of the churches the real meaning of the ecumenical movement? This was the question being asked. It was addressed specifically to the doctrinal section of the Assembly: 'Does the Gospel permit Christians to concern themselves with question of ecclesiastical unity when it is the unity and reconciliation of mankind which alone is relevant in 1968?' The final report of the section recognized that many felt that, given the present needs of the world, the traditional search for institutional church unity is 'irrelevant'. Inevitably perhaps the solution proposed was a compromise, but the debate had shown how radical were the questionings about the premises of the ecumenical movement which had for long been tken for granted (see below, pp. 503–12).

Another debate which ended in compromise was that on the mission of the church. For a decade, as has been seen, the issues of mission and unity had been wedded, but there remained fundamental uncertainties as to what actually *is* the mission of the church – uncertainties which inevitably inhibited the actual plans made to pursue the mission. There are those who still feel that the church's mission is solely concerned with 'the preaching of the Gospel', with converting individuals and with drawing them 'out of' the world and 'into' the church. But there are also those who feel that the mission of the church and of its members is to be 'present' in the world and by this presence to reform the world and its ways in accordance with the will of God. Between the two extremes there are many variations and many arguments. The debate is perhaps inescapable and it was no doubt right that it should be carried on in public at Uppsala. But it is symptomatic of a 'failure of nerve' at every level of the life of the churches. Just at the moment when the churches are all talking about their task primarily in

terms of mission they find that they don't know what that
mission is.

A third theme which emerged at Uppsala is that which
has come to be known as the 'Humanum' debate. At
every turn, as the quotations already given have shown,
the Assembly found that it was concerned with mankind
– with what mankind is or should be, with where mankind is going, with how men and women should live. In
theological terms this means that the churches now find
that they need to re-examine the Christian doctrine of
man if they are to have anything worth saying to men
and women in the world. The section on world economic
and social development found that 'the central issue in
development is the criteria of the human'. That on international affairs declared that 'the church must speak out
... where human lives or human dignity are endan-
gered'.[41] That entitled 'New Styles of Living' stressed the
fact that two thirds of the world's population live in 'sub-
human' ways and that Christian ethics must lead to a
fuller development of human potential. In sum, as the
newly elected Chairman of the Central Committee was to
say, 'the unity of mankind is the context and substance of
the efforts of the Church to manifest its unity'.[42]

All this led to the recognition that a field of study that
would be fruitful for several aspects of the work of the
World Council and of the churches would be what came
to be known as 'studies on man'. There had in fact been
some dissatisfaction because since 1963 the post of Director of the Division of Studies had been vacant and
because on successive occasions it had remained un-
filled. This led some people to say that the W.C.C. was
becoming more 'activist' and that the intellectual and
theological undergirding of its work was going by de-
fault: in fact there is no disguising that at this time
various organizational and policy tensions were appearing within World Council circles. At Uppsala it was decided that the Division of Studies should be suspended

for three years (some of its work being undertaken in
other divisions) pending the awaited report of the Structure Committee, which, it was recognized, might very
well make radical suggestions about the future structure
of the whole movement. Meanwhile a special project was
set up for the studies on man, or the Humanum. The
overall purpose of this study was later defined as: 'to enable the church to find its way in helping man to find his
way'.

Two other organizational changes must be mentioned
as having taken place at Uppsala. The first was the
appointment of a new Associate General Secretary responsible for relations with National and Regional
Councils of Churches. This was a recognition of the importance of the development of less centralized ecumenical relationships, which must, as will be seen later, figure
largely in any re-assessment the W.C.C. now makes of its
work.

The second was the appointment of staff within the
Division of Ecumenical Action to concern themselves
with Christian education. Previously the World Council
had kept out of the educational field because of the existence of a World Council of Christian Education. Recently, however, a joint study had been undertaken by the
W.C.C. and the W.C.C.E., and this had led to closer collaboration and the idea of a possible merger. Such a merger was in fact approved at the Canterbury meeting of the
Central Committee in 1969 by the creation of a Division
of Education and Ecumenical Action.

One thing, however, did not get done at Uppsala. The
setting-up of a secretariat on race relations had been
mooted, but it was decided not to recommend the idea to
the Assembly because of shortage of funds. Despite this
fact the Assembly asked for positive action in the field of
race relationships. This led to a Consultation at Notting
Hill, London, which received wide publicity because of
an incident where the Archbishop of Canterbury re-

buked from the chair a particularly vociferous and militant coloured speaker – and subsequently apologized for his action. Acting on the recommendations of this Consultation the Central Committee meeting at Canterbury in 1969 set up a Programme to Combat Racism.

The programme was backed with considerable resources, indicating the priority given to it by the W.C.C. A general budget of $150,000 p.a. for five years was to come from income for the staff of the project and the financing of research, inquiries and consultations. In addition a Special Fund was created for the support of anti-racist projects. $200,000 was voted to this fund from reserves, despite the fact that the Finance Committee pointed out that this would run the reserves dangerously low in the event of any emergency affecting W.C.C. income, and that such a move might itself 'have a negative effect on future income'.

The programme was described by the committee in the following Biblical terms:

Our programme is not against flesh and blood. It is against the principalities, against the powers of evil, against the deeply entrenched demonic forces of racial prejudice and hatred that we must battle. Ours is a task of exorcism. The demons operate through our social, economic and political structures. But the root of the problem is as deep as human sin, and only God's love and man's dedicated response can eradicate it. The World Council's programme is but part of that response.... By God's love, by the power of his Holy Spirit, some day, soon, we shall overcome.[43]

Having seen their task in these apocalyptic terms the W.C.C. can hardly have been surprised when their programme ran into opposition. In 1970 the Executive Committee, on the advice of its International Advisory Committee, voted $200,000 to various organizations from the Special Fund. The policy was all along 'to support organizations that combat racism, rather than welfare organizations which alleviate the effects of racism'. In making the allocations the Executive Committee had its eyes open.

The Executive Committee is well aware that some of the organizations supported are combatting racism with violent means. However, it notes with appreciation that these organizations have given the assurance that they will not use these amounts received for military purposes, but for conscientization, education and social welfare.[44]

Some of the bodies supported were in fact revolutionary movements which were appealing for support for the government of 'liberated' territories. The W.C.C. ran into a storm of protest over this action, as was presumably to be expected. But the 'personal comment' of Miss Pauline Webb, an English Methodist member of the Executive Committee, is presumably typical of the thinking of the committee.

The Fund must be seen to be a symbolic act – symbolic of a commitment that has very often been expressed by Christians ... but words have little effect until they become deeds. . . . The Fund is symbolic in another sense in that it represents an acknowledgement of the fact that the struggle against racism is not just a matter of charity or good-will, but it involves the transfer of power. The oppressed races of this world do not want our help – however kindly meant – they want the power to attain their own dignity and full humanity. . . . Inevitably, in some situations the struggle will involve the use of force. The Churches have never entirely denounced the use of force. They have recognized the possibility of 'the just war'. Now they are recognizing, painfully and penitently, the possible inevitability of 'the just revolution'. In any case, the alternative to being aligned with those who use violence to resist oppression seems in these days alignment with those who use violence to defend their own privilege and affluence and to perpetuate injustice. . . . In view of the fact that the majority of Christians are among the white, wealthy, powerful peoples of the world, it is surely not inappropriate that by this small symbolic act the World Council of Churches might in penitence put a tiny balance-weight on the other side.[45]

In the event most of the member churches have ratified
the policy.

THE FUTURE OF THE WORLD COUNCIL

It was generally felt at Uppsala that the W.C.C. had
reached a turning point in its history. And it was generally agreed that changes were necessary and that the
Council must avoid the danger that institutionalization
creates vested interests and a static outlook, a danger
against which it has always warned its member churches.

What then of the future of the World Council? Two
things are clear. First, the post-war generation which took
over from the pre-war pioneers and which has been responsible for the building-up of a formidable organization is now bowing out. This was dramatically illustrated
by the death, on the very eve of Uppsala, of Dr Franklin
Clark Fry, the Chairman of the Central Commitee for
fourteen years. But there were many other leaders of his
generation who were appearing for the last time at
Uppsala. Even more significant, the first and at that time
only General Secretary, Dr Visser 't Hooft, retired in 1965,
after guiding and directing the movement since his
appointment in 1938. The appointment of his successor
was bound in any case to be difficult. In the event it was a
most unhappy experience; Dr Fry, in the notes which he
left at his death, described it as 'buffeting', a mild word to
use of the struggle which actually took place before the
eventual appointment of Dr Eugene Carson Blake, an
American Presbyterian and ecumenical leader with long
experience in the counsels of the W.C.C. However, Dr
Blake's reign will necessarily be relatively short. The
stage is now set for a new generation of leadership to take
over in the early seventies – by which time they will
certainly be faced with crucial decisions if the World
Council and the ecumenical movement generally are use-
fully to survive.

In the second place, it was generally agreed at Uppsala that a General Assembly on such a scale is efficient neither as a legislative nor as a thinking body. Legislative bodies which meet only sporadically and briefly are never satisfactory, for they have no chance to develop a corporate entity; either they must rubber-stamp the recommendations of their officers, or they must run the risk of irresponsibly, and perhaps ignorantly, throwing out their carefully prepared work. But by the Uppsala meeting the Assembly was in any case a hopelessly unwieldy body for serious deliberation. The membership of the World Council had grown as follows: at Amsterdam 147 member churches, at Evanston 174, at New Delhi 197 and at Uppsala 235. This meant that there were 704 delegates at Uppsala compared with 351 at Amsterdam – together with 400 other participants with a right to speak, though not to vote – and an overcrowded and highly contentious agenda had to be packed into a fortnight!

The function and working of the General Assemblies of the future is therefore bound to be revised. But more will have to be thrown into the melting pot than this. Two serious criticisms can be made of the W.C.C. as it has developed between 1948 and 1968. In the first place it is often out of touch with the general thinking of its member churches. Time and time again its studies and its recommendations have seemed impracticable and inapplicable to the life of the local church. It is true that congregations are often conservative and inward-looking and that the W.C.C. has a proper prophetic task to stir them into more realistic activity. This prophetic role for the W.C.C. is the more important now that the ecumenical movement has become 'respectable'. Church leaders and most clergy pay at least lip-service to the idea of church unity and there is a danger that a unity will be aimed at which does not carry as its partner other marks of reform and renewal. Undoubtedly the task of the World Council – and one which was recognized in the sixties – is to keep saying that unity will not be enough. This has been the significance of the fact that during the sixties many of its officers were recruited from the ranks of the most radical and impatient young church leaders.

On the other hand it must be admitted that the World Council and its officers have tended to develop a life of their own somewhat divorced from that of the member churches. They have moved from study to study, from concern to concern, from slogan to slogan and from panacea to panacea – all expressed in the latest fashionable ecumenical jargon – with seemingly little reference to the facts of local church life. If the gap between the Council and the grassroots in congregations is too great, nothing will happen, or worse still the local churches will feel a positive, and in some ways justified, antagonism for Geneva and all its works. What is more the image of the whole ecumenical movement will suffer.

It is, as so often, a question of communication. The conferences and consultations of the W.C.C. often remain as so much paper and so many resolutions. Unless they are absorbed into the thinking of the member churches, and more important their congregations, it is difficult to avoid the question whether the effort and, more particularly, the expense were justified.

The second criticism of the W.C.C. – and one of which, to be fair, it is itself acutely conscious – is that it remains after all these years still a predominantly *western* affair. It is true that, since the advent of the Orthodox, it is not now so much the religious equivalent of N.A.T.O. But even with the Orthodox, the debate is still western; indeed with the Orthodox it is even more western, since historically the Orthodox Churches stretch further into the western past, while geographically the Orthodox have no real experience of the 'third world' of Asia and Africa. The churches of Africa, Asia and Latin America are still relatively silent in the World Council debate and the

youth delegates who, meeting on their own before Uppsala, said that 'imperialism and paternalism are perpetuated by the structure and theology of the W.C.C.' were
not so wide of the mark.[46] It is true that for the first time
the Chairman of the Central Committee is a non-
westerner, M. M. Thomas from the church of South
India, but one swallow, even one Chairman, does not
make a summer; something more far-reaching needs to be
done before the World Council really becomes a *World*
Council in the sense that its debates reflect the fact that
more than half of its member churches are from the third
world.

The solution to both these problems, that of communication with the member churches and that of de-westernization, seems to lie in de-centralization from Geneva.
The imposing structure which has been created in the
years leading up to Uppsala has probably served its turn.
Devolution would now seem to be the order of the day;
devolution to the various area Christian conferences,
such as the E.A.C.C. and to national Councils of
Churches, which have not grown at the same rate as has
the central body. If thinking and planning is done more
locally and regionally the W.C.C. runs less danger of being cut off from its grassroots. Moreover more people will
be involved; the World Council has tended to be the
same people meeting over and over again and this itself
has led to inbreeding and has inhibited the diffusion of
ecumenical ideas. Already, before Uppsala, there was a
move in this direction: for example the Faith and Order
Commission was becoming more concerned to stimulate
local unity discussions, while the Division of Studies,
finding itself bogged down in a study of 'Christianity and
other religions' in what it felt to be a western discussion
which was going to lead back to the 'Tambaram stale-
mate', handed that part of its work over to centres in
Africa and Asia. It is difficult to avoid the conclusion that
this should be only the beginning of a whole process of

devolution even though there will still be many things which can only be done at a 'world level'.

Devolution may very well mean diminution. The W.C.C. may get smaller. Indeed it may *have* to get smaller. So far its remarkable growth and the whole network of its expensive operations has been supported largely on American money. In the eight years between the New Delhi integration and 1969 the budget for the W.C.C. without the Divisions of World Mission and Inter-Church Aid grew from $719,300 to $1,320,000; in the same period the Inter-Church Aid budget increased from $1,200,000 to an estimated $1,700,000 p.a. This remarkable growth has been made possible by the fact that in America, unlike Europe, the churches have not until recently been shrinking. It has been possible, therefore, within reason for the W.C.C. to count on ever-increasing American support. But these halcyon days are now numbered, if not already past. The general mood of American expansionist confidence, from which the Council like so many other agencies benefited, is on the wane. Further, in America now, as in Europe earlier, the churches are entering on a period of decline. There is another factor, pointed out by the new General Secretary at Uppsala: the voting strength in the Council has passed away from North Atlantic control. Policies are being pursued on such things as race and world poverty which are not popular in the well-heeled American churches. (Already such 'liberal' policies have reduced the income of the Anglican church in America by more than 10 per cent.) America is in fact now less willing, as well as less able, to foot the World Council bill. Already at Uppsala operations which had been planned were having to be abandoned for lack of financial support and the Programme to Combat Racism has had to draw heavily on reserves. Dr Blake had foreseen that 'the role of the W.C.C. will be reduced in the next period'.[47] For the moment the wealthy churches in Germany and Scandinavia are partly filling the vacuum left by decreasing American support, but it is doubtful whether this will continue.

There are, then, many problems facing the World Council as it is at present organized. Recognizing this, a Committee on Structures was set up some time before the Uppsala Assembly. It was only able to make an interim report in 1968, but completed its work and made its recommendations in October 1970. It listed the problems facing the W.C.C. under four main headings: the need for new structures, the present ones having been conceived in 1954; the need for increased regionalization and decentralization from Geneva; the need for economy and a 'reduction in that part of World Council activity which is dependent on the official contribution of the churches'; the need to change 'the pattern and method of ecumenical work' to relate it more effectively to 'the current crises in the Christian faith and in the life of the church'.[48]

In considering the question of structures the committee listed a number of needs, all implying criticism of recent W.C.C. functioning which would seem to be justified. These were chiefly that the new structure of the Council 'must greatly increase the flexibility and manoeuvrability of the staff' ... 'must surmount the old separation between study and action' ... and 'must maintain the historic paradox of the World Council as both a council of churches and a dynamic "frontier" movement'.[49] The solution proposed is the regrouping of the activities of the Council in three main 'Programme Units'. The rationale for this is presented in a fine piece of ecumenese:

The Structure Committee is not merely recommending a regrouping of traditional activities but the deliberate placing together of traditional activities in creative tension. At the same time, provision is made for co-ordination, mutual support and correction between the several parts.... The divisions which have characterized the structure since 1954 are therefore eliminated in favour of Programme Units conceived along quite different lines. Within the three Programme Units the various specific functions of the Council find their place, not as departments but as more flexible sub-units. These latter are not conceived as permanent: rather they may undergo alteration as need arises. . . . The staff of the Programme Units will conduct their activities in a collegial fashion.[50]

The first Programme Unit is on Faith and Witness; it takes in Faith and Order, World Mission and Evangelism, Church and Society and the newly developing interest in Dialogue with Men of Living Faiths and Ideologies. The second is on Justice and Services, comprising the Churches' Participation in Development, International Affairs (the old C.C.I.A.), the Programme to Combat Racism and Inter-Church Aid. Thirdly Education and Communication puts together Education, Renewal Action Groups, Communications and Publications, and Relations with Regional and National Groups.

The Structure Committee was obviously much concerned with the feeling expressed at Uppsala that that sort of General Assembly was an unsatisfactory form of meeting. It recommends smaller working groups at Assemblies and more careful preparation. It also recommends ways and means of ensuring that there is more non-western representation and that the preponderance of church officials at Assemblies is modified in favour of parochial clergy, lay people, women and young people. These hopes are also applied to other committees, such as those of the Unit Programmes.

On the matter of financial retrenchment the Committee has no very definite recommendations beyond advocating more careful and more centralized budgeting. Similarly the question of decentralization and communications with the regional and national manifestations of the ecumenical movement is left for future working-out.

All these recommendations were accepted with only minor amendments by the Central Committee meeting at Addis Ababa in January 1971. They are at the time of writing in the process of being implemented. It will take time to tell whether they will prove effective; but it is difficult to imagine that they will prove sufficiently realistic if the churches themselves and their support for the W.C.C. continue to decline as they have in the past five years. Much will depend no doubt on the appointment of the new General Secretary which was also set on foot at Addis Ababa.

Another question was considered by the Structure Committee without any firm future policy being recommended. This is the question, which has been becoming increasingly urgent, of the relationship between the W.C.C. and the various international confessional bodies of the churches. The point has already been made that most of the major traditional denominations – and not Rome alone – have now developed strong world confessional agencies. Outstanding among these are the Anglicans, based on the Lambeth Conferences which take place every ten years, the Lutheran World Federation, with its headquarters in Geneva, the World Methodist Council, with its powerful American base, and the Presbyterian and Congregationalist bodies, which were united in 1970 into the World Alliance of Reformed Churches. At first the W.C.C. and ecumenists generally tended to deprecate such bodies, fearing that international organization of individual denominations would inhibit the growth of local ecumenical strength. This was at about the time of the New Delhi statement of 1962, with its emphasis on the unity of the church as that of 'all in each place'. More recently, however, the W.C.C. has seen the necessity of coming to terms with the world confessional bodies, recognizing that for better or worse they are part of the world Christian scene. It has also recognized that the 'all in each place' slogan may have represented something of an over-emphasis on the locality of the church at the expense of its universality.

More recently, too, the world bodies have begun to be

more positive in their attitude to the ecumenical movement in general and the W.C.C. in particular. This can be seen in two ways. First in the general encouragement and help given to local church union negotiations and second in the continuance of financial support and intercommunion fellowship to the resulting union churches which formerly contained the denominations in question. In this respect the year 1968 marked something of a watershed. The Lambeth Conference in that year gave a belated recommendation for full intercommunion with the C.S.I. and accorded a similar accolade of approval to other church union schemes in the pipeline, such as North India and Lanka (Ceylon). Similarly in 1968 the Lutheran World Federation, which had previously been exceedingly cautious in giving its encouragement to churches to engage in union negotiations, became more generous and encouraging in this matter.

A further development has been the involvement of the world confessional bodies in ecumenical discussions with each other. Previously their ecumenical activity had been in encouraging or watchdogging their member churches in local negotiations. Now they have embarked on discussions themselves on a world level. The main and most important examples here are the various Joint Working Groups between various confessional bodies and the Roman Catholic church, which (since Rome has not gone so far as local negotiations) is the only way to enter into ecumenical dialogue with that church (see below, pp. 408–17).

But there are also a number of cases of bilateral conversations between non-Roman confessions. An example is the conversations between Anglicans and Lutherans which were inaugurated in September 1970. It was felt specifically that such 'conversation between Anglicans and Lutherans on a world wide basis ... would not replace local discussions but in fact stimulate them'. This could certainly be the case where Anglicans and

Lutherans are side by side locally but not in union negotiation. The world bodies also believe that they can provide theological expertise and a wider view which may be lacking in local churches: 'It has become more and more evident that many serious theological and ecclesiastical problems cannot be solved locally; for although regional and national churches are independent in many respects, they must always bear in mind the common faith and practice that links the world.' Local churches might be forgiven for thinking that this is simply one more attempt by the west to maintain control and keep western viewpoints to the fore, but however that may be there is certainly one area in which these bilateral discussions are important. This is the establishment of relationships between churches where they are not neighbours in the same locality, but where mutual recognition and action would be a source of strength. (For instance, in the case of Anglicans in England and Lutherans in Germany.) Such relationships can presumably be negotiated only bilaterally but, once negotiated, they would bear fruit in and through the W.C.C. The World Council, therefore, as the expression of the universality of the church, is bound to be concerned with the international confessional movements about which formerly it had its doubts.

NOTABLE NON-MEMBERS

The Roman Catholic Church

This brings us to the most vital question at the moment facing the World Council – the possibility of its being joined by the Roman Catholic church. The general effect of the second Vatican Council on the Roman Catholic church and its place in the ecumenical movement will be described later. Here it is only necessary to discuss the relationship of the Roman Catholic church with the W.C.C. In 1960 Pope John XXIII set up the Secretariat for the Promotion of Christian Unity and from then the official maintenance of ecumenical relations with the Roman church was made very much easier. It was this Secretariat who appointed observers to future World Council meetings and who invited official observers from the W.C.C. to Vatican II. The ecumenical result of Vatican II was in the words of Cardinal Bea, the head of the unity Secretariat, that 'from now on ecumenism is an essential part of the pastoral action of the whole Catholic Church'.[51] In the past there has been doubt on both sides whether Rome's doctrine of the church would allow of her joining the World Council, since to do so does imply some recognition that the other members are in their own way 'churches' and this might not have been possible for Rome. But these doubts are now dispelled and Rome 'accepts that this dialogue should take place on an equal footing (*par cum pari*) between churches which accept the same Lord'.[52] Such a statement represents what would have seemed before Vatican II an incredible *volte face*, a position which would have been adopted only by a few individual Catholic theologians and not by the church officially itself.

The way seems open, therefore, to Rome joining the World Council. But so far it has not happened. A Joint Working Group between the Secretariat for Unity and the W.C.C. was set up in 1965 which proposed the following areas of collaboration:

a. practical collaboration in the fields of philanthropy, social and international affairs
b. theological study programmes which have a specific bearing on ecumenical relations (Faith & Order)
c. problems which cause tension between the churches (e.g. mixed marriage, religious liberty, proselytism)
d. common concerns with regard to the life and mission of the church (laity, missions, etc.)[53]

There was certainly plenty of scope here, and on these lines steps have been taken to forge links between the various departments in the W.C.C. and their opposite numbers in Rome, and several conferences have taken place. The most important and successful was a joint conference in Beirut in 1968 on the theme 'World Co-operation for Development', which brought together the strongest possible Christian team to discuss this burning subject. Among other things the conference led to a large-scale educational campaign by all the churches to lay the Christian responsibility for world development before the members of all the churches. One of the organizers of this campaign was a Jesuit priest seconded by Rome to work under the W.C.C. in Geneva. On a more practical level, in 1966 the W.C.C. and the R.C.C. set up a joint committee in India to co-ordinate anti-hunger work; to-gether they have been appealing for and administering funds in a large project known as Action for Food Production.

But the question of Roman Catholic membership of the W.C.C. remains. In 1967 the Joint Working Group gave it as their opinion that 'for the moment the common cause of Christian unity would not be furthered if the R.C.C. were to join the W.C.C.'.[54] Pope Paul on his visit to Geneva in 1969 spoke of the question as 'not yet ripe for decision'. The Joint Working Group reporting to the Canterbury meeting of the W.C.C. Central Committee in 1969 again stressed the difficulties and urged further co-operation on the present lines. In particular it pointed to the advantages of Roman Catholic participation in national and local Councils of Churches. There is now, however, a sub-committee specifically considering the question. Certainly there would be very great difficulties. For Rome membership would mean a further step along the road of ecumenical dialogue, just at the moment when it seems that the pope may be trying to slow down the pace of change; at the moment indeed when the conservative forces may be blaming the movement of revolt on many fronts in the R.C.C. on the association of the liberals and rebels with ecumenical thinking.

On the World Council side, too, there would be very great difficulties: the unified nature of the R.C.C. would mean that technically her representation would be much smaller than her numbers warrant. On the other hand her membership is about the same as that of all the W.C.C. member churches put together; if Rome were properly represented there would therefore be a danger of her swamping the World Council, especially as her delegates would presumably speak with a more united voice than those of other churches. There would also be great administrative and psychological problems, not to mention the theological ones. In fact if the R.C.C. did join the W.C.C. the character of the latter would be inevitably changed.

To shelve the question of Roman Catholic membership in favour of a policy of co-operation and gradual growing together is, therefore, probably a policy of wise caution. But one wonders whether caution is really the best ecumenical policy. While it continues it will look as if 'Rome is not prepared to take the plunge'; moreover as Father Thomas Stransky, a member of the Secretariat for Christian Unity, has said:

Continued absence of R.C. participation in the W.C.C. might intensify a non-Catholic ecumenism which is implicitly moving toward a Protestant–Anglican–Orthodox unity over and against the R.C.C. The danger of 'non-Roman ecumenism' within the W.C.C. seems as great as the danger of a 'Roman' ecumenism outside of it. The temptation of the R.C.C. and the W.C.C. to think of the R.C.C. as either the centre of ecumenism or as the 'entirely different partner' in ecumenical endeavours could easily grow stronger. . . .[55]

In other words if the ultimate aim of the ecumenical movement is to embrace all the churches, including Rome, the situation as it now exists is artificial; it would be better to end it before the joints become too set. Moreover it would seem better to face all the undoubted difficulties now, rather than to do it later and again go through all the teething troubles which have followed the entrance of the Orthodox on to the W.C.C. scene. No one can deny that these troubles are in a good cause, but equally no one can deny that they set the general 'ecumenical dialogue' back. Surely it would be better to take one bite at the cherry rather than two, especially as so often it proves easier for the 'churches of the west', including Rome, to talk to each other than for those churches to talk to the Orthodox.

Extreme Protestantism

Rome is not 'in', but she is nearer to being in, and she is much more ready to co-operate with the W.C.C. than some other strong churches with powerful and effective missionary operations. The conservative evangelicals, or fundamentalists, are still suspicious, for reasons which have been described. Very often they are united among themselves and organized in a way which cuts across denominational boundaries. When this happens they are tragically non-cooperative and indeed positively antagonistic both to ordinary non-fundamentalist churches and to all sort of ecumenical activity, as for instance in Christian Unions and Evangelical Unions working in colleges and universities throughout the world. The largest church organized on a fundamentalist basis is the Southern Baptist Convention of America, which, with its world-wide ramifications, follows a policy of non-cooperation ecumenically and is not a member of the W.C.C., though some of its members, such as Dr Billy Graham, probably wish that its policy was not so strict. This, and other churches, are members of the World Evangelical Fellowship and send observers to World Council meetings who urge a stronger and more strict Biblicism, interpreted unfortunately according to their own (unrecognized) tradition.

Another American and world-wide church which refuses W.C.C. membership and maintains a general policy of non-cooperation is the Lutheran Church of the Missouri Synod, with its allied Lutheran churches; this movement represents perhaps two million members (against the Southern Baptists' eight million or so). Here the divisions are not so much Biblical as confessional. The Lutheran churches have always tended to be wedded to their strict interpretation of Christian doctrine according to the confessional statements of the Reformation and later, and the Missouri Lutherans are the strictest of all and feel that Christian co-operation is not possible without absolute doctrinal verbal agreement.

Then again the Pentecostalist churches have on the whole stayed aloof from the W.C.C., though they like the other bodies described send observers to some of its meetings. The two Pentecostalist swallows mentioned as joining the W.C.C. at New Delhi did not make a summer, though another large Pentecostalist church joined at the Canterbury meeting of the Central Committee in 1969. This was a church in Brazil with more than a million members. When its leader, Manoel De Melo, was asked the reasons for this change of policy his reply was that the World Council needs Pentecostalist membership for its own good.

> I attended the Fourth Assembly of the World Council in Uppsala, and I observed the way they conducted their committee meetings and their services. To me it was very boring. ... I think *they* are 'underdeveloped'. I felt as though I were standing in 'the valley of dry bones' and that what was needed was some 'wind' to blow over them to revive them again. That's the reason we are joining the World Council of Churches: they need some 'pentecostal fire'.[56]

De Melo may well be right in general terms that the World Council needs something to revive it and to renew its fire. As far as Pentecostal membership is concerned the absence of the great majority of the Pentecostalist churches is a serious matter, a weakness second only to the official absence of Rome. Pentecostals do not steer clear of the W.C.C. and of the ecumenical movement in general for rigid doctrinal reasons, as do the Southern Baptists and the Missouri Lutherans. By the very nature of their belief in spiritual experience they are able and willing to be flexible and *un*dogmatic. But by the same token, as the quotation just given shows, they find the work and spirit of the W.C.C. alien and meaningless, worlds apart from their own understanding of Christianity. For this reason the great majority of Pentecostal churches do not so much reject the World Council and all it stands for as simply ignore it – although De Melo did also acknowledge that one place of common ground was joint concern in political and social matters:

What good does it do to convert a million people if at the same time the Devil unconverts ten million through hunger, disease and military dictatorship? These sorts of things one can't overcome by holding wonderful religious services, but by organizing one's forces and joining with others who have similar interests. We must join now with other Protestants and even with Roman Catholics to help each other.[57]

It is reckoned that there are thirty million Pentecostalists in the world. They are strongest in Brazil, where one fifth of the voting population are Pentecostals; in Chile, where the percentage is nearly as great, Pentecostalists are required to become members of the Socialist or Communist parties. They are growing rapidly in the United States, in Europe, in Scandinavia and even in Russia. Perhaps their greatest potential is still in Africa. One American church historian has said that by the year 2000 'there will be more Christians in Africa and Latin America than in the rest of the world combined. And the majority of these Christians will be of the Pentecostal type.'[58] Above all the Pentecostalist churches convert the unprivileged, proletarian working classes in a way which is almost unknown in the 'respectable' Protestant denominations – and even in the R.C.C. – imprisoned as they are in a middle-class captivity. While the majority of the Pentecostalist churches remain indifferent to the W.C.C. and to movements towards church unity the ecumenical cause cannot be said to be truly representative of world-wide Christianity.

Beyond the Pentecostalists there are hundreds of fringe sects in America and the Third World whose non-interest in the ecumenical movement is reflected in their non-membership of the W.C.C. (see above, pp. 151–3). The negatives are descriptive and typical: the main concern of such sects is to 'keep themselves unspotted from the world'. In this context this means in their eyes keeping well clear of the World Council and all its works. Again there are exceptions. The Kimbanguist church in the Congo (which has many Pentecostalist affiliations) joined the W.C.C. in 1969. This happened only after a good deal of negotiation in which doubts were expressed on the World Council side and by some of the more 'respectable' churches in the Congo at the Kimbanguist lack of a written confession of faith – doubts which would be seen by the sect as typically literate and middle class and as irrelevant to their situation. But the Kimbanguists persisted and in the end succeeded. During the negotiations their Congolese leader, Diengiende, explained his motives. They were not, as some had said, financial; his church had always stood on its own feet. They were theological:

We realize that an African church is not really a 'church'. There is only a *universal* church. And because we want to belong more to *all* the churches, both historically and horizontally in time, you might even say belong to the 'catholicity' of the church, we want to belong to the World Council of Churches. If you exclude us because we might spoil the 'doctrinal purity' of your organization, then we regret that very much, but we would still remain your friends.[59]

Once again one ecumenically-minded swallow from among the sects does not make a summer. There are not many sect churches which would have such a vision of the 'catholicity' of the church. But the quotation is another reminder that if the World Council is truly to represent the universality of the church it may have drastically to revise its western and traditional stance.

More positively antagonistic to the W.C.C. and all its works is the organization known as the International Council of Christian Churches which together with the American Council of Churches is the creation of one man, Carl McIntyre, an extreme fundamentalist and the founder of his own Bible Presbyterian Church. McIntyre does everything he can to discredit the World Council and to put as many spokes as possible in the ecumenical wheel. He is particularly active in trying to prevent the formation or handicap the work of national Christian councils. His methods can only be described as those of the smear campaign. To him 'Billy Graham is "modernist" and "apostate", the Revised Standard Version of the Bible is "the work of Satan and his agents" ... and the leaders of the W.C.C. are alleged to be ... at one and the same time "modernist", "Communists" and "Romanizers"! '[60]

Such language is most effective among some of the 'younger churches', where in any case it stands to do most harm, but British observers of the activities of Dr Ian Paisley have good reason to know that it is not difficult to rouse violent anti-ecumenical feelings in the extreme Protestant fringe.

But undoubtedly the greatest danger to the ecumenical movement in general and the W.C.C. in particular is the feeling, which is widespread – and not only among young people – that it is 'running out of steam'. Ecumenical leaders themselves are talking about a 'post-ecumenical age'. Here is how the portents were described by Dr Visser 't Hooft to Uppsala:

> Is the relationship which the churches have in the ecumenical movement more than a pale reflection of the unity they should have? And is the progress towards full unity not so slow that it reveals rather a fear of unity than a great and passionate conviction about the essential oneness of the people of God? And must we therefore not admit that the ecumenical movement has had its time, and that we have now entered into the 'post-ecumenical' age in which Christians will have to make their contribution and render their service to the world through other, less cumbersome, channels?[61]

Like a good debater Dr Visser 't Hooft was putting up the questions in order to be able to answer them to his satisfaction. But they need to be taken seriously.

Certainly the World Council needs to recover some of its early fire in the belly. Certainly it seems to be missing the great prophetic leaders such as William Temple. Certainly it needs to devise ways and means of getting into closer touch with the man-in-the-pew and even with the parson-in-the-pulpit. Certainly it needs to de-westernize and de-centralize. Certainly it has problems of membership and structure. If it fails to produce answers to some or even to any of these questions it may find itself being by-passed as the voice of the ecumenical movement.

But one wonders if the malaise is not deeper than these things, or a combination of them. On the question of de-westernization for instance, the W.C.C. will undoubtedly continue to seek to de-westernize. But there is more to it than putting a respectable number of Asians, Africans and Latin Americans on to committees, and holding conferences in those countries. These things, certainly the latter, have been going on for some time, and there have been many Asian leaders in the W.C.C. But they were westernized Asians and the committees, even if they took place outside Europe or North America, retained western procedures – western and middle-class. The reactions of

the Pentecostalists and the African sects to their involvement with the W.C.C., quoted above, show how much it
has been conditioned by the historical circumstances in
which it was born and has grown to maturity. But those
circumstances have now changed.

The World Council of Churches is the institutional
response of the institutional western churches to their
conscience about their disunity. But the institutional
churches of the west are in a state of drastic decline as
institutions. It looks as if they will not for much longer
be able to support the institution they have created, certainly not at the level to which they have raised it. It
could be that the churches will collapse as institutions
before the work of their ecumenical institution has born
its fruit in unity; it could be that in the struggle for survival they will give the priority to their own self-preserva-
tion. It almost seems that the self-denying ordinance by
which the World Council refused to initiate or take part
in actual unity discussions may prove in the end its
greatest weakness. There simply was not the time to
proceed in matters ecumenical in the way that the
churches did, keeping the W.C.C. apart from negotiation
and confining its task to aid and consultation between
the divided churches. It could be that much of this work
of mutual support and consultation which the W.C.C. has
done – and for the most part done very well – was work
which should not have been given immediate priority.

Certainly such work would remain to be dealt with by
a World Council of Churches acting for regional and
national churches *after* they had reached unity at that
level. Clearly some sort of council for united autonomous
churches in communion with each other will be a feature
of united Christendom. Consultation and mutual aid at
a world level will continue to be necessary. A world
council of united churches might also have a function in
preventing future schisms or ecclesiastical 'drop-outs'
through the work of theological explanation and com-

munication. How such a world council might develop must depend on the place and position of Rome in the future. It could be that a future united world church would grow out of Roman Catholic structures decentralized further and faster than can as yet be envisaged in the Roman process of change – and allowing a greater measure of autonomy for national and regional churches than as yet seems possible. Or it could be that the World Council itself could be the matrix of an international federation of churches, giving shape at last to a genuinely ecumenical – or world-embracing – Christian fellowship; there are not a few progressive Roman Catholics who would welcome the idea of a world church *not* geographically centred on Rome. Obviously if the future world church is to include Protestant churches of the left the World Council is the more promising umbrella. But equally obviously it is the Roman Catholic church which in these days of religious decline has the greater survival power.

For the fact is that speculations of this sort are based on the assumption that the World Council is going to continue as an effective ecumenical force in the world – and that is an assumption which can no longer be made. The centre of religious gravity in the non-Roman Catholic Christian world may be moving away from the traditional white Euramerican Protestant churches faster than is at present realized. If it is, the effective future of the World Council of Churches may be at risk. Unless the World Council can reform itself, streamline itself and move significantly in the direction of a Christianity that is non-white and non-middle-class it may not survive to be the *World* Council which so far it has only been in an embryonic form.

CHAPTER SEVEN

Union Negotiations

The final and terrible difficulty is that churches cannot
unite, unless they are willing to die.

BISHOP STEPHEN NEILL *after the inauguration of the
Church of South India*

THE CHURCH OF SOUTH INDIA

THE Church of South India (C.S.I.) was inaugurated,
after nearly thirty years of negotiation, in 1947. Its com-
ponent churches were the South India United Church
(itself a union of Presbyterian and Congregationalist),
the Methodist Church of South India and the South
India dioceses of the Anglican Church of India, Burma
and Ceylon. For the first time since the sixteenth century
the great divide between episcopal and non-episcopal
churches springing from the Reformation had been
bridged. The importance of the C.S.I. union was not so
much the method by which this was done – for the
method has not in fact been followed by subsequent
union schemes – as the psychological effect of the fact
that it had been done at all. The background and history
of the negotiations leading to the service in Madras on
15 August 1947 have been superbly described by Bengt
Sundkler;[1] during the course of the long-drawn-out
struggle so many issues were raised which recur time and
time again on the road to unity, especially when Anglicans
are involved, that it is worth giving the outlines of the
story in some detail.

The spring which both set in motion the quest for
unity and kept it going over the years was the recognition
of the futility of divisions in the church when it is in a
missionary situation. The first proposals for union came

from South India Anglicans meeting in 1919 at Tran-quebar. They drew up the document which became known as the Tranquebar Manifesto. It contains the classic statement of the folly of a divided missionary church.

We believe that the challenge of the present hour in the period of reconstruction after the war, in the gathering to-gether of the nations, and the present critical situation in India itself, call us to mourn our past divisions and turn to our Lord Jesus Christ to seek in him the unity of the body expressed in one visible Church. *We face together the titanic task of the winning of India for Christ – one fifth of the human race. Yet, confronted by such an overwhelming responsibility, we find ourselves rendered weak and relatively impotent by our un-happy divisions – divisions for which we were not responsible, and which have been, as it were, imposed upon us from with-out; divisions which we did not create, and which we do not desire to perpetuate.*[2]

The writers of this bombshell were, it will be noted, Indians, and the drafter was, in fact, Bishop Azariah. But the sentiments could be shared by non-Indians and non-Anglicans. At about the same time G. S. Phillips, a Con-gregationalist missionary, wrote

I have lived in a station where the Christian Church was represented by a feeble handful, despised by the great mass of surrounding Hindus in a sacred city of Saivism, and that feeble handful broken into three portions, Lutheran, Anglican and South India United Church, over the communion question. You can scarcely imagine how insane seem our ecclesiastical divisions in those circumstances.[3]

And the divisions were due, as the Indians recognized, 'to the accident of having been baptized in one of these Sec-tarian Churches'.[4] This was the story of one South Indian layman:

My father was a convert to Christianity and he is still a Lutheran. My mother was a convert too, but she was a Congre-

gationalist and then became a Lutheran.... I was sent to a
Puritan College, where I came under the influence of Calvinistic Puritanism ... while as a university student I had great
partiality for a Methodist church service. ... My wife belonged
to the Anglican Communion. Her parents and some of her
relatives are Anglo-Catholics; a few of her relatives are Roman
Catholics.[5]

It was, therefore, Indians who provided the impetus for
the negotiations and over and over again through the
years it was Indians who insisted on their continuing when
the westerners were ready to give up hope. Of one crucial
moment in 1923 Bishop Palmer wrote, 'we really *dare not*
suspend negotiations, because the Indian demand for
union is so insistent. If we broke off the sessions of our
Joint Committees, the Indians themselves would pursue
the matter and would, I believe, settle it one way or another.'[6] Similarly when the western theologians on the
Joint Committee felt themselves on the rocks in 1931 they
were driven forward by the threat of one of their Indian
colleagues: 'The Christians of India might have to secede
if the foreigners place many insurmountable obstacles before them.'[7] It must also be remembered that this was a
time of mounting Indian nationalism, to which of course
Indian Christians were not immune. From the first, and
throughout the negotiations, the Indians had a vision of
a church which was not only united, but also Indian and
so independent. Divisions were of the west; unity in the
church was a natural bedfellow to nationalism in the
state, though Indian Christians may have been too polite
often to say so to their western brothers. It is no coincidence that the same country was first in the field both in
the struggle for unity and in that for independence. Nor
must nationalistic feelings be discounted among the motives in other union schemes.

Not that the 'foreigners' were so hopelessly drag-
ging their feet, for all the outburst of one disgusted
Indian committee member – 'Is the union to be wrecked

for a dozen missionaries?' It has been said that ecumenical leaders are converted individually to the cause and certainly one after another of the South Indian missionaries became advocates of the union after the realities of the Indian situation had loosened up their western theological concepts. A. M. Hollis, for instance, the first moderator of the C.S.I., came to South India as a missionary of the S.P.G. and was in the Anglo-Catholic tradition; but his contact on the one hand with the Protestantism of Tinnevelly and on the other with Hinduism showed him 'what idolatry really is; ritual without conversion is the devil'.[8] So when the crunch came in 1943 he was able to say to his diocese in Madras, 'Loyalty to our past can be disloyalty to God's will now.'[9]

But the missionaries' employers, the home boards of the various missionary societies, were not so easily converted. Sundkler notes that 'it is characteristic of the difference in temper between South India and Britain that the Board Secretaries and advisers, with the notable exception of the Church Missionary Society, were as a rule reticent'.[10] Moreover the societies were representative of the churches and dependent on them for money. The arena of the debate was thus greatly enlarged and became no less than the British churches themselves, where the various missions had their headquarters, with the addition of some interest from Germany and Switzerland – for the Basel Mission had a stake in the South India United Church. Because the issues being debated in South India were so important in terms of western theology, and because the roots of the problems ran so far back into European church history, they raised great interest, and at times inordinate passion. Moreover two of the initiators of the scheme, the Anglican Palmer and the Congregationalist Bartlet, returned to posts in England before the negotiations were half-way through, and they and other well-known British theologians became the theological advisers of the Europeans in the South India front line. So much was this situation taken for granted that one of the staunchest missionary negotiators, J. J. Banninga, wrote to Bishop Palmer in 1938: 'The battle should be fought in Europe rather than here.'[11]

But still in the end it was the South Indian Christians who had to take the decisive step, knowing full well that if they waited for ever they would not be able to satisfy everyone in the west. 'Some obscure persons in South India,' wrote Palmer to *The Times* in 1933, 'are willing to make the first attempt to end that division [that is 'between Catholic and Protestant']. They are like men asking leave to go over the top. They know that they may die in the attempt, and that their attempt will fail if they are not followed.'[12]

At the beginning of the twentieth century the Christians in South India were divided between Roman Catholics, the various ancient eastern churches which have already been described (pp. 103–6), Baptists, Lutherans, Methodists, Anglicans and members of the South India United Church, plus a number of smaller missions. In South India Christians in fact formed a larger proportion of the community than in the rest of the continent. But more important than this as the background for a reunion movement, the South Indians shared a common 'Dravidian' culture of race and language. Sociologically therefore a unity movement for South India made sense. Christian missionaries from the uniting churches had for some time been operating on a 'comity' basis, that is they concentrated their work in different areas, and tried not to poach each other's members. This had worked reasonably well, but inevitably there was some overlap and the increasing mobility of the population was all the time destroying the effectiveness of comity arrangements. As early as 1912, at a local follow-up conference to Edinburgh, Bishop Whitehead of Madras suggested that comity was not enough: what was necessary was unity.

Came the war and the next milestone was the Tran-quebar conference of Indians from the Church of India, Burma and Ceylon and the South India United Church. These were the two largest churches in the area and the Manifesto led to the first Joint Committee in 1920. The S.I.U.C. was itself a recent (1901) union of Presbyterians and Congregationalists and one of the recurring problems was that its British missionaries and its own congregations tended to be steeped more in their own old traditions than in the unity of the new church; over the years new generations of Presbyterian and Congregationalist missionaries had to be assimilated into the discussion. There were also some American Congregationalists and it was found that they were invariably less antagonistic to Anglicanism in general and episcopacy in particular than their British brethren. The S.I.U.C. included a Basel Mission area with its roots in Germany, while in 1923 the Methodists joined the negotiations. The C.S.I. bag was, therefore, pretty mixed, especially when one remembers that the Anglican missionary backing was divided between the 'high-church' Society for the Propagation of the Gospel and the 'low-church' Church Missionary Society.

The Tranquebar Manifesto had suggested a union based on the Lambeth Quadrilateral, including the historic episcopate, but accepting 'the spiritual equality of all members' of the uniting churches and incorporating Congregational and Presbyterian elements as well as the episcopal. It protested that 'we aim not at compromise for the sake of peace, but at comprehension for the sake of truth'; it announced that 'full liberty would be claimed for individuals on the extreme wing of each body to maintain their present views and practices'.[12] It was a tall order – and one which no other church had managed to fulfil. The man who more than anyone else was the architect of the scheme which fulfilled it was E. J. Palmer, the Bishop of Bombay. He was of the Anglo-Catholic school and 'his was without any question the greatest theological mind applied to the South India problem'.[13] He agreed that there was no future in compromise: 'no, not concessions, but convictions on all sides,' he was continually telling his colleagues on the Joint Committee. But his principle was what he felt to be the true principle of the ordering of the Catholic Church: 'The church is built on a definite rule, but there are exceptions to the rule; both the rule and the exceptions are necessary.'[14] It was on this liberal, charitable, pragmatic principle – known to the ancient church as the doctrine of 'economy' (see p. 84) – that the South India solution was built.

It was first of all agreed that the Church of South India would be an episcopal church, in the tradition of the historic episcopate. It was also agreed that the major problem was how to accomplish this without unchurching the non-Anglicans and to all intents and purposes absorbing them into the Anglican church. This was where all former schemes had run aground. The first idea, produced by the Congregationalist Professor V. Bartlet, another great scholar, was for a service of mutual commissioning of ministers for work in the united church, carried out by both bishops and presbyters of the old churches. But Palmer would have none of this: 'The service was camouflage ... a pestilent muddle.'[15] It was felt that it would not be right for the different sides to approach the same service with different intentions and understanding. For some Anglicans it would be the episcopal ordination of those who had never been ordained before; for free churchmen it would be a widening of the orders they held already. This is a difficulty which has continually bedevilled services of this kind down to the Anglican-Methodist service of reconciliation which was rejected in 1969.

Palmer produced another solution, pushed on by his knowledge of the impatience of the Indians. He proposed

that the united church should be inaugurated by the consecration of bishops and that its government and all
future ordinations should be episcopal. (It was a considerable help that it was widely agreed that episcopacy
was a form of government which would best suit the
Indian mind and temperament.) But during an interim
period all the ministers of the uniting churches should
be accepted as ministers of the united church, without
any form of commissioning or ordination, as long as they
accepted the constitution and basis of the united church
with its episcopal structure. This was putting the principle of economy into practice – the rule, episcopal
government and ordination; the exception, the interim
period. (At first Palmer suggested fifty years, but this was
later modified to thirty.) The interim period was what
Palmer described as 'our boldest step'; but it had the
advantage that 'it recognized that union of living
churches had to be a living process; the division of centuries could not be overcome by a single act, however
dramatic; there had to be an interim period ... of growing together'.[16]

Not everyone on the Anglican side liked Palmer's solution, and in order to make it more acceptable another
idea was evolved, which was typical of the South India
scheme. This was 'the pledge'. By it the various parties
promised that in the interim period nothing would be
done which would offend the conscience of any congregation or minister. The most significant thing about this
was the mutual trust which it implied. In practice its importance was that, for instance, no ex-Anglican parish
which had scruples about it would have a non-episcopally
ordained minister thrust upon it, nor would an ex-Con-
gregationalist area be subjected to high-church Anglican
ministrations. (Later in fact there was some trouble
about interpreting the pledge: Anglicans tended to
think that their parishes should never normally have a
non-episcopal minister, whereas the others held that a

general mix-up was essential to the process of growing
together.)

Once this essential solution to the problem had been
accepted the basis and constitution of the united church
were worked out and produced in the scheme of 1929.
This was to be revised in 1931, 1932, 1933, 1934, 1939 and
finally in 1942. There is no need to go in detail into these
revisions, but since a number of points came up which
tend to recur in unity negotiations, especially those
where the episcopal–non-episcopal bridge has to be
crossed, these points and their importance will be described. Basically what was happening was that the non-
Anglicans, having conceded at the outset the principle of
episcopacy, were trying to cover their tracks and insert
what they felt to be essential safeguards to their reformed
position. In particular this was seen in a tug-of-war between Bartlet and Palmer, now both back in England.
They were each patristic scholars and appealed to the
early and undivided church; but Bartlet looked to the
church of the second century, where he felt episcopacy
had not developed so far as in Palmer's model, which was
taken from the fourth century. Palmer, on the other
hand, believed that all the churches including the Anglican must die, and that what would be reborn would be
not a new church but a renewal of 'the one Great
Church' in India. He felt that the various 'concessions'
made to the non-Anglicans were moves away from his
ideal vision of this church.

The first issue was the episcopate and the understanding of it. Here the basic idea was the acceptance of the
historic episcopate in a constitutional form and with no
implied or required theory about its nature. This was in
fact no more than the Anglican position, since the differing schools in the Anglican church take opposing views
about the nature and importance of episcopacy; there is
no official view and it is understood that none is required

of Anglicans as long as they accept the practice of episcopacy. It is important that this same latitude of opinion is made clear to non-Anglicans embarking on union negotiations and this has been the custom ever since the South India scheme.

Apart from the finer points of the arguments whether bishops are the *esse*, the *bene esse* or the *plene esse* of the church (that is whether they are essential to the very being of the church – the Anglo-Catholic view; or whether they are a good form of church government, but not essential – the low-church view; or whether they are the ideal and fullest form of government for the 'perfection' of the church – the mediating view) see pp. 169–71) Anglicans have felt that there are two practical sides to episcopal government. In the first place the single bishop in his diocese is the symbol and personification of the unity of the church; as a member of the 'College' of bishops of the universal church he represents the rest of the church to his diocese, and he also represents his diocese to the rest of the church. This view of the episcopate was safeguarded in South India by the acceptance of the idea of episcopacy. Secondly, because of their succession from the earliest times bishops represent the continuity of Christian doctrine and are in a sense its guardians. For this reason Anglicans have tended to feel that in matters of faith and morals the bishops acting together should have final powers of veto and approval. This became an issue during the 1930s. The non-Anglicans, with their fears of 'prelacy' and autocracy, were determined that the episcopacy established should be not only 'constitutional' but 'democratic'. On this the issue between Bartlet's second-century and Palmer's fourth-century patterns was most clear-cut. In the end the 1929 proposals on the synod were revised in 1932 so that the relationships between the whole synod and the house of bishops were a careful system of checks and balances and the power of initiation of important questions was effectively removed from the bishops. Whatever the details this is an issue which is likely to play an important part in ecumenical discussions, though it should be noted that with the acceptance by the Church of England of synodical government (that is church government in which the laity have a share) some of the sting of the controversy may be drawn.

Another issue which was raised with the introduction of episcopacy was the part to be played by presbyters in the united church in functions which in an Anglican church are reserved to a bishop but in reformed churches are performed by presbyters – that is consecration of bishops, ordination and confirmation. Here again the non-Anglicans pressed strongly for presbyters to share the functions with bishops – one aspect of the idea of 'bishops-in-presbytery'. Once again there was very nearly dead-lock, until it was pointed out that in any case the proper theology is that 'the true consecrator is God'.

These were the main questions which were – and re-peatedly are – raised by the introduction of episcopacy. Even more crucial, perhaps, was the question of what was to be made – or said – of non-episcopal orders and minis-tries. It will be remembered that in 1920 the Anglican Lambeth Conference had acknowledged the 'spiritual reality' of non-episcopal ministries and that the bishops had expressed themselves ready in the case of a satisfactory union scheme to accept from other ministries 'a form of commission or recognition' (see above, pp. 210–12). South India proceeded along the same lines, though it rejected the idea of 'supplemental ordination'. The extreme wing of the S.I.U.C. wanted a formula accepting the 'spiritual equality and validity' of the non-episcopal ministries. The moderates wisely rejected the idea of validity as a form of definition, partly because 'equal validity' would be a red rag to Anglo-Catholics, and partly because it accepted a definition of the problem in somewhat legalistic terms. On the other hand it was eventually felt that an acceptance of the 'spiritual efficacy' of non-episcopal ministries, which was satisfactory to Anglicans, was too neutral and colourless. In the end the following formula was evolved:

The uniting churches recognize that Christ has bestowed his grace with undistinguishing regard on all their ministries and has used them greatly to his glory. All are therefore real ministries of the Word and Sacraments in Christ's Church.[17]

But this was not the end of the problem. It was not only a matter of theoretical formulas but of practical actions. The reformed churchmen felt that the Anglicans should demonstrate their acceptance of the efficacy of non-episcopal sacraments by accepting the sacraments themselves in acts of intercommunion. This is a perennial problem: it is difficult for the free-church-man to believe that an Anglican really accepts his ministry in good faith if he refuses to join him at the altar. Many Anglicans would accept this and are ready to practise intercommunion as a sign of the unity in Christ which already exists, even between divided churches. On the other hand many others, and not Anglo-Catholics only, have felt that intercommunion can be practised only between churches which are in communion and that to attend each other's sacraments before union or communion has been established is at best woolly-mindedness, and at worst to 'act a lie' and demean the sacraments. One party, in fact, holds that intercommunion is the path to union; the other says that it can come only as the fruit of union.

The problem was raised by the non-Anglicans early in the negotiations: 'The refusal of the Anglican Church to have intercommunion is a real offence to me,' said one missionary. 'What then is the scheme but an absorption into that church? If we can't recognize each other even so much, is there much use in trying for union, while the necessary presuppositions are missing?'[18] Yet in so far as the Anglican church had a policy, it was against intercommunion. It therefore took some time and not a little courage for the Anglican leaders to move, not to general intercommunion, but to allowing intercommunion on obviously appropriate occasions. This they did, partly on Palmer's principle of Rule and Exception, and partly because they felt that the time had now come when the three churches were definitely pledged to move forward to union. In England this created a furore among the Anglo-Catholics and Lang, the Archbishop of Canterbury, expressed concern. But in South India the effect of the decision was to convince many who had felt antagonistic to the Anglicans that they were now acting in good faith: 'We felt that the ice had been broken, and that a beginning had been made.'[19] The idea that there comes a stage in unity negotiations when the churches are sufficiently committed to each other to allow some intercommunion as part of the move to union has since been accepted as a regular milestone on many roads to union.

'What then is this scheme but an absorption into that [that is the Anglican] Church?' This was undoubtedly a fear which was at the back of many minds, and it was coupled with the feeling that the Anglicans were approaching the reunion negotiations, and their non-Anglican colleagues in them, with that sense of 'superiority' which has been such a damnable heritage from four centuries of British church history. Three more things helped to persuade those who felt themselves, even in India, to be non-conformists that the Anglicans were 'on the level' about the negotiations. In the first place in 1927 the Anglican Church in India ceased to be 'the Church of England in India'; it became a self-governing province of the Anglican Communion and ceased to be the established church in India. Secondly it came to be seen that those dioceses which joined the C.S.I. would no longer be Anglicans; there was no question of absorption, the new church would not be a part of the Anglican Communion. Third, and perhaps most significant, it became evident early on in the negotiations that the Anglicans were not going to insist on the acceptance of the Church of England Prayer Book as the norm for the worship of the future church. In those days Anglicans were not so restive about the Prayer Book as many of them have since become; in fact it would not be unfair to say that it was something of a sacred cow. This willingness to give it up was, therefore, for non-Anglicans, with their memories of church history, an unexpected sign of grace.

But it was not only the Anglicans who had to sacrifice a sacred cow. In the 1930s a new generation of Congregationalist missionaries arrived on the scene, determined to do battle to preserve what they took to be the vital element of Congregationalism, the right of the layman to celebrate the Holy Communion. This point has always been important for the more convinced Protestants engaged in the search for unity: it came up repeatedly, for instance, in almost a century of negotiations for Methodist unity in England. 'The universal priesthood of all true believers' was one of the great battle cries of the Reformation, and of the struggle to free the church from clerical domination. As a practical issue it got narrowed down to the idea that any Christian could approach God without the intervention of a priest – and hence to the idea that the celebration of the Holy Communion was not necessarily a priestly function, but was something which was the 'inalienable right' of any Christian believer. Here was another crisis which nearly landed the scheme on the rocks. In the end, however, it was agreed that while the ministry of each and every Christian is important and all share in the total priesthood of the church, this does not mean that within the church there are not specialized functions for certain qualified people.

All share in the heavenly high priesthood of the risen and ascended Christ, from which alone the Church derives its character as a royal priesthood. No individual and no order in the Church can claim exclusive possession of this heavenly priesthood.... God is the God of order; it has been his good pleasure to use the visible church and its regularly constituted ministries as the normal means of the operation of his Spirit.[20]

This definition did not deny the old war cry, as might have happened in more controversial days; instead it accepted its positive value and put it in a new context which was both more rational and more theologically sound. This controversy is therefore an example of how the process of seeking unity has the effect of producing a fuller and more complete theological understanding in place of controversy and half-truths. The South India solution to this problem also showed a proper sense of the place of the laity, or whole people of God, many years before this became a key concept in ecumenical thinking.

The controversy over lay celebration showed all too clearly one of the dangers of the long-drawn-out process of negotiation; the new missionaries who had fought so hard for their beliefs had not been through the earlier process of growing together on the Joint Committee. Another danger was that during the long period theological fashions changed, so that old battles had to be refought on new fronts. At the beginning of the plans it had been agreed that it was order, the question of the ministry, which was going to be vital to success or failure – rather than faith. Palmer in any case had felt that 'there is no room for confessional churches in the idea of the Great Church'.[21] In his vision of a revivified early church the doctrinal positions of the Reformation were irrelevant. The basic belief of the united church was therefore defined rather vaguely as 'the Faith which the Church has ever held in Jesus Christ', and the ancient creeds were described as 'witnessing to and safeguarding the faith and containing a sufficient statement thereof for a basis of union'.[22] Such a vague and un-spelt-out formula also suited the liberals at this time of liberal theology and general sitting-loose to credal subscription. But it did not suit the continentals reared in the Reformation tradition. And by the thirties the theological pendulum was swinging the other way and a new Biblical orthodoxy was the order of the day.

Once again, therefore, the ground had to be re-covered. The result of the Basel missionary Streckeisen's efforts was not a full continental confession, but was at least a more elaborate doctrinal basis than the former scheme had been. But the point is relevant to all unity negotiations. Is it enough simply to accept the creeds, which are themselves in any case doctrinal formulations of a certain age of church history, and are not acceptable *in toto* to many sincere Christians? Or should the united church take the bull by the horns and attempt some doctrinal formulation suitable for its time and its place? In which case the danger will be that that formulation may itself soon become dated. Or is it best to attempt some agreement on the ultimate authority for belief, such as is represented in the whole question of the relationship between scripture and tradition? Many believe that this is the least that can in all honesty be done. Since the time of South India different schemes have suggested differing answers to these questions. South India at least made the provision, in line with its general policy, that it could further formulate its position in the future, after unity.

These were the main questions which occupied the time between the original scheme in 1929 and the final one in 1942. Each new draft which came out from the Joint Committee had to be referred in detail to the separate uniting churches according to their own varying machinery for discussion; this could mean that the discussion proceeded at differing rates and one church could send new suggestions back to the Joint Committee before another had even considered the original proposals. Churches, like everyone else, have to work through committees and constitutional procedures and these committees only meet every so often. Unity negotiations are bound to be a slow business. South India was further slowed down – not to say bedevilled – by the constant reference to the 'home base' in particular and in general to the world-wide church, which was watching the state of play very closely.

For instance in 1943 the Metropolitan of India was forced by Anglo-Catholic opposition in his own province, which had to make the final decision, to ask all the other provinces of the Anglican Communion whether, if the scheme went ahead, they would '(a) break off communion with the Church of India, Burma and Ceylon and/or (b) refuse to be in communion with the C.S.I.'.[23] This caused a furore in England. One deputation to Archbishop Temple, headed by Lord Quickswood and including T. S. Eliot, described the decision as 'the greatest crisis in the Church of England since the Reformation'. The Superiors of the Anglican monastic orders addressed an Open Letter to the Archbishop saying that if it accepted the plan the Indian church would be 'condoning an Act of Schism' and threatening the secession of a large number of Anglo-Catholics.[24] Neither Temple nor the Church of England were to be bullied into cutting off relations with the Church of India. But the feeling in England and the rest of the Anglican church that the C.S.I. had not achieved a perfect union by allowing non-episcopally ordained clergy to minister in the united church was sufficiently strong for full communion to be withheld from the C.S.I.

The theological debate continued to rage and turned at first mainly on the place of episcopacy in the Church. Faced with the fact of the Church of South India the Anglo-Catholics adopted their most rigid position: only a church with complete episcopal government in the apostolic succession and universal episcopal consecration and ordination can be a true church with valid sacraments and guaranteed salvation.[25] By this test the Church of South India failed. But a reaction set in against this extreme position and it could not be maintained. Slowly the position of the Church of England and of the rest of the Anglican Communion has modified and a greater measure of intercommunion has been allowed.

It was not only that theological opinion was swinging in England and elsewhere. The Church of South India was proving itself. When Anglo-Catholic visitors went to South India they found that the bishops there were nearer to their idea of true 'fathers in God' than their opposite numbers in England; relieved of the trappings of prelacy – however unwanted – and of the crippling administrative burdens of huge dioceses and endless committees, they were able to fulfil their functions as chief teachers and chief shepherds in unmistakeable ways whether they were 'ex-Anglican', 'ex-Methodist' or 'ex-United Church'. Once again practice was confounding theory. This church was in many ways more truly episcopal than the Church of England.

After its inauguration the C.S.I. also set an example to the Christian world in the field of worship. It had been agreed that it would draw up its own liturgies and this it proceeded to do. But instead of producing yet another version of the Anglican Prayer Book, which would have been the easiest course, the C.S.I. went back to first principles and produced something which was, quite literally, much more radical. The communion service which emerged was quickly recognized as being a breakthrough in combining the best of the old traditions with a freshness and a genuinely South Indian character which made it highly suitable as a vehicle for contemporary worship. One distinguished Roman Catholic scholar declared that it would be acceptable as a Catholic text for the mass and the South Indian example has been followed in liturgical revision in many churches, not least in the Church of England, which has at last seen that the old Prayer Book has many theological faults and weaknesses. Above all, of course, the use of the new services has had a unifying effect in the congregations of the Church of South India itself.

Thirdly between 1961 and 1963 a commission of the C.S.I. set about a re-appraisal of the church's condition and of its task and produced a report which has been widely hailed as one of the most realistic pieces of thinking that any church has produced about itself in recent years.[26]

These are just three examples of the way in which since its inauguration the C.S.I. has shown that it has found new life and new vitality in its mission in India – the purpose which the negotiators had in mind during all the years which led up to the act of union. Before the inauguration a committee in the Church of England appointed by William Temple to report on the union scheme had criticized it as being too western and not sufficiently radical.

The Scheme as it now stands suggests too much an attempt to reconcile divergent western traditions, instead of asking rather what form of faith and of Catholic order an indigenously Indian Church ought to be developing.... Instead of taking for granted the need to combine the 'contributions' of the Episcopalian, Presbyterian and Congregationalist traditions, its authors might in more radical fashion have sought to go behind and beneath all these to the form of the Church as it appears in the Bible and in the early centuries.[27]

These criticisms were at the time justified and the reasons for the weaknesses seen in the scheme can readily be understood in view of its history. But since its inauguration the C.S.I. has done a great deal to meet and rectify these points. The first Moderator of the Church of South India, Bishop Michael Hollis, has claimed that the South India method is the right one: do not plan everything for the new church in advance of union; achieve union and then in a period of growing together leave the church free to find renewal and true unity.

The essential aim of any viable plan must be to make it possible for life in unity to begin, leaving many decisions to be taken by the united church. The act of obedience involved in this submitting to God's will, as we experienced in South India, releases fuller resources of understanding for those who enter into union without any deliberate abandonment of what they hold to be true but with deep awareness that everything will look very different when unity has been brought about.[28]

This seems like a wise and thoughtful policy. Yet in South India the policy of leaving the unification of the ministry as one of the matters on the agenda of the 'new' church, rather than as something tackled before the inauguration, has led to complications. Even now the Church of England and other Anglican churches have arrived at only limited intercommunion with the C.S.I.; for instance only episcopally ordained presbyters of the C.S.I. may celebrate the Holy Communion in C. of E. churches when in England and then only if they agree to do so in Anglican churches only.[29] This sort of thing may seem trivial or pettifogging, but it is the way that church rules work, and this being the case other schemes since South India have attempted to solve the problem of full communion with the Anglican church from the outset of the union.

Thus South India is important not only for its positive achievement which has been repeated in the experience of many other churches seeking unity, but also negatively because where – or if – it failed other schemes have sought to avoid its mistakes. In another way South India was important. It showed what was involved, and what people must be ready for, in the search for unity. This has been best described in a moving passage by Bishop Stephen Neill. Technically he is describing all union negotiations but in fact he must be drawing heavily on his own experience as one of those involved in the final years before the South India inauguration in 1947.

1. The making of divisions in the Church is easy; the repairing of them is far more difficult.

2. The work of planning church union cannot be hurried; even when a division is comparatively recent and does not touch fundamental issues, a whole generation may elapse before the difficulties can be honestly and satisfactorily dealt with.

3. Union must always involve some loss; but union can never come if those who are seeking it are asking themselves all the time 'How much do we stand to lose as the price of union with these people?' instead of asking 'How much shall we gain through accepting their treasures as our own?'

4. The difficulties that have to be faced are strangely varied; but, where the will to unity has been strong and honest, there is hardly any difficulty that has not yielded to treatment.

5. It may be worthwhile to wait many years in order to reconcile a conscientious minority which is unable to accept a plan of union; but such a minority cannot claim for ever the right to frustrate the will of the majority. The most agonizing problem in the search for unity is the decision as to the circumstance, if any, in which unity can be rightly purchased at the price of fresh divisions.

6. Almost every united church will suffer, after union, the severe testing of a long period of unification. This cannot be avoided, however careful the preparation for union may have been; but, faced with patience and humility, it can be a period of great value, provided that every possible step is taken to ensure that nothing is lost of the heritage of any of the uniting churches.

7. In spite of the difficulties and frustrations that unity may involve, in the period under review no united church has been dissolved, and the vast majority of those who have entered into union would affirm that it is unthinkable that they should ever go back to their previous state of division.

8. The final and terrible difficulty is that churches cannot unite unless they are willing to die. In a truly united Church there would be no more Anglicans or Lutherans or Presbyterians or Methodists. But the very disappearance from the world of those great and honoured names is the very thing that many loyal churchmen are not prepared to face. Much has already been achieved. But until church union clearly

takes shape as a better resurrection on the other side of death, the impulse towards it is likely to be weak and half-hearted; and such weak impulses are not strong enough to overcome the tremendous difficulties in the way.

9. The attitude of the churches therefore should be neither one of timid resignation, as though nothing could be done, nor of adolescent optimism as though the problem was already nearly solved. What is needed is sober realism, that takes account of all obstacles, but also recognizes that to faith and obedience, in response to the clearly defined will of God, the word 'impossible' does not exist.[30]

Those words were written soon after the inauguration of the Church of South India. Nothing that has happened since has shown them to be wrong.

CURRENT NEGOTIATIONS

The inauguration of the Church of South India was in 1947. Since then there have been constant unity negotiations in every part of the world. There has been a number of acts of union, but no major unions except, in 1970, that of the Church of North India. This is undoubtedly disappointing – not to say disillusioning. At one time after South India it seemed as if the tempo was really increasing, but hopes of a number of unions inspired by the example of South India have proved unfounded. The lesson of South India, that unity takes a long time, is still true. On the other hand there are some encouraging signs. In the first place negotiations between episcopal and non-episcopal churches are now, if not the rule, certainly no longer the exception; in fact this has been one of the reasons that progress has been slow; it has seemed worthwhile in a number of cases to slow down discussions in order to make them more inclusive. Secondly a number of negotiations are aiming at unity in the early seventies; quite soon therefore the picture, which has seemed largely static for over twenty years, may change rapidly. Thirdly there has hardly been a single case, in literally hundreds of schemes, where discussions have totally broken down; there have been delays and set-backs, but virtually no break-downs.

The remainder of this chapter will describe current unity negotiations under three headings: first an analysis of the issues which have to be faced in almost any major unity scheme; second some examples of the various types of negotiation according to the churches involved; and third a survey by areas of the current scene. All the time it must be remembered that unity negotiations do not take place in a vacuum. There is a growing corpus of knowledge and experience which can be made available to those embarking on the quest for unity. On a personal level, for instance, a Church of England missionary, the Reverend T. S. Garrett, was transferred from South India to Nigeria when the churches of that country started serious unity discussions in the well-founded belief that his experience in the united church would be of great value in the negotiations – the danger, of course, being that this would help to impose a western/South India pattern on a Nigerian situation. By 1967 the amount of common experience which could be shared made it worthwhile for the World Council to mount a Consultation on Church Union Negotiations at which twenty-seven different union conversations from twenty-six countries were represented. This consultation was felt to be very valuable; it was repeated at Limuru in April 1970.

Less specific but no less influential has been the general turn-over and advance of ecumenical thought in the life of the W.C.C. The New Delhi formulation of unity 'all in each place' (see above, p. 250) was felt to be a spur to actual union negotiations and has been quoted as the aim of several of them. Similarly the Faith and Order discovery at about the time of the Montreal Conference of 1963 – that it is better to discuss doctrinal matters *ab initio* (that is from a common search for a contemporary formulation) than on a comparative basis – has had its influence. For instance the negotiators in Australia working on these lines felt it would be possible to give priority to a discussion of the faith to which the church would bear witness, rather than, as has sometimes undoubtedly happened, by-passing questions of faith and concentrating on those of order. 'It cannot be denied,' writes one of the leaders of these discussions, 'that we shared in the new impetus and new hope which came into Faith and Order discussions between Lund and Montreal.'[31] Other unity discussions have been influenced in the same way and it must be remembered that those who are involved in the life of the W.C.C. are also likely to be to the fore in actual down-to-earth unity negotiations.

Discussions at the level of the national Council of Churches have also had an influence. Sometimes, for instance, the initiative for starting unity negotiations has come from a call for action at a Council of Churches conference: in 1964 a Faith and Order conference in northeast India led to a church union scheme being sponsored by the Christian Council, and there are other examples, though it has to be said that such schemes do not seem to have the same drive as those which are more firmly rooted in the initiative of individual churches. Again, the Faith and Order Conference of the British Council of Churches at Nottingham in 1964 produced an idea which has since had important repercussions on unity negotiations throughout the world. This was the agreement of the churches to covenant 'to work and pray for the inauguration of union by a date agreed amongst them'. This idea of covenanting for union as a definite step of committal to union between churches has been widely adopted and in some cases has been the basis of intercommunion – just as in South India the Anglican participants felt that at a certain stage intercommunion was justified. Thus in Rhodesia the covenant has been felt to be an important

stage in unity negotiations and, once it has been accepted
and affirmed by the various churches, baptized and con-
firmed members of the negotiating churches will be able
to receive communion in any of the churches concerned
'as an immediate and visible sign of our fellowship and
an earnest of full communion to come'.[32] Similar
arrangements have been introduced into the negotiations
in Ceylon and in Ghana, both particularly significant
and therefore important to the negotiating churches because the Anglicans concerned come from the 'high-
church' wing who do not take intercommunion lightly.

Lastly and most recently among the outside influences
which have affected negotiations, there has been the interest of the Roman Catholics. As yet the Roman Catholics are not involved in any specific unity negotiations
and it is even early days for them to send observers to
many discussions. But one example of the influence of
Roman Catholic comments has been important: in the
English Anglican/Methodist scheme the production of
an Ordinal setting up the service for ordaining ministers
in the united church was of vital importance. Roman
Catholic comments were invited, and as a result of them
the first draft of the Ordinal was modified. Subsequently
one Roman Catholic writer suggested that the new Ordinal might be adopted in the Roman Church, since it was
superior to their own rite! It is to be hoped that there
will be more examples of this sort of collaboration with
Roman Catholic theologians in the future, since clearly if
as many points as possible are ironed out in schemes
which do not include Roman Catholics, there will be less
difficulties later when the Roman Church may be participating. (Quite apart from the fact that in any case R.C.
theologians may have useful lessons to teach their non-
Roman brothers!)

RECURRING PROBLEMS

(i) Ministry

In unity schemes certain themes tend to recur and these constitute the main problems with which the negotiators have to deal. Some have already been discussed as they were faced and overcome in South India. Those which are currently on the agendas of the various negotiating churches will now be described. The mixture varies according to the ingredient churches. Where Anglicans are involved there will be much heart-searching about the means of uniting the churches through their ministries; where Lutherans are participants the theological beliefs of the united church are bound to be hammered out; and so on. But an overall pattern does emerge, especially as the majority of countries nowadays have Anglican/non-Anglican schemes, and these are in any case the plans which are most likely to be fruitful for the future.

The question of finding an acceptable ministry in the united church remains a major problem. Here the South India experience has been a determining factor. Because of the anomaly that the united church contained among its ministers some who had not been episcopally ordained, various branches of the Anglican Communion have felt to this day that full communion with the C.S.I. is not possible. This has influenced all the other Anglican churches embarking on discussions with non-episcopal churches. Wanting to maintain after union full communion with the rest of the Anglican Communion they have looked for a solution which would provide a unified ministry which from the inauguration of the united church would be acceptable to Anglican churches – which they have usually interpreted to mean acceptable to the Church of England. This means some form of unification of ministries which can be achieved in several ways: for instance there might be some form of mutual ordination which would amount to the idea of 'supplemental' ordination, or of conditional ordination, that is ordination which starts with the phrase 'if you are not already ordained ...'; but this is psychologically very difficult and would be unacceptable to many Anglicans as implying a slight to their existing orders.

Yet the problem remains: how to achieve some form of 'episcopal ordination' for those not already so ordained without ordaining them afresh and so casting doubts on their previous ministry. The first union scheme to find a solution to this problem was that of Ceylon, or Lanka. Discussions had been in progress since before the war and in 1955 a scheme was drawn up. The essential starting point of this scheme was the recognition that 'since the ministries of all separated communions are by the fact of separation limited, the ministry can recover fulness only by the union of all the parts of the one body'. So the unification of the separated ministries takes place *after* the union of the churches has been declared and in the context of the new union. But, unlike South India, there is no delay between union and unification. The bishops elect of the new united church are consecrated by three bishops and are then commissioned to act in the united church by ministers of the old churches; they then receive into the presbyterate or diaconate of the united church the clergy of their own dioceses.

The rite is not to be understood as re-ordination or 'supplemental ordination'.... The profound centre of intention is openness to what God wills for this ministry. This is indicated in the declaration by the uniting ministers. They declare: 'In the conviction that God wills one Communion and fellowship of all who believe in his Son Jesus Christ as Lord and Saviour, I, believing myself to have been duly and lawfully ordained within the ... [former] ... Church to the Ministry of Word and Sacraments in the Church of God, am humbly prepared to submit myself to God and through the laying on of hands

317

with prayer to receive from him such grace as it may be his will to bestow upon me for my ministry within the Church of Lanka as Presbyter in the Church of God.' It is thus intended that *each* person receives what is necessary, in God's will, for him to minister in the new church (not merely the non-episcopal participants); further it is open to each to believe what he will about what others, as well as he himself, receive. In a real sense this is a new rite without precedent in the history of the Church; but this is so because never before has there been attempted as today unification of churches so diverse in nature, and not merely the absorption of one or more by another. In the South India Church this will take place over thirty years; if one wishes it from the outset, as in these more recent schemes, some such totally new approach is needed. But since precedent cannot be found for it, neither should it be identified with some form of ordination – it is *sui generis* out of a new situation in the life of the church.[33]

Three things must be underlined about this scheme. In the first place it is not based on the idea of joining the churches together to get the best solution by an amalgam of the gifts of each, as has tended to be the approach in some cases. Instead the idea is that the uniting churches go back, as it were, to scratch and ask God to give what he alone knows is needed for the united church. In the second place, as this is worked out in the unification of the ministries, it means that in the unification rite the clergy put themselves into the hands of God and accept what he gives without questioning the details of what exactly this is. By this means the difficulty of how to achieve 'episcopal ordination' without 're-ordination' is overcome. But it means that there is ambiguity in the rite; while it does not say exactly what is happening it will be interpreted in differing ways by different partici-pants. Thus 'high-church' Anglicans will undoubtedly be thinking that 'free-church' ministers are receiving episco-pal ordination (and so effectively being ordained for the first time), while these ministers will be thinking that their former ministries are now being extended for service in the new church. It was this ambiguity which was rejected as a means of uniting ministries at an early stage of the South India negotiations (see above, p. 297) and it is this ambiguity which makes this form of unification of divided ministries unacceptable to some people, and especially to some Anglo-Catholics. They say that to use such a rite as this is to found the new church, if not on a lie, at least on a prevarication, and that it is dishonest and even blasphemous. Others, including those Anglo-Catholics who are willing to accept this means of unification, reply that in any case what God does at any sacrament – and particularly the exact means by which he does whatever he does – is always a mystery in the theological sense that it is beyond man's comprehension and description. Therefore, they say, the rite of unification is only applying in these special circumstances the sort of belief with which people will approach, for instance, the sacrament of Holy Communion. Add to this the fact that this is a unique service for an exceptional circumstance, and any ambiguity there is will certainly be covered by the principle of 'economy', by which it will be recognized that in an imperfect situation, a perfect solution will never be found. What is all-important is the positive result which has been achieved: 'A minister was ordained by Christ in a situation of division, and now his ordination is ratified by and united to the normal organ of ordination in the (united) church.'[34] This sacrament, like all others, must be thought of 'less as the imparting to [the individual] of some quasi-physical object or quality which he did not possess before than as the setting of him in a new relation to the Church ... or the intensification of a relation which has been previously set up'.[35]

The third point which must be noticed about the 'Lanka solution' is that it is basically a formula which appeals to, and was required by, Anglicans. Anglicans form 60 per cent of those Christians who are taking part in the Ceylon scheme, and the Anglican diocese is a markedly high-church one which had always made it clear that it disapproved of the South India scheme and would not be willing to take part in any union which would have the effect of cutting off the united church – and the Anglicans in it – from the Anglican Communion. The 1958 Lambeth Conference gave general approval to the scheme though asking for some modifications and clarifications on points of detail. In 1961 the two Convocations of the Church of England gave the scheme a less easy passage. In each case the upper house (of bishops) approved it but the lower house (of clergy) either voted against it or gave such limited approval as to constitute an adverse vote: the clergy of Canterbury were willing to approve only if it was made clear that 'episcopal ordination is being conferred on those who have not already received it'. By 1963, however, the emendations suggested had been accepted and the Anglo-Catholic opposition was happy to accept the new scheme for Ceylon – though they would not accept a similar proposal when it came to the English Anglican/Methodist vote in 1969.

The Lanka solution became therefore in its main outlines the pattern for other union schemes. North India and Pakistan accepted it, as did Ghana, and during the fifties it was agreed that this should be the basis of Anglican/Methodist negotiation in England. Likewise the early discussions in New Zealand, Canada and the United States have accepted this premise. Still more significant, the Nigerian churches changed horses in mid-stream; they had been working towards a union on the South India pattern and even in 1955 had had a visit from the Moderator of the C.S.I. to commend the scheme to the church in Nigeria. But despite the fact that Anglican missionaries in Nigeria come mainly from the C.M.S. and are therefore low-church rather than high-church, the pressure of Anglican opinion at the end of the fifties swung the Anglicans in Nigeria in favour of a Ceylon-type scheme. Not that Ceylon has been accepted in every detail. World-wide Anglican pressure has been enough to make this the most acceptable solution to most negotiators, but where the Anglicans do not have such a majority as in Ceylon it has not always been possible for the Church of England convocations to call the tune! The actual details or machinery of the unification rites do, therefore, differ. In North India, for instance, where Anglicans form only 20 per cent of the negotiating churches, the Anglican delegates did not feel able to press through all the amendments suggested from Canterbury. Nevertheless the basic fact remains: the unification of the participating churches, followed immediately by the unification of the ministry by the laying-on of hands, including episcopal hands – though with an 'ambiguous' formula – has become the generally accepted solution to the problem of how to unite churches of the episcopal Anglican tradition with churches in the various Protestant or reformed traditions. (In the case of the Anglican/Methodist scheme for England the unification of the ministries, along the general lines already described, preceded the full unification of the churches, as will be seen later – pp. 367–71.)

It has already been seen that the renewed interest in the priesthood and ministry of the whole people of God has done much to draw the sting out of the old controversies about the ministry of the 'specialist' clergy. The Church of South India found a theological formula to cover this point and almost every scheme of unity prefaces its chapter on the ministry with a section on the priestly ministry of the whole church in worship, mission and service. Thus the Ghana scheme, in many ways one of the most vivid and urgent, says:

The negotiating churches believe that the Church is a royal priesthood through which the risen and ascended Christ continues his high priestly work. All its members are called, in virtue of their union with Christ, to a priestly ministry; both godward, in the offering of spiritual sacrifices, gifts and prayers for mankind; and manward, in the showing forth by life and word of the glory of the redeeming power of God. No individual and no one order in the Church can claim exclusive possession of this priesthood. The negotiating churches believe that within this ministry of the whole church Christ has given a special ministry of the word and sacraments.[36]

In view of this insistence on the prior ministry of the whole church, including or indeed especially the laity, it is surprising how often unity schemes omit the laity from the initial unification of the churches. It seems that the negotiators have become so obsessed with the minutiae of the machinery for unifying the clergy that they have left the laity out of their calculations. (Perhaps this reflects the fact that the negotiators themselves tend to be 100 per cent clergy!) The lesson has been learned that lay people must be interested in and brought along with negotiations at every stage, and elaborate measures are undertaken to achieve this even in comparatively 'primitive' countries, where education and communications are concerned, such as Ghana. In Ghana, too, the congregations of the various negotiating churches have made their covenants for union. But when it comes to the union the laity tend to be given only a passive role. They are, no doubt, part of the congregation at the service of unification, but they are not involved in the way that the ministers are; there is no rite or ritual which commits them to the new church as their clergy have been committed. But ought not congregations to share the same experience as their clergy? Often the central unification service has to be repeated locally, so that all the clergy are covered, but even here the laity in congregations are hardly involved in an active capacity. Only the Canadian scheme proposes 'a congregational act whereby the laymen in each parish re-affirm their faith and with prayer and blessing pledge themselves to the united church'.

There is another way in which negotiations about the ministry have so centred on 'the fact though not the theory' of the continuity of episcopal ordination that other important considerations have been neglected. Anglicans insist on the threefold ministry of bishops, priests and deacons and it is this ministry which is now being generally accepted as the norm for united churches. But for centuries the Anglicans, like the Roman Catholics, have not really had a proper diaconate. (The problem is in fact more serious for Anglicans than Romans in view of the Anglican lip-service to the threefold ministry, where the Romans would frankly say that as far as they are concerned the essential ministry would be that of pope, bishops and priests.) The diaconate has been simply a stepping stone to the priesthood; virtually no one has remained permanently a deacon and there are no real functions for the ministry of a deacon in the church. But in almost every case this meaningless Anglican shibboleth about the diaconate as a constituent part of the essential threefold ministry has been transferred into the scheme for the united church. Deacons tend to be left out of the unifications rites, which indicates the value put on their ministry, and no attempt is made to re-think the function of the diaconate, or to make its ministry meaningful. In this can be seen an unhappy example of the fact that unity schemes are still western-dominated and accept western premises and western shortcomings. Australia seems to be the honourable exception – a scheme in which Anglicans are only observers! There the negotiators have had much intensive discussion on the function of the diaconate in the contemporary church.

The ministry of presbyters, as increasingly they are coming to be called, is clearly a matter which no scheme can ignore. It is generally agreed that the priestly or presbyteral function is the ministry of the word and sacraments. But even if sacramental doctrine is not discussed in dangerously great detail, there is still the vexed ecumenical question of how many sacraments there are. Without going into too great detail on this question, it can be said that in a number of schemes the presbyters' functions have specifically included the 'ministry of reconciliation', which can be taken to include auricular confession – an old Protestant battle ground and a ministry which many Anglicans hold to be of vital importance.

On the other hand in some places Anglicans have had to come to terms with the idea of the ordination of women, another highly controversial matter in the past. Traditionally some Protestant churches, such as the Congregational, have ordained women to their full ministry, but the ordination of women has been anathema to Catholic thinking, and Anglo-Catholics have set their faces against it, partly because of the fear that the ordination of women would present very great problems in any future unity negotiations with Rome. But the fact that unity negotiations in which Anglicans are involved now include churches which ordain women means that the question can no longer be avoided. The Ghana scheme – where the Anglicans are notably of the Anglo-Catholic tradition but are at the same time a very small minority of the negotiating Christians – envisages a fully ordained diaconate of women; the discussions in New Zealand have implicitly accepted the ordination of women as presbyters; while the Canadian doctrinal commission can see no 'theological reason' against the ordination of women. Other schemes in which Anglicans are involved will undoubtedly have to face the question.

(ii) Baptism

An even more fundamental question has been raised by the widening of the spectrum of churches which are now willing to take part in unity schemes. This is baptism. The C.S.I. broke new ground in including the Anglicans. But at the other end of the scale there was no question of Baptist participation. More recently the

Baptist churches have been willing to take part in wide-ranging unity schemes, rather than concentrating on seeking closer ties only with members of their own particular branch of the Christian fraternity. Thus Baptist churches are involved in negotiations which include Anglicans in Ceylon, North India, Ghana and New Zealand. Baptists are on the whole strongly congregational in their view of the church. That is to say the essential unit of church government is the local congregation; the individual congregation has a very great measure of autonomy, for instance in the 'calling', or appointment, of its minister, and the connection between congregations of Baptists is on a loose federal basis. But this does not represent a major problem for unity negotiations. Schemes have already been evolved which include churches with a strong congregational basis, such as the Congregationalists themselves. In any case the Congregationalists and Baptists are moving all the time in the direction of a stronger feeling of what is known as the 'connectional' element in the church, that is the feeling of belonging to a church which is at the same time rooted in a specific congregation and also part of a national and world-wide fellowship – and governed as such. Similarly at the other end of the scale Anglicans are no longer able to talk in terms of the diocese as the fundamental and essential unit of the church (which incredibly enough many have continued to do in England despite the fact that the size of English dioceses means that the average member of the Church of England is hardly aware of the life of his diocese or the name of his bishop). Thus it has been possible to base many church union schemes on the idea of combining episcopal, presbyterian and congregational elements in the ministry and government of the united church.

The fundamental belief of the Baptists, and of churches allied to them, and the tenet which provides their whole *raison d'être* as separate churches, is the insistence on adult baptism. Basing their teaching on the New Testament they reject infant baptism, which has been practised by the church from the earliest, if not from New Testament times. Baptism they say is the sign of the individual's faith in Christ; it is the sacrament of his forgiveness, his new life as a follower of Christ and his membership of the church. It can therefore only be the act of a mature and responsible believer; to baptize unknowing children, even with the best intentions of devoting them to the service of Christ and nurturing them in the Christian faith, is to debase the sacrament on which Christians – and especially those in the Catholic tradition – place so much emphasis. For Baptists a belief in the practice of adult or believers' baptism is the mark of the true church, in much the same way as the continuance of bishops in the apostolic succession is the mark of the true church for a high-church Anglican. Just as such an Anglican driven to a logical extreme might say that without bishops there can be no sacraments and therefore no salvation, a Baptist might feel bound to declare that only an adult converted believer can receive true baptism and that therefore only in a church practising exclusive adult baptism can salvation certainly be found. Thus for Baptists to approach unity negotiations with non-Baptists has something of the same Rubicon character which marked out the C.S.I. union for Anglicans. Baptists can be seen facing up to the reality of this situation in a moving statement by the Churches of Christ in New Zealand.

Because of this desire to find the way of reconciling the practice and meaning of Baptism in the ... Church of New Zealand, the Associated Churches of Christ are asked to indicate in what way those who hold exclusively to believers' Baptism can accept infant Baptism as real Baptism. Obviously they do not and cannot accept infant Baptism as regulative for themselves in practice, but they do accept it as an existential order of the church because it is acceptable for a very great part of it, which they recognize as belonging to the Body of Christ. ...

Though Churches of Christ are convinced that certain indispensable elements of Baptism, such as response to the divine grace in desire for God's forgiveness, and confession of personal faith in Christ by word and by self-commitment . . . are not apparent in the rite of infant Baptism . . . we believe nevertheless that those who practise it sincerely hold the intention of keeping the commandment of Christ to 'make disciples, baptizing them in the name of the Father and of the Son and of the Holy Spirit'. . . .

Furthermore we must recognize in the lives of those who come to communicant membership by this route those whom God has accepted and blessed. . . .

Since we are thus impelled by an honest facing of facts to recognize that a considerable section of the Church has acted (even though we believe unadvisedly and not according to the order of the New Testament) to bring people through infant Baptism within the life of the Church . . . their Baptism is therefore factual, it is real, even though it may not be of good order, according to our understanding of scripture and of predominant pre-Nicene practice. To think otherwise would be to constitute a condition too terrible to contemplate. . . . There is no occasion to make immersion on a profession of faith absolutely essential to a Christian.

If Churches of Christ are prepared to acknowledge that other Christian Communions are in fact real Churches, though sadly all of us are deficient through disunity, then logically it must follow that their Baptism is in fact real Baptism. . . . If however we are prepared to allow two practices of Baptism to co-exist meanwhile within one Church, instead of as at present within divided forms of the Church, then both for the sake of love and truth the reality of each other's Baptisms should be accepted.[37]

The wordiness of this statement is perhaps a measure of the heart-searching which went into its preparation. But the message is clear: faced with the fact that there are undeniably Christians in other denominations the Baptists have had to concede that churches without their own essential pre-requirement are nevertheless true churches. It is the same process which overtook many

Anglo-Catholic upholders of the apostolic succession and which has faced Roman Catholics in their dealings with 'separated brethren'. In the face of the facts of ecumenical experience some devoutly held theories have to be modified.

The modifications suggested in those schemes which include Baptists are along the lines sketched in the last paragraph of the New Zealand statement. In general provision is made in the united church for both believers' and infant baptism. Some schemes exclude the possibility of the same person being baptized in infancy and in later life, on the theological grounds that baptism is an unrepeatable event; but others on pastoral grounds allow that a person who feels the need for baptism as an adult may receive baptism even though he was baptized in infancy. In any case there are reasons why this problem may not be so severe in the future. In the first place as Christianity declines in those countries which are traditionally 'Christian' the practice of infant baptism may decline at the same time, so that infant baptism becomes the exception rather than the rule, as is already the case in countries where the church is in a recognized missionary situation. Already the Church of England in its new baptism services has declared adult baptism to be the norm on theological grounds even though it is still the exception in practice. Secondly, current theological thinking is showing that Christian initiation cannot be confined to the single event of baptism: inwardly a person will become a Christian in various ways; outwardly his initiation will include baptism, instruction, confirmation and Holy Communion. With the acceptance of episcopacy in uniting churches confirmation will become increasingly important and the whole question of the adult believer's profession of faith, which is the basic truth held by the Baptists, will be increasingly emphasized. Thirdly many non-Baptists are becoming worried about the practice of 'indiscriminate' infant baptism.

(iii) Conservative v. Radical

There is another problem which faces the architects of all church union schemes. More and more discussions are coming to be based on the idea that the united church will not be so much an amalgam of all the best features of the old churches, as a new embodiment of the united people of God in that place. This is in any case the natural result of the idea that the united church will start from a common act of penitence and renewal. In Canada, for instance, the union negotiators declare that 'we are united in our intention to bring into being, not a merger of two existing ecclesiastical bodies, but rather a new embodiment of the One Church of God'.[38] The problem then is this: how radical can the negotiators be in seeking such a new embodiment of the church? This question reflects the turmoil which in any case already exists in Christian thinking about the nature and work of the church in contemporary society. It is also true that many of those who are most devoted to the ecumenical movement would tend to be radical in their answers to the questions being asked, while on the other hand among those who have to vet church union schemes, and finally to vote for them, there will be many whose approach is cautious and conservative. Nowhere was this more dramatically seen than in the rejection in 1957 by the rank and file of Scottish clergy and laity of the unanimous recommendations of a somewhat academic committee negotiating with English and Scottish Anglicans for a union based on the idea of bishops-in-presbytery.

It is unlikely that any of the members of the Joint Conference which produced this unanimous report expected the proposals to receive easy and speedy acceptance. It is certain that all of them were surprised by the nature of the reaction which the Report provoked in Scotland. The cry 'no Bishops' seems to have run through the land with the vehemence of a 'No Popery' battle-cry.[39]

The lesson of this sharp rebuff to ecumenical hopes is that negotiating committees must be broadly based with a fair representation of all the likely shades of opinion, and that they must be careful not to get in their thinking too far ahead of the churches they represent.

There is another problem in reconciling the old and the new in union schemes. On the one hand there is the desire not for 'merger' but for 'a new embodiment of the church', on the other there is the natural desire of the old churches to conserve in the new church – even to present to it – all that they believe to be most precious in their own heritage. This again has the makings of a radical/conservative struggle. The cautious commentator for the bishops of the Lambeth Conference of 1968 has this to say:

> The Anglican attitude towards any re-union scheme tends to be conservationist. But a scheme should be scrutinized not only for its faithfulness to the past, but also for its openness to the present and future.[40]

Speaking of the Ceylon scheme after the Church of England criticisms had been met he says:

> I do not think that there are any problems about the Scheme for the Anglican. Indeed there seems to be a slightly dated air about it now ... and sometimes there seems too much willingness to stereotype traditional Anglican practice, e.g. over the definition of deacons.[41]

On the other hand where a scheme is clearly cast on radical lines, as for instance in the United States, the same writer makes very definite warning noises to the Anglican bishops:

> As one would expect the winds of change are more evident in these consultations, than in schemes with a longer pedigree, e.g. the realization that parish congregations need to be supplemented by special task groups. But the general trends in

doctrine are not encouraging from an Anglican point of view. . . .[42]

The plea by Bishop Hollis that churches should be left as free as possible to work out the details of their life as a united church obviously puts a premium on a South India-type union, and as has been seen the C.S.I. has steered a very positive course since its inauguration. But even if a Ceylon-type union is accepted and ministries are united at the inauguration of the new church, there is still ample opportunity for the negotiators to think constructively and flexibly about the nature of the church in contemporary society – provided their attitude is not over-preservationist.

A few examples can be quoted. In the first place a union scheme gives a church a chance to consider what its size and area of operation ought to be, bearing in mind such secular factors as the political, national and cultural background. Thus it was the fact of a common culture in South India which made it logical for the C.S.I. to be formed as a separate church on the Indian sub-continent. But this still meant that as far as Anglicans were concerned the remaining church covered India, Pakistan, Burma and Ceylon. This may have been tolerable in the days of the British raj, but it is clearly ridiculous now the same church is operating in four different states with different political attitudes and different religious cultures – Hindu, Muslim and two types of Buddhist. Union schemes have made it possible to rationalize this situation and to think in terms of different churches for each country.

Some examples of the ways in which the opportunity for rethinking the purpose and structures of the church has *not* been taken have already been given: for instance, the general failure to try to find a meaningful ministry for the diaconate. The 1968 *Survey of Church*

Union Negotiations reports on this problem 'a general uneasiness, not to say anxiety, with the present and former structures of the church':

It is increasingly realized that the structures of the past were historically conditioned, adequate perhaps for one era, but in no way holy in themselves. Thus the need for flexibility of structure, for imagination and experimentation . . . is receiving greater attention. This need, to cite one example, caused the Consultation on Church Union in the United States to delay and modify its formulations for many months after it had reached substantial agreement on the principles of Faith, Worship, Sacraments and Ministry. Having made this positive point, however, it must be mentioned that a corresponding openness to restructure ministry is not yet apparent. Although the need for new forms of ministry is recognized, the schemes generally presuppose the adequacy of the traditional three-fold formulation of ministry. . . . Accompanying this phenomenon, and related to it, is the general short shrift given to the ministry of the laity.[43]

The Consultation on Church Union in the United States is here singled out for praise: another example of its 'openness' is that in laying down 'Guidelines for the Structure of the Church' this scheme formulates the principle that structures should reflect at the same time continuity with the past and 'free openness' to the future, so that the church's structures can be functional in order to serve its contemporary mission in a situation of rapid social change. With this in mind the C.O.C.U. has decided to 'move into union on the basis of a plan of union and then prepare and adopt a constitution only after a period of experience in union'.[44] This is to adopt Bishop Michael Hollis's recommendations with a vengeance, and to leave details to be worked out in faith by the united church to an even greater extent than was attempted in South India. It will be interesting to see whether such radical openness can be maintained in later stages of negotiation or whether more cautious preservationist tactics in the end prevail – or, thirdly, whether some churches will back out of such an open-ended scheme.

Another scheme which seems to be willing to think experimentally about the future is the Canadian: here special attention is being given to the ministry of deacons and of women, and the whole 'function of the church in a technological and increasingly urbanized society' is being considered. Similarly in Australia and New Zealand the negotiators are thinking along fresh and – in the sense of going back to the roots – radical lines about some of the questions which have already been discussed. It will be noticed that the most forward-looking schemes are those taking place in churches which are living in a western and post-Christian society. This is no doubt partly due to the fact that in these circumstances western theologians are more prepared to be radical than the leaders of the younger churches, where, ironically, the older western traditions sometimes last longer. It is partly also because the schemes in the younger churches are on the whole some ten years further along the pipe-line than those in the western churches, and reflect the thinking of their time, with an attendant danger of 'setting up an elaborately devised archaism'.[45] In any case this whole question underlines the fact that the reunion movement is both set in and part of the whole turmoil which is changing the life of the churches today.

(iv) Doctrinal Agreement

The question of the search for a doctrinal basis of uniting churches is both a matter which is vital in itself and also one which illustrates many of the points just discussed.

There are several possible approaches to this question. When reformed churches – particularly those with a continental background – come to it they have tended to do so from the point of view of their denominational confessions of faith, traditional or more modern. This is particularly true of the Lutheran churches, as will be seen when the Lutheran/C.S.I. negotiations are discussed. Other reformed churches have tended to move away from a strictly confessional outlook since the time of the C.S.I. negotiations, but even where they have some schemes still show the signs of an original approach which was based on the traditional Reformation confessions of faith. Thus the Japanese united church, the Kyodan, which reached a shot-gun unity in 1941 (see above, pp. 217–18), produced in 1954 a confession of faith which on analysis can be seen to be based on 'Lutheran and Calvinistic orthodoxy'.[46]

Another way of preserving links with the Reformation is to acknowledge and even to incorporate the old confessions in the basis of the new church as part of the way in which the Catholic and **Apostolic** faith has been handed down to the present united church. This was done in the North India/Pakistan scheme, where it was claimed that their presence in the scheme would 'secure the continuity of the United Church with the Churches from which its membership will be derived'.[47]

But on the whole a Reformation-orientated confessional approach to unity has been on the wane in recent years. This is partly because the churches themselves have felt that they do not wish to be saddled with outdated confessional baggage, and partly because they have come to see that confessions of faith are useful not so much as tests of orthodoxy in times of division but rather as integral parts of worship and springboards for teaching in times of unity. For these purposes the old confessions are less than useful.

But the strongest reason for the reaction against the Reformation confessional approach has undoubtedly in practice been Anglican pressure in church union negotiations. Anglicans are not very proud of their own Reformation doctrinal basis, the Thirty-Nine Articles (which in

334

any case have real authority – and that a tenuous one – only in the Church of England). But they have always stood out in church unity negotiations for the authority and place of the Nicene and Apostles Creeds. Their own doctrinal position has been largely based on worship and these creeds have traditionally figured largely in that worship. Thus they were an essential part of the Anglican formula for reunion, the Lambeth Quadrilateral. The reformed churches, on the other hand, had no such tradition and at first regarded 'these old creeds' with some suspicion (see above, p. 204). But from the time of the C.S.I. negotiations the creeds came to be accepted as the doctrinal basis of unity and, very often, as the 'sufficient' statement of faith. Looked at one way this approach can be seen as being an Anglican victory, or at least a victory for the Anglican outlook. It embodied the Anglican assumption that it is neither desirable nor really possible to demand too close a verbal acceptance of detailed doctrinal statements. On the other hand, looked at more positively, this approach made progress possible. It safeguarded the idea of the creeds as a part of worship. It avoided divisive argument on western-orientated details. It provided what many came to see as an essential link between the new united church and the ancient united church of Christendom. It safeguarded the 'Catholic' outlook for future negotiations with Rome – and even, though to a lesser extent since it was the 'western' creeds which were accepted, with the Orthodox. Above all in practice it made possible what was at the time so important for Anglicans – the concentration of negotiations on matters of order rather than of faith, the questions of episcopacy, and of the uniting of the churches and of their ministries.

Thus a credal confessional basis became the norm for unity negotiations, especially where these included Anglicans, from the time of South India until quite recently. The South India approach is echoed, though of course with minor modifications, in such schemes as those of Ceylon (Lanka), North India (though see above), Ghana, Rhodesia, Nigeria, Tanzania, and the West Indies. Even in Zambia, where Anglicans are not a party to the negotiations, the same approach is used. Finally, and 'as one born out of due season', this is the approach of the Anglican/Methodist scheme in England.

A glance at this scheme illustrates other characteristics which are to a greater or lesser extent common to this method of reaching doctrinal agreement wherever it has been adopted. The scheme is set out in a book of 178 pages. Of this the chapter 'Agreement in Doctrine' occupies twenty-three pages. Of these, seven give the basic text; the remainder are appendices. In effect these seven pages are an elaboration of the statement that 'assurances with respect to doctrinal standards having been mutually exchanged, each church would declare itself satisfied that the other maintained the apostolic faith and proclaimed the apostolic gospel'.[48] The conclusion is reached that 'we are convinced that any impression of major doctrinal tension between the two churches, or of fundamental doctrinal uncertainty in either or both at the present time, would be quite false'. This somewhat negative but hopeful conviction is the doctrinal basis for reconciliation and union. It is not spelled out, and the fact that it was not was one of the reasons for the rejection of the scheme by the two more doctrinally authoritarian parties of the Church of England. Instead there is some insistence, both in the text and in the appendices, on the question of the authority which underlies doctrinal belief and through which agreement is reached. In other words the basis of the argument is shifted from *what* is believed to *why* whatever is believed is believed.

This is a common feature in all the schemes which adopted what might be called a minimal and credal approach to doctrinal unity. The place of scripture will be defined in some way as 'the supreme standard of faith and morals in the Church'.[49] The creeds will be mentioned and it is probable that some reference will be made to the part played by 'tradition' in interpreting, safeguarding and conveying the apostolic faith. The South India union baulked this question, but other schemes from Lanka on have included this typically Anglican approach. (It will be remembered, too, that the Montreal Faith and Order Conference of 1963 acknowledged the importance of tradition in the life of the church – see above, p. 256.) Thus the Anglican/Methodist scheme, after a section called 'The Supremacy of Scripture', goes on to 'The Value and Limitations of Tradition'. As might be expected from the heading the negotiators approach this explosive western Catholic-*v.*-Protestant issue very warily: tradition 'will enrich the Church from age to age'; it can 'yield many rich insights into the meaning and application of Scripture'; 'it may rightly be called the living stream of the Church's life'; '*but*, venerable and valuable though it is, tradition ... by itself exercises no authority.... Tradition, however high and holy, can never stand by itself.' It must always be tested by the scriptures.

Other topics which are regularly treated in some detail in this type of approach to doctrinal agreement are the traditionally divisive doctrines of the ministry and the eucharist. On the ministry, as has been seen, the air has been very much cleared since the emergence at the time of the South India negotiations of a common view that all human priesthood must be seen within the context of the prior priesthood of Christ and the subsequent priesthood of the whole people of God, lay and ordained. Following from this it has not been difficult in these schemes to reach agreement, provided that the position on episcopacy goes no further than 'the fact and not the theory' – that is that episcopacy (usually constitutional episcopacy of some form but with invariable episcopal ordination) is accepted, but no doctrine of episcopacy is insisted on, an agreement which could not in any case be found in the Anglican church itself.

The doctrine of the eucharist, previously so controversial, is one of those subjects on which in recent years the churches have found themselves converging more and more on to common ground. Thus, provided that the historical disputes and the shibboleth words are avoided, it is usually possible to arrive at some sort of formula of agreement. Nevertheless, after stating various principles and asserting 'common ground', the Anglican/Methodist Scheme has to conclude on a note of caution, or perhaps of realism:

We reaffirm the claim of the 1963 Report, made in the light of these common affirmations, that 'in the interpretation of Holy Communion as well as Baptism there is, amid divisive issues that must not be shirked, an impressive measure of agreement between us'.[50]

This paragraph is typical, in fact, of the approach on matters of doctrine of the schemes mentioned from C.S.I. through Lanka and many churches in developing countries where Anglicans are involved, and up to the English Anglican/Methodist scheme. The approach is largely historical, recognizing the divisions since the Reformation and referring to them and to their continuing existence in the beliefs of many of the clergy and laity involved in the union – yet at the same time claiming a sufficient measure of agreement to move forward to union, without on the other hand trying to articulate this agreement into a contemporary statement of the Christian faith.

It is this type of approach which has recently fallen out of favour among those responsible for negotiations in various 'western' churches, other than Britain. The implicit feeling seems to be that it is not enough to refer to the post-Reformation past, to reach some measure of agreement and then to agree to differ within a comprehensive framework. That is to shirk the church's duty to confess a faith which will be meaningful to the contemporary world. In particular some schemes have stressed the missionary aspect of doctrinal unity: the church cannot expect its message to be heard unless it has stated in clear terms what that message is: the inauguration of a united church is an opportunity for the new body to lay its faith on the line. Clearly this is brave thinking, and moreover thinking into the future rather than rehashing the past.

Equally clearly there are dangers in this approach. In the first place theological fashions change. A confession which reflects the thinking of today when the union is being negotiated may look dated by tomorrow when the union is consummated. In that case the new church may be saddled with a doctrinal albatross which may prove a source of embarrassment as the church journeys into the future. It may be easier to travel light, to profess adherence to the creeds, however dated they are, and then allow contemporary but not authoritative interpretation. In the second place the attempt to arrive at an acceptable formulation of Christian belief may prove fatally divisive. It is true that those negotiators who have so far embarked on the attempt seem to have been relatively successful in that they have come up with agreed statements. But none of these statements has so far been accepted by the rank and file of the churches who have to vote the union. It has already been seen that ecumenical negotiators tend to be thinking in a different world from the constituencies of their churches, witness the out-of-hand rejection of the Anglican/Presbyterian scheme in Scotland in 1957.

The fact is that the majority of those who are chosen for union negotiations by their churches are inevitably people who are in any case caught up in the ecumenical world and share a common outlook and language acquired in the W.C.C. and in national councils of churches. This outlook and language has not necessarily penetrated to the grassroots level where the final decisions are taken. The confessions and agreed statements drawn up by those union schemes which have opted for this method of advance are, to a greater or lesser extent, radical and 'forward-looking'. Will they be accepted when they are put to the vote?

The first union scheme to produce a contemporary confession of faith was the United Presbyterian Church in the U.S.A. This union of Presbyterian churches came into being in 1958 and, with three million members, is the largest Presbyterian church in the world. Its confession was not produced until 1967, though work had been started on it at the inception of the church. The confession makes a break at once from the insistence on the authorities underlying Christian belief – scripture, tradition and the rest. It starts, as do the traditional Presbyterian confessions, with God and with his work of reconciling the world.

Uniting churches which have followed suit and produced their own confessions of faith as part of union negotiations include those in Australia, New Zealand, Canada, the United States and, most recently, the C.S.I. and the Lutherans in South India. Naturally the confessions differ in emphasis, though all reflect current theological thinking. The Australian document *The Faith of the Church* has been influential as being one of the first in the field and having produced a great deal of historical and theological documentation. The New Zealand scheme produces a succinct section, 'The Faith of the Church', covering the standards of faith, the doctrines of God, of man, of new life in Christ, of the church, the sacraments, the ministry, the world and of Christian hope; there follow more extended sections on the church's worship, sacraments, ministry and government. The Canadian doctrinal statement is most remarkable as having a strong missionary emphasis and as underlining the necessity of communicating the faith in modern conditions of technological and urbanized society. It is emphatic in not producing a take-it-or-leave-it package deal of Christian faith: 'We stand beside all men. We too are bewildered and challenged by the questions men ask.' Only after some of these questions have been detailed does the Canadian declaration go on to outline its own faith.

Undoubtedly the most remarkable contemporary confession of faith yet to emerge from a union scheme is that of the negotiating churches in the United States. This scheme was formerly known as the Consultation on Church Union: now it has reached a definite Plan of Union it calls itself the Church of Christ Uniting. (The same initials C.O.C.U. serve both phases of the scheme.) The plan does not contain a doctrinal confession as such. Rather, the whole document is written in theological terms. It is as if the negotiators were saying 'this is what the Church ought to be like, and this is what our church will be like – and for these theological reasons'.

The scheme is prefaced with a rousing slogan for the uniting churches as they 'begin anew' ... 'a company of the people of God celebrating the one God ... seeking under the Gospel for Christ's mission and service in the world'. 'We open ourselves ... to renewal from the Holy Spirit' and 'struggle against racism, poverty, environmental blight, war and other problems of the family of man' – words which very precisely fix the date of origin of the scheme. The plan starts by setting out its objectives, giving priority to 'the celebration of God's grace' and 'mission in the world' as 'the primary characteristic of the church's life on every level'. For this mission 'the united church must be structured with flexibility far beyond that existing in any of the uniting churches'.[51] Other objectives are mutual enrichment, continuing ecumenical relationships, the protection of diversities and liberties in the church, and 'maximum openness ... for continuing renewal and reformation'. The plan goes on to describe the church, under the heading 'What it Means to be God's People'. The church is seen both as the continuation of the apostolic community and as a body rooted in, and responding to, contemporary history; it is described in Biblical terms and then in theological terms as catholic, evangelical and reformed. Next comes a chapter, 'What it Means to be Members in This Community', stressing strongly the elements of personal committal and discipline.

Only now is there a section on 'The Living Faith', setting out in fairly conventional terms the authorities for faith in scripture, tradition and creeds, reserving the right after unity to produce a contemporary affirmation of faith and, rather oddly at this point, appending a passage against racial discrimination based on the belief in the fatherhood of God and the brotherhood of man. There follows a section on worship which starts with a relatively long passage on general principles, stressing the fact that 'in the united church there will be room for wide variety and manner' of worship and that 'each parish, subject to to the general norm, will be free to work out its forms of worship'.[52] Compared with this what is said about the sacraments is kept short and uncontroversial.

Ministry comes next, starting with the now-familiar theme of 'The Ministry of the Whole People of God', and going on to a long section of the ministry of the laity, which boldly asserts that 'the laity has fundamental responsibility for the Christian mission'. The pages on the ordained ministry place at the outset a welcome emphasis on the fact that 'the whole church bears a continuing responsibility toward every minister, from his first approach to ordination until the time of his death'.[53] The threefold ministry is described for the most part in terms of the functions of presbyters, bishops and deacons in that order, the order being given, according to the Ordinal, 'with a definite intention to avoid the implication that the different offices are simply ascending steps in a hierarchy'[54] – which seems a somewhat whimsical idea. Episcopacy is described as corporate, personal and collegial in character, with special stress on the last, though it is somewhat difficult to see the difference between the corporate and the collegial elements: the constitutional checks and balances between the episcopal college and the rest of the church are not so closely defined as in some union schemes, such as that of Ghana. The ministry of deacons is somewhat sketchily described: clearly the negotiators are still in some doubt on this matter, though the principle is laid down that the diaconate will not be an automatic stepping stone to the presbyterate and that most deacons will not be the paid functionaries of the church.

The structure and organization of the united church is described in a long chapter headed 'Organizing for Mission'. The fundamental unit is the parish, which will be made up of congregations and task forces, which are groups of Christians organized not on a locality but on an interest basis. The intention is that the individual congregation will be spared the 'competitive drive' to provide a comprehensive programme for every need, and so personnel and plant will be used more economically and effectively. Above the parish is the district, which is the sphere of operation of the bishop, though the word diocese is avoided. It is evidently envisaged as small enough to allow effective personal oversight by the bishop. In turn, districts are grouped together in regions, which 'will be related to natural areas of non-metropolitan and metropolitan population clusters' – the sociologists have obviously been at work! It is the regions which are to provide the main administrative and specialist services of the church. Lastly there is the national set-up which is seen primarily as the seat of the supreme legislative assembly of the church.

A short section now indicates that the united church

will continue to be concerned with possible future union with other churches and that it will continue relationships with the world bodies with whom its constituent churches were in membership.

Lastly a chapter, headed 'To Move in Pilgrimage', is devoted to the actual process of the inauguration of the united church. Any two of the nine churches which have drawn up the plan can decide to move ahead into union. There will then be a transitional period until the constitution of the Church of Christ Uniting has been adopted. 'This period will afford an opportunity for all the participants to solve small problems and large, to learn new ways, to discover one another, to lose suspicions, and to gain a sense of the single mission commanding us all.'[55] The period is obviously also seen as a breathing space during which legal and constitutional problems are worked out. The actual service of inauguration is in many ways similar to the English Anglican/Methodist scheme. The churches are solemnly united before the ministries, indicating that the one act governs the other. The ministries are then united by mutual recognition and by a prayer asking 'that each ordained minister may be so blessed by God as to receive the graces and gifts available to the ordained ministries in all of the uniting churches, together with such further enrichment as he may need for servanthood and mission in the united church'.[56] Representative ministers then all lay hands on each other in turn and in silence. Among these representative ministers will be bishops: new bishops for the united church will be consecrated according to the Ordinal already drawn up, which provides that at every act of ordination 'representatives of all offices of the ministry, including the laity, shall participate in the laying on of hands, thus signifying that ordination is an act of the whole church' (as well as ensuring the continuity of episcopal ordination).[57]

This is the outline of what is probably at the time of

writing – 1971 – both from the theological and the practical point of view the most original plan of union yet devised. It is, moreover, a scheme which has both been very carefully thought out and also remains in many respects, such as doctrinal formulation, surprisingly open-ended. It can be said to represent the best of responsible liberal thinking about the church at the present stage of theological planning. What the precise status of the scheme is, and what its future may be, will be described later in the chapter.

The attention given in the C.O.C.U. plan to the stage of transition from plurality to union among the churches is a reminder that in any scheme of union there will be formidable legal and constitutional issues to be faced. Union negotiators have been slow to recognize the importance of this factor. This naïvety has resulted in bitter acrimony in some schemes and unlooked-for delays in others. It will be remembered that in the pre-war United Church scheme in Canada a body of dissentient churches was able to fight a bitter rearguard action over property and finance which both soured and delayed the in-auguration of union and which resulted in some Presbyterian churches remaining to this day outside the united church (see above, p. 216). Similarly in Nigeria union was stultified at the last moment by dissentients fighting on constitutional issues. Thirdly in England and Wales a union between the Congregational and Presbyterian churches was delayed because it was discovered that the necessary legal and parliamentary arrangements could not be got through in time to make a final vote in 1970 practicable.

These examples are enough to indicate that church leaders will in future negotiations have to pay more attention to the details of the legal complications which follow from a union scheme.

DENOMINATIONAL APPROACHES

The examples which have so far been given in the analysis of the issues being raised in current union movements have mostly been taken from plans covering the ecclesiastical spectrum from Anglicans to Baptists. Inevitably these are the schemes of the greatest significance for the future. But it would be wrong to think that they are the only, or even the majority of, the negotiations in progress. Of the forty-eight listed in the 1968 *Survey of Church Union Negotiations*, only seventeen may be said to be reasonably inclusive in their scope. Some examples will now be given of other types of negotiation and of their characteristics.

In the first place there are unions between separated churches of the same Christian family. These may have arisen because of chance quirks of missionary history. Thus in Upper Burma the Methodist church was a British foundation and the Methodists there were members of the British Methodist Conference, whereas the Methodist mission in Lower Burma was founded from America and carried membership of the Conference of the United States. In order to unite, each church has first to gain freedom from its home base, and although union was originally mooted in 1962 the union is still not completed: the organizational details of combining the two different missionary traditions are presumably posing problems. In any case it is now hoped that the conversations may be widened to include Baptists and Anglicans.

Another example of tidying-up within a confession can be quoted from Switzerland. In 1965 the Reformed National Church of the Canton of Vaud and the Free Reformed Church of the same Canton were reunited after a break in 1847 on a church/state issue similar to that which had split the Church of Scotland at about the same time; the remarkable thing about this union was that it was brought about by a vote of the *political* electorate of the Canton – and that Roman Catholics were encouraged by their bishops to vote for it 'as a sign of their solidarity with their Protestant brothers'!

Lutherans have tended to split among themselves even more than have the Reformed churches. These divisions have usually been over details of doctrine expressed in the various Lutheran confessional statements. A Lutheran approaches reunion from the point of view of seeking exact verbal doctrinal agreement, and this makes negotiations difficult even within a general Lutheran framework. Very often, therefore, Lutherans aim not at unity but at federal relationships in terms of what is known as 'pulpit and altar fellowship' and of membership of the powerful international Lutheran World Federation. But there are a number of negotiations for closer union than this. In Australia, for instance, there are two Lutheran churches both stemming from the arrival of Silesian Lutherans from America in 1838 and 1841; one is in fellowship with the American Lutheran church and one with the Lutherans of the Missouri Synod, a church of the utmost doctrinal rigidity, which has considerable world-wide missionary ramifications and which tends wherever it is found to be strictly non-cooperative in the ecumenical movement, to the point for instance of refusing to join in meal-time grace where other churches are represented. These negotiations, therefore, highlight many of the problems typical to Lutherans seeking unity. It is agreed that union can be based only on 'unanimity in the pure doctrine of the Gospel and in the right administration of the sacraments'. What areas must this doctrinal unanimity cover? In Australia it embraces such things as the events at the end of the world, the doctrine of the Papacy as Anti-Christ and practical matters such as marriage with the deceased wife's sister. It is agreed that unity based on anything short of unanimity on such matters as this would be 'sinful unionism'. Yet despite difficulties, such as these, inter-Lutheran negotiations are proceeding in such countries as South Africa, the United States and Canada. In America the various Lutheran schisms have been slowly consolidating round the two main blocks of the Lutheran Church in America and the Missouri Lutheran Synod and there is now even some fellowship and co-operation between the two main opposing federations.

There are also some cases where Lutherans will join negotiations taking place between churches of different denominations, the next type of scheme which must be mentioned. Thus in Aden there was in 1963 a union between two Arab congregations with mission backgrounds from the Church of Scotland and the Danish Lutherans respectively; the result is a united church comprising some twenty or thirty people but firm in its declaration that in the hostile Arab and Muslim environment it is an independent entity – probably the smallest church in the world.

More significantly negotiations have been going on between the C.S.I. and the Federation of Lutheran churches in South India. From its beginning the C.S.I. declared that it could not be satisfied with the measure of unity it had so far found, and started to look for more inclusive union. As a result, as long ago as 1947 feelers were put out towards the local Lutherans – and more recently towards other churches such as the Mar Thoma Syrian Church and various Baptist churches. Negotiations with the Lutherans have been elaborate and time-consuming and, as so often happens in these cases, one side has sometimes been discussing a draft formula which has already been rejected or modified by the other.

At first the Lutherans took the view that the C.S.I. was disastrously weak doctrinally speaking, and that in concentrating its efforts on crossing the bridge of episcopacy the C.S.I. had sacrificed the 'pure milk of the Gospel'. The C.S.I. on the other hand was unwilling to swallow a lot of Lutheran – and therefore western – doctrinal formulas. But as the representatives of the two churches started meeting they found that the doctrinal differences were not as great as they had thought. In fact 'a great change in Lutheran evaluation of the C.S.I. has taken place since 1947'.[58] Similarly the C.S.I. has been more willing to embark on doctrinal formulation especially as it became clear that this might take the form of a contemporary confession of faith. A major step was the preparation of a joint catechism and more recently a draft constitution was drawn up, which includes a concise statement of faith and a longer confession in an appendix, as in the New Zealand arrangement. The actual wording also owes something to the New Zealand model, though there are also many signs that traditional Lutheran doctrinal positions have been respected. Episcopacy is agreed on, though there is to be no re-ordination in the United Church and no required theological belief about the office. In January 1970 the C.S.I. commended this draft constitution to its dioceses for study. It will be, to say the least, interesting to see how the Lutheran churches react, since this series of negotiations could be something of a breakthrough in Lutheran ecumenical relations.

Lest it be thought by English readers that too much space is being given to the Lutheran part in the ecumenical movement, a reminder may at this point be in place: Lutherans compose, after the Orthodox, the second largest non-Roman family of churches in the world, one tenth of the total world Christian population as compared to the Anglicans' one twentieth (see p. 19).

So much, then, for the typically Lutheran approach to inter-confessional unity negotiations. The typical attitudes of Anglicans and Baptists to such schemes has already been discribed. Where Lutherans, Anglicans and Baptists all stand aside from negotiation the schemes currently being debated fall into two main categories; there are those where the two main-stream traditions of the Reformation, that is Presbyterians and Congregationalists, are seeking reunion, and those where the uniting churches come from the more extreme Protestant churches, such as Evangelicals or Baptists – though the really extreme left-wing sectarian churches are still excluded. In the case of the Presbyterians and Congregationalists the main historical dividing line is between the strongly 'connectional' or corporate nature of the Presbyterian church, based on its high conception of the place of the ministry in the church, and the emphasis put by the Congregationalists on the autonomy of the local congregation, with a consequent playing-down of the awareness of the wider corporate nature of the church. In fact, as has already been said, this emphasis on the local congregation has for some time been breaking down in face of the pressures of modern society. Negotiation is therefore more likely to centre on the nature and function of the ordained ministry and the corporate government of the church.

In some places the problems are more organizational than anything else; in Scotland, for instance, this has so much been the case between the Church of Scotland and the Congregational Union of Scotland that the latter church reported of the draft union scheme that 'as presently framed it seems more an absorption of one denomination by another than a true union drawing on the traditions of both denominations'.[58] Even so organizational problems which are rooted in history and tradition take a lot of ironing out; it may be easy in theory to recognize that there are non-theological factors in church traditions which prolong disunity and to deplore the situation; but in practice the factors are facts – obstacles which have to be overcome with patience and good-will.

WORLD SURVEY

It remains to conduct a rapid geographical survey of current union negotiations to complete this picture of the world-wide movement towards unity. The situation is changing fast and some of the information may already be out-of-date but at least a sense of the general picture will be conveyed. Details will be given only of schemes which have not so far been adequately described and are of particular importance or interest.

In Africa almost every country has some sort of unity negotiations in progress. In the Cameroons a scheme between French and English-based Presbyterians and others led to a schism in the French church by a group of die-hard Presbyterians who claimed to preserve the true tradition. Such a schism in the course of negotiations happens remarkably rarely and the remaining churches hesitated to continue, but have now done so. Ghana, Tanzania and Kenya, Malawi, Zambia and Rhodesia all have widely inclusive schemes, which count in the Anglicans, in various stages of progress. That in Rhodesia, however, has recently suffered a set-back, probably for political reasons. The others are reasonably well advanced, especially Ghana and Kenya-Tanzania, which are both at or near the covenant stage and have both gone a long way in drawing up, and even using, experimental joint liturgies. More recent negotiations have started in Sierra Leone and South Africa. The latter is a putting together of talks which had formerly been proceeding separately. The Dutch Reformed Church is not included. The negotiators are looking largely to Canadian and New Zealand models.

In Uganda the situation is different because this predominantly 'Christian' country is for the most part divided between Anglicans and Roman Catholics, and although relations are good and improving there can as yet be no question of union discussions. The Nigerian unity scheme has already been partly described. It changed at an advanced stage of negotiation from a C.S.I.-type scheme to a modification of the Ceylon plan giving immediate unification of the ministries. This was in 1963, and by 1965 the authorities of the three churches concerned, Anglican, Methodist and Presbyterian, had given approval to the revised scheme. The inauguration of the new church was planned for December 1965. However at the last moment the Methodist negotiators asked for a postponement of the union since it had become clear that to proceed would divide the Methodist church. Three Methodist congregations in Lagos had initiated lawsuits to prevent the union and while these were pending it was felt that it was impossible to proceed. Two months later the political troubles began: the government was overthrown and in time the Biafran war of secession ensued. Negotiations ceased and there is no news of their having recommenced since the end of the war. When they do it seems certain that more will be necessary than simply taking up the threads where they were laid down in 1965.

Elsewhere in Africa there are other less broadly based union schemes. In general the picture is one of slow but steady ecumenical progress among the major churches. The Congo is the exception. Here on 8 March 1970 the Conseil Protestant du Congo became the Église du Christ au Congo. This was a very different process from the other unions and plans described in this chapter. There had been no slow negotiations leading to consensus and unification. Almost with a wave of a wand, certainly with little more than a stroke of the pen, the national Council of Churches had turned itself into a united church. A large number of churches and missions are involved and in fact in this predominantly Catholic country they are largely of a pronounced Protestant bias. In the event the union reached is hardly of the 'organic' nature generally aimed at; there would in any case not have been time to have achieved this. The former churches are now called 'communities' and maintain much of their old authority and independence. Nevertheless there is a central organization and the 'communities' are being grouped into local synods. It may be that the new church will grow into unity more quickly after this union than through the normal process of negotiation.

The Congo is also remarkable as the home of many of the largest sectarian and nationalistic churches which have broken away from the traditional and highly westernized denominations (see above, pp. 151–3 and 285–7). It is reckoned that there are some five thousand of these sects, involving seven million Africans – that is about a quarter of the Christian population of the continent. In many ways the sects reproduce the characteristics and beliefs already described in America, though with a heady extra mixture of primitive African culture. As has been seen most of these sects eschew the ecumenical movement, though four of the least extreme, in the Congo, Kenya, Rhodesia and Nigeria, joined the All Africa Conference of Churches in 1957, while the Congo church founded by Simon Kimbagu, which now has 200,000 followers, has succeeded in joining the World Council. But the fear these churches have of respectability and of western domination is bound to mean that for the most part they steer clear of unity negotiations. While they do so the cause of local church unity will be much impaired.

In the Near East there have been since 1962 negotiations in Jordan, Syria and Lebanon between Presbyterian, Congregational and Lutheran churches and the Arab Anglican community in those countries. The total number of Christians involved is said to be about 35,000. Inevitably, in view of the political circumstances, the negotiations have been sporadic. That they have continued at all is remarkable. By the outbreak of the Six-Day War in 1967 the delegates had produced a draft constitution of an episcopal church with a system of government with strong lay representation. This has been circulated to the churches but there has been little reaction as yet. A meeting planned for the summer of 1970, after which it was hoped to proceed to the inauguration of the church, failed to materialize.

In Asia the movement to reunion is strong in some places, but weak in others.

The most advanced schemes are to be found on the Indian sub-continent. Here the opportunity is being taken to rationalize the structures of the new united churches according to their political and cultural setting. For instance North-East India now has a unity scheme. This is unusual in that it originated, not with a church-to-church approach, but from the Council of Churches. This was in the early 1960s, after which negotiations seem to have languished, but now the talks have gathered impetus again and a draft Plan of Union is before the churches.

Burma presents a different problem, since the background to the life and very existence of the churches there is strongly Buddhist, coupled with religious nationalism. The Burmese churches are, therefore, in many ways closer to the churches of South-East Asia than to those of the old British India. Baptists (the great majority), Methodists and Anglicans have covenanted to seek union.

The salient features of the plans in North India, in Pakistan and in Ceylon (Lanka) have already been sufficiently described (see above, pp. 317–20). The Lanka scheme which provides for a united ministry from the inauguration of the church has been a model for many others. The negotiating churches are Anglican, Methodist, Baptist, Presbyterian and a diocese of the C.S.I. Between 1966 and 1969 four of these voted for union on the basis of the agreed scheme. The Methodists failed by 1 per cent to get the required 75 per cent approval. The Methodists now seem to be suggesting a two-stage union, starting with mutual recognition of ministries; but the four churches which are in agreement have decided to inaugurate union among themselves in 1972, thus giving the Methodist Conference two more chances to reach the required vote.

The North India and Pakistan schemes have not been without their last-minute difficulties. In these schemes there are seven participating churches who after forty years of negotiation decided in January 1970 to inaugurate the united churches on 29 November 1970. But at the eleventh hour the Episcopal Methodist church raised difficulties. This had been the last church to join the negotiations; it is also by far the largest body concerned. The difficulties were mainly of an administrative nature, turning to some extent on the fact that the Methodist bishops, who were paid on the American scale, would find their salaries drastically reduced in the united church. The Methodists felt that they had not been sufficiently consulted on these and other matters. It was not possible to reach agreement before the set date, and on that date the six other churches went forward into union.

In other parts of Asia the cause of union is less advanced than in India. In Malaysia, following a Christian Council initiative, negotiations began some years ago on a wide basis, including the Lutherans; local difficulties resulted in their coming to an end but church leaders are now hoping to embark on a series of bilateral discussions. Hong Kong is one of the few places where the churches are still growing, but they are at the same time astonishingly varied. There is co-operation especially in education and in the field of the social services, but not negotiation for unity. For different reasons the same is true of Taiwan (Formosa). It would probably be true to say that these small enclave societies, artificial and western-dominated, do not make good seed beds for ecumenical initiative. In Japan and the Philippines the Protestant churches have already found a measure of unity (see above, pp. 217–18). There are no new developments to report in these countries except that in 1969 the United Church of Japan reached a union with that of Okinawa, thus healing a long-standing war wound.

In South-East Asia it is to Indonesia that one looks at the moment for ecumenical action. There the first ecumenical approaches took place in 1946 and in 1950 a National Council of Churches was founded. The N.C.C. protested from the beginning that it saw itself as only a temporary organization, and that it wished to father a united church from the various reformed churches of the country. But the terrible events of the early sixties in Indonesia hardly made a propitious background for further advance. By 1967, however, more definite steps were again being taken. An attempt has been made to arrive at a doctrinal consensus and a draft has been drawn up for an ecumenical synod which will govern a united church in Indonesia. If this constitution is accepted by the N.C.C. it will turn itself into a united church. It will thus have reached a form of federal rather than organic unity somewhat similar to that in the Congo. It is perhaps worth commenting that the background to the two unions is not dissimilar. In each case there is a strong nationalism coupled with political instability. In each case western missionaries, with their ingrained habits of negotiation and committee work, are absent. In each case the churches concerned are notably at the reformed/Protestant end of the ecclesiastical spectrum. Neither as non-westerners nor as Protestants are they primarily concerned to wait for administrative tidiness or full organic union in the face of the urgency of the need for unity in a hostile environment.

In Australasia and the Pacific there are important ecumenical developments. In Papua there are negotiations for a united 'central Protestant church'. The main features of the New Zealand and Australian schemes have already been mentioned. The course of the New Zealand negotiations is interesting in that when conversations between the main Protestant churches were already far advanced in 1964 the Anglican province asked to be allowed to join the scheme which was evolving. At the time this slowed things up, since inevitably a lot of ground had to be re-covered; but it was felt that some delay would be amply justified in view of the prospect of achieving a wider union eventually, rather than taking two bites at the cherry. The New Zealand Plan of Union is now being discussed at both local and central levels. After any suggested revisions have been incorporated the churches will then decide whether they are ready to proceed to unification. Meanwhile there is a great deal of ecumenical co-operation: New Zealand, for instance, is one of the many places to lay good ecumenical foundations through the work of a Joint Theological College.

The Australian negotiations have taken almost exactly the opposite course. The original – and continuing – negotiating churches are the Congregational, Methodist and Presbyterian. Yet the scheme as it was first drawn up envisaged church government by bishops-in-presbytery. The negotiators evidently felt that they should create a church which would be open for future ecumenical development. In the same vein the bishops were to be consecrated by C.S.I. bishops. In this way they would not only be in the tradition of the historic episcopate, but also the Australian church would have shown its determination to think outside Australia and towards Asia and to be thought of as 'not an Australian sect with its own peculiar order, but by faith, aspiration and commitment ... a part of the Church of God'.[59] Not surprisingly the Anglican church in Australia took an interest in these negotiations; but in the end the Anglicans decided not to participate, except by sending observers. Anglican thinking is to wait for the smaller union, which could occur in 1974, and then start separate negotiations with the united church – a strategy which may reflect the very great numerical preponderance of the Anglican church in Australia, and perhaps the outlook which goes with it. There will, therefore, be two bites at this particular cherry. But meanwhile the idea of bishops-in-presbytery has been dropped in the latest revision of the Plan, though it is claimed that the section on church government still makes it clear that oversight in the church is 'personal as well as conciliar'. In place of the special relationship with the C.S.I. mention is made of all the neighbouring churches in Asia and the Pacific. With these changes the union goes forward and voting is due to begin in 1971.

In Latin America the soil is particularly sterile from an ecumenical point of view. This is because the continent has been until relatively recently reckoned a Christian area by virtue of the overwhelming dominance of the Roman Catholic church there. The Edinburgh Conference of 1910, for instance, 'declined to regard it [Latin America] as a mission field'.

This meant that for a long while the ecumenically-inclined historic churches more or less kept out. The missionaries who flooded in were those who refused to treat Roman Catholics as Christians, who had no concern for comity arrangements, and little interest in one another. (Of the 134 missionary agencies who have sent missionaries for training ... over the last twenty-eight years, only thirty have been affiliated with the National Council of Churches of the U.S.A., forty-nine have belonged to non-ecumenical associations, and fifty-five have been wholly independent.) Many missions were virtually founded on a basis of anti-Catholicism.[60]

In other words these missions have been mainly of a sect type; almost by definition they have not been interested in the visible unity of the church. Where there has been any attempt at common action it has often been on an anti-Catholic basis: in Haiti, for instance, 'the uniting issue for the Council of Evangelical Churches is ... anti-

Catholicism'. With such churches 'to recognize real changes in the Roman Catholic Church today ... would seem to threaten their very *raison d'être*'. In fact and in summary:

> In spite of its preponderating power and traditional attitudes the Roman Catholic Church in Latin America is far more ready for ecumenical dialogue and co-operation than are the Evangelical Churches.[61]

Where there have been the tentative beginnings of co-operation the initiative has come from the R.C. side.

Nor are these Protestant churches very much more friendly to the ecumenical movement in general as represented by the World Council of Churches and all its works.

> The very term 'ecumenical' tends to be a word of abuse in Latin America. The fact is that the enemies of the movement got in first, and queered the pitch with their calumnies [see above, pp. 246 and 287]. Their chief accusations are that the World Council is pro-Communist, liberal in theology, guilty of the heresy of Universalism, activist instead of spiritual, and friendly to the Catholic Church. Of these sins the last is the worst.[62]

Nor is it against the W.C.C. only that this anti-ecumenism operates ... 'but against the ecumenical spirit, attitudes, theology and movements, on the national level'. Where there are local federations of churches they can often be not only anti-Catholic but also anti-ecumenical, in the ordinary sense of that term. The fact that the Haiti federation of Protestant churches originally at its foundation in 1969 proposed to call itself a 'Council of Truly Evangelical Churches' is the tell-tale. In this context 'Truly' means 'sound', 'conservative evangelical', 'fundamentalist', 'non-liberal' and in general don't-touch-the-W.C.C.-and-its-member-churches-with-a-barge-pole. This is a spirit which even affects in Latin America churches which are normally in the ecumenical camp, such as the Presbyterian.

On top of all this, where there are Protestant churches they are, apart from the Pentecostalists, usually scattered single missions or even congregations which are hardly large enough or corporate enough to be able to mount a union operation, even if they wanted to. There are, however, one or two small schemes in hand: in particular eleven churches in Argentina and Uruguay met in 1970 to discuss unity.

In the northern (British-influenced) Caribbean ecumenical advance has been slow for rather different reasons. Here the predominant churches are the Anglican and the Roman Catholic, though the major Protestant denominations are also represented. The Anglicans are markedly Anglo-Catholic and have been very slow to give a lead, as in view of their majority position was incumbent on them; even W.C.C. activities have been minimal. In 1965, however, the Anglicans in the West Indies and the Methodists in the Caribbean area started negotiations based on the Anglican/Methodist plan in England, though in some ways more forward-looking than that scheme. After the 1969 failure of the English parent model it was hardly surprising that the West Indian discussions slowed down. However in 1969 a wider group, including Roman Catholics, was formed to discuss covenanting for unity and at the same time a local Caribbean Christian Conference was mooted. If these plans bear fruit some long-overdue ecumenical activity may be the result.

In Canada the ecumenical scene has been much simplified since the formation of the United Church of Canada in 1925 (see above, pp. 215–16). Apart from the Roman Catholics and the sects this leaves to all intents and purposes the Anglicans, Lutherans and Baptists, plus one or two small churches such as the Disciples of Christ (see above, p. 150) and the continuing Presbyterians who have never joined the United Church. The Lutherans have been engaged on a federal agreement which involves 97 per cent of their number and which may continue into a more organic form of union.

The United Church and the Anglican province have been involved in negotiation since 1943, and have recently been joined by the (much smaller) Christian Church, that is Disciples of Christ. These discussions have already been characterized as being very open-ended and much concerned with the church's witness in contemporary society. For these and other reasons some Anglicans have approached them with caution. When an Anglican (*sic!*) negotiator writes of the Apostles Creed – no less – that to make assent to it a condition of church membership 'would be thought by many United Church people an offence to intellectual honesty and an impediment to the work of Christian education and mission', other Anglican eyebrows are sure to be raised.[63] In any case some Anglicans have been saying that 'Rome is where the action is' and that it would be better to concentrate ecumenical advances on that front. It is not surprising, therefore, that at times these long-drawn negotiations have proceeded somewhat desultorily. Recently, however, more energy has been shown, though the Anglicans seem to have stacked the cards against the scheme by saying that an adverse vote from a single diocese will act as a veto for the united church. The four negotiating Commissions – the Church in the World, Doctrinal, Constitutional and Liturgical – have produced draft reports; these are now to be the subject of an educational programme in the churches on a very big scale. Inter-church study groups are to be set up in every locality where this is possible, and it hoped in the end to muster as many as 3,000 such groups – probably the biggest experiment in ecumenical education ever undertaken. On top of this the interest of non-members is invoked through numerous public meetings and the use of the mass media. Clearly this programme will take some time and no exact dates for future progress have been suggested.

In the United States there is a great deal of ecumenical activity, as would be expected with the churches in such a state of multiple division. There are negotiations going on separately between Methodists, Presbyterians, Moravians and Lutherans who have all at one time or another split inside their denominations. There are negotiations between Baptists and Methodists and even to some extent between some of the sects. Over-arching all these is the Consultation of Church Union, or Church of Christ Uniting, which has already been described in some detail. The Consultation started in 1962 between the United Presbyterian Church, the United Church of Christ, the Protestant Episcopal (Anglican) Church and the Methodist Church. Since then there have been at least annual meetings and other denominations have been gathered into the fold, so that nine churches are now represented. In some cases other union plans have been shelved so that the Consultation can be concentrated on. At one time the negotiators felt that there was a generation of work ahead of them, but recently the face of things has changed. In 1969 a draft Plan of Union was drawn up and by 1970 the present plan was offered to the annual plenary meeting. This was achieved by nineteen representatives of the churches giving a week in each month to drafting over a twenty-month period – an indication of priorities which might serve as a model to other negotiating committees. It is reckoned that by 1972 a revised Plan of Union will be ready to be submitted for decision to the churches concerned. Meanwhile a full-scale education programme, similar to that in Canada, is being launched.

We come finally in this brief world survey to Europe

and Great Britain, the home and source of the divisions which are so slowly now being mended throughout the rest of the world.

In Europe there is very little progress to report. In 1968 a union was consummated across the East/West German boundary between a German Methodist and a German Evangelical church, both of which had their separate roots in the United States. Four Lutheran Free (that is non-established) churches, having found that they have no fundamental doctrinal differences, have agreed on union in 1971. In France tentative discussions between Lutherans and Reformed seem to have arrived at deadlock.

Unity Negotiations in Great Britain

Unity negotiations in Great Britain differ from most of those in the rest of the world in that they are bilateral rather than multilateral. The reason for this is largely fortuitous in the way that conversations between the various churches were set up after the war. It may be that where the divisions between the churches trace back directly to historical and theological roots (instead of being inherited by chance as in the 'mission' churches) it is easier and more logical to work on a one-to-one basis; on the other hand it can be said that the fact that the British churches have not grasped the nettle, as the Americans have, and embarked on a multilateral scheme, is evidence of a lack of ecumenical urgency in a country where the missionary task of the church is still not seen in its stark true light.

Ireland is to some extent the exception. Conversations began there in 1965 between the Church of Ireland (Anglican) and the Presbyterian and Methodist churches of Ireland respectively; in 1968, however, it was decided that it would be more rational – let alone more economical in time and money – to continue negotiations on a tripartite level. The conversations are still in the initial stages. Discussing the traditional dividing issues of Scripture, Church, Sacraments and Ministry, they have failed to reach agreement on episcopacy and on the appointment of lay members to pastoral office in the life of the church – that is the eldership issue.

In Wales the Anglicans and Methodists have had a scheme which has kept roughly in step with that proceeding over the border. The Welsh Methodists were part of the Conference which voted in favour of the Scheme; this vote has now been ratified by the Welsh Synod. The independent Anglican province showed deep divisions about the plan, the laity being much more in favour of it than the clergy. The governing body has, however, approved a move towards the inauguration of Stage One of the proposals.

The Congregationalists and Presbyterians are also in negotiation, having had an intercommunion relationship since 1951.

There have also been moves towards a wider general union of the churches in Wales, including the Methodists and Baptists but excluding the Anglicans. In 1967 a Scheme of Union was presented to these churches; the Baptists found it unacceptable but the other churches are now working on amendments. Alongside all this the major denominations in Wales, from the Anglicans to the Baptists, responded seriously to the call from the Nottingham Conference in 1964 to covenant for unity. A Committee has now agreed that the Churches are in sufficient agreement to covenant for unity and has produced a draft covenant for solemn notification in 1974. During the course of these negotiations much anti-Anglican feeling was revealed, but some progress has been made in a relaxation of Anglican rules on intercommunion – an issue which the report highlighted as important for further progress. With so many conversations afoot in Wales, and with some churches involved in two or three of them, it would not be surprising if the unfortunate church members felt a little overwhelmed at the conflicting possibilities being presented to them.

The situation between the Church of England and the Church of Scotland has already been touched on. A working party, largely composed (as far as the C. of S. was concerned) of academics, published in 1957 a paper on *Relations between Anglican and Presbyterian Churches* in both countries. This proposed, as a basis for inter-communion, the adoption of 'bishops-in-presbytery' in the Church of Scotland and of a more corporate and conciliar practice of episcopacy in the Church of England. It also suggested that the Church of England should adopt a form of eldership, that is specially commissioned laymen with a permanent part in the government and pastoral oversight of the church. Of the four churches concerned, only the Episcopal church in Scotland accepted this report. In Scotland at large it caused a furore largely fomented by a virulent campaign of opposition in the Scottish *Daily Express*. (Lord Beaverbrook was the son of a Canadian manse.) Matters were not helped by the fact that the Church of England showed hardly any reaction to the report. As a result even ecumenically-minded Scottish leaders felt with a certain sense of despair that the proposals about elders were being virtually ignored in such a way that it was difficult not to suspect that the Church of England was approaching the whole affair with that sense of 'superiority' which non-Anglicans are quick to look for. In the event the report was rejected by the General Assembly of the Church of Scotland in 1959.

It was a matter of back to the drawing board. New conversations were started, but some lessons had been learned. In the first place the new Church of Scotland representatives were more typical of the parochial life of the church. Secondly it was more clearly recognized that the end in view must be unity at a national level: that is to say the Church of England and the Presbyterians should be united in England, the Church of Scotland and the Episcopalians in Scotland, while the two new national churches would be in communion with each other. To this end the new conversations addressed themselves to certain thorny and traditional questions, the nature of which showed how much the debate was still covering familiar ground. These were such matters as the distinction between unity and uniformity – always a tricky point, especially as many churches fear that negotiations with Anglicans will amount to a take-over bid which will swamp their own individuality – and the meaning of validity of orders and sacraments, and of the apostolic succession. Despite the fact that the questions were largely traditional it is significant that for the answers the members of the various committees were willing to learn from general ecumenical experience and even from particular unity negotiations; they acknowledged a debt for instance to an Australian document on the nature and function of the church – a state of affairs which would have been to say the least unlikely a few years earlier.

The conversations came up with some fresh answers to the stale questions. They formulated the important principle that 'at certain points unity demands uniformity, at others diversity working towards a single end'; they said that 'validity' might be an acceptable term to describe the law of a particular church or denomination, but was hardly one which could be applied to ecumenical discussion – a lesson learned long ago by those plans which have been based on a mutual acceptance of ministry and sacraments; they acknowledged that in the past and even today unity discussions have been 'far too much dominated by clerical attitudes and actions'; they agreed that, while a minimal form of church establishment might be desirable, the Scottish pattern was preferable to the English as it gave greater freedom to the church to rule its own life.

The result of these renewed conversations was reported in 1966 and since then specific union negotiations have been set on foot between the Church of Scotland and the Episcopalians in Scotland. The background to these negotiations is now distinctly more promising, with increasing mutual trust between the churches and even co-operation in some parishes in new housing areas – but it is always possible that the Scottish *Daily Express* may return to the fray. Meanwhile in Scotland more general multilateral conversations involving six churches have also started since 1966; they are studying the methods adopted in South India and New Zealand. To complete the picture, in 1969 a Plan of Union between the Church of Scotland and the Congregationalists was rejected by both churches.

This brings us lastly to the situation in England. Here the Congregationalists and Presbyterians have had inter-communion since before the war, but until recently this fellowship has not stimulated any more definite moves to organic union. In 1963, however, the churches voted to start moving towards union, a move which was delayed (as has been seen) by legal and constitutional difficulties. In May 1970, however, the annual assemblies of the two churches voted by the required substantial majorities to accept the proposed scheme for consideration by local member churches. Presbyterian churches will have to opt *out* of the united church and Congregationalist to opt *into* it – a significant survival of the Reformation insistence by the independent churches on the autonomy and self-sufficiency of each gathered congregation (see above, pp. 139–40). The scheme involves only some 250,000 Christians but if it continues to completion – which at present is planned for October 1972 – it will be the first union in Britain since the Reformation to take place across denominational frontiers.

Anglican/Methodist conversations began in 1956 and

proceeded via an interim report to a definite scheme published in 1963. The essence of the Anglican / Methodist plan was that it was the C.S.I. solution turned upside down. That is to say, instead of a union of the churches followed at an interval by the union of the ministries, it started with a unification of the ministries, followed at Stage Two by the union of the churches. This solution goes back to the suggestion made in 1946 in the famous 'Cambridge Sermon' by the then Archbishop of Canterbury, Dr Fisher, that the Methodists and Free Churches should 'take episcopacy into their system'. During the fifties it was tacitly agreed in England, as elsewhere, in response to Anglo-Catholic pressure that a unified ministry should be the basis of the scheme. The reason for the delay between Stage One (unification) and Stage Two (union) is that, in the words of the scheme, 'nothing else is practicable'.

During the time of their separation the Church of England and the Methodist Church have lived in isolation from one another. . . . Most members of both churches have grown up in ignorance of each other's ways. Differences of approach to worship and order often turn out on close and friendly examination to be superficial and insignificant, but meanwhile they loom large in the minds of many clergy, ministers and lay people. So it would not be possible for the two churches to become effectively one, in full fellowship together, through a single act of unification in the near future. . . . The imposing of union before the members of the two churches were fully prepared for it would bring bewilderment and bitterness in plenty, and this cannot be the right way to proceed.[64]

This paragraph constitutes an appalling admission of the failure of the ecumenical movement at the grassroots; but the situation being what it is, the conclusion is probably wise.

After the unification of the ministries there would be a period of intercommunion, a time of growing together in understanding, which should lead to full organizational union at Stage Two. The form that this ultimate union would take has not been so much as sketched in the present scheme. The first hurdle to be negotiated is that of the unification of the ministries. It is admitted that there are various problems on both sides, but it is hoped that once Stage One has been achieved these will be resolved in the period of growing together before Stage Two. These problems are such things as, on the Methodist side, doubts over the establishment of the church, different approaches to some ethical problems such as drink and gambling, and the use of fermented wine at the Holy Communion; on the Anglican side they concern the fact that Methodist laymen are occasionally allowed to celebrate the Holy Communion, and doubts about the way the consecrated elements of bread and wine are disposed of in the Methodist church after the communion service – both these items reflecting Anglican fears that in the Methodist tradition the sacraments are not treated with the same respect as in the Anglican. Anglicans have also expressed concern that the Methodists allow the re-marriage of divorced people in church – although Anglican practice on this matter must surely soon be modified in a more tolerant direction.

But the over-riding problem is the initial one of the unification of the ministries at Stage One. Here the service of reconciliation has been several times altered and improved so that it is now probably the most carefully worked out of all the services of this type in current union schemes. The latest proposal places a much greater emphasis on the reconciliation of the churches as a whole, of which the unification of the ministries is a part, and in accordance with current thought lays great emphasis on the missionary nature of the united church. The service starts with an act of commitment to 'the pledged purpose of our two churches to become one'. This is followed by acts of penitence, thanksgiving and renewed covenant. After this the total membership of each church is received into fellowship with the other. This is the essential act of reconciliation, within the context of which the act of integration of the ministries takes place. This is done by a united prayer by all the bishops and ministers taking part on behalf of the two churches:

We offer ourselves wholly to thee, asking that thou wilt renew in us thy blessing already given, and that thou wilt transcend the differences of our calling and make us one by bestowing upon us what thou knowest us to need for thy service as Bishops/Presbyters in thy universal church and in the coming together of the Church of England and the Methodist Church.[65]

This corporate prayer is then followed by the laying-on of hands by Methodists on Anglicans and vice versa *in silence*. The service, therefore, not only makes no judgements about past or future ministry, it makes a positive point of putting the whole question into the hands of God.

This central service is followed by local services on the same lines and by the consecration of the first Methodist bishops. In the course of the negotiations it was seen that the preparation of an Ordinal of services for all ordinations in the united church would be an essential part of Stage One, so that all future consecrations and ordinations would take place within the context of the new life of the reconciled church. The new Ordinal has met with general admiration (see p. 315) and as Anglicans tend to look to liturgical forms for an expression of doctrinal belief they have noted with satisfaction the fact that the services of the Ordinal express quite clearly what they consider to be the traditional 'Catholic' teaching on the ministry.

It was not over the Ordinal but over the Service of Reconciliation and Unification of Ministries that the scheme ran on to the rocks in 1969. It had been decided that a 75 per cent majority in each church must be obtained before the plan could be said to be acceptable. In the Methodist church there had been steady opposition from a number of convinced Protestants who saw the scheme as a sell-out to the Church of England which was not satisfactorily committed to the Protestant position. Nevertheless when the day came the Methodist Conference, meeting at Birmingham, voted 76 per cent in favour of the scheme. The same day, 8 July 1969, the joint Convocations of the Church of England, meeting in London, voted only 69 per cent in favour; 38 bishops voted for and 5 against, 225 priests voted for and 111 against. There had been indications in the dioceses and in the Church Assembly, which included lay people, that the majority would not reach the required 75 per cent, but the issue remained in doubt until the last moment. The vital 6 per cent was a matter of 21 votes and it is probable that that number of voters at least were not themselves opposed to the scheme but were frightened at the idea of a minority as large as 20 to 25 per cent who could not be carried along with it – some of whom had declared that they would continue as an independent church and seek legal means to be granted at least a proportion of the property and income of the Church of England.

The opposition came from the two extreme wings of the Church of England. The conservative evangelicals disliked the scheme and voted against it on the grounds that once the churches are reconciled it is unreasonable, unnecessary and unscriptural to insist on the unification of the ministries by the laying-on of hands. In other words they reject what has become the current Anglican approach to union in favour of a C.S.I.-type solution. But the unification of the ministries solution has been insisted on by the 'high-church' section of the Church of England and there is no doubt that, if this approach had not been adopted, the voting against the scheme among high-churchmen would have been much greater. Those who did vote against it on the opposite wing to the

Evangelicals were the rigid Anglo-Catholics, for whom the careful – and even positive – ambiguity of the service of unification was not satisfactory. They wanted a clear statement through the wording of the service that what was being done was the essential episcopal ordination of the Methodist ministers. They complained that the proposed method of unification was based on prevarication and was therefore unacceptable if not positively blasphemous.

The conscientiousness of both these opposing views must be accepted, however much it may be felt that it is tragic that it was a combination of two entirely different standpoints which brought the scheme down. The honesty of each party in saying that it desires union may also be accepted. In this vote the Church of England found itself between Scylla and Charybdis. Neither extreme party was able to accept the view that a totally logical and water-tight solution was in the circumstances impossible. Neither was able to feel that in the over-riding interest of the unity of the church the application of the principle of 'economy' might be possible.

Note that each side represents in its different way the authoritarian traditions in the Church of England: the conservative evangelicals appeal to the absolute authority of the Bible; the Anglo-Catholics to that of the church with its episcopally ordained ministry – however much in practice they often reject the guidance of the bishops. Both parties are therefore psychologically conservative and likely to be resistant to change. It is difficult to avoid the conclusion that in voting against the scheme each party was voting against change and trying to preserve the Church of England intact according to its own outlook. The evangelicals had made it clear that among other things they regretted the fact there was no mention of the Thirty-Nine Articles as the basis of the united church; the Articles are the Protestant high-water mark in the history of the Church of England and the evangelicals have always claimed to be the party which truly upholds the Protestant tradition in the shifting sands of Anglican history. The Anglo-Catholics are pinning their colours to the mast of the nineteenth-century view of the episcopal ministry and the apostolic succession as the only true test of the church – a view which is permissible within the Church of England but not obligatory. Each side is appealing to the past. In claiming that its views must bind the whole church each side is implicitly denying the historic fact that the Church of England is a widely comprehensive church, where various parties can live together and where differing views on certain important but inessential and uncertain matters can be held within a general framework of agreeing to differ.

The Methodist vote is in one sense a vote about the nature of the Church of England. Not for the first time at a moment of crisis the tail is wagging the dog. In this case it is a Siamese tail. In the last century the two parties came together to resist intellectual change in the face of Darwinianism, Biblical criticism and the like. In 1969 they came together again to reject the change which may be thought to be most typical of – and necessary to – the church of the twentieth century.

At the time of the rejection of the scheme the Archbishop of Canterbury, who had given a vigorous lead in its favour, complained repeatedly that the opposition had failed to produce any positive counter-proposals. Since the opposition was an alliance of the two diametrically opposed wings of the Church of England it seemed unlikely that they would be able to produce an agreed alternative scheme for union. However four leaders of the opposition, two from each party, have now done so in the form of a book entitled *Growing into Union*.

In criticizing the scheme its opponents make some shrewd and palpable hits. Three in particular may be mentioned. First they complain that the scheme had been a centrally directed one and one which had not had much local support (as was shown in the final voting) and even less really local impact. In a sense this was true; the attempt to gain local understanding and arouse local interest in a way which would lead to local action had been less than is the case with the programmes now being launched in Canada and the United States, or even in the local education which has preceded the Ghana union scheme. It is also probably true that 'although a change in the Church of England was at issue, it was not one that would have proved costly in the average parish'.[66] Moreover it is fair to criticize this scheme as ignoring the need of expressing or finding union at the local level. On the other hand it is hardly reasonable to complain that a union scheme has been produced by church leaders, as its opponents seem to do. How else is such an idea to come forward and be promoted in the churches concerned?

Second – and related to this – the writers assert that the scheme does little or nothing to produce a reformed as well as a united church. For instance nothing is done to reduce the size of Church of England dioceses in order to make possible the proper working of personal episcopacy. This criticism seems valid, especially when it is allied to the further complaint that, although the real crunch of the union will take place at Stage Two, there have as yet been no indications of what is proposed at Stage Two. This is particularly serious in that

The biggest objection to the two-stage Scheme was that it postponed every tricky question *except* that of the ministry. If there were really a deep-felt desire for union in the two churches, then a bold programme for reform could have been put before them.[67]

The writers' greatest wrath is saved for the plan for the unification of the ministries and the introduction of episcopacy into the united church. In general they feel that episcopacy is being produced not as a theologically felt necessity, but as a *deus ex machina* formula for unity.

We are all haunted by a view of apostolic succession which is mechanical and isolated from the Church's total life.... To isolate episcopacy as something which can, so to speak, be injected into a Church without organic relation to its faith, liturgical practice and pastoral structure is not only to reduce episcopacy to 'gimmick' or mascot status, it is to empty it of its historic meaning and to invert its real purpose. Episcopacy is not an accolade bestowed on the Church as a finishing touch or a final decoration, nor is it a trifle of which a Church should make as little as possible lest its members be offended.... It is a part of the visible Church's developed bone structure – no more, and no less.[68]

This accusation about the introduction of episcopacy could be levelled against any of the schemes in which Anglicans have been involved and which have been based on the adoption of a united episcopal ministry from the inauguration – from Lanka down to the English plans. The accusation of 'gimmickry' and 'injection' in the unification service might be understood if it came from a non-Anglican source. But this form of unification was preferred to the South India method precisely at the insistence of the Anglo-Catholic party in the Church of England. It seems, therefore, to say the least, ironic that the Anglican/Methodist scheme should be rejected by Anglo-Catholics on this ground.

The more specific objection is against the Service of Reconciliation itself, which is described as a 'bog of illogic', and a 'magnificent double-think'. Fundamentally it is that the service neither proclaims itself as a re-ordination of those who are not in episcopal orders, nor really accepts the validity of the orders of the participating ministers as they stand. The critics are also at pains to show that the whole business of a united ministry after the service will be difficult to administer. It will be necessary to keep a record of who has been 'reconciled' and who has not; the service will have to be repeated for those coming into the country – say from America – and wishing to minister in the united church. There is much play with the idea of 'bishops at the customs' and 'customs-protected brand of orders' for any church which adopts this method of unification. This is all very well, but it is difficult to avoid the feeling that it is logic-chopping, and that in applying this ruthless logic the opponents of the Anglican/Methodist scheme have failed to learn what must surely be the basic lesson of all ecumenical negotiation. That is that disunity creates a situation which is itself so abnormal that to demand a totally logical and water-tight method of arriving at unity is to cry the moon. Somewhere along the line there are bound to be loose ends and untidy solutions which may be accepted in the context of the search for unity. Moreover the achievement of unity is a once-for-all thing, which does not create worrying precedents. As the Lanka negotiators say of their service of reconciliation: 'precedent cannot be found for it ... it is *sui generis* out of a new situation in the life of the church' (see above, p. 318).

Nevertheless there are obviously better and worse ways of finding unity. What is the positive alternative offered by the representatives of those who rejected the Anglican/Methodist suggestion? Basically they suggest that if churches can reach doctrinal agreement, they could then proceed to unity in an episcopal church without any service of reconciliation or unification of ministries. They particularly criticize the Anglican/Methodist scheme as being theologically weak and having skated round the problem of finding unity in doctrine. Describing themselves as ' "conservationist" rather than "conservative" ', they see in the theological approach of the scheme 'doctrinal minimalism'. The 'minimalist spirit' is typical of the liberal approach in all ages, 'and the modern concern for church reunion has given it a new lease of life'.

Against the 'minimalist' method, which is to find 'what is the minimum of agreement in belief that is necessary for this purpose', the conservationists wish to substitute an approach based on 'a contemporary declaration of faith for a united church'. Such a contemporary confession will be 'orientated to current forms of misbelief':

It must be possible to know in advance that as a corporate body a united Church will stand for the historic faith in its fullness, and only a contemporary confessional statement ... will make this possible.[69]

It may be felt that such a statement aimed evidently at rebutting modern minimalizing heresies will be negative rather than positive, but the writers make a brave attempt to produce a doctrinal statement which will satisfy the divergent theological positions they represent. On some such agreement as this a united church for England is to be based. Once such doctrinal agreement has been reached their suggestion is that the church may be inaugurated and after that individuals or groups may join it. They envisage existing congregations joining corporately or new congregations of the united church being set up, especially in new or 'mission' areas. This will be a one-stage scheme which will happen alongside the existing denominations. In fact in effect it will create a new 'ecumenical' denomination in the country. The new church will be 'reformed' in that it will have got rid of many of the abuses of the contemporary churches. It will be episcopal, although the practice of episcopacy will be 'overhauled to bring it into line with the theory'.[70] At first two or three dioceses will be needed for the whole country; but, as the new church grows and the old ones decline, these will be further subdivided. Such things as the Church of England cathedrals will be among the longest survivors of the old order – and, as the Archbishop of Canterbury has remarked, he himself will be the last person to be able to join the new united church.

The strengths of the scheme are its local basis, its vision of reformed church structures, and its challenge to churches and to Christians to die in order to be reborn into unity. But the general opinion has been that these theoretical gains cannot offset the practical disadvantage of the idea. It is unworkable. It would lead to administrative, legal and even personal chaos. The writers of *Growing into Union* criticize the official scheme as illogical and administratively untidy. Their own alternative makes the official plans look a model of practicability. Moreover – and this they do not deny – their own plan for a united church in England would be a very slow process. This being so it is difficult to avoid the conclusion that the period of ecclesiastical chaos while the new and old churches existed alongside each other would provide the final *coup de grâce* for organized religion in the country. If time were no problem and the country was generally Christian and church-going the scheme might be a starter. But time is of the essence, and that being so there is little wonder that it has not been deemed worthy of serious consideration.

Before the rejection of the Anglican/Methodist scheme it was being said that a negative vote would set back the cause of church unity in Britain by a generation. This was probably an exaggeration – although the vote certainly makes the covenant made at the Nottingham Faith and Order Conference to attempt to bring about union in the British Isles by 1980 seem wildly over-optimistic. It will be difficult to modify the scheme in such a way as will make it acceptable to those who rejected it in 1969. It seems more likely that in a year or two it will be reintroduced with minor changes in the hope that wiser counsels will prevail at the second time round. Meanwhile in most English dioceses the bishops have issued instructions making intercommunion and the exchange of pulpits easier. If the opportunities thus given are taken at the parish level it could mean that the period of growing together, which was to have begun after Stage One, will begin now. Thus when Stage One does come there may not need to be so long a delay before Stage Two follows on. In the long run therefore it could be that Stage Two – full organic union, which is after all the essential goal – will not be so long delayed as at first seemed certain when the result of the vote on 8 July 1969 was known. But this will depend, as all union ultimately depends, on work and study at the local level – and there is little evidence that this is taking place on any significant scale.

It is in fact precisely at the local level that the negative vote may have its most damaging effect. Some people are disgusted; many are impatient. In some places there has been talk of open rebellion; in some places co-operation between Anglicans and Methodists has gone too far for progress to be held up now. Young people especially in universities and colleges are among the most impatient. But rebellion against church rules and seemingly irrelevant clerical leadership is preferable to the more likely result – which is sheer disillusion. There are many people in England – again especially among the young – who are disillusioned by the churches' inability to change themselves to a role suited to the twentieth century. Some are leaving the churches because of this disillusionment; others are inhibited from joining them. The rejection of the Anglican/Methodist proposals cannot but add to this disillusion, even if ultimately the scheme goes forward. For the moment the negotiations are in abeyance. If the Church of England brings the scheme forward again the vote will now be taken, not in Convocation, but in the new national Synod, which includes lay people. It is too early yet to say what the temper of this assembly will be. At its foundation a New Synod Group was formed, which is devoted to supporting the scheme as it at present exists.

The scheme was the first Anglican/non-Anglican union to be voted on since the inauguration of the

Church of South India in 1947. That union was hailed as a breakthrough. But more than twenty years have passed and, with the recent exception of North India, no others as yet have followed. It is true that union is a slow business; it is true that a number of schemes, which have been in the pipeline longer than the English plans, are due to come to fruition soon. But still some will think the pace too slow. They may be wrong to think it, but the fact that they do so means that they are bound to be disillusioned. And meanwhile the rate of decline of the churches is accelerating. There are many factors beyond the control of the churches which make their task difficult and their very survival uncertain. There are also some factors over which they do have control. Unity is perhaps the chief of these. It seems ironic that they should make their own task harder.

'UNITY IS NOT ENOUGH'

This book is about the search for Christian unity known as the ecumenical movement. Its brief does not extend to a discussion of what happens to churches *after* they have united. But it may be well to include a brief mention of some of the difficulties which churches have to face after union.

One point has been made so many times that it may even have been laboured. This is the fact that ecumenical leaders in the past decade have never tired of saying that union is only one aspect of church renewal: a church which is reunited but not in other ways reformed will not be a church which has fulfilled the aims of ecumenists, the aim summed up in the slogan 'one church renewed for mission'. Unity, as the sociologists have not been slow to point out, is not a panacea for ecclesiastical success: it will not automatically be followed by conversions and full churches.

The preceding analysis of current negotiations for

union has made it clear that some are conservative (or even conservationist) in character, whereas others have a more built-in reforming spirit; the opportunity of union is taken to rethink church structures in a modern context. Among the more conservative schemes was the Anglican/ Methodist proposal in England, so far as it had developed when the vote went against it. Among the more radical schemes is C.O.C.U. in the United States. But in either case there may be a danger that a union scheme has been so long in negotiation that when it comes to fruition it will in fact reflect the ideas of a past generation; if the basic ideas put forward at the beginning of the negotiations have become ossified without substantial change, this is bound to happen however 'advanced' those ideas were when they were first produced. Thus some people were already saying at its inauguration that the United Church of North India was 'an old man's church'.

An old man's church is one that is not inherently likely to push ahead with reform and new ideas – or even with those essential changes and economies which can be made as a result of union. Such changes should be an essential consequence of any union scheme. But they are not always made. In 1960, twenty-eight years after the British Methodist union of 1932, the Chairman of the Methodist Conference for that year summed up the post-union situation on one vital factor – that of closing churches which had become unnecessary and duplicatory since the union.

There is a widespread impatience ... at the continued tolerance on the part of Conference of the redundancy which is strangling our effectiveness.... Let me give two examples, which are typical, not exceptional. There is one city which contains within its boundaries fifty-nine Methodist churches, considerably more than the Church of England possess. Congregations are small and we could well do with half of them. I visited a town recently with a population of 17,000 where there are four large Methodist churches, none of which have an average congregation of fifty. . . . Methodist union took place twenty-eight years ago. When Conference decided that union at the circuit and society level would be a matter for local action, they could never have dreamed of such a sequel. The laity of the three churches ought never to have voted in such numbers for union unless they intended to consummate it locally. . . . In area after area, the appeal and often the direction of Conference has been flouted. Worship of bricks and mortar has supplanted the worship of the living God.[71]

Here it was the local churches which failed to take the steps which should in all logic have followed union. There can also be problems with organizational growing together at the centre which can hold up effective unity after a formal act of union has taken place. In 1957 in the United States the Congregational Christian church and the Evangelical and Reformed church reached union. Negotiations had been going on since 1942 but had been held up by a protracted law-suit by dissident churches on the result of which much future planning had depended (see above, pp. 216 and 315). The two churches were in fact very close in doctrine and in 'policy' or understanding on questions of church and ministry. A union seemed, therefore, logical and easy. What was perhaps not realized at the time was that the bureaucratic and organizational methods of the churches had for historical reasons developed along very different lines. Different committee structures had led to different assumptions, understandings and relationships within the churches. A study has been made of the post-union process of growing together in the united church which shows how difficult were some of the problems which had to be faced. The study leads to the following conclusions.

This study of one segment of the United Church shows that the problems raised by the institutional unification of the churches differ from the problems raised by differences in doctrine, ways of worship, and 'church order'. . . . In institutional integration doctrine and formal church order are of limited

importance. . . . Institutional procedures have their own autonomy, their own reality and stubbornness. . . . Nor does a deep
commitment to church unity and enthusiasm for its actualization dissolve the problems of institutionalism. All the leaders
who work in the agencies studied are committed to the United
Church; none have opposed its consummation, and many have
worked hard to bring the union into being. But even when
union has become a fact of history at one level it must still be
worked out in political negotiations. . . .

The unification of churches at the institutional level is
created and takes place in the context of tension. Differences
in conception of purpose and 'style of life' . . . differences in
economic resources, size and social status of denominations,
create an imbalance in social power, and will be interpreted
in this way in spite of pledges to ignore them. Staff members of
the uniting churches represent the interests of previous patterns of organization, traditional ways of work and personal
loyalties. . . . These institutional issues are settled by processes
of negotiation that are frankly political and business in character. . . . At least as much time and energy is required for business and political processes as for discussions about doctrine
and purpose. . . .

Many aspects of the new church – its particular tasks and
patterns of work – will take shape as the patterns or forms of
organization are revised according to the purpose and functions that develop in the course of institutional unification.[72]

In sum this study underlines the fact that the achievement of unity is only the beginning of the road of
unification, with its consequent adjustment of the life
and effectiveness of the united church. It also suggests
that the supporters of the C.S.I. type of union scheme
have been right in claiming that its chief strength was
that, by fixing as few details as possible before union, it
left matters open-ended so that the new church was free
to develop in new ways after union (see above, pp. 309–10;
this is the whole argument of Bishop Michael Hollis's
book *The Significance of South India*).

But even the C.S.I., for all the hopes which were felt at
the time of its inauguration, has had its difficulties. In 1964

– seventeen years after that inauguration and the same year as the publication of the much-praised self-survey of the C.S.I., *Renewal and Advance* (see above, p. 309) – the Reverend Mark Gibbard paid a three-month visit to the C.S.I. His report on what he saw was most favourable – but it was not starry-eyed. His final conclusion, as the title of his book suggests, is that *Unity is not enough.*

Church unity, though essential, is not alone enough. Before the inauguration of union and soon afterwards it looked as if unity by itself would give the Church new zeal and insight to extend the Kingdom of God, but this has not been so to any considerable extent ... Unity without inner renewal will not equip churches for mission.[73]

CHAPTER EIGHT

The Roman Catholic Church and the Orthodox Churches

Knowledge prepares the way for love: love leads to unity.

POPE PAUL VI, *at the opening of the Anglican Centre in Rome, 1966*

THE SECOND VATICAN COUNCIL

THE negative attitude of the Roman Catholic church to the ecumenical movement in the first half of the twentieth century has already been described (see pp. 207–8). This attitude was based on the teaching that the Roman church is the only true church and its sacraments the only valid sacraments. The only possible basis for reunion was that Christians individually or churches corporately should rejoin the Roman church. Any other form of ecumenical activity was dangerous because it implied the recognition of some sort of status for non-Roman churches and was labelled indifferentism, that is the error of thinking that there could be any compromise on the absolute position of Roman Catholic teaching. In practice this meant that Roman Catholics eschewed all forms of ecumenical activity, even to the extent in many cases of refusing to say the Lord's Prayer with other Christians; in theory it meant that the Roman Catholic church was committed to a rigid and extremely conservative doctrine, not only on ecumenical matters but on many others – doctrines which stemmed from the absolute authority of the papacy and its teaching.

All this has changed dramatically in the last ten years – it could even be said unbelievably if it had not in fact happened. The hinge of the change was the papacy of Pope John XXIII (1958–1963) and the work of the Second Vatican Council (1962–1965), called by him but continued under his successor, the present Pope Paul VI. How far the change in attitude usually attributed to Pope John had in fact really begun under his predecessor Pius XII is a question which need not concern us here. Certainly it did not seem at the time that a more liberal attitude was being allowed – let alone encouraged. Such well-known Roman Catholic thinkers and scholars as the two Frenchmen, the Jesuit Teilhard de Chardin and the Dominican Yves Congar, were both 'disciplined' in the 1950s; but the fact remains that they and other 'liberal' or progressive teachers like them, such as the German Professor Hans Küng, were publishing their work and through it reaching and influencing a great number of people. Moreover there were a number of movements current in the church – Biblical theology, patristic studies and the liturgical movement – all of which were having a liberating influence on Roman Catholic theology and helping to change its balance and emphasis (see above, pp. 224–8). All this was important because it meant that when the Vatican Council did meet there was an articulate and even a semi-organized body of progressive opinion which was able to stand up to and resist the steam-rollering tactics of the conservative theologians who were at first entrenched in most of the main policy-making positions in the church and the council – and particularly of course in the Roman Curia itself. If there had not already been an undercurrent which was in favour of some liberalization and change, Vatican II would have continued in the conservative and authoritarian tradition of Vatican I (see pp. 181–3). As it was Vatican II gave the liberals a platform they could not otherwise have hoped to have found and enabled them in the end to set the church on a course of reform, which is still being worked out with a good deal of trauma and indecision.

Two examples of the way in which the Council made possible the mobilization of progressive opinion and consequently set the Roman Catholic church on new theological courses may be given. At the beginning of the Council the all-important question of the sources of revelation was being debated; the Fathers had before them a schema – or draft – drawn up by a commission which was markedly conservative in its composition, and presented by the arch-conservative Cardinal Ottaviani. One by one the progressives rose to criticize it: it was dogmatic and unbending in its tone where it should be pastoral; it perpetuated the explosive and theologically dubious idea that there are two sources of revelation; it was based on outdated Biblical teaching and was condemnatory in its attitude to much modern Biblical scholarship; it had been composed by a 'packed' commission from which the great German Biblical scholar, Cardinal Bea, the head of the Ecumenical Secretariat, had been excluded. The conservatives, led by Ottaviani, fought back and claimed that, while their draft might be amended, it could not be rejected *in toto*. Someone said that His Eminence was prevaricating: 'all the world knows it'.[1] Finally Pope John intervened: the schema was withdrawn and a mixed commission, which would include Bea and members of the Unity Secretariat, was appointed to redraft it.

The second critical clash between conservatives and progressives took place a year later and concerned the question of religious liberty. Here the tactics were reversed. The progressives had produced the original schema and the conservatives were opposing it. It was widely thought that the original draft had been the work of the American Father John Courtney, who had earlier been disciplined, probably at the instigation of Ottaviani. In any case it was anathema to the conservatives. They did everything they could to avoid or delay the vote, which would almost certainly go against them. The Secretary General of the Council, Archbishop Felici, was punningly accused of an 'infelicitous plot' and on more than one occasion there was uproar in the Council. At the height of the crisis a spontaneous petition to the pope was signed by 1,400 bishops – and their cause prevailed.

Your Holiness:
With reverence but urgently, very urgently, most urgently [this is more forceful in the Latin original] we request that a vote on the declaration on religious liberty be taken before the end of the session of the Council, lest the confidence of the world, both Christian and non-Christian, be lost.[2]

This quotation shows how aware the Council Fathers were of the eyes of the world being on them – and this in itself is significant. Hitherto it had been the tradition of the Roman church to work *in camera*. Decisions and pronouncements would be prepared by the Curia (the Vatican civil service) and there would be very little open debate or knowledge of how they had been arrived at – beyond the inevitable gossip that takes place in such conditions. The result was that the church had presented a monolithic face to the world; Roman Catholic – or certainly Roman – teaching seemed to be uniform and unchanging, even to an exaggerated decree as far as outsiders were concerned. One of the effects of the Council was that its debates were widely publicized and it was possible to see that there were cracks in the façade of unity, that there were wide varieties of opinion even at the very top of the church, among the cardinals themselves.

Seen in this light the very fact of calling the Council was an immensely courageous decision. Even more courageous were the policies of the progressives among the bishops. It is all too easy for liberal-minded Christians of

other churches to approve and applaud the liberal plat-
forms being promoted at Vatican II. There has been a
tendency, especially among Anglicans, for Christians of
other denominations to congratulate themselves that
'Rome is at last seeing the light', that she is belatedly
setting about reforms which other churches undertook a
century, or even four centuries, ago. What these touch-
line critics forget is that Roman conservative policies
have on the whole been extremely successful: there has
been less of a flight from organized Roman religion than
from other churches; discipline has been maintained to
an astonishing extent; the policy of maintaining orthodoxy in order to protect simple people from the ravages
of doubt seemed largely to have paid off; it had even had
the effect of attracting many intellectuals, as witness the
steady stream of conversions in England from the mid
nineteenth to the mid twentieth century. To advocate
abandoning this policy was therefore an act of great
courage. To the conservatives it was an act of supreme
folly – an attitude which must make one more sympathetic to the last-ditching of Ottaviani and his followers.
No doubt the progressives had lately seen the writing on
the wall for the attitude of battening down the hatches,
which went back over a century, to the time of Pius IX.
Their leaders came mainly from Holland, France, Germany and Austria; they were the first to see the growing alienation of the industrial working classes and the
decline in the number of conversions and in vocations to
the priesthood. But for all that their attitude was very
courageous, especially when one remembers what a complete *volte-face* it represented for the official policies of
the church and how it meant attacking entrenched positions in the Vatican.

There is no doubt that in taking the stance they did
the progressive leaders were swayed by considerations of
not so much policy as of truth. They advocated their
changes because they believed that what they wanted to

see was theologically right and would therefore be to the good of the church and ultimately of the world. It is more than probable that Pope John himself did not foresee how the floodgates would be opened by the calling of the Council; nor probably would he have relished the course which events finally took. His own theological position was not progressive. But none the less he had called the Council for the well-being of the church. 'The Church was to be the Council's preoccupation and theme, first looking inwardly (*ad intra*) at herself for *aggiornamento* [an almost untranslatable word meaning roughly 'bringing up to date'] and renewal and then, thus refreshed and brought up to date, looking outwards (*ad extra*) to all men to give them renewed faith, hope and love from God the source of their, as well as the Church's, whole being.'[3]

The Agenda

It is important to remember this about the Council. It was not summoned primarily with the ecumenical movement in view. It was first and always a domestic affair for the Roman Catholic church to put its own house in order. During the process the ecumenical issue was seen to be important, but it was the church's own concerns which were paramount. This explains why the agenda did not include a number of issues which must have been given priority if the Roman church's relations with other Christian bodies had been the primary concern. Thus such issues as the doctrine of grace – with its explosive overtones of the meaning of justification – and the doctrine of the eucharist – with a history of controversy about transubstantiation and the sacrifice of the mass – were avoided. This was in fact a mercy, since the Council in this way avoided giving new life to what are really now old quarrels. There was one exception to this rule – the work of the Council on revelation, which resulted in one of the four major doctrinal pronouncements, or Constitutions, of Vatican II. This was an issue which could hardly be avoided. It was not so much a question of adopting a position in a long-standing controversy with the Protestant world. It was more a matter of Roman Catholics clearing their own minds – though the process is of course of intense concern to the non-Roman churches.

Since the Council of Trent there had been doubt whether Roman Catholic teaching favoured one source of divine revelation – the Bible only, the Protestant war-cry – or whether the Council had added another source, the tradition of the church (see above, pp. 134–5). Vatican I had done nothing to clarify the position and indeed in the nineteenth century the waters had been further muddied by the debate, started by Newman, over whether, and in what way, doctrine could 'develop' from its original 'deposit' in the teaching of the Apostles. This question is clearly one of vital importance to the whole ecumenical movement, for it concerns the very basis of Christian truth, around which all worth-while ecumenical debate must ultimately turn.

It also raises the fundamental question of the authority of the church, not only as the guardian and interpreter of Christian truth, but also, in the conservative Roman Catholic view, as the source of Christian doctrine. As has already been said the progressives objected to the first, conservative, draft of the schema on revelation partly because it seemed to perpetuate the theory of two sources of revelation. This was a place where, as it was remarked, the opposing sides 'never really encountered each other'. But in the event the subject of scripture and tradition was dealt with in a way which would be acceptable to most modern non-Roman Catholic thinkers. There is only one final source of the revelation of God, Christ himself. Scripture and tradition belong together and interpenetrate each other in 'handing down' – the original meaning of tradition see pp. 89–90) – this original revelation from the apostles. 'Sacred tradition and sacred scripture form one sacred deposit of the word of God. . . . Sacred tradition, sacred scripture and the teaching authority of the church . . . are so linked and joined together that one cannot stand without the others.'[4] (It will be remembered that the Montreal Faith and Order Conference of 1963 went so far as to talk of the church existing 'by tradition alone' – see above, pp. 255–6.) There is no growth in tradition; all things necessary to salvation were contained in the original deposit; but under the guidance of the Holy Spirit there can be growth in understanding of the deposit.

Thus the Constitution on revelation pronounced soberly on these fundamental concerns of Christian truth. When it came to speaking of the background and contents of the Old and New Testaments the document was, by modern Biblical standards, more disappointing: the Bible seems once again to be made subservient to the traditional teaching authority of the church and a highly cautious attitude is adopted in the exposition of its essential message. Nevertheless there is no direct condemnation of modern liberal Roman Catholic scholarship as had earlier seemed likely and the conclusion is reached that 'easy access to Sacred Scripture should be provided for all the Christian faithful'. Modern translations of the Bible are commended and the idea of ecumenical co-operation in translation is envisaged. All this is cautious and indeed lags behind much modern R.C. thought and practice. But at least it is not retrogressive; the door is not closed. There is the possibility of further development within the Roman Catholic church itself and future dialogue between Roman and non-Roman scholars. Much depends in fact on what happens in this field after and as a result of the Council.

The same is true of the Constitution on the church. In

fact it could be said of all the work of the Council. From an ecumenical point of view, and from that of an outsider, the main achievement of Vatican II was that it stopped any further anti-ecumenical drift in the Roman church, adopted on the whole a cautious but positive position and left the door open for future advance. If this sounds like damning with faint praise, it should be said at once that compared with the previous Roman Catholic stance on all the questions it discussed Vatican II represented a vital change of position. But the fact remains that the follow-up is all-important.

This point is made about the Constitution of the church by an 'insider', the Abbot of Downside:

The value of the Constitution of the Church is largely potential. It is a document not immediately directed to practical changes. But its worth for the Church and for the future of Christianity will depend largely on our willingness to understand and communicate its message, and to give practical expression to its implications.[5]

Primarily *De Ecclesia* was the result of the Roman Catholic church looking at itself in the light of its current theology.

It canonized a striking fresh definition of the Roman Catholic Church – a self-definition heavy with consequences both for the domestic economy of Roman Catholicism and for its stance in the world.... The significant transformation of Roman Catholic ecclesiology is an indisputable fact. This transformation may be summarily described as a shift from the juridical and institutional emphasis of the past four centuries or more to a primarily theological and missionary vision of the church.[6]

It was this shift which represented the great victory for the progressive point of view. Bishop de Smedt of Bruges, one of the great orators of the Council, had described the church as being dominated by three devils, clericalism, juridicalism and triumphalism. Clericalism may be defined as the domination of the church and its thinking by its professional hierarchy to the exclusion or detriment of the work and problems of the laity. Juridicalism is the habit of mind of thinking of the church, of its life and membership, in legal terms, imposing rules and regulations rather than encouraging freedom and organic growth. Triumphalism is the danger of applying to the church and its activities the worldly criteria of power and glory, rather than the Christ-like pattern of humility and suffering. No one would pretend that the Roman church has a monopoly of these particular devils. The point here is that Vatican II attempted to exorcize them.

It is true that the critical reader can spot in the Constitution some echoes of the old ways of thinking and speaking about the church; a complete change was hardly to be expected. But for all that the essentials of the doctrine of the church are set out in such a way as is now generally understood to be in accordance with Biblical thought. In the first place ecclesiology is seen to be dependent on Christology: that is to say the church's understanding of itself must depend on its doctrine and understanding of Christ, his nature and work. This is laid down in the opening words of the document which give it its name, *Lumen Gentium*:

Christ is the light of all nations. . . . By her relationship with Christ, the Church is a kind of sacrament or sign of intimate union with God, and of the unity of all mankind. She is also an instrument for the achievement of such union and unity.

This quotation contains the seed of the second vital doctrine about the church, known theologically as its eschatalogical nature. The church is a 'sign of intimate union with God', but it is also 'an instrument for the achievement of such union'. The idea of the church is linked to the idea of the kingdom of God; partly in that in the church since the coming of Christ the kingdom already exists, and partly that the church's task is to bring about the kingdom – or rule – of God.

Its goal is the kingdom of God, which has been begun by God Himself on earth and which is to be further extended until it is brought to perfection by Him at the end of time. . . .

The third idea in the *De Ecclesia* which is essential to the understanding of the church is the Biblical idea of the People of God, and linked with it the insistence on 'the common priesthood of all the faithful, originating in their baptism'.[7] We have seen that this idea of the priesthood of all the people of God in the mission and work of the church, once a divisive battle cry, has been the source of much fruitful and unifying thought in the work of the World Council and of many unity schemes. To find it reappearing here as the basis of the Roman Catholic church's teaching shows how much has happened in recent years to create a common theological basis for the ecumenical movement. More than this, the other key ideas set out in the Constitution are indeed axes laid at the root of 'triumphalism'; that is to say they could imply – even if they do not make altogether explicit – a very different idea about the authority of the church, and authority in the church, from that which has recently dominated Roman Catholic thought.

Two other sections of the Constitution on the church are of vital importance both in the development of the Roman Catholic church's own thought about itself and as affecting the attitude of other churches to Rome. The first is the question of the Virgin Mary, to which the eighth and last chapter of the Constitution is devoted. It was an open secret that many of the 'conservatives' were hoping that the Council would see another step forward in defining doctrine about the Virgin Mary. On top of the definitions of her Immaculate Conception (1854) and her Assumption (1950) (see above, pp. 181–2) they hoped that she might be defined as the mediatrix of all grace and as 'co-redemptrix' with Christ. One English bishop said as much in a pastoral letter before setting out for the Council. 'He is a disappointed, but a wiser, man as a result of the Council. For not only was the escalation of Marian doctrines deliberately halted, but Christians outside Rome could note with satisfaction a real endeavour to bring Marian doctrines and devotions within a compass which would not distort the totally Christocentric nature of our faith.'[8] It need hardly be said that if any move had been made which had the effect (or looked as if it did) of putting Mary in place of Christ in the Christian scheme of things, this would have severely set back the ecumenical cause and added to the already considerable distrust of Rome among Protestants.

What in fact happened was that the idea of a separate definition of Marian doctrine was rejected and Rome's teaching about Mary was placed firmly within the context of the doctrine of the church. She is not set up as a rival or equal of Christ: 'No creature could ever be counted as equal with the Incarnate Word and Redeemer.... The Church does not hesitate to profess this subordinate role of Mary.' Instead she is seen as typifying the church in its ideal response to the grace of God: 'a pre-eminent and altogether singular member of the Church, and ... the Church's model and excellent exemplar in faith and charity'. To press this point home the Constitution warns the faithful against exaggerated, emotional and credulous devotions to Our Lady, while commending true devotion and imitation. In doing so it particularly mentions the danger of giving a wrong impression of Catholic doctrine to 'separated brethren'. When one remembers the pressures for further extreme definition of Marian doctrine, especially from the more backward parts of the Roman Catholic church, this level-headed teaching is the more remarkable.

The second area of doctrine on which the Constitution had to clarify, or even correct, preceding work was on the matter of the government of the church, and of authority in the church. Vatican I had defined the infallibility of the pope speaking *ex cathedra* in matters of faith and morals (see above, pp. 182–3). This definition had undoubtedly been unsatisfactory, partly because it had not been made clear which papal utterances were to be reckoned infallible, and partly because it had left uncertain the relationship between the pope and the bishops in the government of the church. Vatican I had been a victory for the infallibilists in so far as it had seemed to spell the end of the 'conciliar' idea of the church, whereby final authority lay with a general council and thereby with the general consensus of the feeling of the bishops of the whole world. The infallibilists had rushed the definition of papal infallibility to the head of the agenda of Vatican I and the Council had had to break up before it was able to deal, as it had meant to, with other aspects of the doctrine of the church. This task now fell to Vatican II. But on the question of authority and government Vatican II was working on very different premises from those of Vatican I. It was within the general context of the doctrines already described that the Constitution on the church came to consider the question. It was the idea of the apostolic, or missionary (the root meaning of apostolic), nature of the church which governed what was said about episcopacy. Christ had entrusted the continuance of his mission to the apostles and they in turn to successors among whom 'the chief place belongs to those who, appointed to the episcopate in a sequence running back to the beginning, are the ones who pass on the apostolic seed'. The bishops are not to be thought of individually, but corporately, as a 'college': 'in the episcopal order the apostolic body continues without a break'. This idea of the corporate function and importance of the episcopate, rather than the old individualistic and 'tactile' theories of apostolic succession, is one which has recently been favoured by high-church Anglicans, and the above quotation from *Lumen Gentium* might have been written by a number of Anglican theologians.

What *Lumen Gentium* does not make so clear is the all-important question of the relation of the college of bishops to the pope. It merely says that ultimate responsibility for the church is shared by the bishops with the pope:

> Together with its head, the Roman Pontiff, and never without this head, the episcopal order is the subject of supreme and full power over the universal church.

The position and powers of bishops were spelled out more fully when the Council came to consider the Decree on the Pastoral Office of Bishops. During the debate the Fathers were asked whether they considered episcopal consecration to be the highest sacramental order. This was a vital question. It is hardly an exaggeration to say that since Vatican I and the infallibility decree, bishops had been, as it were, a depressed class. The vital ministry had been the pope, with his supreme powers of authority and government, and the priesthood, which exercised the day-to-day on-the-spot ministry of the sacraments. Bishops had been those to whom the pope had delegated certain powers for the smooth running of the church – a situation which hardly accorded with the doctrine or practice of the early church (see Chapter 2). But when the Council Fathers voted overwhelmingly that episcopacy was the highest sacramental order in the church, they redressed this balance. As Abbot Butler sees it:

> Although it was the doctrine of collegiality that stole the headlines the crux of the Constitution's teaching on the episcopate is perhaps contained in the affirmation that a bishop receives in his consecration the 'fullness' of the ministerial priesthood derived from Christ.... Thus episcopal authority is not something received from the Pope, but something given directly by God in the sacrament of holy orders.[9]

This was clearly an important principle to establish, for it could be seen as implying the doctrine of collegiality in the government of the church and even open the way in theory to a recognition that the pope among the bishops was *primus inter pares* – the first among equals.

But further than that beyond enunciating the idea of collegiality the Council did not go. Here again everything would depend on how matters developed after the Council; the idea could remain an empty form of words or it could be the beginning of a shift in doctrine and power.

For the moment ecumenical observers had to take comfort from the fact that the whole emphasis of the Council's description of the work of bishops (and also of priests) is pastoral rather than authoritarian. Another hopeful ecumenical portent was seen in the Constitution on the liturgy. Here such controversial doctrines as the sacrifice of the mass and transubstantiation were bypassed and the emphasis was placed on such things as the simplification of the mass, on the need for experiment and if necessary for variety between differing traditions and cultures, and on participation by the worshippers – all trends which made the non-Catholic observers feel that there is a steady drawing-together between hitherto divided traditions.

We come now to the Council's explicit work in the ecumenical field. This was enshrined in the Decree *De Ecumenismo*, but in many ways even more important was the Declaration on Religious Liberty, which laid down more far-reaching principles than *De Ecumenismo* and which can in fact be said to provide the context for it. It has already been seen that the debate on religious liberty was one of the resounding victories of progressives over conservatives. The traditional teaching of the Roman Catholic church (see above, pp. 208 and 261) is briefly that there is no such thing as an inherent right to religious liberty: in countries therefore where the Catholic church is dominant there is – or should be – no religious liberty, though where it is not dominant it will claim liberty for its own opinions. There can in fact be liberty only for truth, as defined by the church. The position was summarized during the debate by the Spanish Cardinal Arriba y Castro:

Only the Catholic Church has the duty and the right to preach the Gospel, and therefore proselytism by non-Catholics among Catholics is illicit and must be obstructed not only by the Church but by civil authority itself.[10]

On this doctrine many Vatican political policies have in the past been based. The opposite point of view was put forcibly at the Council by the English Cardinal Heenan:

We must be clear on this: it is completely absurd to say that error has no rights and that only truth has them. Rights are rooted in persons, not in things.[11]

This statement may seem obvious to a Protestant coming from a liberal democratic background, but for many of the conservatives from Catholic countries it was heresy and folly which would spell the ruin of the Catholic church – indeed Cardinal Arriba y Castro prophesied precisely this ... 'the ruin of Catholicism'. Nevertheless the liberal position carried the day.

The change of outlook was based, as Cardinal Heenan emphasized, on a recognition of the basic rights of the human being. The title and opening words of the Declaration stress this – *Dignitatis Humanae*: religious liberty is an expression of the dignity of the human personality. It applies individually and corporately: 'The freedom or immunity from coercion in matters religious, which is the endowment of persons as individuals, is also to be recognized as their right when they act in community.' The only limiting factor to such freedom is the recognition by all parties that tolerance must be mutual and must not be abused; the criterion for such mutual tolerance within society is 'the just demands of public order'. All this applies to liberty within the state and secular society and there is no specific mention of the rights of the individual to liberty within his membership of the church. But many commentators have observed that, once the principle has been accepted that human dignity demands individual liberty, it must apply to membership of religious as well as secular societies. They hope, in other words, that the idea of liberty will 'spill over' within the Roman Catholic church in ways which could have positive effects ecumenically. One example may be given. The Declaration accepts the principle that parents have a right to determine the religious training given to their children. But, despite much pressure and the undoubted fact that the rule constitutes the greatest single sore in ecumenical relations, the Roman Catholic church still insists that in a 'mixed' marriage the non-Roman party must sign before the ceremony a promise that any children will be brought up in the Roman Catholic church (though see below, pp. 420–24).

It has to be admitted that, compared with the Declaration on Religious Liberty, the decree on ecumenism is a disappointing document. This was another case where the debate was of greater significance than the final pronouncement, where the decree shows signs of trying to patch up a compromise between two positions which are so far apart as to be almost irreconcilable, and where in the event what was *not* said was more important than what was said. It was of the utmost importance for instance that the old clear-cut absolutist position of *Mortalium Animos* (see above, p. 207) was not repeated. Instead the decree to some extent spells out the theological position laid down in *De Ecclesia*. There a delicate tightrope balance had been drawn between the old claim that the Roman Church possesses the monopoly of truth and a more ecumenical approach to the problems of Christian disunity. The true Church of Christ

subsists in the Catholic Church, which is governed by the successor of Peter and by the bishops in his communion, although many elements of sanctification and of truth may be found outside of its visible structure, which, as gifts belonging to the Church of Christ, are forces impelling toward catholic unity.... The Church recognizes that in many ways she is linked with those who, being baptized, are honoured with the name of Christian, but do not possess the faith in its entirety or do not preserve unity of communion with the successor of Peter.

These links are said to be a belief in the Trinity, baptism and other sacraments, episcopacy, and Christian zeal. Corporate Christian bodies enjoying these characteristics are described as 'Churches or ecclesiastical communities'. This represents a significant advance on former Catholic thought which, in order to emphasize the uniqueness of the Roman Catholic church, had been unwilling to grant the title of a church to other Christian bodies. But once again the change is cautious and everything will depend on how matters work out in the future.

The decree on ecumenism was in a way the first stage in this working out. It contained an acknowledgement that in the divisions of the church 'both sides were to blame' and a recognition of the fact that the Catholic church itself suffers from the divisions of Christendom: 'The Church itself finds it more difficult to express in actual life her full catholicity in all its aspects.' There is the recognition, too, that though the Catholic church preserves the fulness of unity, there is still the possibility that this unity will increase – a typical example of the contradictions in the decree between the desire to maintain the old Roman position and the willingness to go some way to meet the facts of disunity. There is an acknowledgement, several times repeated, that the church is called 'to that continual reformation of which she always has need'.

The teaching of *Lumen Gentium* on 'separated brethren' is repeated and to some extent enlarged. 'One cannot charge with the sin of separation those who are at present born in these separated communities . . . and the Catholic Church accepts them with respect and affection as brothers. For men who believe in Christ and have been properly baptized are brought into certain, though imperfect, communion with the Catholic Church.' It is admitted that separated churches can possess the means of grace: 'In ways that vary according to the condition of each church or community, these most certainly can engender a life of grace and, one must say, can aptly give access to the communion of salvation.' But on the other hand it is claimed that these means of grace 'derive their efficacy from the very fullness of grace and truth entrusted to the Catholic Church'. Once again the tightrope is almost too narrow to permit balance. Looking to future unity the decree lays down principles which will appeal to any Christian who believes that unity will depend on comprehensiveness rather than uniformity: 'While preserving unity in essentials, let everyone in the church . . . preserve a proper freedom in the various forms of spiritual life and discipline, in the variety of liturgical rites, and even in the theological elaborations of revealed truth.' There is – wisely no doubt – no attempt to define what are the essentials.

It is when it comes to practical proposals for ecumenical action that the decree is most disappointing. Ecumenical activity is to be encouraged and the control of such things as joint services is to be left to local bishops – an encouraging sign. Catholics are reminded that they should seek to understand the beliefs and practices of separated brethren and that theological discussion should be 'on an equal footing'. Moreover theology should be taught 'with due regard for the ecumenical point of view ... not polemically', while Catholic teaching should be presented in such a way as neither to cause offence nor to water down the full Catholic position; on the other hand it is once again emphasized that there is within Catholic teaching such a thing as 'an order or hierarchy of truths'. This phrase, which was not in the original draft of the decree, has been described by the Catholic theologian Karl Rahner as 'one of the great actions of the Vatican Council', and by the Protestant Oscar Cullmann as 'the idea containing the most [ecumenical] promise'. But so far it is only a phrase (though see below, p. 437) and it has to be admitted that the rest of this part of the decree does not take us very far – until one once again remembers how far in fact they had taken the Roman church from its completely negative attitude to the ecumenical movement.

It was known before the Council ended that the promulgation of the decree on ecumenism would be followed by a Directorium which would lay down in greater detail rules for ecumenical action throughout the world. It seems therefore that it was recognized that the decree did not provide a satisfactory basis for future ecumenical activity. It was too ambiguous. The more hopeful points, from an ecumenical point of view, have been cited, but there were also many passages which seemed to echo the old attitudes. The conservatives had fought hard, and beliefs which have been held unchallenged for literally hundreds of years do not die easily. The decree is therefore marked by ambiguities and contradictions which 'cluster round the fact that [it] set out to do something which it was impossible for Roman Catholic theology to do, given its actual resources and state of development in the 1960s'.[12] In its ecumenical thinking, even more than in other aspects of its work, Vatican II represented a staging post rather than a destination. Everything would depend on the road followed by the Roman Catholic church after the Council.

AFTER VATICAN II: THE ECUMENICAL DIRECTORY

The Ecumenical Directory, which had been announced during the Council, did not appear until 14 May 1967 – two and a half years after the promulgation of the decree on ecumenism. The length of this delay and the reasons for it are pointers to the fact that the ecumenical mills in Rome will grind slowly. The original draft was prepared in May 1965 by the Secretariat for Promoting Christian Unity and was then examined by the Commission for the Doctrine of the Faith; in March 1966 it was sent to the Episcopal Conference. In June 1966 the Secretariat examined all the comments so far made and prepared a revised draft which then went back to the Doctrine of the Faith Commission. Lastly in 1967 a joint conference representing many sections of the Vatican Curia approved the final text.

The 1967 directory is in fact only Part I of the document and further parts are promised for the future, the possibility of 1970 or 1971 being mentioned. Part I calls for the setting-up of commissions or secretariats to promote ecumenical activity in every diocese, or at some other appropriate level; these should include lay men and women besides clergy. It also calls for commissions of bishops assisted by experts on a national level. All this was a welcome extension throughout the church of the ecumenical initiative which had started in Rome with the foundation of the Secretariat for Christian Unity.

The directory then deals with what for many years had been a vexed question – 'the validity of Baptism conferred by Ministers of Churches and Ecclesial Communities separated from us'. Previously it had widely been the custom that when a man or woman wished to join the Roman church from another church he received 'conditional baptism', that is baptism prefaced by the words 'if thou art not already baptized'. Unhappily the

Roman authorities very often made no attempt to inquire of his former church whether or not he had in fact been baptized. The effect of this was often to give the convert the psychological feeling that his Christian life in his former church up to the time of his conversion counted for nothing, and generally speaking to give the impression that Rome discounted the baptisms of non-Roman churches. Obviously the practice was ecumenically disastrous. For some years certain Catholic theologians had been saying that since in Catholic doctrine all baptisms are one and Christ is the true baptizer (see above, pp. 97–8) the practice was doctrinally unsound as well as ecumenically deplorable. It was therefore a great relief when the directory declared unequivocally 'indiscriminate conditional baptism of all who desire full communion with the Catholic church cannot be approved. The sacrament of baptism cannot be repeated and therefore to baptize again conditionally is not allowed unless there is prudent doubt of the fact, or of the validity, of a baptism already administered.'[13] This ruling quoted, and sprang from, the Vatican II recognition of the baptisms of other churches. It removed a legitimate grievance felt by other churches and paved the way for greater understanding.

The rest of the directory deals with the question of fostering ecumenism between Catholics and non-Catholics by allowing the former to take part in worship with 'separated brethren'. When again one remembers that until recently such activities on the part of Roman Catholics were frowned on as 'indifferentism', this encouragement is the more remarkable. A distinction is drawn between the Orthodox and all other non-Catholic churches. Because the Orthodox possess 'true sacraments' and are 'very close' to the Catholic church in matters of faith, it is permissible in certain circumstances for Catholics to receive Orthodox sacraments and for them to welcome individual members of Orthodox churches to their own sacraments; the circumstances where this would apply are when either party is cut off from the ministrations of his own church, or even when there are special cases of public duties, family relationships or even friendship. But it is emphasized that 'it is fitting that the greatest possible attention be given to "reciprocity" '.[14]

With other non-Catholic churches the rules are more cautious: Catholic sacraments can be given to a non-Catholic cut off from his own church only *in extremis*; otherwise there can be no sharing of sacramental worship and Catholics are even forbidden to preach at the sacraments of other churches, and *vice versa*. Otherwise, however, attendance at other churches' worship is permitted and the ministers of non-Catholic churches are allowed to take a public place in Catholic worship and Catholic priests at non-Catholic services – a rule which has made possible the hitherto unthought-of presence of the clergy of both sides at the ceremony of a 'mixed' wedding.

THE PRESENT: JOINT WORKING GROUPS

So much for the directory. How far its provisions have been put into practice in various local situations will be considered later. Meanwhile other examples of the central activities of the Secretariat for Promoting Christian Unity must be described. For its official relationships with the official representatives of other churches and Christian bodies with whom it is 'in conversation' (as opposed merely to sending observers) the Secretariat uses the Joint Working Group. Thus there are regular meetings of a Joint Working Group between the R.C.C. and the W.C.C. The facts of growing co-operation between the R.C.C. and the W.C.C., especially in matters of social concern, and the question of Roman Catholic membership of the W.C.C., have already been discussed (see pp. 279–83). Here it is only necessary to outline some of the other topics which are considered by the R.C.C./W.C.C.

Joint Working Group: these include such subjects as the date of Easter, the role of women and of the laity in the church (both matters of great concern to the W.C.C.), international affairs and the explosive issues of religious liberty and proselytism. In June 1969 the pope paid a visit to the World Council headquarters in Geneva; on this occasion he made what was thought by many to be a disappointing statement:

We are here among you. Our name is Peter. Scripture tells us which meaning Christ has willed to attribute to this name, what duties he lays upon us: the responsibilities of the apostle and his successors. But permit us to recall other titles which the Lord wishes to give to Peter in order to signify other charisms. . . .[15]

The pope went on to say that the question of Roman Catholic membership of the W.C.C. was not 'so mature that a positive answer could or should be given':

The question still remains a hypothesis. It contains serious theological and pastoral implications. It thus requires profound study and commits us to a way that honesty recognizes could be long and difficult.

The General Secretary of the W.C.C. subsequently stated that since by its very constitution the W.C.C. does not require any church to forsake its fundamental convictions in assuming membership, he did not find the pope's firm 'Petrine' stand discouraging; but it hardly seems that for the moment official relations between the W.C.C. and the R.C.C. will progress much beyond the Joint Working Group.

The first J.W.G. between the Roman Catholics and other confessional bodies was that set up with the Lutherans. Between 1965 and 1967 a Joint Working Group was examining the possibility of conversations and co-operation. This led to the formation of a joint Study Commission which has held three meetings, at

Zurich in 1967, at Bastad, Sweden, in 1968 and at Nemi, Italy, in 1969. The participants have been mainly scholars and the discussions have taken the form of papers on subjects which would traditionally have divided the two churches, such as the question of the continuity of Christian teaching as it is understood in the Catholic church against the Lutheran insistence on the renewed event each time the Gospel is proclaimed. It has been agreed that in the light of modern understanding these questions now look very different from the old traditional disputes, and it has been found in these, as in so many ecumenical discussions, that 'in practically all the questions dealt with agreement and differences did not coincide with confessional boundaries'.[16]

Obviously there are differences of emphasis, but at this level of donnish discussion it has been found that many theological positions are converging; for instance the Lutherans are no longer unable to accept the fact that there must be some authority behind church teaching; what they do not like is the fact that an infallible authority 'intends to speak in a way which binds for all time in its doctrinal statements';[17] but this problem of the unchangeability of Rome's dogmatic statements is precisely one of the points which has been worrying some of the more progressive Catholic theologians (see below, pp. 434–6). Another subject of debate has been the Lutheran belief that there is a 'centre of the Gospel' – that is a vital doctrine which regulates the whole of Christian teaching, such as the Reformation doctrine of justification – and how far this can be related to the Vatican II idea of a 'hierarchy of truths'. In general at the end of the third conference the participants felt that 'thus far it can be stated that the chances of a mutual understanding are very great as long as one attempts to deal with present day problems and questions': so far, perhaps so good, but all this is in the realm of debate and the urgent conclusion is that 'it seems more important to be concerned even now about how this discussion can have real influence on the two confessions'.[18]

Roman Catholic/Anglican discussions followed on the visit of Dr Michael Ramsay, the Archbishop of Canterbury, to Pope Paul in March 1966. At the end of that meeting the two leaders announced that 'they intend to inaugurate between the Roman Catholic Church and the Anglican Communion a serious dialogue which, founded on the gospels and on the ancient common traditions, may lead to that unity in truth for which Christ prayed'.[19] In January 1967 a Joint Preparatory Commission met at Gazzada, near Milan. It was generally agreed that the delegates set to work with a real sense of urgency: 'We have gone on with our divisions long enough,' said the Anglican chairman, the Bishop of Ripon. The most remarkable outcome of the meeting was the drawing-up of a set of practical recommendations which 'add up to a vigorous reshaping of existing practices of collaboration and discussion between Anglicans and Roman Catholics'.[19] In effect these recommendations called for more frequent meetings; study and discussion of common problems between the local representatives of the two churches at every level; the fostering of ecumenical co-operation at universities and colleges and collaboration between theological colleges; the joint use of churches wherever possible; and the use of common texts and formulas in church services.

Clearly, as the Secretariat for Christian Unity put it at the time, 'their full adoption would put us forward several decades at a blow'.[19] The problem was to get local action. The R.C. authorities circulated the proposals to their world-wide national episcopal conferences and asked for reactions: on the whole there were very few straight negatives, but some of the suggestions were greeted with modified rapture. But reaction is not action, and there is still a long way to go before local co-opera-

tion of the sort envisaged is a fact. It does not appear that
the Anglican Communion has acted as vigorously in
recommending the proposals as the Roman Catholics.

The Joint Preparatory Commission met again at
Huntercombe Manor in England in September 1967;
here the discussion was more academic and doctrinal, and
particularly centred on the root question of the authority
of the Bible in the church. At the third meeting at Malta
over the New Year of 1967/8 the Commission felt that it
was now possible to plot 'some course towards unity'. The
necessity of scholarly work at the doctrinal differences
separating the churches, alongside practical local measures for growing together, was stressed.

The result of all this was that the preparatory work
was over. A Permanent Joint Commission between the
two churches was formed – the point of the word 'permanent' in the title being that the Commission is now
seen as remaining in being until union or full intercommunion is reached between the two churches. This commission held its first meeting at Windsor in January 1970.
A full report on this meeting and its proposals is not
yet available, but some summary can be given of the
current state of Anglican/Roman Catholic relationships
throughout the world. In general it can be said that it is
in the 'Anglo-Saxon' countries that matters are furthest
advanced. This may be partly a reflection of the fact that
the membership of the Joint Preparatory Commission has
been almost exclusively Anglo-Saxon, plus of course some
European Roman Catholic members. It may also be a
reflection of the fact that in the younger churches the
authorities are more hesitant about the wisdom of encouraging their less sophisticated native members to embark on the uncertain seas of ecumenical dialogue. In
any case in Africa and Asia co-operation has hardly got
beyond the formation of joint episcopal committees and
the exchange of pulpits. But in South Africa vigorous
steps are being taken to carry out the Gazzada recom-

mendations. In Australia there is a good deal of consultation and collaboration. The same is true in the British Isles: in Scotland there is talk of drawing up a common service of baptism; the Archbishop of Canterbury has set up a special committee for R.C. relationships, while a meeting of Roman Catholic diocesan ecumenical advisers urged the church leaders to interpret the Ecumenical Directory liberally where possible; there are a number of shared buildings, and the possibility of joint building projects is bearing fruit at such places as Thamesmead. Some people feel that England is still not taking the lead that might be looked for, but others feel that progress is bound to be slow where the burden of history is so heavy and where the memory of distrust and recrimination is so recent.

However that may be, it is in the New World that Anglican/Roman Catholic relationships have progressed the fastest. This is especially true of Canada – so much so that some Anglicans are now said to be seriously asking whether they had not better go slow on union negotiations with the United Church of Canada in order to concentrate on the further development of relations with Rome. In the United States representatives of the two churches have been meeting officially since June 1965 and had had seven joint sessions by December 1969. Questions of belief about baptism and the eucharist have been considered and it has been agreed that in the contemporary climate of theological thinking there is little difference between the two churches. This led some to ask why intercommunion is not immediately possible and, while this was felt to be rushing the fences, it is known that joint celebrations of the Holy Communion, that is, concelebration, do take place. Furthermore it was felt that 'there was no basic difference of understanding' on such topics as the necessity and role of the priesthood and its relationship to the laity.

In wishing to push ahead towards an official policy of

'mutual recognition of ministry' with the inevitable consequence of intercommunion, the American commission recognizes that the next issue which must be taken up is that of the validity of Anglican orders. Here the commission quotes the report of the Malta meeting of the international preparatory commission: 'We believe that the present growing together of our two communions and the needs of the future require of us a very serious consideration of this question [that is of the traditional judgement of the Roman Church on the validity of Anglican orders] in the light of modern theology.'[20]

Since this question of Anglican orders is essential to future progress it must be briefly explained. In 1896 the papal bull *Apostolicae Curae* declared Anglican orders invalid, with the consequence that Anglican communion services were invalid and could not be means of salvation. The issue had been raised at Rome in the hope of forwarding the Anglican cause, but after a good deal of Vatican politics the exact opposite had happened. The condemnation had not been on the grounds that the apostolic succession had been lost at the Reformation, for it was accepted that this had not happened. Instead Rome found that Anglican orders were invalid because the Ordinal by which they were conferred was deficient in its theology of the ministry and sacraments. The Church of England, it was said, did not 'intend' to do in ordination what the Catholic church does. It seems, therefore, reasonable to say, with the American and international commissions, that if agreement could be reached about the theology of the sacraments, of the church and ministry, then the Roman Catholic objections to Anglican doctrine at the Reformation might be waived and Anglican orders henceforth found valid according to contemporary understanding. This, too, is the significance of the fact that Roman Catholic theologians were asked to comment on the proposed new Ordinal for use in the united Anglican/Methodist

Church in England (see above, p. 370); if Catholics were happy about this Ordinal as a statement of doctrine and 'intention' there would be one less barrier in the future to the recognition of Anglican orders.

There can be little doubt that these detailed theological discussions taking place in America must have an influence on the thinking of the international permanent commission, especially as many of the same people are involved on both commissions. Indeed it has already been said that at the first, Windsor, meeting of the international commission it was the Americans and the English who found themselves talking different languages rather than the Anglicans and the Roman Catholics!

Meanwhile alongside all this talk one practical step of great significance must be noted. In 1969 the Roman Catholic Episcopate in the South-East Pacific announced that they were willing to admit to communion by acts of 'economy' Anglicans who were cut off from the ministrations of their own church. It is noteworthy that this rule applies to Anglicans and not to members of other non-Roman Catholic churches; and of course the great distances involved in the Pacific make this sort of act of economy and of charity more urgent there than anywhere else in the world. Nevertheless this act can be described as an important breakthrough and the first application of the statement in *De Ecumenismo* that the eucharist can be seen as a means to, as well as an expression of, unity.

Conversations between the Roman Catholic church and the World Methodist Council were set on foot in 1966 and the first joint commission took place in October 1967. The usual process of pin-pointing differences and areas of convergence took place, and the point was especially made that the discussion should be concerned with the life and problems of the present day. For all that, further meetings in London and Malta in 1968 and 1969 respectively trod the well-worn ground of the doctrines of

414

authority and the ministry, each meeting having been prepared for by smaller sessions of scholars at Cambridge and Oxford. At the end of 1969 in a progress report it was agreed that scholarly discussion on the great dividing themes must continue, but it was also hoped that matters of more everyday concern to both churches might be added – such as the Christian home and family, and practical Christian life and spirituality in the contemporary world. It was recognized that the discussions were excessively centralized and it was hoped that area meetings might be arranged. It was the usual picture of friendly and even fruitful discussions which might have seemed miraculous a few years ago, and yet which seem agonizingly slow given the situation which faces both the churches:

Measured against our age-old estrangements, our progress in ecumenical experience in the past three years has been swift and surely led by the Spirit.... But measured against the exigencies of our churches and the challenge of our times, we are vividly aware of the distance that still lies between us now and our professed goals. We know too well that the latter stages of the ecumenical dialogue are more formidable than the early ones, requiring of us redoubled efforts and devotion, not merely to the work we have to do together, but to the tasks of educating our people and communicating to them something of the joys and inspiration that have been vouchsafed to us.[21]

The last Joint Working Group to be set up is that between the R.C.C. and the World Alliance of Reformed Churches – the international body which speaks for both Presbyterian and Congregational churches. Here in fact in some places (Holland, France, Switzerland and the U.S.A. for example) official conversations at a local level had preceded the international dialogue. Preliminary discussions took place in 1968 and 1969 and a programme of full meetings is now envisaged from 1970 to 1973. The main themes chosen, as being the most suitable for

R.C.C./Reformed debate, are the doctrine of Christ and that of the church.

Enough has now been said to be able to trace a common pattern in these Joint Working Groups between the Roman Catholic church and the various bodies representing the great church families of the western world, and to assess the strength and weaknesses of this way of going about things. In general all the groups have found that their churches are faced throughout the world with the same problems, such as the need for reform to meet the fact of secularization, and a marked decline in the number of men entering the ministry. Some of the more impatient members of the groups have argued that the logic of this is that the churches must adopt the 'Lund Principle' that the churches do everything together unless they are forced by conscience and theology to continue to act in separation. But the Joint Working Groups – let alone the local churches – have not got that far. In a way these groups are much more like the ecumenical efforts of the non-Roman churches in the 1930s. On the R.C. side at least many of their leaders have been courageous pioneers, men like the great Cardinal Bea, the first head of the Secretariat for Promoting Christian Unity, and Cardinal Willebrands, the present head. For the rest the members of the various groups have largely been dons or ex-academics; even when in the case of the Anglicans these have been promoted to the episcopate their former academic posts are mentioned to prove their respectability! Inevitably in these circumstances the discussion has tended to centre on the great historical divisive issues. The various groups have emphasized the need for discussing contemporary issues, and especially issues where the various churches find themselves facing common problems, but for all that the greater part of the discussion has in fact centred on the traditional bones of contention –

though it is true and encouraging that these have been found less serious than in the past.

Another drawback of the somewhat donnish composition of the Working Groups is that they are hardly representative of the ordinary life of the churches and of the effective centres of power and decision-making at the various levels. The report of the R.C./Lutheran working group goes so far as to comment that 'a persistence of institutional and structural divisions counters a widespread doctrinal consensus'.[22] On the Roman Catholic side the actual hierarchies, bishops and ecclesiastical administrators, are on the whole conservative and are unlikely to be willing to proceed at the speed hoped for by the Joint Working Groups. There would be exceptions to this – for instance in Holland – but Britain, where the hierarchy is certainly cautious, would be typical of many national episcopal councils. On the non-Roman side there is the danger that the members of the Working Groups will be chosen for their sympathetic attitude to the Roman Catholic church and its teachings and will not be representative of other sections of their respective churches. Certainly this would seem to be true of the Anglican delegations both on the international and the American commissions. It seems doubtful whether the widespread doctrinal agreement reported from America would in fact truly reflect the feelings of large sections of the American episcopal church.

THE FUTURE: THE HEART OF THE MATTER

It seems that three further developments are essential if the process of growing towards unity between the Roman Catholic church and other churches is not to get bogged down at the stage of academic discussion in top-level Working Groups. In the first place there must be much more local discussion and, above all, co-operation at every possible level, national, diocesan and parochial. It is urgent that the R.C./Anglican proposals made at Gazzada should be carried out at all levels and not only between R.C.s and Anglicans. The Gazzada proposals, suitably adapted, could be a blue-print for relationships between the R.C.C. and other churches. It has already been seen that in Canada and the United States a good deal of progress has been made at the national level. This progress has begun to engender the necessary impatience which could begin to shift the slower-moving church authorities and entrenched opinion; it has also had a recognizable influence on the discussions of the international commission. The Roman/Anglican situation in Canada and the United States needs to be echoed all over the world.

National discussion and co-operation is not enough. It must be repeated at the diocesan and parochial level – and of course the appropriate adjustments have to be made in the case of churches which do not share the R.C. and Anglican hierarchical structure. One hopeful example can be quoted from England and Wales. There in May 1968 the Roman Catholic Ecumenical Commission reminded diocesan ecumenical commissions that

there can hardly be a department of a diocesan curia whose work is not full of ecumenical possibilities, e.g.: planning for building of all kinds; the running of schools, including the teaching of religious doctrine; the youth commission; liturgical and musical commission; the Chancery itself.... There will be need of two-way traffic. The D.E.C. will need to know of events and developments helpful to those engaged in promoting ecumenism; and it will need to find ways of bringing ecumenical possibilities to the notice of other 'departments', urging the principle: 'if we could be doing it together, we should'.[23]

At the same time at the parish level the commission urged the joining or initiating of clergy 'fraternals' and of local councils of churches, and the formation of house groups which 'make ecumenism a real meeting of people'. Here again the policy is summarized as 'a constant reconsideration and serious application of the Lund Principle of always doing together what conscience does not oblige us to do separately'.[24] In fact in many ways it could be said that the relationship between Roman Catholics and other churches has now reached the stage at which non-Roman churches found themselves at Lund in 1952. It must also be said that it is to be hoped that the R.C.C. and the churches they work with are more willing than were their predecessors to put the Lund Principle into practice!

Secondly, therefore, the position will improve only if the churches concerned can work together on joint practical projects. In the case of the Roman Catholics, as in all ecumenical discussion, the context of all effort is the need to work for greater effectiveness in Christian witness in an unfriendly world. Collaboration on practical problems (even if these are in fact scholarly projects!) is necessary if the various negotiations are to shed their academic clothes.

One particularly promising area of collaboration has been in that of Bible translation and distribution. Taking as their text the Vatican II emphasis on a wider use of the scriptures in the vernacular throughout the church, the Roman authorities started in 1966 to explore the possibility of collaborating in this field with the world-wide interdenominational Protestant Bible Societies. There were not a few preliminary difficulties to be overcome: the Roman Catholic and Protestant churches accept different canons of authoritative books, the former including and the latter excluding the Apocrypha; the two traditions have established over the years different methods of reaching agreement on the basic text; they have evolved different ways of translating proper names. These and other differences present real problems, yet by 1968 a Joint Working Group of the Bible Societies and the S.P.C.U.

reported that it should be possible, 'given a significant measure of good will and a concern for Christian unity', to produce a common Bible, common translations and even mutually acceptable helps to understanding and commentaries.[25] This development, linked as it is with the feeling that such collaboration is an urgent need for the missionary work of the church, is of the greatest importance. It is co-operation in ways like this at every level which will have the greatest effect in cancelling long-standing traditions of ignorance and suspicion.

The third necessity, and in the end no doubt still the most difficult, is doctrinal agreement – and more than mere agreement, or agreement to differ, on formulas – a general coming-together between the churches in their attitude to authority and its exercise in the church. Professor Owen Chadwick, who was one of the Anglican participants at the early R.C./Anglican meetings, wrote at about the time of that at Gazzada:

The divide remains in this century. It is no longer quite such a chasm, nor are its terms quite the same. But in my view the rights of liberal divinity, and its relation to the authority of the Church, is even now the most momentous single question which confronts the divines upon either side.[26]

This question of 'liberal divinity' and its opposite, the authoritarianism which is usually seen as characterizing the Roman Catholic attitude, is a matter not only of theology but of differing approaches to practical questions of Christian living. This point is best illustrated by reference to the vexed question of 'mixed marriages'. One by one and at every level Joint Working Groups between Catholic and other churches report that the Roman Catholic attitude over mixed marriages between Catholics and members of other Christian churches is the greatest single practical stumbling block to further ecumenical advance. In the past the Roman Catholic rule here has been absolute: the wedding must take place in a Roman

Catholic church, and if the non-Roman party does not 'convert', he or she must before the wedding sign a promise that the children of the marriage will be brought up as Roman Catholics and that he or she will do nothing to hinder the partner in the practice of the Roman Catholic faith; at the same time the Roman partner was required to sign a promise that he or she would do everything possible by prayer and example to convert the non-Roman spouse to Catholicism after the marriage.

These regulations, while lightly undertaken by some, caused a great deal of grief and perplexity to many, and were generally thought of by non-Roman Catholics as intolerable. On the other hand it was not as easy for the Roman church to change them as was often assumed by the others. To non-Romans they are disciplinary regulations which can be altered by a change of practical policy in the ecumenical interest. But to the Roman church canon (or ecclesiastical) law which sets up and enforces such regulations is itself a branch of Christian doctrine and a vital part of the life and teaching of the church; therefore its regulations cannot be as lightly changed as non-Romans would hope. It is this marriage of theology and practice in the Roman church which makes so diffi- cult the safeguarding of that 'liberal divinity' and ethos which other churches take for granted.

Two examples, among many, of the approach to the problem of mixed marriages may be given. Switzerland, where the population is so mixed religiously, is a country where the question touches many individuals. In 1967 a mixed commission of Roman Catholics and Protestants asked some searching questions which implied substan- tial changes in Roman Catholic practice. In particular they suggested the acceptance by Rome of the validity of mixed marriages where they are celebrated in a non- Roman church, provided that certain conditions (such as the acceptance of life-long union and neither party being divorced) were fulfilled. On the question of the religious upbringing of children the commission had this to say:

> In this respect there is need to study closely and draw out the implications of the conciliar declaration on religious liberty. The excommunication of the Roman Catholic who without dispensation agrees to give a non-Catholic education to his children is a question which concerns the discipline of the Roman Catholic Church. The study of a modification of this rule would however make an essential contribution to rapprochement between the churches.[27]

This quotation clearly shows the hopes which can be pinned on Vatican II's Declaration on Religious Liberty as the sharpest end of the liberalizing wedge.

The single church which has gone farthest in negotiations with Rome about mixed marriages is the Anglican; this may be a reflection of the fact that Rome does recognize that in certain ways the Anglican church stands apart from the Protestant world and does – for example on the question of marriage – maintain a mind which is more 'Catholic' than many other reformed churches. In November 1968 a joint committee reported 'a remarkable degree of agreement' on the doctrine of marriage. (The Anglicans concerned had in fact bent over backwards to emphasize Anglican teaching and practice on the indissolubility of marriage, and this at a time when many Anglicans are pressing for a more liberal attitude on the remarriage of divorced people.) This agreement led the committee to 'hope that, having regard to the special place given to the Anglican Communion in the Decree of Ecumenism, special consideration will be given to our recommendations concerning Anglican–Roman Catholic marriages'. These recommendations were chiefly that the validity of a marriage celebrated in either church should be recognized and that no more should be asked of the Anglican party to a mixed marriage than 'that he knows of the obligation in conscience of the R.C. party and at least does not rule out the R.C. baptism and education of the children'.

In these circumstances a pronouncement on mixed marriages from Rome was eagerly awaited. It came in the form of a papal '*Motu Proprio*' on 25 March 1970. A Roman Catholic still has to obtain a dispensation to marry a non-Catholic, otherwise the marriage is illicit; on obtaining this dispensation he has to make a promise 'to do all in his power to have all the children baptized and brought up in the Catholic Church'. The non-Catholic partner is told of these promises but does not have to make any of his own. There are certain concessions about the marriage ceremony in a mixed marriage in a Catholic church, but none about allowing the validity of a marriage in a non-Catholic church, while a wedding in which Catholic and non-Catholic clergy take part is expressly forbidden. On the other hand some latitude is given to national hierarchies in the practical application of the new regulations.

Speaking of these new regulations at a press conference Cardinal Heenan of Westminster said: 'The *Motu Proprio* makes a welcome concession by no longer requiring promises from the non-Catholic. It is undoubtedly a genuine effort to remove causes of bitterness. But, in fact, neither the *Motu Proprio* nor subsequent episcopal norms can solve the dilemma of the partners. The problem of mixed marriages between Christians will be solved only when Christendom is re-united in one faith.'[28] This is true, but meanwhile other Catholic reaction to the *Motu Proprio* has not been so favourable. The Roman Catholic periodical the *Tablet* headlined its editorial comment 'half a step forward'; it then went on to quote the well-known Roman Catholic M.P., Norman St John Stevas, whose views are by no means always outspokenly 'progressive':

This is nothing less than a repudiation of the whole ecumenical movement. . . . The whole tone of the decree is to my mind legalistic and lacking in love and charity.... Could not someone in the Curia have conceived of the whole matter of a mixed marriage, not as an 'imperfection', but as a magnificent opportunity to create a real ecumenism where it most matters, in the heart of the Christian family?[29]

The same number of the *Tablet* carried even more critical comment from the leading German progressive theologian, Professor Hans Kung.

Rome has once again committed itself to positions which, theologically and practically, are largely out of date and which cannot be held in the long run. All this is at the expense of the Church's credibility and authority, since it is at the expense of the human being concerned.... A fundamental solution of the mixed marriage question has again been postponed for an indefinite time.[30]

The 'fundamental solution' which Professor Kung would like to see would include three things all of which, he says, are within the bounds of theological and practical possibility. These are: the recognition of all mixed marriages without the necessity of dispensation, the use of an 'ecumenical marriage rite', and a decision about the upbringing of children which would give real freedom of conscience. Until such a solution had been reached he went so far as to urge Roman Catholic priests to sabotage the new regulations by refusing to apply for any dispensations for mixed marriages – a suggestion for which he was subsequently rebuked by the French liberal elder statesman. Yves Congar. (See below, pp. 522–3.)

The Question of Authority

The question of mixed marriages has been dealt with at some length partly because in itself it is the greatest single obstacle to the improvement of relationships between the Roman Catholic church and other churches; and partly because it illustrates the difficulties the

Church of Rome has in approaching the question of 'liberal divinity' and the related matter of liberal practical attitudes. So many Roman Catholic doctrines are tied up for practical purposes with traditional and binding canon law.

At Vatican II, Bishop de Smedt of Bruges named the trinity of devils dominating the church, 'clericalism, juridicalism and triumphalism' (see above, pp. 393–4). Liberalizing or progressive thinkers within the church are hoping to move away from a view of the church as an authoritarian institution, in which the lives of the members are bound by rules, towards a more humble and organic view of the Body of Christ. Recently scholars have traced the beginning of 'juridicalism' to the eleventh and twelfth centuries: faced by an attempt by royal and lay powers to subjugate it, the church reformed itself and gained much new strength; but in doing so it borrowed many ideas about power and authority from the secular world. 'This man orders us about as if we were his bailiffs,' said a German bishop of the great reforming pope, Gregory VII (1073–85).[31] Before that time, writes Professor R. W. Southern,

Men went to Rome not as the centre of ecclesiastical government but as a source of spiritual power. The 'power' was St Peter's. . . . This power brought many men to Rome who would have no thought of going there when Rome became the centre of the everyday government of the church. Several English kings, for example, made the pilgrimage to Rome before 1066; after 1066, not one.[32]

It was about this time that men began to think of the church as 'a spiritual hierarchy culminating in the Pope';[33] that the canon law assumed new and vital importance; that the church claimed to dominate the state – clericalism, juridicalism and triumphalism.

All these tendencies were strengthened in the struggle at the Reformation and in the new fight against political and theological liberalism in the nineteenth century. It is only in recent years that the premises have been questioned. It seems therefore that the question resolves itself once again into whether the liberalizing or 'progressive' – call them what you will – forces which found a platform and achieved so many changes of direction at Vatican II can maintain and increase their influence. Once the Council was over, the advantage tended to pass again to the central Roman bureaucracy, which is for the most part conservative and opposed to reform – certainly to rapid reform. Here the Synod of Bishops could be of crucial importance. The Synod was set up by the Council to continue the association of the episcopate with the pope in the government of the church, which is seen at its fullest in a Council. The details of how the Synod would work were left vague by Vatican II; it seems that at each meeting the progressives have had to struggle to get their voices heard and their policies discussed in much the same way as, on a larger scale, they had to fight at the Council itself. Thus the vital matter of agenda for the brief meetings was in the hands of the pope and the Curia and, for instance, the question of the celibacy of the clergy, which the liberals regard as being high on the priorities for discussion was not included until 1971. At the 1970 meeting, however, the Synod was given its own continuing secretariat. This should mean that it will have a greater measure of independence of the Curia so that the work of the progressive elements in the Synod will not be in danger of being thwarted or held back by the slower-moving conservatives of the central bureaucracy.

In all this the fact cannot be escaped that it is the influence and attitude of the pope himself which is the greatest single factor for or against change – and therefore affecting the speed of the *rapprochement* between Rome and the rest of the Christian world. Here it cannot be denied that the present pope, Paul VI, seems to be on the whole cautious and opposed to change. It is true that he has made some necessary and in fact overdue reforms in the Curia itself; he has moved in the direction of simplicity against much in the traditional papal outlook which could be labelled as triumphalism; he has made some imaginative gestures, especially in his foreign journeys, which have been very successful from the public relations point of view.

But when it has come to matters which progressives in his own church would regard as the crunch, he has almost always proved conservative. Indeed the tone of many of his pronouncements has been not only conservative but beleaguered and frightened. This is perhaps not altogether surprising in an elderly man, faced as he is with a decline in the church (as shown in the decreasing number of ordinations among men and vocations among women) and in actual rebellion from an increasing number of priests who give up their orders, an almost unheard-of thing a few years ago. These are not matters which concern this book except in so far as they indicate a crisis of and for authority in the Roman Catholic church – with the consequence that the way the crisis is resolved, either in a liberal or a conservative direction, must affect the Roman stance in the ecumenical movement.

The best authenticated example of the present pope's conservativism is over the question of birth control: the pope was known to have been advised to modify the strict Catholic rules by the commission he had set up to discuss the matter; the doctrinal *volte-face* which justified such a change had been published in Catholic periodicals; yet in coming to his final conclusion he sought the advice only of known conservatives – and the result was pleasing only to people of that ilk.

In the very extended correspondence in *The Times*, which followed the publication of the encyclical, not a few people commented that this papal decision, which looked so much like a fiat of arbitrary authority, might have precisely the effect of undermining the authority of the pope and of the church. For if it proved that the rules insisted on by the pope could not or would not be kept by a large number of lay people (and especially intelligent lay people), then this would eat like acid into the credibility of papal authority. 'I am in no doubt,' wrote a Benedictine priest on 6 August 1968, 'that the encyclical will be found dramatically to have forced the pace as to what authority in the Church is and how it works.'

This has proved true, at least in England. The reaction to *Humanae Vitae* led directly to the foundation of the Catholic Renewal Movement. At first this started as a – mainly lay – protest movement against the encyclical but later 'the Catholic Renewal Movement was formed because it was instinctively realized that the birth control failure was symptomatic of a deeper problem of authority and attitudes affecting the Church's mission and indeed ... the Church itself'. So the movement has broadened out, tackling at the local level 'problems like lack of consultation with parents over the running of church schools, misuse of authority in parish life and the right to question decisions and advocate changes'.[34] Here is just one example of the fact that the way the 'crisis of authority' in the Roman church is solved could have great importance for this cause of unity.

Theological Roots

As so often in this book the unity of the church is seen to centre on the doctrine of authority in the church. At a theological level this problem can best be highlighted by quotations from the monumental book *Ecumenism*, by the French Dominican scholar Bernard Lambert. Fr Lambert is not as progressive as some who have written on the subject but he is by no means conservative, let alone reactionary; his thought can be said to be typical of a cautious but hopeful R.C. approach to ecumenical matters. In approaching ecumenism from every conceivable point of view he returns over and over again to the

problem of authority. The cardinal difference between
Rome and non-Roman churches is that Rome believes
that the authority of Christ, first shown at the supreme
'eschatological' moment of his incarnation, continues in
the church since his resurrection and ascension. Non-
Roman or Protestant churches believe that the incarnation was a once-for-all moment and that the church,
while it has some authority, cannot have the authority of
the continuing presence of Christ.

The standpoint of the Catholic Church is dictated by a view
of the eschatological realities as present and active in the
historical Church. . . . This is the very crux of the disagreements
among Christians. For Protestantism, the historical Church and
the eschatological realities are two things which encounter and
touch each other, but remain for ever separate. For Catholicism
the Church is the Kingdom of God, in its initial stage, and on
pilgrimage, but real.[35]

The essential difference between Protestantism and Catholicism lies in the notion each forms of the relation between Christ,
the Omega reality, and the Church. . . . Christ came to this
world and was seen as the minister of salvation, the supreme
pastor. . . . Therefore, says Protestantism, all ministerial activity
has been accomplished. . . . All that remains is to bear witness
to this. . . . The various ministries in the Church are thus
ministries of witness. . . . Catholicism, on the contrary, holds
that Christ's presence as minister is a reality . . . the eschatological realities substantially keep their identity, but are committed and shared. In fact it is this word *presence* that provides
a key to our differences. . . . The eschatological realities and the
fact of presence are again seen to be the central question.[36]

The purpose of the magisterium (that is the teaching
authority of the Church) is to be the permanent presence
of the teaching of Christ and the apostles . . . the purpose of the
Church's government is to maintain Christ's presence as grasp-
ing the world in order to recapitulate it in Himself.[37]

The root of the difficulty between Protestantism and
Catholicism lies in the interpretation of the Presence, for it is

the meaning given to this that determines acceptance or refusal of the visible mediation of the Church.[38]

What separates us, then, Catholics and Protestants, is not faith in the Presence ... but it is the interpretation of the meaning of the presence, its mode of manifestation to us and our way of entering into it.... We say there is only one presence and it is the same whether manifested in the Church in her pilgrim state or in her final state.... In Protestantism, on the contrary, this Church, the Body of Christ, could not be the Kingdom of God on earth in the pilgrim state. The Church of faith and the Church of history are incompatible.[39]

The decisive word underlying this (Protestant) standpoint (on unity) that has now acquired the status of common agreement in ecumenical Protestantism is the verb 'to manifest'.... The unity of the Church on earth is a sign of the unity achieved in Christ.... The Church of faith and the Church of history are two distinct realities. The Church of history has the importance of a sign of the Church of faith, but no interior continuity connects them.... Catholicism, too, has found the secret of its unity and the decisive motive of its concern for Christian reunion in this same reality. But there is disagreement as to its nature. Protestantism holds it to be transcendent but extrinsic; Catholicism believes that it is transcendent, but that the historical process has a part in it.[40]

These quotations have been given at length because, although they may contain an element of caricature, they do underline the nature of Protestant and Catholic differences over the vital problem of authority. The Roman church can claim authority because it has certain basic beliefs about the relationship of the church to its Founder, and beneath that certain beliefs about the nature of time and of history. The Protestant churches must resist these claims because they do not share the beliefs.

The basic difference between the churches on the matter of authority has been put another way by the General Secretary of the World Council of Churches, Dr Eugene Carson Blake:

To put together ... the Holy Spirit on the one hand and Catholicity of the Church on the other is itself to come to grips with this central question. The ethos of evangelical Christianity has always depended upon a belief that God the Holy Ghost was not confined in his action to the visible structures of the established Catholic Church. Martin Luther could not have taken his stand without the confidence that the Holy Spirit was his guide to the understanding of the Word contained in the Scriptures. John Calvin developed his ecclesiology and his sacramental theology on a high doctrine of the Holy Spirit. And the farther to the left you go in Protestant theology, the more is ecclesiastical theology directly understood to be dependent upon whether or not the Holy Spirit is actively present with Christ's people guiding and inspiring. The Pentecostal Churches with whom the World Council is seeking closer relations and better understanding are clearly at this theological pole. The very word Catholic, however carefully you define it, has for nearly 500 years caught up connotations which contradict this evangelical understanding of the Holy Spirit at almost every crucial point. ... This is still a central issue in the ecumenical movement.[41]

The approach is slightly different from that of Fr Lambert but the fundamental point dividing the churches is the same. Is Christ, working through his Holy Spirit, to be completely identified by his presence in the visible Catholic church, or can the Spirit work outside the visible church, even at times to judge and condemn it? It may be that to put the question so is somewhat to caricature it. But at least it takes the problem of authority to its fundamental roots.

And the tracing of the differences back to their roots also shows a hopeful way ahead. If the root ideas can be shown to be not incompatible but complementary, then it may be that the doctrines which have sprung from them will also be seen to be complementary, so that some agreement can be reached. This is the whole point and aim of ecumenical 'dialogue'.

It has already been seen how the decline of controversy

and polemics coupled with greater scholarly understanding has made it possible for such dialogue to come to agreement on various questions which have traditionally been bones of theological contention between Catholics and Protestants. There are examples in the various Joint Working Groups, and in the discussions between Anglicans and Roman Catholics in the United States. Another example has been in the remarkable amount of agreement reached – and actually reduced to sets of written theses – by a French and Swiss Catholic and Protestant group, known as the *groupe des Dombes*, which has met almost annually since its foundation by Fr Couturier in 1937. A description of Fr Couturier's own contributions to these 'exchanges', as he preferred to call them, is typical of the way in which dialogue must be seen, if it is to be fruitful:

When clashes occurred, he lifted the debate to a higher level in search of a synthesis. The theological specialists at first sometimes protested, but upon reflection would be amazed at the pertinence and profundity of the interjection: Father Couturier, they would feel, had glimpsed, beyond the classic differences, even beyond the plain Yes-No, a hidden similarity, a common direction, a germ capable, God willing, of providing the first beginnings of an agreement.[42]

In these various dialogues the theologians concerned have reached agreement on such questions as scripture and tradition, apostolicity, justification, priesthood, baptism and the eucharistic sacrifice. Which is not to say, of course, that the agreement has spread from the selected theologians to the great mass of the clergy and laity of the churches. Nor have the questions of the 'new' doctrines, defined by the Roman Catholic church since the middle of the nineteenth century, been subjected to the same amount of dialogue and discussion as the more traditional points at issue. These are the Immaculate Conception of the Blessed Virgin Mary (defined 1854), the In-

The Roman Catholic Church and the Orthodox Churches

fallibility of the Pope (1870) and the Assumption of the
Blessed Virgin Mary (1950) (see above, pp. 181–3). These
issues are not likely to lend themselves to discussion and
agreement as easily as those already mentioned. In the
first place they are not old controversies, half buried in
the silt of history, but contemporary theological issues
which divide the churches and which have arisen since
the churches were divided; nor are they matters of
opinion and therefore capable of flexible treatment on
either side; for the Roman Catholic church they are *de
fide*, matters of belief essential to salvation. Lastly they
are on matters which tend to polarize theological thinking and make splits across which it is particularly difficult
to build bridges of theological understanding. The dogmas about the Virgin Mary rouse all the Protestant suspicions about Roman Catholic 'idolatry', and more seriously the fears that the uniqueness of the person and
place of Christ in the Christian scheme of things is being
attacked. (Even the Orthodox, who in their worship and
general outlook are not afraid to give the 'Bearer of God'
high honour and reverence, dislike the definition of the
Assumption because it is accepted that the belief was
unknown in the earliest ages of the church.) However,
Vatican II did nothing to satisfy those who hoped Mary
might be defined as Co-Redemptrix, but rather redressed
the balance by insisting on her place in the church (see
above, p. 396). The Constitution *De Ecclesia* said in discussing the 'Mother of God' that when she 'is invoked by
the Church under the titles of Advocate, Helper, Media-
tress, this, however, is to be so understood that it neither
takes away from nor adds anything to the dignity or
efficaciousness of Christ the one Mediator.... The
Church does not hesitate to profess this subordinate role
of Mary.'[43]

This makes a possible starting point for a dialogue
which may allay Protestant fears and reach some understanding, but there is no denying that the two dogmas

433

already defined make *rapprochement* much more difficult.

The infallibility of the pope further provides difficulties for Protestants, focusing as it does the whole question
of the authority of the church; it is also a constant bone
of contention to the Orthodox, whose whole history mili-
tates against the acceptance of the supremacy of the pope.
Nor is it possible for those who dislike the doctrine to
draw much comfort from the fact that it has been in
practice somewhat ineffective: in the first place there is
the difficulty of deciding when the pope is speaking
infallibly, and in the second there is the logical fact that
infallibility is difficult to arrive at because a 'definition'
will always need interpretation, and that interpretation
will need further interpretation, and so on. Yet the fact
remains that papal infallibility sums up all that Protestants (and even Orthodox) most dislike about the
Roman conception of the authority of the church. Even
'high' Anglicans, with a strong sense of the authority of
the church wherever it is located, prefer to the concept of
infallibility that of indefectibility – the idea that the
gates of hell will not prevail against the church. Thus the
late Dr Austin Farrer:

> I prefer to put it differently, and more sympathetically, since
> I hope I share the faith which I suppose the idea *de facto* to
> express. ... I prefer to call infallibility by another name, which
> enables us to bring it right down to earth. Our faith is that
> God is infallible, the Church is not; she is indefectible. ... I
> will have infallibility, if it is indefectibility cast into the guise
> of a Kantian idea (that is an 'ideally perfect model'). But I
> shall need to be assured that the utterances which dogmatized
> the Immaculate Conception and the Corporeal Assumption
> need not be held incorrigible.[44]

Here Dr Farrer puts his finger on what is perhaps the
single most vital issue in the ecumenical debate. Roman
Catholic authoritarianism has tended to be based on the

old idea that 'when Rome has spoken, the case is closed'. That is the last word – and that word is 'incorrigible', in that it is perfect for all time and unchangeable (or unreformable) in any circumstances. It is this attitude which makes it so difficult for Rome herself to shift, even when perhaps she wishes to. This, for instance, is part of the difficulty for the pope when it comes to revising the teaching about birth control; his predecessors have spoken in no uncertain terms against it. Even more is this true in the case of defined dogmas such as the Immaculate Conception and the Corporeal Assumption of Our Lady. Rome has spoken. . . . There can be no question of a historical re-assessment or an admission that the doctrine is of only relative importance. There is no room for debate or for minimizing manoeuvre.

Or at least that used to be the position. But even here there is now the possibility of change. Vatican II, for instance, spoke in places about the Bible and certain books of the Bible in ways which were in fact condemned in highly authoritative papal pronouncements at the turn of the century. These pronouncements have not been denied or reversed; they have simply been tacitly dropped. The assumption presumably is that times have changed; but whatever the assumption the fact is that the thin end of the wedge has been inserted into the problem of incorrigibility.

There are some Roman Catholic theologians who are willing to extend this idea and allow that even defined dogmas may be capable of being treated relatively. Thus Fr Robert Murray, s.j.:

The Catholic Church has gone so far, in official documents, in recognizing both the full ecclesial status and the authenticity of doctrinal witness of the Orthodox Church that the Decree of Ecumenism can say that the divergent theological formulations of East and West 'are often to be considered as complementary rather than conflicting'. If this is to be taken seriously it must mean that, for example, we will ask the East to respect the

doctrine of the Immaculate Conception as a formulation valid
for the Latin West ... while we will allow them to be content
with their way of expressing Our Lady's role in the economy
of salvation. A future united council might, if necessary, find
a united formula, or might simply allow alternatives, as
Florence did on the Filioque; and so the varying insights of
the *sensus fidelium* in different parts of the Church would be
respected. Is this to say that we must abandon the doctrine of
irreformability? I do not think so. We shall still say that a
formulation where the Church's infallibility was engaged is
true for all time. It was the product of an action in the past
when the doctrinal lense of the Church was focussed on a part
of the deposit of faith and an exposure was made.... The
picture was made.... It is of permanent value.... But to say
this is not to say that precisely that answer to the question in
that context remains exclusively determinative, or even
specially relevent, for the Church in another era and another
context; sometimes it may be so, while sometimes there must
be another focussing of the doctrinal lense, and with all respect
to the former formulation, a new one must be sought.[45]

This is to introduce with a vengeance the idea of historical relativity into the conception of doctrinal definitions.
Probably there are not at the moment many Roman
Catholic theologians who would go so far as this statement. But from the ecumenical point of view it does seem
to point the most promising way ahead.

Crystal-Gazing

The Decree on Ecumenism of Vatican II spoke of 'an
order or hierarchy of truths' within Catholic teaching
(see above, p. 404). This phrase seems to introduce the idea
of relativity. In earlier ecumenical thinking, such as *Mortalium Animos*, Rome had condemned the idea of trying
to differentiate between those doctrines which were fundamental and those which were not. Since the Reformation this has been a, if not *the*, Protestant approach to
church unity. But for Rome it has spelt 'indifferentism',

and thus has been anathema. For Rome Christian doctrine has been Catholic doctrine, one and indivisible. But with the phrase a 'hierarchy of truths' it seems that there may be a wind of change. Inevitably Protestants pounced on the idea; probably they have made too much of it; certainly it will need much working out. But again it seems the way ahead.

In a sermon preached at Great St Mary's Church, Cambridge, on 18 January 1970, Cardinal Willebrands, the Secretary of the Secretariat for Promoting Christian Unity, seems to have introduced another idea into the debate, along the same lines. After mentioning the 'hierarchy of truths' and saying that 'diversity of theological approach and explanation is legitimate and can be acknowledged within the unity of faith', he went on:

May I invite you to reflect on a notion which, it seems to me, has received much fruitful attention from the theologians recently? It is that of the *typos* (a Greek word) in its sense of general form or character, and of a plurality of *typoi* within the communion of the one and only Church of Christ. . . . In the Decree on Ecumenism we read: 'for many centuries the churches of East and West went their own ways, though a brotherly communion of faith and sacramental life bound them together. . . .' . . . The words 'went their own ways' point in the direction of the notion I would like to develop a little more. What are these 'own ways' and when can we speak of a *typos*? . . . Where there is a long coherent tradition, commanding men's love and loyalty, creating and sustaining a harmonious and organic whole of complementary elements, each of which supports and strengthens the other, you have the reality of a *typos*. Such complementary elements are many. A characteristic theological method and approach . . . is one of them. . . . A characteristic liturgical expression is another. . . . It is through such seated realities as these, and not because of mere territorial or national boundaries, that we can find the expression of a typology of Churches. . . . If within one nation two *typoi* are so closely related, that in a situation of full communion between them, Providence draws them into coalescence, the authentic and strong elements of each will take their place in an enriched unity.... Obviously the very existence of different *typoi* added to external causes and to mutual failures of understanding and charity can also set the stage for separations. Through the grace of God the ecumenical movement is creating understanding and charity and restoring unity between those who have grown asunder. The life of the Church needs a variety of *typoi* which would manifest the full Catholic and apostolic character of the one and holy Church.

In this passage Cardinal Willebrands seems to be saying that uniformity is not essential for communion in a united church. He even seems to be suggesting that quite widely differing traditions can be tolerated between churches in communion with each other, and that if such churches then move into closer union their differing viewpoints when united will result in positive gain and enrichment. Here again we have an idea which would hardly have come from an authoritative Roman Catholic leader a few years ago.

The idea was taken a little further with special reference to the Church of England by Bishop B. C. Butler in a sermon in Westminster Cathedral. Commenting on the fact that Vatican II recognized the Anglican Communion as having a special place in Christendom, and looking into the ecumenical future, the Bishop said:

What do we in fact expect other than some sort of co-existence with one another, of the Catholic western rite as it exists today in this country ... and an 'English rite' with its own bishops, liturgy and theological tradition? Both rites would acknowledge the primacy of the successor of St Peter, but each – presumably – would have its own 'patriarch' or the equivalent.[46]

Bishop Butler acknowledged that all this would presuppose a measure of agreement on matters of faith, but insisted that Roman Catholics must not demand anything 'not absolutely essential to Catholic faith'. Even so there would have to be some 'convergence of doctrine'.

The question of orders would also arise and the bishop felt that changes in Catholic sacramental theology 'may make it possible to reverse the judgement given against the ordinations of Elizabeth I's reign by Leo XIII' (see above, p. 413).

Bishop Butler's ideas are bound to carry weight, since he is generally reckoned to be the leading 'intellectual' among the English Catholic bishops. What he is foreseeing in C. of E./R.C. relationships is in fact a type of 'uniat' scheme. The uniat churches are churches of eastern Christendom which are in communion with Rome and acknowledge Roman supremacy while retaining their respective languages, rites and canon law on such things as communion in both kinds and the marriage of the clergy. In many ways, therefore, the uneducated faithful of uniat churches may hardly know that they are ultimately under the jurisdiction of Rome. The origin of these uniat arrangements goes back to the Middle Ages and at various times up to 1860 a number of small Orthodox churches with long national and cultural traditions have acknowledged the Roman primacy on these terms. The idea is understandably not popular in the main Orthodox world, especially as some of the uniat churches are dissentient breakaways from the great Orthodox patriarchates. Altogether there are seventeen such churches, numbering perhaps eight million people. Their existence has been made much of by Rome recently: their bearded, oriental-looking bishops were, for instance, much in evidence at Vatican II. It is obviously felt that they provide precedents for future ecumenical action; certainly they are what Cardinal Willebrands would call *typoi* of churches. There may be a way ahead here, but the Eastern uniat model would need a good deal of modification before it could be transplanted to English soil.

Two points can certainly be made about an extension of the uniat arrangement as envisaged by Bishop Butler.

In the first place uniat arrangements have been confined in the past to churches of the 'eastern rite', and also of a pronounced Catholic – albeit eastern – character. Negotiations for a 'western' uniat church would inevitably be very different, though such an arrangement would obviously be easier in the case of the Church of England than of a more thorough-going Protestant church. Secondly uniat schemes are much more likely to work in the case of a relatively strong, national (even established) majority church than with one which did not have these characteristics; it was admitted by Bishop Butler, for instance, that uniat proposals were not looked on with favour at the Windsor J.W.G. meeting by the Anglicans from North America, where the Anglican church is a minority in the religious conspectus, and therefore does not have the same feeling of confidence in maintaining future independence which Church of England leaders might feel about such a scheme.

A further point may be added. The uniat idea suggested in Bishop Butler's sermon does not fulfil the World Council's ideal of the unity of 'all in each place'. It proposes for England two churches, existing side by side – the continuing Roman Catholic and the uniat Canterbury patriarchate. In Cardinal Willebrand's language these would be two *typoi* – though presumably they might eventually merge into the richer unity foreseen by the Cardinal.

The proposal has now been tabled. In fact it is not a new suggestion, since the idea of a Canterbury patriarchate came up at the conversations which were held at Malines in the 1920s. It must be taken seriously, especially as it does seem to suggest a way by which the Church of England – and presumably by extension other churches – could recover the unity of western Christendom without being 'swallowed' or absorbed by Rome or losing their own individual traditions.

The Church of England has a precedent of its own for

arriving at full communion between two churches of differing traditions. This is the Bonn Agreement of 1930 between the Church of England and the Old Catholics, the principles of which were later applied to full communion concordats between the Philippine Independent Church and various branches of the Anglican Communion (see above, pp. 219–20). The essence of this arrangement is that the churches acknowledge that each holds the essentials of the faith and so agree to full communion, while recognizing that there remain between the churches wide variations of tradition, devotion and practice. It is a scheme of this sort, one supposes, which Anglicans might hope to make the basis of *rapprochement* with Rome. The 'doctrinal convergence' mentioned by Bishop Butler would still be necessary and the question of orders would undoubtedly raise its head, but such an arrangement would presumably stop short of full papal allegiance – or imply something like the recognition of the pope as *'primus inter pares'* – and thus from the non-Roman side be easier.

We are now frankly crystal-gazing. But even the fortune-teller cannot avoid questions of chronology. Are discussions between Rome and the various churches going to go forward at such a rate that agreement is reached in some cases *before* those churches have lost their identity in national united churches? Or will the non-Roman western churches speed their rate of reunion so that in the end it is a matter of union or full communion between Rome and a number of united national churches? It is difficult to tell. Certainly there are said to be some Anglicans in Canada who feel that priority should be given to discussions with local Roman Catholics rather than with the United Church of Canada. Perhaps the final answer to this chronological question will not be either/or but in some places one timing and in others the other. Nevertheless it still seems most probable that the first major unions will be between non-Roman churches of the western tradition in various national or cultural situations – South India, North India, Ghana, Australia, the United States and so on. Presumably if and when that happens concordats for full communion between these churches on some sort of Bonn basis will not be difficult to arrive at.

The next step will then be union or full communion with Rome. (This is not to say that the Joint Working Groups between Rome and the various individual churches are wasting their time: the chronology *may* turn out differently and in any case now and for a long time to come all efforts at understanding will have their value.) Whether this will be achieved by organic union, or by agreements along uniat or 'Bonn' lines, remains to be seen. Probably first will come full communion by a method which is neither uniat nor Bonn, but something in between. Certainly the fact that the united churches will be episcopal with orders in the apostolic succession will make union between them and Rome less difficult than union between Rome and Protestant churches (of whatever tradition) would have been. Equally certain is it that both sides will have to be ready to change in their presentation of their own fundamental beliefs to the other, and in their understanding of the beliefs held dear by the other. It may have seemed in these last pages that the onus was being put on Rome to hasten the change of attitude which is already apparent in some quarters. But such a change only has the effect of putting Rome *within reach* of the reformed churches. There will have to be change, too, on their part.

But what is most certain of all is that to think of a unity which falls short of unity with the Roman Catholic church is folly.

THE ORTHODOX CHURCHES

It will have been noticed that, in talking about the relationship of the Roman Catholic church with various other Christian communions, nothing was said of the Eastern Orthodox churches. This is because there is no Joint Working Group between the R.C. church and any Orthodox church. Nor is any Orthodox church involved in official 'conversations to unity' with any other denomination. The position of the Orthodox churches must now be reviewed.

The Decree on Ecumenism of Vatican II made it clear that Rome recognizes that she shares many ancient and 'catholic' doctrines with the churches of the Orthodox east. This means that Rome looks at the Orthodox churches and the non-Roman churches of the west in different ways. This fact was spelt out in the Ecumenical Directory: the Orthodox possess 'true sacraments' and are 'very close' to the Catholic church in matters of faith; so in certain circumstances of pastoral need Catholics may receive Orthodox sacraments and *vice versa*, and it is hoped that these arrangements will be reciprocal (see above, p. 406). This is certainly a significant move, and one which follows logically on one of the final acts of Vatican II, when the anathemas against the Orthodox churches, which had stood since 1054, were solemnly lifted.

There is, therefore, now in theory limited intercommunion between Rome and the Orthodox east. But no steps have been taken to make this intercommunion any fuller. There have been visits by the pope to Jerusalem in 1963 (including cordial exchanges with Orthodox leaders there) and to Istanbul in July 1967. Here the pope and Patriarch Athenagoras of Constantinople conversed, shared in worship and exchanged gifts and speeches. The ecumenical task ahead was described in a message from the pope as follows:

Now after a long period of division and reciprocal incomprehension, the Lord grants us that we rediscover ourselves as sister churches. . . . In the light of Christ we see how urgent is the necessity of surmounting these obstacles in order to succeed in bringing to its fullness and perfection that unity – already so rich – which exists between us. Since we both profess 'the fundamental dogmas of the Christian faith on the Trinity, the word of God made flesh of the Virgin Mary' as they 'were defined in the ecumenical councils celebrated in the East' . . . and since we have in common real sacraments and a hierarchical priesthood, it is necessary first of all that in the service of our holy Faith we should work fraternally, seeking together those forms which are suitable and progressive toward development and actualization in the life of our churches of that communion which already exists, though imperfectly. It will then be necessary on both sides and through mutual contacts to promote, deepen and adapt the formation of the clergy, and the instruction and the life of the Christian people. It is a matter of knowing and of respecting each other in the legitimate diversity of liturgical, spiritual, disciplinary and theological traditions by means of a frank theological dialogue, made possible by the re-establishment of brotherly charity in order to attain accord in the sincere confession of all revealed truthes.[47]

The pope's visit was returned when Patriarch Athenagoras went to Rome in October 1967 and much the same pattern of events followed, though on this occasion Cardinal Bea took the opportunity to stress that unity would be hastened as both churches pursued their own paths of renewal. It must be admitted that, with all the gifts and speech-making, no very urgent plans for *rapprochement* between the churches were proposed at these meetings; and no further or more concrete steps seem to have been taken since. Other visits to Rome by leaders of other Orthodox churches have taken place, and the pope and Orthodox leaders exchange messages on special feast days, but there matters rest.

Nor are any of the Orthodox churches in very close touch with any other world denominations. Traditionally the Orthodox and the Anglican churches have felt drawn towards each other. Certain high-church Anglicans, especially, have felt that Orthodoxy provides an expression of Catholicism alternative to Rome and lacking those Roman 'additions' to the faith and practice of the ancient church which Anglo-Catholics find difficult to accept. Despite societies for mutual understanding, such as the Fellowship of St Alban and St Sergius, traffic between the churches has, except for the occasional ceremonial visit, been largely confined to individuals. This is partly because in the very nature of things it is not easy for the two traditions to be brought together to learn about each other; and partly because when this does happen the old psychological and mental division between east and west becomes all too apparent (see above, pp. 117–19) and Anglicans find themselves baffled by the spiritual world which the Orthodox inhabit.

For these reasons relations between Orthodox and Anglicans have not progressed very far. Anglicans have always hoped to receive Orthodox recognition of Anglican orders, but no very clear conclusion on this subject has ever been reached, partly because of the difficulty of getting an agreed pan-Orthodox statement on any question (see above, pp. 115–17). As long ago as 1922 the church of Constantinople made a declaration which seemed to accept the validity of Anglican orders; this was followed by similar statements from Jerusalem (1923), Cyprus (1923), Alexandria (1930), Romania (1936) and Greece (1939). But these statements have not been followed through in practice and Anglican clergy who join the Orthodox churches in question are re-ordained. They cannot be the basis of intercommunion between Anglicans and Orthodox because of the prior Orthodox insistence on unity of faith. Again as long ago as 1935, owing largely to the efforts of Bishop Headlam of Gloucester, reasonably close relations with the Orthodox church of

Romania were established and a conference at Bucharest led to a concordat, though not to intercommunion. Revolution and war intervened to stop the development of this movement, but it is now felt that there may be a possible point of ecumenical growth here. There exists a pan-Anglican Commission for Orthodox relations which holds a full meeting nearly every year with additional regional gatherings. The Orthodox churches have something of the same nature, but not on a pan-Orthodox basis. These bodies exchange papers and questions on such matters as eucharistic doctrine, Anglican orders and the comprehensiveness of Anglican doctrine, which is a matter of bafflement to the Orthodox who cannot understand how the Anglicans can combine in one church such extremes of Catholic and Protestant opinion! As yet no official Anglican/Orthodox ecumenical conversations have taken place. But a joint meeting of the sub-committees is planned for September 1972, which it is hoped will make final preparations for the official opening of the dialogue.

But if matters move slowly on the Anglican/Orthodox front, they are hardly moving at all between the Orthodox and any other churches, though there are some contacts at a theological level between the Orthodox and Lutherans. An exception is negotiations between the Orthodox and the Old Catholics which have reached much the same stage as those with the Anglicans. Some explanation of this tardiness of the Orthodox to get involved in the ecumenical movement must be given. In the first place there is the fact, often commented on by western observers, that the Orthodox churches (except perhaps in Greece and Romania) seem hardly to have started on the *aggiornamento* – or modernization – which is so much a part of the life of western churches. It has already been mentioned (see above, pp. 113–14) that the feeling of continuity and lack of change form precisely one of the strengths of

Orthodoxy. By that token it is the more difficult for the Orthodox churches to take account of what seem to westerns to be the facts of modern life. And one of the undoubted facts of modern ecclesiastical life is the ecumenical movement. Added to this there is the factor, already commented on (see above, pp. 117–19 and 263), that deep as are the divisions in western Christendom, they are at least divisions on western subjects and westerns know what is at issue when they are under discussion; but eastern tradition split from western long before these divisions, and western ecumenical dialogue tends to be carried on in terms which have little meaning for the Orthodox.

Secondly there is the fact (which again has often been mentioned: see above, pp. 115–17) that Orthodoxy cannot be thought of – or treated with – as a single whole. There are eight autocephalous churches, not to mention their various branches in the western world, and any approach has to be made to these churches separately. A pan-Orthodox movement is very slow in forming and it can by no means be said that Orthodoxy speaks with a single voice on such important detailed questions as, for instance, the validity of Anglican orders. Before embarking on conversations with other churches, they want to try to reach a common mind among themselves. There are internal jealousies and questions of precedence in Orthodoxy which partly account for this lack of mutual consultation. The political background must also be remembered: the oldest Orthodox churches are in countries where they have been for centuries under the domination of Islam, and where contacts with the west have been difficult; the strongest are in Russia and other countries behind the Iron Curtain and, inevitably, their freedom for meeting with the west is limited.

But the Orthodox are slow at embarking on dialogue with other churches above all because of their watertight dogmatic position. This is how Timothy Ware, a converted English Orthodox priest, begins a chapter headed 'The Orthodox Church and the Re-union of Christians':

> The Orthodox Church in all humility believes itself to be the 'one, holy, Catholic and Apostolic Church', of which the Creed speaks : such is the fundamental conviction which guides Orthodox in their relations with other Christians. There are divisions among Christians, but the Church itself is not divided nor can it ever be.[48]

In spelling out this unity of doctrine Fr Ware quotes with approval the Archbishop of Canterbury's summary of the Anglo-Russian Theological Conference at Moscow in 1956.

> The Orthodox said in effect : '. . . The Tradition is a concrete fact. Here it is, in its totality. Do you Anglicans accept it, or do you reject it?' The Tradition is for the Orthodox one indivisible whole : the entire life of the Church in its fullness of belief and custom down the ages, including Mariology and the veneration of icons. Faced with this challenge, the typical Anglican reply is : 'We would not regard veneration of icons or Mariology as inadmissible, provided that in determining what is necessary to salvation, we confine ourselves to Holy Scripture.' But this reply only throws into relief the contrast between the Anglican appeal to what is deemed necessary to salvation and the Orthodox appeal to the one indivisible organism of Tradition, to tamper with any part of which is to spoil the whole, in the sort of way that a single splodge on a picture can mar its beauty.[49]

From these premises it is difficult for the Orthodox to arrive at any other ecumenical conclusion than that 'before there can be reunion among Christians, there must first be full agreement in faith'.[50]

The slowness of the development of ecumenical interest in the Orthodox church is in one way less serious than it might be. In most countries where the Orthodox church is strong it tends to be the only church on the ground. (This is especially true now that Protestant churches have for the most part given up proselytizing in the Middle East; it is however less true than some might think in Russia, where there is a vigorous and growing Baptist church.) This means that on the whole the Orthodox churches do not have on their doorstep an urgent ecumenical problem, challenging them to unity, as is the case in almost every country in the west and in the developing nations. This is no doubt another reason for Orthodox ecumenical backwardness. There are, however, some exceptions to this rule. There are some areas of eastern Europe which have been traditionally disputed between Roman Catholic and Orthodox loyalty and where the two churches overlap; this is one of the reasons why the limited intercommunion established by the Ecumenical Directory is important. There are also strong Orthodox communities in North America and in Australia, and these have so far stayed aloof from the unity negotiations in those countries, which is a serious matter; worse still the Orthodox are divided among themselves, owning allegiance to differing European patriarchates. This situation is most obvious in the United States (see above, pp. 115–17); there the Greek Orthodox form the majority and are strongly Hellenistic. The situation is somewhat alleviated by a Standing Conference of Canonical Orthodox Bishops in the Americas, but the Orthodox churches in America and Australia have a long way to go to solve their own internal differences before they can enter effectively into the unity negotiations in these places where they do form part of the picture of Christian divisions.

Meanwhile, of course, the growing Orthodox participation in the life of the World Council of Churches is of great significance. There the Orthodox voice is increasingly being heard and respected, while on the other side Orthodox participation in the W.C.C. will break down the barriers of suspicion and ignorance which have been growing up between the east and west for so many centuries. Already, as has been seen, the Orthodox at the

W.C.C. are able to join in the debates and play their part in the formulation of conclusions instead of letting the debate go on, only to register a dissentient vote when the resolution is passed, as they used to do.

There can be little doubt that, although this new type of Orthodox participation may for some time yet slow down the process of the ecumenical old hands of the west arriving at agreement (in terms, perhaps, of western ecumenical jargon), the east has its contribution to make. In the first place the point must be made that, where the western churches are now preoccupied with living in a newly hostile environment and finding the answer both to survival and witness in these circumstances, for the eastern churches this is no new experience; to hundreds of years of living under Islam they have recently added survival under an atheistic communist regime. When the west, therefore, complains at the inability of the east to come to terms with contemporary society, it may be forgetting that essentially the east did this centuries ago!

The doctrinal continuity of the Orthodox churches has been mentioned more than once. Here it need only be repeated that no Christian witness could be truly ecumenical, in the sense of world-wide, which did not contain the elements of the essential eastern outlook. In the past the Orthodox have had a highly dogmatic approach to ecumenical debates, tending simply to equate the Catholic faith with the Orthodox understanding of it; but now, as has been said, the Orthodox are more willing to join in the discussion so that there is hope that the outcome will be a true synthesis. Moreover, though unchanging and to some extent still unyielding on doctrinal matters, the Orthodox can be surprisingly flexible on practical ones. In the early church when there were many schisms and disputes in the east the practice grew up that diocese A could be in communion with dioceses Y and Z, even though these latter two were not in communion with each other (see above, pp. 84–5). Logically if Y was out of communion with Z, A would have to choose between one and the other, but the eastern church realized that logic was not always the happiest weapon to apply to ecclesiastical disputes. This application of charity – or sense – to override logic was known as 'economy', and it is the application of this principle which enables the Orthodox church to be flexible on practical matters. Economy has been otherwise defined as 'the housekeeping policy of the Church' and it presupposes that 'the church is the authoritative body which can freely regulate her policy towards her means of grace and interpret them, not of course contrary to the word of God expressly commended in the New Testament, but independently of any particular view which may prevail at the time, in such a way as to meet the needs of the time.'[51] Thus for the Orthodox economy is not a mere ignoring of ecclesiastical or theological principle but is a conscious act of the church in the interest of charity – an idea which perhaps goes a little further than the definition of the Anglican Lambeth Conference of 1948 – 'a technical term representing administrative action to meet a temporary situation without prejudice to any principle of ecclesiastical order'.[52] The more positive idea of what 'economy' means was very well expressed by Archbishop Athenagoras of Thyateira in a speech in 1970:

For this reason, the Orthodox Church, discerning beyond the Canons, which are always conventional, and looking beyond Canon Law, which is always surrounded by the Mystery of Economy, and proceeding primarily with love, and being strengthened by faith, and mindful of the analogy of God's evident activity towards the separated factions of the Old Israel, feels and proclaims the presence of the Holy Spirit as active among those who are outside her walls, and considers them as being with her, and within her own domain on account of their Baptism and on account of their faith in Jesus Christ, the God-Man. For this reason the Church calls those who are outside herself Christians. She recognizes their societies as

Churches. She knows more than the theologians, the canonists and the professors.[53]

This use of Economy allows a very different attitude to non-Orthodox churches than that traditionally adopted by the Orthodox – though such a charitable view would by no means be universally accepted by 'the theologians, the canonists and the professors'. It is already evident in the meetings of the World Council that strong differences of opinion are beginning to develop between the Orthodox themselves, with the church of Greece adopting a particularly conservative line.

Another card which the Orthodox churches have to play into the ecumenical pool is that of an ancient, Catholic and episcopal church which did not take the step of centralization taken in the west by Rome (see above, pp. 98–100). The Orthodox churches are what might be called *locality*-centred and the bishop in his diocese is the centre of the locality church. There is a resemblance here to Anglicanism, but the resemblance should not be pushed too far. Anglican churches are basically western and of a reformed mentality, and in any case Anglicanism still retains to a large extent (especially in England) the medieval Catholic abuse of vast dioceses, where the bishop cannot hope to be a true father in God and the 'ecclesiastical person' (that is, *persona* in the Latin sense of focus and representative) of a locality. On the other hand western reformed churches would, no doubt, feel that in the Orthodox world church government is too much in the hands of bishops, and the Orthodox insistence on the authority of councils of bishops undoubtedly runs counter to the developing idea of synodical church government by representatives of bishops, clergy *and* laity – or, as much ecumenical thought has put it, the combination of episcopal, presbyteral and congregational systems.

But without doubt the greatest contribution the

Orthodox have to make to the ecumenical church is in terms of spirituality. From the theological viewpoint the Orthodox churches look dogmatic and perhaps old-fashioned; but the reverse of this coin is that dogma or belief is linked to piety through the liturgy. Western observers at Orthodox services find that this world and the heavenly world of God, Christ and the saints are brought together in a way which is new to them. It is this power of the liturgy to transcend ordinary life and make real the spiritual world which, they feel, must be responsible for the astonishing history of survival in the Orthodox churches through many centuries and different styles of persecution. Nor is Orthodox spirituality confined to its corporate expression in the Liturgy; the Orthodox have often been able to imbue their followers with a remarkable – and remarkably simple – individual piety, such as the 'Jesus prayer' used by thousands of Russian peasants. It may be above all this spirituality, corporate and individual, which Orthodoxy has to bring to the ecumenical movement – though it does so at a time when many ecumenical radicals are demanding forms of contemporary piety and its liturgical expression which are much freer, less churchy and traditional than has been the case in the established western traditions.

The Oriental Orthodox Churches

Finally a word must be said about the Oriental Orthodox churches, as they are called. In so doing the wheel will have come full circle, for these were the first churches to move away from the church of the Ecumenical Councils – over the Monophysite issue in the fifth and sixth centuries (see above, pp. 101–6). These churches (which some prefer to call non-Chalcedonian, that is as not accepting the findings of the Council of Chalcedon in 451) comprise: the Syrian Orthodox centred on Damascus, with its offshoot in India; the Coptic Orthodox, with its roots in Egypt; the Ethiopian Orthodox, an entirely African church and one of the most ancient in the world; and the Armenian, with its history of survival through persecution and political and cultural change. They may seem to the western churches remote and more than half buried in the sands of history and of the desert, but they have been described as follows:

Here is a phenomenon of the most immense significance for the total body of Jesus Christ – 22 million Christians rooted in the human and cultural soil of some of the most strategic regions on earth, having survived untold onslaughts and persecutions, basing themselves on the same Holy Bible of the Orthodox, Catholics and Protestants, and wholly faithful to what was delivered to them by at least the first three Councils.[54]

Recently a remarkable movement has arisen among these churches. They have moved away from their insularity, or what the west would think of as their intensely self-centred and backward-looking life. This was shown in an inter-church conference in Addis Ababa in January 1965, in which the leading spirit was the Emperor Haile Selassie. The findings of this conference read not at all like those of churches half buried in the sands of time, but much more – perhaps *too* much more – like the work of a western ecumenical deliberation. The churches were self-critical of their 'archaeological' attitude and the key words were recovery, rediscovery and renewal. They recognized how much theological education they needed to undertake and the chapter headings of the report of the conference indicate in what directions this would be: 'The Modern World and Our Churches'; 'Co-operation in Theological Education'; 'Co-operation in Evangelism'; 'Our Relations with Other Churches'; 'Instituting a Machinery for the Maintenance of Permanent Relations among the Churches'; 'A Statement on Peace and Justice in the World'.

It seems in fact that as a result of this conference the

Oriental Orthodox churches have discovered not only each other, but the rest of the Christian world. That, at any rate, was the hope of the leaders. Warm things were said about the ecumenical movement, and one by one these churches have been joining the W.C.C., which brings them into touch with the ecumenical world. At the end of the conference an attempt was made to set on foot a healing of the original schism between these churches and the rest of the Christian world:

> Concerning the Christological controversy which caused the division, we hope that common studies in a spirit of mutual understanding can shed light on our understanding of each other's positions. So we decide that we should institute formally a fresh study of the Christological doctrine in its historical setting to be undertaken by our scholars, taking into account the earlier studies on this subject as well as the informal consultations held in connection with the meetings of the World Council of Churches.[55]

This may look at first like one more among many thousands of such pious conference resolutions. But, coming from churches which for centuries have been known mainly for their self-sufficiency and seen as an attempt to heal the oldest breach in Christendom, it is none the less remarkable.

It would seem that the first bridge to try to build is with the Orthodox churches, with whom the non-Chalcedonian churches share so much. This is in fact what is happening. Informal discussions have been set on foot to prepare for more formal negotiations – the usual cautious approach! In 1967 at Bristol – a neutral venue with a vengeance! – representatives of the churches met and came to the remarkable conclusion that they shared a common faith. Once again the barriers may be more traditional, cultural and historical – and above all the sheer inertia which clogs so many ecumenical hopes. But at least a start has been made.

CHAPTER NINE

The Grassroots: Inertia and Impatience

> ... like those Orthodox theologians who were discussing
> the sex of angels when the Turks were at the very gates
> of Byzantium.
>
> *A Paris student on the attitude of church leaders to the
> unity of the church*

THE last three chapters have presented a gloomy picture
of the current state of the ecumenical movement. The
World Council of Churches is at a turning point in its
history, recognizes the fact, but seems uncertain what to
do. It has become an established institution, is large and
top-heavy and is over-centralized, with its centre still too
much in the west. It is one thing to diagnose these ills,
but another to reform them without sacrificing the real
work of the Council and so losing the baby with the bath-
water.

The movements for organic union between churches
all over the world seem to be slowing up. Since the South
India breakthrough nearly twenty-five years ago nothing
of comparable significance has happened. The North
India scheme has at last been inaugurated; the C.O.C.U.
negotiations in the United States seem to be the most
hopeful and fast moving in the world and there are
promising developments in New Zealand; but by and
large the pace is desperately slow and this slowness carries
the seeds of disillusion.

The work of Pope John and the Vatican Council
started a romantic period between the Roman Catholic
Church (or parts of it) and the other churches of Christendom; but the period is now over and we are beginning
to see that it will be a long haul before any marriages are
consummated.

All the time there are many churches on the extreme left such as the Pentecostalists and the independent churches in Africa, which are the fastest growing (indeed virtually the *only* growing) churches in the world, and which are for the most part uninterested in the ecumenical movement; indeed they are a further development in the nineteenth-century movement of division in the churches.

The millions upon millions of words which have been written and spoken in the World Council or church union discussions which have so far been described have this in common: they are all the work of church leaders of one sort and another – bishops, moderators, presidents, chairmen, theologians and occasionally laymen who, when they reach the ecumenical heights, tend to become so clericalized that they virtually lose their lay status. Of course some lesser lights have been involved in ecumenical pioneering, but they have usually gone on to higher things in the ranks of their own churches – and from there (be it said) have provided valuable ecumenical statesmanship. But in the main the movement has been the work of church leaders. And it has been their constant complaint that the ecumenical vision has not really spread to the rest of the church, the workaday clergy and the lay people. Indeed the very fact that when such people do become involved they are labelled 'ecumeniacs' is some indication of the status of the movement in the churches at large, or (as the jargon goes) at the grassroots.

This chapter will describe the movement, such as it is, at these grassroots and give some picture of what happens when ordinary clergy and lay people become involved in it. It will not be possible to give a world-wide review of all the evidence of such ecumenical activity; but the main types will be described and examples given.

NATIONAL AND LOCAL COUNCILS
OF CHURCHES

The first stage down the ecumenical ladder from the top rungs, such as the W.C.C., is the national Council of Churches. Many national councils of churches now have a long history and in them thousands of clergy and laity have received their ecumenical apprenticeship. On the other hand the more prestigious the N.C.C. becomes, the more likely it is that the representatives on it of the various churches will be the same people as are involved in World Council and unity discussions. Thus there is the ever-present danger that ecumenical concern will remain in the same few hands, especially when one remembers the laziness of committees in co-opting old hands rather than looking for new blood.

National Councils of Churches vary in their composition and functions according to the circumstances in the country concerned. Roughly speaking their member churches will be the same as those in membership of the W.C.C.: that is to say basically the main reformed churches but not including some of the main Lutheran bodies, the powerful Southern Baptists and other churches on the Protestant left. Since Vatican II the Roman Catholics have been becoming more involved in N.C.C.s, especially in Asia and Africa, either as observers or, increasingly, as full members. In India for instance, the Roman Catholics are now full members and are playing a very active part, especially in such things as co-operation in the very extensive programme of Christian education at all levels from university to secondary school. In all the R.C.C. are members of ten national Christian councils.

One of the earliest national councils was that founded in the United States in 1908 (see above, p. 186). This was planned less on a consultative basis (as is typical of most N.C.C.s) than as a federation of churches. It has, therefore, over the years achieved considerable autonomous powers and built up a sizable programme, especially as a service agency. It is responsible for a good deal of co-operative overseas missionary work; but its major operation has been the vast programme at home and overseas of the American branch of Inter-Church Aid, known as Church World Service. On the consultative side the N.C.C., with so many member churches and such great distances involved, is a cumbrous affair, and the criticism has lately been made that it has been slow in developing new types of ecumenical programmes, such as joint missions in urban areas. (It did, however, sponsor important parts of the Delta Ministry scheme, in which the churches united in the Mississippi delta area to educate and encourage the poor black populations to claim their rights as people and citizens, a campaign in which Martin Luther King was involved at the time of his assassination.) It may be that with the changes now taking place on the ecumenical scene the N.C.C. of the United States will have to assume, as some are urging, 'an entirely new entity'.[1] It is certain that its operations will be severely curtailed by reason of financial difficulties. If it fails it could be that significant contemporary ecumenical leadership will pass into other hands, a danger present for many established ecumenical organizations.

In the developing countries the typical role of the national council of churches has been somewhat different. On top of the normal functions of consultation and the developing of mutual understanding and confidence between the churches, the N.C.C. has often been called on to act as the mouthpiece for all the churches in dealing with a hostile or unfriendly government. Thus, for instance, if the government of Malaysia or Tanzania embarks on a policy which will be to the detriment of Christian schools, opposition from the churches will be much more likely to be effective if it is united, and the council of churches speaks with a single voice. The same is true in a number of fields, such as broadcasting, land tenure and even basic human rights. It is for this reason, no doubt, that Roman Catholic membership of national councils has progressed faster in non-western than in western countries. Even where the government is not unfriendly co-operative planning and speaking can be a help in official negotiation, let alone to the actual Christian mission. Thus in Hong Kong the Christian Council has – belatedly – agreed on a comity policy in planning churches and schools in the newly developing towns, so that the ground is covered and there is a minimum of competition – a policy which is welcomed by the government as making their own planning easier and more rational than the old law of the Christian jungle. The councils of churches have been involved in another important programme in many developing countries, especially in Asia: this is the sponsorship of educational schemes to encourage Christians to think positively about what it means for a newly independent country to find its 'nationhood'. The churches have been so western-based that it was natural that nationalistic leaders should be doubtful about the loyalty of Christians to the new regimes; natural, too, perhaps, for native Christians to be the least eager in the cause of independence. In many countries, therefore, such as Ceylon, studies in this subject have been an important part of the work of the National Christian Council.

The British Council of Churches was not founded until 1942, an indication not only of the fact that the European countries were on the whole the slowest to respond to the ecumenical vision, but also of the fact that this tardiness is to be expected in a country where one church dominates all the others – compare the United States. In Britain too, and for the same reasons, the B.C.C. is still pathetically weak and powerless, underfinanced and under-staffed. The churches have been slow in committing themselves to its work in ways which really count, that is in people and money, and in programming or policies which could affect their own lives.

Nevertheless the B.C.C. has been growing in activity and prestige and its statements on such things as the South African cricket tour of 1970 and the sale of arms to South Africa have had to be taken as the consensus of British Christian opinion. (Although if a gallup poll of all the people in church on a particular Sunday were taken it is doubtful if a 'left-wing' opinion on these particular issues would emerge, many churchgoers being conservative in their opinions; the fact is that the B.C.C. or any ecumenical organization will tend to be supported by church members who are to the left of the majority.) One notable advance has been the growing number of local councils of churches. In Britain this growth has almost reached mushroom proportions: in 1950 there were 119 such local councils, in 1960, 300, and at the most recent count in 1969 there were 700. The establishment of such local councils of churches is almost entirely confined to Britain and the United States. It is perhaps the most hopeful feature in the ecumenical life of these western countries, especially since, of course, it represents the real grassroots movements and involves the local clergy and the man-in-the-pew. Local councils of churches vary very much in their strength and activity. Some are little more than ministers' fraternals meeting for discussion and Bible study; some plan the exchange of pulpits and the local shape of the week of prayer for Christian unity; some sponsor processions of witness or even full-scale local missions; some undertake community activities such as housing societies (like that in Notting Hill), the local Samaritans Group to help people tempted to suicide, or good-neighbour schemes for the lonely or the aged; some have even been the beginning of united total ministry to the neighbourhood. Everything will depend on the quality and enthusiasm of local leadership, the amount of time clergy and laity are willing to devote to the work, and the commitment of the local churches in terms of money and personnel. If a local council of churches remains weak in real commitment it may even end by *hindering* ecumenical development. It will often be a question of priorities, of a choice between the established work of the denominations and the experimental work of the council. Will the vicar release a valued Sunday School teacher (when this particular commodity is in any case in desperately short supply) to prepare and lead an ecumenical study group or a locality good-neighbour scheme? That is the sort of issue which is often the crunch.

Two particular high-water marks of B.C.C. activity must be mentioned. The first is the Faith and Order Conference held at Nottingham in 1964. This was a particularly well-organized affair, with a real attempt to get wide local grassroots representation and with a number of preparatory regional conferences leading up to it. The theme was 'One Church Renewed for Mission'. This theme was typical of the current outlook in ecumenical circles at the time (see above, pp. 262–71). It was not just a matter of the unity of the church for its own sake. The unity movement is part of a renewal movement, and unless unity marches with renewal the point of the operation is lost: because the point of the operation – the end product – is the Church's mission to the world. This was the context in which the B.C.C. placed the Nottingham Conference, and in which the discussions took place. One unexpected thing emerged at the last moment from the conference: the delegates present covenanted with each other and with God to work for the unity of the churches in Britain by the given date of Easter 1980. This was the beginning of the idea of covenanting for unity, which was later used in a different context in church union negotiations. For instance in Ghana at a certain stage in the negotiations the uniting churches covenanted together not to cease or withdraw from the discussions until they were consummated in unity. It is this sort of committal of churches to one another in a covenant situation which has made it possible for Anglican churches, as in Ghana, to embark on intercommunion. Whether or not the Nottingham covenant for unity in Great Britain by 1980 will be fulfilled remains to be seen – though at the present rate of progress it seems unlikely.

Secondly, in the spring of 1967 the B.C.C., with the (ecumenical) Conference of British Missionary Societies, launched a major ecumenical study programme for groups throughout the British Isles. It was called 'The People Next Door'. Its object was twofold: first 'to introduce to the man in the pew the wealth of fresh thinking and creative experiment which is going on among the churches in the ecumenical movement', and second 'to test the relevance of the ecumenical insights in the local church situation'.[2] The programme was ambitiously mounted with film-strips, gramophone records and other audio-visual aids in each study kit, and carefully prepared over a period of two years or more. In many ways it was like a similar Church of England programme, 'No Small Change', in the Lent of 1965 – but the Anglican programme, which had been a pioneer effort, had been mounted in a matter of months. The Anglican study had been followed by 150,000 people in England alone and in the early days of P.N.D. the hopes were for as many as two million people throughout the British Isles. In the event some 85,000 people took part.

What went wrong? In the first place, without doubt, the fact that the whole programme was ecumenical. Despite the careful preparation the fact remains that ecumenical lines of communication are not so effective as the purely denominational ones used for the 'No Small Change' campaign – though these were rusty enough. Furthermore there seems no doubt that the very fact that the course *was* ecumenical meant that in many cases it did not get the all-important support from the clergy which it needed to be viable in any particular district. Reports of clerical non-cooperation were common: 'we met with no interest and even active hostility from some ministers' . . . 'At the start the clergy and ministers (except one) were lukewarm' . . . 'Decrease in numbers largely due to lack of clergy support' . . . 'without being spiteful, I feel that some of the clergy in our area could have done much more to get the campaign going'.[3] There was another reason, many felt, for clerical lukewarmness. The study was specifically planned for *lay* people and clergy were not allowed to sit in on, still less to chair, the groups – though they could form groups of their own. This led to clerical suspicion, especially among the type of clergyman or minister who thinks of the laity as *his* people and dislikes 'his' people showing initiative in church matters (see above, pp. 56–60).

All things considered, therefore, the tally of 85,000 participants was not too bad for a first attempt – especially as the church coverage was in fact widely ecumenical. At an early stage permission had been given for Roman Catholics to join the groups even though they had no part in preparing the study. Final numbers of the major denominations were as follows: Anglicans 35,126, Baptists 3,415, Congregationalists 5,865, Methodists 13,844, Presbyterians 3,023, Roman Catholics 5,558, Salvation Army 315, Quakers 596. The Presbyterian count includes the Church of Scotland and is perhaps the most disappointing; presumably it represents suspicion north of the border of a London-based operation! Altogether 1,360 people came from other churches including Brethren, Orthodox, Moravian, Lutheran, Dutch Reformed and Copts.

There were, of course, criticisms of the syllabus and a sense of failure to complete some of its requirements. But the most general comment was that it had been an 'eye-opener'. People had made friendships across denominational barriers, which are known to have persisted. (One of the most striking finds of the course was how far people's friendships came from within their own church circles and how few of the participants even *knew* people who were not churchgoers; one group spoke of 'the esoteric circles of the Christian Church'.) Meeting in each other's houses they had discussed beliefs, modes of worship and the possibility of common action. 'Things will never be the same again in the village' . . . 'this course has done more to promote Christian unity in this area than anything else which has happened in the last 100 years' . . . 'We straightened out a lot of funny ideas we had about our individual denominations; if this had been the only object of the meetings, we have certainly achieved it' . . . 'Reports from all the groups left us in no doubt that their members had found a new dimension in their Christian thinking'.[4]

The follow-up plans that were made for further study, joint local action and the rest need not here concern us. What was significant was the very large number of recommendations that were made repeatedly to the churches for ecumenical progress and the tone in which they were made. Urgency and impatience were constant. Anti-clericalism was also recurrent. 'The course raised hopes that lay people will take matters into their own hands and speedily do something really effective. . . . The danger is that it will be dismissed as just another academic exercise and a great deal will depend on the quality of the follow-up' . . . 'Please, a sense of urgency about church unity. . . . This is a very dangerous project for the establishment. You parsons had better watch out – you may find the laity demanding unity if you let us get together like this' . . . 'The chief stumbling-block to unity is the clergy and ministers. All clergy ought to attend courses on Christian unity run by laymen' . . . 'We feel the barrier between ministers and laity is greater than that between denominations. All the clergy are too burdened with administrative responsibilities to cope' ... 'It must be recognized by clergy that the activity resultant from our proposals might be at the expense of normal church activities' ... 'We must ensure that the activities we undertake are in place of existing ones, *not* additional. We do not want to come to our ecumenical activities worn out by our denominational ones' ... 'It seems that if the actions listed are to become realities then time has to be found. "Finding time" means simply a reassessment of priorities on our time. If the course leads us to this question, "What are our priorities?", then it will have been time well spent.'[5]

The actual recommendations can be divided into those relevant at local, regional and national level. At the local level the stress was on things being done ecumenically on the 'Lund Principle' of doing everything together unless conscience and principle made it impossible. There was much talk of shared worship and of what was to be gained by the denominations learning from each other; ecumenical house groups, study groups, retreats and surveys were urged; there could be co-operation and ecumenical planning in youth clubs, Sunday School training, publicity and mission to the area generally; numerous ideas were put forward for ecumenical service to the community. 'At the regional level most of the suggestions involved joint planning of church life. There were suggested schemes for amalgamation of churches and the sharing of buildings, for combined work in new areas, for the setting-up of team ministries and for the appointment of regional ecumenical officers. ... At the national level there was no doubt at all of what seemed to be a priority request of numerous places. This was the plea that intercommunion should be authorized as soon as possible.'[6] Beside this the churches were urged to consider the total strategy in an ecumenical context of church building and use, the viability of denominational church schools and the necessity of combined theological training. There were also many demands for the strengthening of the B.C.C. and the widening of its activities.

The P.N.D. programme has been described at length because it is perhaps to date the most ambitious scheme undertaken to arouse the interest of the laity in matters ecumenical. Furthermore it shows what happens when the interest and concern of the laity are aroused. The demands made by many of the P.N.D. groups were radical and far-reaching, providing, indeed, an 'agenda for the churches'. The sharing of churches, one of the questions which came up repeatedly, had already been on the agenda of the Church of England. In 1965 a commission had reported to the Church Assembly in cautious and conservative terms on this subject: it emphasized the traditional view that the establishment of the Church of England ensured that through the parochial system every person in the country is under the spiritual care of one of the church's representatives, the local vicar. This made the sharing of churches difficult, though certain steps in that direction were suggested. The putting forward of this old-fashioned and now completely impractical view as a handicap to ecumenical progress was a disappointment to many people and in 1967 a new Bill was passed which did make joint ownership legal. It is at least possible that the knowledge of lay feeling as it was focused in the P.N.D. reports had some effect on the Church of England legislators. Similarly the very strong demand for a change in attitude towards intercommunion may have had some influence on the change in Anglican thought on this subject in recent years (see below, pp. 497–503).

On the other hand it would be rash to claim too much for the results of P.N.D. It must be remembered that only 35,000 Anglicans took part throughout Great Britain compared with 150,000 in the Church of England alone for the 'No Small Change' programme two years earlier. If the C. of E. could have been mobilized for P.N.D. in the same way as for 'No Small Change' one wonders what would have been the effect on the Anglican/Methodist vote in 1969. It is true that that vote was in the hands of the clergy, but a strong mobilization of local lay opinion in favour of the proposals must have had its effect. In the event that is the very thing which did not happen.

It is generally speaking true that the laity are more willing to move towards unity than the clergy, who are concerned about detailed matters of faith and order. Though the laity had no vote in England on the Anglican/Methodist proposals, in Wales they did have a share in the decision: 'All the lay votes in the six diocesan conferences approved of the scheme, the clerical votes in three of the dioceses disapproved of it.'[7] Again, a remarkable survey has recently been made among Episcopalians in Scotland on attitudes to intercommunion, a subject judged to be the vital next step on the agenda in the P.N.D. reports. Of the clergy 18.9 per cent wanted stricter rules in the matter, but only 5.7 per cent of the laity. At the other end of the scale 34.6 per cent of the laity wanted unqualified intercommunion, against only 12.8 per cent of the clergy. In every vote clergy attitudes were more 'conservative' than lay, with very little variation between dioceses. Moreover the report remarked that 'if an attempt is made to correlate the laity's practice in communicating at non-episcopal services with the degree to which clergy discourage or encourage this practice, it will be seen that there is no marked relationship in either case'.[8] This seems to bear out the conclusion that with or without clerical instruction the laity would wish to push ahead to unity. The question is how hard will they push. It is here that instruction or education will make the difference in ensuring that lay pressure is both informed and enthusiastic and this was a prime objective of the People Next Door campaign.

But the Secretary of the B.C.C., Bishop Kenneth Sansbury, saw dangers in the very success of the campaign:

There is evidence that a good deal of frustration was experienced in the Church of England after the No Small Change campaign. People ... made their recommendations and waited for their implementation. And by and large nothing happened. There is a lot more evidence that, if P.N.D. ends the same way, frustration will give way to despair. Many thinking lay people are likely to lose faith in the Church altogether and vote with their feet. Either they will join in one of the local ecumenical groupings, which may well develop, or else they will keep a personal faith in Christ, but drop out of the life of the organized church altogether.

The Churches are making great efforts to bring their structures and patterns of life up to date, but they have to wrestle with strong conservative forces and progress often seems desperately slow. Yet our society is changing fast, and it is clear that only a Church that has its priorities right ... has a chance to survive.[9]

It is a picture which is by now familiar. Too little and perhaps too late. The irony is that when the churches, after bemoaning so long the fact that the laity are not involved in the ecumenical movement, achieve at last some improvement, then there is a real danger that these lay people may retire in disgust at the slowness of the progress being made.

ECUMENICAL EXPERIMENTS

(i) *Throughout the World*

This section will describe a number of typical experiments being undertaken on an ecumenical basis throughout the world. It does not attempt to be comprehensive but simply picks out a number of things which are being done, and hence can be done.

The bodies originally sponsoring these experiments vary greatly. Some will be W.C.C. projects. Others will be sponsored by a national or local council of churches. Others, again, will have started as the project of a single church and become ecumenical when it was seen that their scope was too ambitious to be coped with in any other way. Indeed very often it is the size of the problem being tackled which has forced an ecumenical solution upon it. Only ecumenical action, even with all its attendant difficulties of patience, timing and communications, makes sense. But the common factor to all these experiments is that they give people at the grassroots level – junior clergy and lay people – ecumenical experience and training. They give them the taste of working together. Very often they fire enthusiasm which is carried on to the higher levels of ecumenical responsibility. Again, it will be noticed that many of these ecumenical experiments are of a pioneering nature. Very often it is the new things, where there is no tradition of denominational action to be broken down, which get done ecumenically. And being new things, pioneer projects, they tend to attract the more forward-looking young Christian leaders. Thus it is that the ecumenical cause finds good recruits – a factor which has been important throughout its history.

Traditionally one of the places where Christianity has failed to make its presence felt is in industry. The Gospel, it is said, has been irrelevant to industrialized man. The old western parochial system, based on man's place of living, has ignored his place of work. These matters were faced in England in the 1930s by such experiments as the Sheffield Industrial Mission, which cut free from the parochial system and concentrated on placing priests in factories and involving the church in unions and in places of decision-making in industry – not to preach and convert, but to listen and understand and, precisely, to be identified. The Sheffield Industrial Mission was an Anglican concern, but more recent experiments have been on an ecumenical basis; the Coventry project, for instance, is in the hands of an ecumenical team, and there is an ecumenical 'Industrial Mission Association' which brings together all those working in this field.

In some places abroad the church has recently geared its mission to a newly developed industrial society, and done so on an ecumenical basis. In such places industrialization can be amazingly sudden and can bring with it overwhelming problems to the simple people swept up in it. An example is the industrialization of an area about a hundred miles north-east of Calcutta as part of India's plans for the growth of heavy industry. There within a matter of years primitive villages become towns with populations of hundreds of thousands; jungles are erased and vast steel plants take their place. People 'find themselves cut off from the village and the village life that they were used to. They find they are uprooted from the moral sanctions of the village, its culture and traditions, and they find themselves in a completely different set-up. They were tillers of land and over-night they find themselves surrounded by an industrial world.'[10] Durgapur is one of these townships and there in 1963 the churches established an Ecumenical and Social Institute. The emphasis was on training Christians to find their feet and take their place in the new industrial situation, making sure that the church did not become a refuge from the factory floor; to train lay leadership and so 'to attempt through the lay people to bring the love of God to bear upon every part of the life and society of Durgapur'.[11] The constant attempt was to make Christians aware of themselves as Christians and not as members of denominations. The 'area churches' established are to serve all the Christians in the area irrespective of denomination, although care is also taken to provide from time to time in every area specifically denominational worship.

A similar experiment was launched in Port Harcourt, Nigeria, before the civil war there. Port Harcourt was another town of mushroom growth, based on the discovery of oil and gas in the Niger Delta and the subsequent development of the area as a port and as an oil and industrial centre; between 1953 and 1963 it is estimated that the population jumped from 50,000 to 250,000. Here again the churches (that is the co-operating main-line reformed churches) planned their work in the area on an industrial basis and an ecumenical foundation. There were to be two teams, an industrial team and a social welfare team 'with a number of expert workers in specialist fields, health visitors, a psychiatric social worker, a worker for juvenile delinquency and a youth worker'.[12] Personnel and money for these teams were found from the Anglican church in Nigeria, the Church of England, the Church of Scotland and the Methodist church of Nigeria.

Durgapur and Port Harcourt are two examples of industrial and ecumenical mission. Others could be cited, such as new developments in Singapore, though it is perhaps surprising that, with similar situations in so many places, ecumenical action of this sort is still infrequent.

Other ecumenical experiments which have concentrated, like Durgapur, on helping lay people to find and take their Christian place in the secular world have taken place in Germany. These are the Evangelical Academies and the Kirchentag movement. Both these movements have been largely independent of official church sponsorship and have involved people who are not necessarily churchgoers. The numbers they have attracted have been very large – up to 60,000 a year in the case of the Evangelical Academies and as many as 25,000 at a time at the Kirchentag assemblies. The former movement has been particularly active in by-passing the regular residential parochial system and helping lay people to relate their Christian faith to their place of work, while it has been noticeable about the latter that it has been able to transcend political frontiers and has held many of its most successful assemblies in East Germany.

The point has already been made (see above, p. 357) that in many places ecumenical theological training has been an essential foundation for a process of growing into unity which in turn leads to practical proposals for unity. There are now united theological colleges in many parts of the world. Sometimes these have been quite definitely sponsored by unity negotiating committees; in other places, such as Hong Kong, a united theological college has been founded well before specific unity negotiations have begun. In either case the establishment of joint theological training indicates an important ecumenical commitment of the churches to each other.

Seen in this light a number of ecumenical theological colleges in Latin America – otherwise, as has been seen, a somewhat barren ecumenical area – are the more significant. There are united theological colleges – or colleges which engage in a good deal of co-operation – in the following places: Buenos Aires, where the co-operation is on a very broad denominational basis; Quito, Ecuador; San José, Costa Rica; Mexico City, where there is a centre which embraces all the major non-Roman Catholic denominations from Baptists to Anglicans; and Puerto Rico, where the foundations of Roman Catholic and non-Roman Catholic co-operation are being laid. Even more significant, perhaps, is the fact that in August 1970 a conference was held at São Paulo under the auspices of the W.C.C. for theological professors from all over Latin America. Among those taking part were representatives of churches in Latin America which do not usually take part in ecumenical affairs. In short, as a W.C.C. observer ended an ecumenical report on Latin America: 'By far the most encouraging ecumenical feature of the general scene is co-operation in theological education.'[13]

England and Scotland have been almost the last countries to experiment with ecumenical theological colleges. For some time university theological faculties have been on an interdenominational basis – though weighted towards the established church north and south of the border; but the first fully ecumenical theological college was that founded in the autumn of 1970 at the ex-Anglican college of Queens, Birmingham. This is one more example of the backwardness of the churches in the British Isles in ecumenical affairs.

One of the earliest and most esteemed of all united theological colleges was that founded at Bangalore, South India, in 1910. Its work laid essential foundations for the Church of South India itself. In turn its personnel were founder members of the Christian Institute for the Study of Religion and Society which was sponsored by the National Christian Council of India in 1957. In one way this centre was akin to the World Council centres for the study of other world faiths which have already been described (see above, p. 242). The Institute works as the servant of the churches in helping their members in ways which cannot be undertaken on a local or denominational basis; many of its programmes are carried out in other parts of India than Bangalore. Its director, M. M. Thomas, describes the work as follows:

Firstly we have a programme of studying the modern movements of renascence in the other religions of India and of bringing out books and pamphlets to help Christians understand the modern religious environment in which the Church lives in India.... Secondly we arrange formal inter-faith dialogues on religion and society.... Thirdly we have spent a good deal of our energy on defining the Christian approach to crucial issues in the political, economic, social, and cultural aspects of nation-building in the concrete situation of India today and the methods of Christian participation in community development at different levels.... We have an extension programme not only to communicate the result of the study, research and thinking of the Institute to the members of the churches at large, but also to receive from them a knowledge of the crucial issues they face in their daily life and work....[14]

This is an ambitious and sophisticated programme and

an illustration of the fact that to attempt such work on a denominational basis would be not only impracticable but ridiculous in the face of the sort of problems encountered by the churches in India.

Another field in which interdenominational team-work is becoming increasingly necessary is that of communication. Marshall McLuhan's 'global village' demands global communications which are both complex and expensive beyond the resources of single churches – except perhaps the Roman Catholic. In the field of international radio transmitting the Lutherans have been the pioneers, but their work has now been co-ordinated with the Division of World Mission and Evangelism of the W.C.C. There are Christian radio stations transmitting in many languages in Addis Ababa and Manila and smaller units in other parts of the world. Transmitting is only a small part of the operation. The churches have to feed the transmitters and this requires a complicated network of religious radio work throughout the world.

But whatever McLuhan says, the written word is going to remain the primary means of mass communication for a long time. Here the churches have a long record of ecumenical co-operation. The British and Foreign Bible Society was founded on an interdenominational basis in 1804, and has given ecumenical experience to generations of churchmen. Its work has been the translation and distribution of the scriptures throughout the world. An American counterpart was founded in 1816, again well before the real beginning of the ecumenical movement at the turn of the century. More recently the United Bible Societies, the overall Protestant body, has begun to co-operate with the Roman Catholic Biblical Commission, so that once again the work of Bible translation and distribution has registered an ecumenical 'first'.

Bibles are not the only items of Christian literature which need translating and distributing in the course of the church's missionary work. Prayer books and hymn books, theological and evangelistic literature, tracts and Sunday School material, these are just some of the literature projects which make the Christian churches major operators in the field of publishing. Here the churches have been slow to move to an interdenominational basis, no doubt because literature – as opposed to the straight text of the Bible – raises denominational problems. But more and more the churches – especially once again the 'younger' ones – are now co-operating in this field, with considerable financial support from the W.C.C. Christian Literature Fund. An example comes from Tanzania. There in the 1960s at Dodoma the Anglican church in collaboration with the Christian Council of Tanzania established a Literature and Christian Education Centre. Its work, which had in mind the whole of East Africa, included the preparation of radio and film strip material and literature for youth and Sunday School work. On top of this there was publication.

Perhaps an idea of what can be accomplished by co-operation might be illustrated by the book, *I Loved a Girl*, which was written by Walter Trobisch in French for West Africa. It was translated and published by the United Society for Christian Literature (a W.C.C. concern) in English, but its cost was a little high for East Africa and, as it was in English, its sale was limited. The book was therefore translated into Swahili and, with the co-operation of the author and the U.S.C.L. in England, an edition was prepared for the press in Tanzania. The Lutheran Vuga Press, the Africa Inland Mission Press, and the Central Tanganyika Press became joint publishers, and by getting pre-publication orders it was finally possible to go to press with an edition of 25,000 copies.... One could say quite definitely that an edition of five to seven thousand would have been the maximum that could have been attempted had it not been for this very close co-operation brought about through the diocese and the literature secretariat of the Christian Council of Tanganyika.[15]

Here again the folly of uni-denominational and the sense

of ecumenical operation is illustrated. In these days when so many things increasingly demand large-scale financial underwriting ecumenical co-operation is more and more being forced on the churches.

In the developing countries the churches usually laid the foundations of their work alongside and through educational and medical enterprises – schools and hospitals. These older denominational bodies have therefore often been the last to come on to an ecumenical basis. However, with the growing problems of financial stringency and, often, governmental antagonism, the need for ecumenical co-operation is now seen in these fields also. At the least there will be co-operation through national councils of churches in planning new developments, fixing priorities and allocating money made available to the central body rather than to an individual school or hospital. Very often in fact the lives of these fine Christian institutions may be limited. But when there are new foundations they are likely these days to be on an ecumenical basis. Thus, the story of Chung Chi College, Hong Kong. In 1951 the communist government of China took over the thirteen Christian universities in that country. Some of these had been single church foundations, others interdenominational. The same year a group of Christians in Hong Kong decided to found a Chinese college for higher education to meet the needs in that field of the thousands of refugees pouring into the British colony. This was Chung Chi College. It was from the first interdenominational, and despite massive government support it could never have succeeded on any other basis. The College started in the smallest possible way – in the transept of the Anglican Cathedral; but by 1956 it had acquired a separate site and its first independent buildings. In 1964 it was one – and in many ways the strongest – of the three colleges which were chosen to form the new Chinese university of Hong Kong.

Similarly in Hong Kong, the new four-million-pound Christian hospital is an ecumenical venture. Like Chung Chi it draws most of its financial support from the United States, support which would not be forthcoming except on an interdenominational basis.

Another obvious area for ecumenical co-operation is that of social service, with all its many ramifications, of which, of course, medical work is one. Some of the ecumenical work of the churches in this field has already been touched on in describing the programmes of the Inter-Church Aid and World Refugee Service Department of the W.C.C. (see above, pp. 259–60).

Lastly there is the traditional activity of the establishment of the church in the localities where people live. (In jargon more acceptable in ecumenical circles this might be described as the establishment of a 'Christian presence'.) In some ways the pattern of Christian work will be affected by the type of locality in question. These could be categorized very broadly as, besides rural areas (or semi-rural such as country towns), 'downtown' areas of slums or tenement property, established suburban areas, and – in any part of the world the most important – new townships or housing areas. Of these obviously the most heartbreaking are the downtown slums or tenements of condemned housing, which exist in the centre of almost every large nineteenth-century city. Here are congregated those who have least chance in life and who can least take life's chances. In these areas the normal pastoral and evangelistic work of the churches is at its most ineffective. But there are examples – though all too few – of ecumenical teamwork in such areas meeting with relative success.

One such example is the East Harlem Protestant Parish which has been described in a book which is one of the few Christian classics of this century – *Come out the Wilderness* by Bruce Kenrick. Faced with problems of dire poverty, racialism and appalling housing and education, with their social concomitants of racketeering, drugs, crime, unemployment, drunkenness and many other ills, a group of Protestant pastors found that the old denominational divides and patterns were meaningless. Co-operation was the only hope – and the development of a new approach from scratch.

Another infamous 'twilight zone' is the Gorbals, in Glasgow, 'a household word for all the evils of slum life'.[16] Here two pastoral groups, Church of Scotland and Episcopalian, merged into an ecumenical team: 'Friendship over the years and a common mission fused us into one.' This group has become deeply involved in the social and political problems of the area: 'More precisely, we have involved ourselves in a fairly intense battle against the local landlords who exploit to the full the evils of the sub-let housing system in the district.'[17] Out of this in turn has come the foundation of a housing association to buy old property, convert it and let it to needy families. Youth clubs, summer holiday camps and of course much individual work centring on personal and social problems are some of the more 'normal' activities of this ecumenical team.

(ii) In Britain

The rest of this section will describe some other ecumenical experiments in evangelistic, social and pastoral work on a locality basis in the British Isles. For obvious reasons such experiments are more likely to take place in new towns or housing areas than in established urban or suburban areas. The new towns present special problems which call for experiment; a new area is *tabula rasa*, without any backlog of traditions or inherited patterns to be overcome. The established areas are heavy with just such traditions and in them the churches are all too often

479

weighted down with the sheer effort of maintaining themselves and their plant and are unwilling or unable to take the risk of new experiment.

Nevertheless in some traditional localities with well-established patterns of denominational pastoral activity the denominational structure has been broken down in favour of an ecumenical one. Two such places are Desborough, Northamptonshire, and Cotham, Bristol. Other examples could be cited but these experiments have gone particularly far; others have proceeded a certain way along similar lines of co-operation and then come to a halt.

Desborough is a small town in Northamptonshire of some 5,000 people. It has four churches: Anglican, Baptist, Congregational and Methodist. Ecumenical activity there has a relatively long history, going back to such things as joint services before the Second World War. There is no doubt that this early start to ecumenical interest was of great importance. When the seeds of more radical proposals were sown the ground had been well ploughed. A Council of Churches was formed in 1953 – again early as these things went. This is about the stage now reached in thousands of towns and areas in the British Isles. But in Desborough in 1963 it was realized that a Council of Churches was only a beginning. Despite numerous joint activities 'the churches remained apart. What was needed was some irrevocable commitment of the churches to one another so that there could not be the possibility of denominational retreat from ecumenical activity.'[18] It is this feeling of 'commitment' between the churches to one another which is the vital step in local as in national ecumenical progress.

By 1965 the Council of Churches had drawn up a plan of co-operation based on a Declaration of Intent 'to work together for the creation of full organic union of our four churches in Desborough'.[19] This plan involved a practical attempt to take the Lund Principle of 1952 seriously –

that is 'to act together in all matters except those which deep differences of conviction compel them to act separately'. It was recognized that this would mean growth into further involvement. At this time there was no common worship – this was seen as a goal for the future – but there was a joint governing council and carefully worked-out joint committee structures. In 1968 the next step was taken when the Anglican and Methodist councils started working towards 'a united congregation, a team ministry and a single set of premises'.[20] It was recognized that this would involve the selling of the Methodist church and the use of the funds gained for future work including new buildings ancillary to the parish church. Worship was to be on a pattern which included both Anglican and Methodist type services on each Sunday, though the scheme was to be flexible and intercommunion was envisaged (see below, pp. 495–502); the present ministers were to be formed into an ecumenical team.

On 7 September 1969 this scheme was formally inaugurated. (The Baptist and Congregational congregations involved in the earlier stages seem to have dropped out of this development because they were at that time without ministers; also, no doubt, the Anglican/Methodist national conversations were an incentive to this local move.)

Certain things may be noted as contributing to the success of this experiment. The long-standing ecumenical activity has already been mentioned. It seems that there has been a succession of ecumenically-minded clergy who have been willing to enter into a serious partnership. At the same time great pains were taken to involve the entire congregations of lay people at every stage. This was not just a ploy of the ecumeniacs. It was a highly responsible operation as can be seen by the commitment both to thoughtfully worked-out theology and carefully evolved structures. At the same time it was not all theo-

481

logical discussion or committee talk; the participants recognized that the ultimate object was mission in the area and one of the first things undertaken in co-operation was a joint mission. Lastly, it seems that at every stage it was recognized that there was a connection between what was being done locally and the total ecumenical movement: the Declaration of Intent contained these words:

we cannot forever frustrate the will of God; and yet, although we passionately desire to be obedient to God and long for unity in Christ, we recognize that there are still many factors, theological and traditional, great and small, which must be resolved before we enter upon such union.[21]

As a statement of responsible and yet urgent ecumenical principle that could hardly be bettered; similarly the action founded on it seems to have been both urgent and responsible. Yet the fact that this can be done at such a seemingly unpropitious place as Desborough, but is not being done in thousands of similar places, once again demonstrates the strength of ecumenical inertia.

The second example of co-operation in an established area comes from Cotham, Bristol. There a joint Baptist, Congregational and Methodist Church began in 1966. The circumstances conducive to union there were that the Baptist and Congregational churches found themselves without ministers at the same moment. This led them to look seriously at the propriety of continuing two separate operations. When it was known that they had a united congregation in mind the local Methodists asked to join the planning. Describing the events which followed, the minister of the united church, the Reverend H. Bryant, writes:

Certain 'accidental' factors were undoubtedly a help in the smooth course of negotiation. First – though there was some difference in the sizes of the three memberships concerned, any two outnumbered the third! So there could never be a feeling that one body was just swallowing up the others. [The same was true at Desborough.] Second – one set of premises was quite obviously better suited for the united church and in vastly better condition than the other two. This certainly saved a lot of possibly agonizing discussion on choice of premises. But the most important factor of all was a constantly growing sense of the leading – even the driving – of the Holy Spirit which spread through leaders and members of all three churches. . . .

Mr Bryant says specifically that this enabled the participants to move ahead in faith even when there were problems unresolved. In particular this applied to the basic Constitution:

There are places where it has been described as 'purposefully vague'. This is not entirely accidental. There were places where we did not find ourselves, at that time, able to find a form of words entirely acceptable to all of us. . . . So we left a gap. Though there were some things about which we were not sure, we *were* quite sure that God meant us to come together. So we did not try to get a water-tight answer to everything before we made the venture of unity, but decided to go ahead, believing that, *when we were in fellowship together,* we should probably see some things more clearly than we could see them while we were still talking over dividing walls. I suspect that there may be a vital principle here.[22]

It is interesting to find Mr Bryant giving evidence on a local level to the 'South India principle', so strongly urged by Bishop Michael Hollis (see above, p. 309), that churches should not wait for a cut and dried answer to all problems before uniting, but should rather set up flexible structures for the united body to fill out.

Several points emerge from the working of the united church. It has been careful not to become a 'rogue elephant', but has gone out of its way to maintain its contacts with the local and national bodies of the three original constituent denominations. Thus the church sends its representatives to local denominational area meetings, even if those representatives are not necessarily originally members of that particular denomination: for 'in an astonishingly short space of time it became quite difficult to remember what it was like to be apart, and we were (I am sure) much more united than some churches I have known with only one denomination'.[23] Thus, too, the united church has made larger contributions to the central missionary funds of the three original denominations than was the case before union. Secondly, from the beginning the uniting congregations recognized 'that they were not interested in coming together to form a "mere Union Church", but in trying to find the shape of a "new Church" whose worship life and witness would meet the needs of the rather odd and somewhat difficult area in which we are set'.[24] This is the working-out in local terms of the recognition by countless ecumenical leaders and international conferences that the movement to church unity is only part of a larger movement for the renewal of the church. It is the embodiment in a particular area of Bristol of the slogan of the Nottingham Faith and Order conference of 1964 – One Church Renewed for Mission.

(iii) *Areas of Ecumenical Experiment*

The Nottingham Faith and Order Conference called on the member churches of Britain 'to designate areas of ecumenical experiment, at the request of local congregations or in new towns and housing areas'.[25] This was an attempt to force the Lund Principle on the churches in a local context and so to foster ecumenical thinking and activity at the grassroots level, still dangerously neglected in the movement. It was seen that 'new towns and housing areas' would be the natural seed plots for these experiments – for the reasons already discussed – and the remainder of this section will deal with officially designated areas of ecumenical experiment in such areas.

In fact the question of what comprised such designa-

tion took some time to solve. Writing in 1968 in his book
Areas of Ecumenical Experiment the Reverend R. M. C.
Jeffery could say that there were as many as 170 such
areas known to him. Since then, however, closer definition has been given to the term. As a result in his latest
survey (1970) Mr Jeffery can only list fourteen experiments which fulfil the conditions of a designated area.
Desborough is one of these, but the rest are all in new
towns. It is not that there are less experiments in progress. Very few of the 170 have come to shipwreck. It is
rather that there is now seen to be a difference between
an 'area of ecumenical co-operation' and an officially
designated 'area of ecumenical experiment'. The chief
difference is that an area of co-operation 'does not provide for the suspension of present denominational regulations, but would go as far as possible within those
regulations'.[26]

This is not to write off the areas of co-operation; very
much can be done within them in the spheres of shared
worship (and use of churches) and of numerous shared
activities. But a designated area of experiment goes an
essential step further.

In July 1969 a B.C.C. working party met to draw up a
report, 'The Designation of Areas of Ecumenical Experiment'. It was this report which saw that the essential step
was that 'under responsible authority certain denominational traditions are suspended in order that new
patterns of worship, mission and ministry can be undertaken'.[27] Apart from this the most important recommendation of the working party was its insistence that for
these experiments a 'sponsoring body' must be set up to
constitute the 'responsible authority' under whose wing
the operation should take place. The composition of the
sponsoring body will depend on the area in question, but
basically it will consist of nominees of the churches involved in the experiment. Its existence will ensure the
full commitment of the churches concerned to the ex-

periment in the new area, especially as far as finance and continuity of policy and of the personnel of the ecumenical team are concerned. (Lack of continuity and sudden changes of personnel have constituted a major problem in ecumenical co-operation.) The existence of a properly constituted sponsoring body will also prevent the experiment in the designated area becoming a 'new denomination'. It will be able to receive reports and guide overall policy – especially important since by the very nature of the operation ordinary denominational channels of authority will have been suspended. Lastly the sponsoring body will be able to undertake the 'evaluation' of the experiment on which the report is insistent. The fact that this is an experiment, which can be limited in its duration and which is subject to control and evaluation, is an important part of the 'responsibility' of the churches setting it up, and the ultimate deterrent against the creation of a new denomination. In sum, as Mr Jeffery comments, 'It cannot be emphasized too much that the whole basis of areas of ecumenical experiment depends on the existence of a strong sponsoring body. Without the supervision which this provides there will be both a lack of real support from the denominations and a sense of insecurity among the team.'[28]

It has already been suggested that fundamental ecumenical planning and co-operation would be easiest in specifically new towns, where the churches are starting with a *tabula rasa* and with no long-standing traditions of separate denominational work to be broken down. Certainly ecumenical co-operation is the only practical approach, financially and in other ways, for the churches to undertake their missionary responsibilities in the new towns of Great Britain. To cover the expected increase in the population before the end of the century, sixty Government-designated new towns are planned, as well as the expansion of some 300 existing towns. The act setting this policy in motion was passed in 1946. So far work

486

has started on twenty-six towns. A research report has recently been written on how the churches have reacted to the new towns' challenge. Only in Milton Keynes, the most recent new town off the drawing board, have the churches acted ecumenically from the start: '26 towns and 24 years later than the passing of the first New Town Act may be somewhat late in the day, but better late than never,' comments the writer of the report.[29]

The report shows a gradual move in ecumenical planning (and in other radical and fundamental responses to the new town situation) over the years. In Hemel Hempstead for instance, one of the first new towns, designated in 1947, 'there was certainly no idea of any ecumenical approach to planning, for this was too early days for this even to be considered'.[30] The churches simply went ahead separately with their traditional policy of providing places of worship on a generous scale for the population. In the end thirty-five churches were built for 75,000 people; already one of these – only twelve years old – has had to close as a place of worship because it cannot be maintained and financially supported. Nothing could show more clearly the folly of denominational going-it-alone in such a situation.

At Skelmersdale in south-west Lancashire, fifteen years later, matters were somewhat better and a scheme has eventually emerged on an ecumenical basis. That it did so was largely fortuitous and the result of the presence of a few leaders with ecumenical convictions rather than of deliberate planning from the beginning. Firstly the local Anglican suffragan bishop (of Warrington) saw the need of some sort of ecumenical co-operation in approaching the new town. Then the town's Senior Development Officer was a keen Christian layman who had seen the result of ecumenical non-cooperation at Hemel Hempstead and was determined that the same mistakes should not be repeated: 'I was certainly determined that we were not going to perpetuate the stupidity of some of the

New Towns.'[31] The Ministers' Fraternal thus found it-self precipitated into ecumenical planning. It proposed an ecumenical team – but was somewhat vague as to its basis: 'It was agreed that membership be on a sort of United Nations approach. Denominations should retain their identity, but there can be no hard and fast rules at present.'[32] Nothing could show more clearly than this quotation how lack of ecumenical thinking at the grass-roots inhibits real ecumenical action when an opportunity such as is present in a new town arises.

In the event an Ecumenical Centre was planned and built at Skelmersdale, but its aims and objectives, and the vital questions of its finances and staffing, were never really settled. Comparing the somewhat frenzied last-minute ecumenical action embarked on at Skelmersdale with the handling of the same problem at Desborough shows very clearly how real ecumenical progress depends on commitment and patient planning over a consider-able period of time. Summarizing the ecumenical lessons from the twenty-four years of the new town programme, the writer of the report says:

The lukewarm feeling towards ecumenism seems to me to be shared right up to the top levels of authority in the Church. The majority of Church leaders are obliged to make the right sort of ecumenical noises these days ... but of course the ex-pression of ecumenical sentiments and attending a United Service here and there really demands very little of a person. Ask a few of them actually to plan and spend some money together and the colour of their ecumenism is startlingly re-vealed.[33]

From the very few local ecumenical experiments which can as yet be described in Great Britain as truly radical, it would seem that there is much truth in this condemna-tion. Nor is the situation so very different in the United States. A recent book, *The Church in Experiment*, has described the situation there. It lists a number of the more enterprising experiments taking place. In these areas of activity one would expect the ecumenical spirit to be strong. But in fact of the forty-four experiments described only fourteen have an ecumenical basis. In this case the writer puts the blame more on local leadership.

The willingness to co-operate between parishes and their officers is the touchstone for the ecumenicity of church renewal. ... As long as ministers and board members only talk about the ecumenical movement without taking some decisive steps towards killing the germs of divisiveness in the congregations, the impact upon the local parish will be nil.[34]

Local ecumenical action, if it is really to be effective, requires committal in terms of time and money – and it is at this point that the shoe begins to pinch, because this involves a re-appraisal of priorities. Effective ecumenical action is not something which can be added to normal denominational work. People, clerical and lay, are busy, and ecumenical activities will have to take the place of regular ecclesiastical commitments. And if the churches are short of time, they are shorter still of money. New ecumenical projects will have to be at the expense of new – or even of old – denominational ones. It is in facing these issues that the churches have been slow.

Other problems, too, soon arise in any serious attempt at local ecumenical planning. These include the nature of ecumenical clerical teams, the building of ecumenical churches – and the whole thorny question of intercommunion.

An ecumenical parish will be based on an interdenominational team ministry. This is the most important innovation common to all local ecumenical co-operation. A number of experiments have been taking place on denominational lines in 'team ministries', and it seems in any case that this may be the ecclesiastical shape of things to come. In future the church's ministry to a local area will depend on teamwork by a group of specialist lay and ordained people. The old idea of the clerical jack-of-all-trades – the single parson meeting the needs of 'his' area or parish – dies hard. But for bettter or worse the ecumenical parish is inevitably based on a team ministry. There are certainly problems – of training, of leadership and of continuity. Not least at the moment there is the problem, which the churches are being slow to tackle, that the different denominations pay disparate salaries to their clergy. In an ecumenical team, therefore, either there will be the embarrassment of different salaries for the same job, or some of the members will have to make sacrifices to bring themselves to the same level as their less fortunate colleagues. (It will be remembered that the same problem has proved a stumbling block – sometimes as in the case of North India an insurmountable one – in unity negotiations.) None the less it seems certain that in ecumenical co-operation the team ministry has come to stay; and that this is one of the areas where ecumenicity is the agent of other measures of church reform.

Other experiments open to an ecumenical area are in the field of worship. The suspension of ordinary denominational regulations must include the regular forms of worship of the various churches. The maintenance of such forms has certainly been an inhibiting factor in areas which have stopped short at ecumenical co-operation. As has been seen, the result has been that Sunday has seen in the one church a variety of services of the old denominational patterns following each other in quick succession and probably all sparsely attended. When in 1965 the Bishop of Oxford authorized an Anglican priest to embark on an ecumenical experiment with a Congregational minister at Blackbird Leys estate, Cowley, he did so with the following proviso:

With regard to the services to be held in the church, they must be either Anglican or Free Church services and must be advertised as such. Sometimes, however, on Sunday evenings, a joint service, perhaps often having the character of a mission service, could be held, but at least once a month there should

be an Anglican Evensong. I regard it as absolutely essential
that every Sunday morning there should be a Church of England Parish Communion.... In no circumstance could this
service be displaced. There will be ample time for a Free
Church service in the latter part of the morning, if desired.[35]

The bishop was at proper pains to prevent future misunderstandings; but the regulations were to say the least
inhibiting. They meant that, even though the church was
being shared, the congregations remained separate. Now,
however, there is the possibility of shared worship. The
B.C.C. Report makes it clear that it recognizes what the
result of this will be:

Where Churches are committed to working together there
will be a strong desire for reciprocal intercommunion. If ecumenism is to become a reality and not just a word, intercommunion should be accepted as the norm. The responsible
authorities should be generous in granting permission.[36]

The form the joint worship will take must depend on
circumstances. Obviously sometimes it will be the service
of one of the traditions involved; or it may, as at Hale-
wood, Lancashire, draw on various traditions. The fact
that there is now an interdenominational Joint Liturgical Group may be of significance here. There is another
possibility. These new churches in new areas may feel
that none of the traditional forms of worship, nor any
combination of them, is adequate. They may want to
embark on altogether more radical experiment. Presumably this, too, is possible under the aegis of the sponsoring body. It is in this sort of way that unity may go hand
in hand with renewal.

It has already been seen that intercommunion will be
one problem arising out of joint worship (see also below,
pp. 495–503). Another will be the question of church
membership. It is presumed that the original members of
a congregation in an area of ecumenical experiment will
be baptized people with communicant status in their

former denomination. But what of those who are baptized into the ecumenical congregation? To what church do they belong when they leave the ecumenical area and return to the divided churches? And how do they join it?

Lastly the congregations in these areas will inevitably find themselves experimenting in the building and in the use of church plant. The Sharing of Church Buildings Act of 1969 was a notable advance in this field, allowing as it did the shared use of existing Anglican parish churches by a wide variety of denominations. But the Act also allows for new churches to be built on a shared basis, thus giving up the old Church of England theory that through the establishment every part of the country, even a new town, is part of an Anglican parish. There are many ideas current at the moment about the building of new churches, 'pastoral units', movable churches – and indeed non-churches. The 'ecumenical church' adds another factor. So far there has been little experiment in this field. One well-publicized example is the ecumenical chapel at London Airport: there three different chapels (R.C., C. of E. and Free Church) open off a central space which seems not to be intended for use. The architectural design thus emphasizes division rather than unity. (The Chapel at Lancaster University has much the same scheme.) It is to be hoped that joint planning will achieve something better than this in the future. One interesting example of ecumenical planning is that at the new town of Livingston, between Edinburgh and Glasgow. Here there is an ecumenical team for the area comprising Church of Scotland, Methodist, Episcopal and Congregational – with the Roman Catholics as sympathetic observers. As the town grows, new church centres are built. The responsibility for building is that of the various sponsoring denominations in turn, but the churches are designed for ecumenical and community use by a joint congregation.

But there are places where Roman Catholics are more than sympathetic observers. In Great Britain as yet there is only one example of premises shared between Roman Catholics and other churches, apart from London Airport and university chapels. This is at Cippenham, near Slough, where Anglicans and Roman Catholics have built jointly on a piece of land owned by the Church of England parish. But a report of the R.C. Ecumenical Commission for England and Wales in March 1970 discussed shared premises and team ministries for 'mission, work and worship', and more plans for shared premises are in the pipeline. Moreover other parts of the world are further ahead in this respect than Great Britain. A recent survey in the R.C. ecumenical journal *One in Christ* contained details of schemes involving shared premises (both established and new buildings) in Australia, Canada, Guyana, Holland, New Zealand, South Africa, Tanzania, Uganda and the United States. An important factor in the proliferation of these experiments which involve shared premises is that they have a built-in guarantee of continuity. It has been seen that one of the problems of local ecumenical co-operation is that it depends so largely on the people involved: the departure of one member of an ecumenical team can bring an experiment to an end. But once buildings are shared, and the necessary legal arrangements made, it is much more difficult to untie the ecumenical knot.

To sum up, the idea of designating 'Areas of Ecumenical Experiment', with the related idea of shared premises, is so far the most promising grassroots activity evolved, at least in Great Britain. By 1971 there were some thirty areas designated, without doubt a disappointing number and a reflection of the fact that the churches, though receiving the report, have not really as yet given it priority. As usual they seem chary of investing money in experiment.

It is too early as yet to estimate the 'success' of any of

the experiments. Indeed they are no panacea and the areas concerned must be prepared for failures and disappointments – hence the importance of the suggested evaluation of the project. But those concerned have reported a feeling of liberation and new hope, and at least one congregation, Bar Hill, near Cambridge, reports a considerable growth in church membership.

Perhaps the most important aspect of these ecumenical experiments is that they are a sort of field laboratory for the work of the united churches of the future. The original report emphasized the need for flexibility, and no two experiments will be the same. In this way new patterns of local church activity can be worked out on an ecumenical basis which will make invaluable examples for united churches. Union schemes will have less excuse to ignore renewal and reform in setting up their new structures. They will have data for the planning of their work. Meanwhile it must not be thought that even the most radical ecumenical experiment is a satisfactory or lasting solution. Already it is evident that these experiments present as well as solve problems. In the first place what happens to a person who joins and is baptized into one of the newly united congregations and then leaves the area of ecumenical experiment? What church does he belong to among the divided denominations? Secondly, the united congregations are by definition *local* affairs. In a locality they are at the moment the ecumenical answer and should no doubt more and more be taking the place of local councils of churches, which can very often be half-hearted concerns which do little more than act as palliatives to the ecumenical conscience. But they cannot be, and represent, the church at the area level – in a fair-sized town or a considerable conurbation. So the ecumenical area will not have proper administrative backing at the level above itself and the church will not be able to make its united witness in the larger social groupings which certainly present a field for its activities, and call for over-all united church strategy and planning.

Ecumenical areas are admirable experiments in a situation of division. But they are no substitute for organic union.

INTERCOMMUNION

It can be said with certainty that any kind of ecumenical experiment anywhere in the world will sooner or later raise the question of intercommunion. Intercommunion is the practice of members of separate churches being able to receive communion freely at the eucharistic services of another denomination. As soon as Christians from divided churches begin to work together they will desire to express and cement their fellowship (and their recognition of each other as Christians) at the most central and symbolic act of Christian life – the Holy Communion. The B.C.C. report *Areas of Ecumenical Experiment* recognized that joint work and worship would lead to such a demand; the Anglicans and Methodists at Desborough, when they decided on shared worship, realized that the corollary would be intercommunion and decided to seek permission for it. The ecumenical team in the Gorbals took matters into their own hands:

Originally there were two groups representing the two denominations, but friendship over the years and a common mission fused us into one. Then one night we realized that we could no longer remain out of communion with each other, in spite of the official viewpoint of the Church. Since then we have been happily (if illegally) in communion with each other. Thursday evening is the regular meeting of the group. At 7.30 p.m. there is a meal at which we celebrate the Eucharist (alternating between the Presbyterian and Episcopalian rites) after which the group discusses together the common concerns of our work in the area, closing at 10 p.m. with intercession for the life of the area street by street, as well as in the particular crises of individual families.[37]

Clearly the closer people come together in ecumenical fellowship, the stronger will be the demand for intercommunion.

The question of intercommunion is a disciplinary matter on which the proper church authorities have to pronounce. In fact there are two related questions which have to be decided. First, is a church in communion with other churches A, B, C, etc.? If it is then there is no further problem; church members are free to communicate at each other's altars. If it is not, then the church authority has to decide whether individual acts of intercommunion can take place either way. It is this latter decision with which we are here concerned. Traditionally the attitude of the churches to the question has varied. The more 'Catholic' churches have said that the mass is both the means and the expression of the organic unity of the church and that therefore to allow members of churches which are divided to share in each other's communions is to act a lie to the point of sacrilege. Intercommunion must wait for full communion. Churches at the Protestant end of the spectrum have taken the view that baptized and professing Christians share a deep, if invisible, unity which it is proper to express by acts of intercommunion, especially as such acts should have the effect of hastening full organic unity.

These conflicting positions were stated in more theological language at the W.C.C. Assembly at New Delhi:

> For some Christians, the Lord's command 'Do this' is an imperative which over-rides all our divisions. If Holy Communion is the sovereign means of grace for the forgiveness and conquest of sin, then that is true of the sin of division as well. Thus it is intolerable and incomprehensible that a common love of God should not be expressed and deepened by common participation in the Holy Communion which he offers.

> For some Christians the essence of the Christian life is in-

corporation into the Body of Christ realized as fellowship in an organic and transcendent unity of faith, life and love made visible in a pattern of ministry and sacraments which is indivisible. Then it is intolerable and incomprehensible that those who do not share the organic life should expect to share in its eucharistic expression.

In fact this is one of those issues on which Christians are hopelessly divided – and it is no help to say that one view is less true, or less Christian, or even less ecumenical than the other.

In practice, then, the Roman Catholics and Orthodox and many smaller churches in the 'Catholic' tradition, such as the Old Catholics, have forbidden intercommunion: their members may not communicate at other altars, nor will they receive members of other churches at theirs. (For some relaxation of these rules 'by economy', see above, pp. 406 and 443.) Members of the reformed churches on the contrary have practised intercommunion as well as being more ready to be 'in communion' on a church-to-church basis. The Lutherans have been less open to intercommunion following their usual custom of looking for doctrinal safeguards. Some of the extreme Protestant sects, such as the 'closed' Brethren, have only allowed 'table Fellowship' to those of their own persuasion. The attitude of Anglicans has been ambivalent, as might be expected from their stance as both Catholic and reformed. Individually those at the more Protestant end of the comprehensive church have welcomed and practised intercommunion, while those at the other end have maintained a firm Catholic position. But the official position of the church – or rather it should be said the churches, that is the various self-governing provinces – has been against intercommunion.

This has been a particularly vital – in fact sore – issue wherever Anglicans have been involved over many years of ecumenical co-operation and unity negotiations. Reformed churchmen have tended to make it a touchstone of the bonafide-ness (if the word may be permitted) of Anglican intentions: if Anglicans will not practise intercommunion then it must mean that they do not accept the reformed churches and sacraments as true churches and sacraments. If they do accept, as they say, reformed sacraments as 'real' then why do they not 'come clean' and allow intercommunion? In reply Anglicans have tended to say that they are sorry their reformed church friends take this view, that it is a misunderstanding, but they cannot compromise their principles – especially as these 'Catholic' principles are the very thing they most hope to be able to contribute to a united church. Thus the matter has been a crux. It will be remembered that the change of heart of the Anglican bishops in South India to receive communion at 'free church' hands was a turning point in the negotiations (see above, p. 302). Similar actions at a local level have no doubt paved the way for better relationships in many a town and parish.

For many years most Anglican churches have had an exception to their general rule about intercommunion. This has been that on certain appropriate ecumenical occasions authority may be given for an Anglican communion to be celebrated at which non-Anglicans are made welcome. This was a step in an ecumenical direction, but the fact remained that it was not reciprocal: Anglicans could not officially join in non-episcopal services – though of course some individuals did. The result of this was that at many ecumenical conferences the only way to achieve some sort of intercommunion was by means of an 'official' Anglican communion service. In England this was all very well because at least Anglicans were likely to be a majority – though even here the continual repetition of the practice was unhealthy, not least for the Anglicans. Overseas it often led to a ludicrous situation as the Anglicans might be a tiny minority of the Christians present.

There have been, and are, other ways round the problem. One is the practice known as concelebration. In the early church the bishop used to celebrate the eucharist with (*con*) his presbyters, the various celebrants using the same words and the same actions together. This idea has been adapted for joint ecumenical celebrations, and used at a number of places and on a number of ecumenical occasions. Using a single rite ministers of the various denominations bless and distribute the bread and wine together. Looked at one way a joint celebration seems an ingenious way of overcoming the difficulties. Some have felt that it is *too* ingenious, savouring of ecumenical sleight of hand. There could be a danger that if the custom was widely adopted it would blunt the edge of desire to push ahead to fuller union, just as it is felt that this happens when intercommunion is accepted too easily among the reformed churches. In fact, as the Church of England report *Intercommunion Today* says, joint celebrations are really a way of staging intercommunion 'where there is no single authorized ministry but mutual recognition of differing ministries and mutual acceptance of communicants'.[38] Seen in this light it is not so much a pretence of union as a way of showing continuing disunion. In the words of a Roman Catholic theologian, Fr Michael Hurley, s.j.,

A joint celebration ... is emphatically not in the first place a way of making intercommunion acceptable 'by cloaking scruples about the status of the ministries' involved in it. It is first and foremost a means of expressing and enhancing ... the presently imperfect unity of the Church, as it exists in separated Churches whose leaders and members desire in word and deed to overcome separation. ...[39]

The fact that this quotation comes from a Roman Catholic source is a reminder that, although the official R.C. position on intercommunion remains what it has always been, there is a good deal of debate in that church on the subject; in some places, such as Holland, intercommunion between Roman Catholics and Protestants is already being practised.

Another way of expressing unity among Christians short of full union is through the custom known as the Agape meal. In the early church the communion was known as the Agape – or love-feast. In the ecumenical setting the Agape is a fellowship meal. It can be more or less like a 'proper' communion service: the more it is so the greater will be the feeling of unity achieved, but by the same token the greater will be the danger of 'cloaking scruples'. In England and Wales Roman Catholics have been definitely encouraged by their Ecumenical Commission to join in such meals, provided that care is taken that there is no possibility of their being mistaken for the mass.

The matter comes back, therefore, once again to the question of intercommunion – and particularly of the Anglican attitude on the subject – 'the main log in the log-jam for ecumenical progress in England', as one People Next Door Group commented.[40] There is no doubt that in recent years Anglican opinion on this subject has been slowly changing towards a more 'liberal' view. This may be partly due to the fact that the rigid Anglo-Catholic view is less widely held than formerly. (Too much stress must not, however, be laid on this factor; the B.C.C. recommendation about intercommunion in areas of ecumenical experiment met with some strong protests.) It is also no doubt a reflection of the greater emphasis that is now placed on ecumenical concern in the general policy of the church. Thirdly it arises from a theological reconsideration of the issues involved. It can be now said that there is a third position besides the cut-and-dried Catholic and Protestant stances summarized above. The eucharist is increasingly seen in its 'eschatological' context. As such it is a foretaste of the perfection and wholeness which awaits Christians – and indeed the world – at 'the end'. Viewed in such a way in an ecumenical context intercommunion can be understood as anticipating the hoped-for reunion of the churches. This position was put by the Archbishop of Canterbury in a speech on 9 August 1968 at the Lambeth Conference debate on intercommunion:

We ought also to be looking ahead to the plenitude of the Church, and where we and other Christians are really set upon that plenitude, where we have a common understanding of it and a commitment to it in our minds, we can already be doing things in anticipation of that plenitude. The Eucharist in its essential theology has always had its anticipatory trend in which the looking forward as well as looking backward has played its part.

There is a world of difference between intercommunion on the old liberal Protestant get-together lines with no intention of organic unity, and intercommunion in a serious ecclesiastical situation with agreement upon the goal in faith and order. Where that situation exists, I believe it is possible for there to be Eucharistic intercommunion, not with a sense of doing something surreptitious, but with a sense of doing something which does belong to a true understanding of the Eucharist in relation to the Catholic Church.[41]

The resolution of the 1968 Lambeth Conference on intercommunion followed these lines:

The Conference recommends that, where there is agreement between an Anglican Church and some other Church or Churches to seek unity in a way which includes agreement on apostolic faith and order, and where that agreement to seek unity has found expression, whether in a covenant to unite or in some other appropriate form, a Church of the Anglican Communion should be free to allow reciprocal acts of intercommunion under the general direction of the bishop; each province concerned to determine when the negotiations for union in which it is engaged have reached the stage which allows this intercommunion.[42]

This was a significant advance, though as has been seen, some provinces (such as Ghana) had already acted in this way after the establishment of covenants for unity. The Resolution awaits confirmatory action in the Church of England. Despite a commission on the subject resulting in a considerable theological treatise, *Intercommunion Today*, there is no change in the traditional position. In Scotland, on the other hand, the Episcopalian church has also had a commission studying the subject. This is significant, because the Scottish province is traditionally conservative or 'Catholic' in its approach to ecumenical questions. The Commission produced what was in some ways a cautious report, but the recommendation on intercommunion which was subsequently passed by the Provincial Synod must be recorded. It encouraged Episcopalians to share in non-episcopal Trinitarian worship, recognizing that some would and some would not go on to communicate at communion services. It continued to recommend that the Synod

affirm that general intercommunion between the Episcopal Church and non-episcopal Scottish Churches is not at present possible; and yet refrain from passing judgement on those congregations and their clergy which, by virtue of their close association in mission with other Trinitarian Churches, participate according to conscience in each other's Eucharistic services from time to time, where they know they are welcome to do so, effect always being given to the pastoral oversight of the diocesan bishop, acting in accordance with such directions as may be resolved upon by the College of Bishops.[43]

This resolution combines caution and the general upholding of the traditional Anglican principle with permission for responsible experiment under the control of the proper authorities. Thus it allows for intercommunion in such situations as Areas of Ecumenical Experiment, as well in covenant situations. There seems to be no reason why this line should not be further explored. Once again it may be a matter of how much pressure is exerted by informed lay opinion.

ECUMENICAL REVOLUTION

The ecumenical experiments described in the second section of this chapter all had one thing in common. They were, or are, official enterprises of the churches, taking place under the control and with the blessing of the relevant ecclesiastical church authorities. The same point emerged at the end of the section on intercommunion. The Scottish Episcopalian resolution quoted virtually said 'the rules may be broken as long as it is with the approval of the bishops'. That is: experiments are in order as long as they are under control. There is evidence that in other parts of the Anglican Communion, and in other churches generally, controlled experiment is the order of the day. As far as the Anglican church is concerned this may arise from a resolution of the 1968 Lambeth Conference which was 'referred to each province for consideration, as a means of furthering renewal in unity':

We believe that each bishop of the Anglican Communion should ask himself how seriously he takes the suggestion of the Lund Conference. . . . To do so immediately raises the need to review church structures . . . to see whether they can be altered to foster rather than hinder co-operation. . . . It involves also the exploration of *responsible experiment* so that ecumenical work beyond the present limits of constitutional provision is encouraged to keep in touch with the common mind of the Church and not tempted to break away.[44]

It seems that the bishops had seen a red light. They sensed the danger that some ecumenical enthusiasts might give way to impatience and kick over the traces, embarking on experiments which had not got the blessing of the authorities of the churches and so escaped their control. Events have moved so fast since 1968 that the question is now whether it *is* possible any longer to control ecumenical experiments – or at least some of the more radical churchmen who have in the past been the leaders of such experiments.

In the 1967 *Times* correspondence, which was quoted at the beginning of this book as exemplifying the impatience of the laity with the slowness of ecumenical progress (see above, pp. 55–8), one lay woman, writing from the precincts of a Presbyterian theological college, advocated the equivalent of a campaign of civil disobedience:

I think the time has come for lay people in all churches ... to take some definite action. I should like to suggest that we begin a loving and non-violent campaign of 'ecclesiastical disobedience'.

Her suggestion was that lay people of all churches should present themselves for communion at the altar rails of other churches, *without first seeking permission*: 'If we are refused [communion] we should not protest or become angry, but simply come back again and again week after week.'[45] No such large-scale movement as she suggested has in fact taken place, but it is certain that in Britain and elsewhere a number of Christians of various churches (clergy as well as lay people) who are used to working together at the local level have taken their fellowship to the altar rail in defiance of the rules of their denominations. What is more, since the failure of the Anglican/Methodist scheme, most Church of England bishops have made it clear to the vicars in their dioceses that they may give communion to individual Methodists who desire it.

On Whitsunday 1968 a group of Christians in Paris announced an act of rebellious intercommunion to the Cardinal Archbishop of Paris and to the President of the French Protestant Federation:

Brethren, Today on the feast of Pentecost 1968, sixty-one Christians, both Catholic and Protestant, lay people, priests and pastors met together to hear the Word of God and to share the Eucharistic bread and wine. For many years and especially in the course of recent weeks we have for various reasons taken part in the political struggles of our time and have verified there the revolutionary reach of the Gospel. Conscious of our profound communion in the faith, we have been driven to celebrate our many meetings amid workers and students fighting for their freedom by a common sign. . . . By this gesture it is not our purpose to separate ourselves from our respective communities. We simply take note that today the real unity of Christians goes beyond the confessional frontiers. The events we have lived through together for many years and recently in the streets have taken us further towards unity than our many ecumenical meetings for theological discussion.[46]

The sixty-one people meeting in a Parisian flat that day were not simply a group of irresponsible young people, as some of their denigrators tended to suggest. Many of them were mature and respected leaders in their own communities, religious and academic – albeit no doubt of the political left by personal persuasion. The R.C. authorities responded with a condemnation of the action; it was, however, couched in sympathetic terms and no disciplinary action was taken against the R.C. participants. The action clearly sprang from the political turmoil of the time, the revolution in Paris and France which André Malraux called a 'crisis of civilization'. But one participant was at pains to point out that the service should not be written off as a temporary aberration of midsummer political madness. It was

A way of carrying the street revolution into the Church, not in order to imitate that revolution, but to try and break out of the dichotomy which too often afflicts the Church, namely the separation between the 'religious' life and social and political life. What we are experiencing is no longer expressed in the Church's present structure. We challenge that structure. We wish to reinvent it. . . . Instead of talking of 'unusual events', 'prophetic action', 'left-wing Christians' it would certainly be fairer – though of course more disturbing for all the churches – to recognize that we have here a normal, evangelical action which only the infidelity and 'hardness of heart' of Christians still makes impossible.... The 'unusual' and abnormal thing is the division of Christians.... What is scandalous is not that 'left-wing' Christians should have contravened the static stifling regulations of Churches which are short of breath because of years of immobility and complacency. What is scandalous is that the hierarchy, the authorities, the professionals, should fail to realize that the house is on fire and that these problems must be solved as a matter of urgency and not left indefinitely in the study.... The day is not far distant when these Christians who wish to live their faith together ... will separate from the institutional church and will let it get on in peace with the 'ecumenical dialogue', like those Orthodox theologians who were discussing the sex of angels when the Turks were at the very gates of Byzantium.[47]

This is a statement which very fairly describes the position and feelings of those who believe that 'controlled experiment' under the aegis of the 'proper' ecclesiastical authorities is no longer possible. It must however be recognized that the number of people who are willing to challenge the church authorities, and yet remain practising and witnessing Christians in their own way, is very small. There are not many whose Christian committal is strong enough for this. The great majority who feel impatient with the established churches will express their impatience or disgust, not by taking new and revolutionary but still specifically Christian action (such as the Paris Pentecost communion), but simply by ceasing any outward form of Christian practice.

This established, however, it can be said that there are three main factors involved where there are those who are eschewing 'controlled experiment' and indeed the whole institutional life of the churches. Each is reflected in the statement about the Paris intercommunion and each has as a common element the fact, already men-

tioned, that the leaders in ecumenical enterprise have
been drawn from the ranks of the more radical and 'progressive' churchmen especially among the younger clergy
and lay people. Their radical interests have not been
confined to matters ecumenical.

In the first place, as has been repeatedly stressed, during the sixties the ecumenical movement has emerged –
been seen – not just as a thing on its own, but as part of a
larger movement of renewal in the churches. 'One
Church Renewed for Mission' was the cry, not only of the
Nottingham Faith and Order Conference of 1964, but of
virtually all the ecumenical leaders in the sixties. It was
the underlying theme of countless W.C.C. conferences. It
even had the blessing of such 'establishment' leaders as
the Archbishop of Canterbury; speaking just before the
Anglican/Methodist vote in 1969 he said:

I think it is a mistake to be chiefly at discussing unity as such.
We've done it over and over again and just discussing unity as
such generally leads to a kind of deadlock and generally makes
us all very self-conscious. No, why not rather make renewal
prior to unity as a theme? The agenda therefore should be
what we can do to make our own respective churches better
serve God today in their life, their witness, their holiness.[48]

It almost sounds as if the Archbishop were bored with
unity. Many young radical church leaders certainly are.
Unity is for them one renewal theme among many. It is
one which seems to be particularly prone to get bogged
down. It sometimes seems in any case not to be very
firmly attached to renewal. Thus the Anglican/Metho-
dist scheme in England could look rather more like a
piece of ecclesiastical joinery than a vital part in a programme of renewal for the two churches. If this was what
unity really amounted to, was it worth the tears and
sweat? Would not the united church be simply a continuation of the unrenewed life of the separate churches

– just as the united Methodist church continued much in its own ways after the union of 1932 and failed to implement even the most obvious results of union, such as the closing-down of redundant churches? Would it not, therefore, be better to concentrate on those renewal causes which do show some hope of return and give lower priority to the organic union of the churches?

In 1969 the various self-designated 'Renewal Groups' in England, from the Roman Catholics to the Baptists, came together to form a new Christian Renewal Movement, entitled 'ONE for Christian Renewal'. Writing about the new movement in its magazine *New Directions* the Secretary had this to say on the word 'ecumenical' in its title:

denominationalism is dying, even if it seems singularly unwilling to lie down; what is more, Christians are ceasing to relate to ecclesiastical organization at all (the other meaning of 'ecumenical' is to be world-orientated and not merely concerned with the religious club). For some, this will mean moving their fellow church-men in this direction [i.e. presumably the old direction of organic union], for others a local fellowship of Christians whether they belong to a 'church' or not may be more important. Anyway, we tended to drop the word ecumenical in favour of simply 'Christian'.[49]

The syntax may be muddled but the meaning is clear. At least some members of the new movement do not consider the word ecumenical as any longer implying the search for the organic and visible unity of the institutional churches.

The second factor in what can only be called the ecumenical revolution is theological. It is implied in the words just quoted, 'the other meaning of ecumenical is to be world-orientated and not merely concerned with the religious club'. For some time now ecumenical pundits, including various influential W.C.C. leaders, have been talking of 'secular ecumenism'. The thinking behind this movement can be summarized as follows: the secular world is the stage on which the church and its mission are set. Unless the church is so set up ('structured', the ecumenist would say) that its work is relevant to the world, then it is a useless and pointless institution. 'The world must write the agenda', and the church must respond and reform itself accordingly. This is the correct priority of action for the church. It must not start from its own life and interests and work from there; that way lies the danger that it will continue to be a self-absorbed community whose main effort goes into its own self-perpetuation. The world at the moment has certain pressing needs, such as racism and the poverty of the undeveloped nations. The church must be saying and doing something relevant to these needs, and the ecumenical movement within the church must be judged by whether or not it is gearing the churches to helping the world to solve these problems. Ecumenism is concerned not with the one church but ultimately with the one world – the 'global village'. These various concerns were summarized in a question which was considered in the Faith and Order Section of the Uppsala Assembly of the W.C.C. in 1968: 'Does the Gospel permit Christians to concern themselves with questions of ecclesiastical unity when it is the unity and reconciliation of mankind which is alone relevant in 1968?' The report of Section I recognized the existence of a radical reply to this question:

It seems to many, inside and outside the Church, that the struggle for Christian unity in its present form is irrelevant to the immediate crisis of our times. The Church, they say, should seek its unity through solidarity with those forces in modern life, such as the struggle for social equality, and should give up its concern with patching up its own internal disputes.[50]

The final report, while recognizing the force of these arguments, concluded that the curing of the disunity of the church is part of the struggle to find unity for the world. Not all the radicals formerly within the ecumenical movement would accept this conclusion. Some have become convinced of the 'irrelevance' of the movement and have concentrated their efforts on seeking solidarity with 'those forces in modern life' which they see as the last hope for the world.

It becomes evident, therefore, that the third element is the ecumenical revolution is political. Those who are radical in the church tend also to be radical in politics. Some of them in the sixties have despaired of ever persuading the churches to adopt really radical policies and have turned instead to fulfilling their ideals by secular means. How extreme this movement can be may be seen in an article on the underground church in Germany by the German Lutheran minister Rudiger Reitz. He sees one element in the underground church as composed of those who have 'withdrawn from the conformism of the ecclesiastical apparatus' because they despair of 'carrying out reforms in the church'. But they do not go so far as 'political activity of a revolutionary nature'; their action is 'ecclesiastico-political' rather than 'socio-political'. (Herr Reitz has been trained as a sociologist.) The more extreme element in the underground church 'pursue the downfall of capitalism and the building-up of a socialist order of society. Numerous adherents of this wing will have nothing to do with theology, although they have studied it. They undertake activity in the church from purely strategic grounds. The sphere of the church is for them the "institutional sphere of freedom" for the burgeoning of revolution.'[51] For Herr Reitz it is only this more extreme wing which constitutes the true underground church: 'The characteristic of a true underground is that ... a socio-revolutionary guerilla activity of individuals or groups comes from it.'[52]

It may be objected that this is an exaggerated description of a movement in Germany where the ultra-established nature of the church pushes its non-conformists to extremes, and that such extreme groups in any case form a tiny minority. This may be true, though Herr Reitz gives a not unimpressive list of the activities of the underground church. Moreover the foundation issue of the English ecumenical reform action group contains an article castigating some renewal movements as attempts to 'buy the church's place in a permissive, secular society', and calling on the church 'to reject those superficial parodies of real re-birth, and to rediscover its mission as a revolutionary world movement'.[53] The manifesto or Provisional Declaration of the movement is couched in terms which are radical politically as well as ecclesiastically:

We are faced with a world intent on self-destruction, a divided and impotent Church, our personal failure to build the new from the old. Where we are: in a time of world revolution, in a time when denominationalism is dead; in a time when forgiveness and love alone have authority. We now commit ourselves to: total acceptance of one another in Christ; study together the nature of our human responsibility for God's world: social and political action to end poverty, violence and oppression; the re-creation of the new Church – one in witness, worship and structure: support those doing the work of Christ whether inside the Church or out; root the action for renewal in our own local situation.[54]

It must also be remembered that, just as the sixties saw a shift to the left in ecclesiastical radicalism, so political radicalism changed significantly. Describing this change, as exemplified in the break between Bertrand Russell and his erstwhile secretary and colleague Ralph Schoenman, an *Observer* article compares the English liberal-radical tradition and the new movement of revolutionary socialism and concludes: 'Radicalism was changing in the 1960s and becoming the perquisite of a militant minority.'[55] For some Christians the religious and the political radical shift went hand in hand. A minority they may be; but they are the minority potentially most committed to the ecumenical movement. They may now be lost to it.

There now exists, then, a movement which has grown out of the ecumenical movement but is challenging – albeit perhaps in practice rather than theory – the entire basis on which the movement has been founded since the Edinburgh Conference of 1910 – that is the search for the visible and organic unity of the church. Faced with the delays and conservatism of the churches in reaching such unity and reacting to their feeling that in the modern world much of institutional Christianity is irrelevant, some clergy and lay people are taking matters into their own hands. This movement takes different forms according to the differing ecclesiastical starting positions of its participants and the differing social conditions in which they find themselves. In Germany the 'underground church' is an extremist movement politically as well as religiously. In Britain the members of the merging renewal movements, including Roman Catholics, practised intercommunion at their first national conference. In Holland the position would be much the same: there is a good deal of collaboration and intercommunion by radical members of the Protestant and Roman Catholic churches. The same, again, would be true of individuals and groups in the United States, except that there it is easier for a breakaway group to be established as one more sect among many. This is because of the whole pattern of the history of religion in America: 'The very tendency to denominationalism in the ecclesiastical history of North America virtually welcomes underground movements into the official ecclesiastical pluralism.'[56]

This is even true of Roman Catholic breakaway movements. Thus in September 1967 a group of about twenty-five Roman Catholics, dissatisfied with the rigidity of their official liturgy, celebrated with their priest an unofficial mass in a private home in Highland Park, New

Jersey. The priest, Fr George J. Hafner, was suspended by the R.C. authorities, but the group continues. Whatever concrete form they take these different movements all have a common impatience and disillusion with the established procedures of the ecumenical movement's search for unity.

We can now attempt the following summary of the state of affairs at the grassroots among clergy and laity. There are a number of highly impatient and disillusioned people. They may be a small minority and confined mainly to the 'older' churches, but they are among the more committed, informed and courageous Christians and the future may very well lie with them. At the other end of the scale there is still a sleeping majority. These are unconvinced about the importance of unity. In some cases they may be actively opposed to some manifestations or results of the move to unity; they may dislike the views of some of its supporters or they may find that it seems to threaten established positions or ecclesiastical vested interests (see Chapter 1). In between the conservatives and the radicals there are the clergy and laity who, with more or less enthusiasm or knowledge, favour the movement.

It seems that, if the movement to unity is to continue along the lines so far laid down, the essential thing is for the churches to mount educational campaigns to mobilize the apathetic and the unenthusiastic especially among the laity. They will then in turn exert pressure for more urgent action from church leaders; they will also be more willing to experiment in and to implement ecumenical schemes at the vital local level. A number of churches which are involved in unity schemes have learned the lesson that lay people and local clergy must be involved from the word go: this is especially true in churches in the third world, such as that in Ghana. But in the western world, and not least in Great Britain, it still cannot be said that the laity are really *involved* in the ecumenical movement. It is, of course, a question of priorities. There are many things in which the churches wish to educate their lay people – and the lay people and their local clergy tend to become resistant to one campaign after another. It remains to be seen whether unity will hold its own in the priority lists. There is another consideration: educational campaigns to mobilize the laity may involve the risk of mobilizing them to frustration and consequent disillusion if they then feel that the pace is not quickening as it should. When the Secretary of the B.C.C. saw this danger at the end of the People Next Door campaign he was not crying wolf. But it seems that the churches must be willing to take this risk if the ecumenical movement is not either to become the preserve of a militant radical minority, who will wish fundamentally to alter it, or to lose what impetus remains to it – or (paradoxically) both. At the grassroots level, as in every other aspect of the ecumenical movement, progress depends on the willingness of the churches to take risks. For institutions which base their life on a belief in crucifixion followed by resurrection and preceded by the Garden of Gethsemane, they seem strangely unwilling to do so.

Epilogue

IT seems that the movement to church unity is, as of November 1971, in the same position at whichever aspect one looks. The World Council of Churches, the movements to union among non-Roman churches, the *rapprochement* between Rome and the rest, the movement at the grassroots – in each of these branches of the movement a number of similar things are happening.

Partly it is a running-out of steam after the promising-looking progress of the fifties and sixties and the brief general feeling of optimism in the churches at that time. Partly it is a resultant loss of confidence, which is coupled with profound questionings about the validity of institutional religion itself. Partly it is the fact that at the beginning of the seventies in the churches, as in politics and indeed over the whole world scene, there seems to be a decline in the consensus of western liberal opinion and an increasing polarization of opinion. Inevitably this affects the ecumenical outlook and means that many premises which would have been taken for granted ten years ago are now being questioned – the necessity of the visible organic unity of the church among them. At a less radical level there is the change in priorities consequent on the upswing of the renewal movement which is affecting all the churches and within them their ecumenical pundits.

These doubts and misgivings all apply to some extent to church leaders, to the ecumenically committed, to the movement at its official level. To a far greater extent they apply to younger people, who a generation ago would have been ready to step into the shoes of ecumenical leadership and would have assumed almost without question that this was to have high priority in their Christian discipleship. Now they sense that a change of course may be imminent. But in what direction? Even looking simply at the unity movement as it has developed on the lines which one would have thought till recently to be set and accepted, this is now uncertain. And then there are the great question marks. The continued decline of institutional religion? The pattern of contemporary Christian discipleship? Religion in the Third World? Rome? The Orthodox? The sects? The Pentecostal movement?

And still below all this turmoil on the ecumenical surface there is the massive inertia of the ordinary Christian parsons and people. Meeting recently at Louvain in Belgium the Faith and Order Commission of the W.C.C. called for extensive education of church members to prevent disappointments in union schemes when it comes to the voting. Church members are still not alerted to the urgency of the cause.

The obstacles to union are not only or mainly theological or religious. They lie deep in the minds and emotions of men and women who cannot accept the desirability of change and cling desperately to the safety of the institutions and ideas with which they are familiar.[1]

Those words might have been written about the hard facts of ecumenical indifference at any time in the last fifty years. The fact that they were written in August 1971 shows how little progress has been made at those levels where the final votes are taken.

A commentator writing on the American C.O.C.U. negotiations makes this analysis:

Three groups now evident in U.S. theology and religious life generally have been identified ... as the traditionalists, the reformers or renewalists and the revolutionists. Obviously the traditionalists will not be interested in C.O.C.U., nor will be revolutionists who seek answers solely in the secular movements and underground liturgies. The renewalists or reformers are the likely allies of the plan for church union.[2]

Two things must be said about this analysis. In the first place, while it is the reformers who may make the plans (and especially the more radical ones such as C.O.C.U.) it is the traditionalists who at the end of the day will vote on them. In the second place the analysis is probably more true of the churches and of the ecumenical movement in the developed countries than it is of the younger churches where thought has not moved so fast and the situation is not so polarized. But with these provisos the analysis is true for the churches as they seek their unity. The question is: can the reformers and renewalists press ahead with their schemes and convert the traditionalists to them before it is too late and the whole fabric of the movement as it has been described in this book crumbles?

For all these reasons the next decade must be crucial to the movement, as to the future of the shrinking separate churches themselves.

Two last examples of the current situation must be given, since they illustrate the dilemmas of union leaders. The Church of England Synod met in the summer of 1971 and had a number of ecumenical items on its agenda. In the first place, and on the credit side, the Synod in a surprise vote gave approval in principle to admitting full members of Trinitarian churches to communion at Church of England altars. The Canon which will complete this measure comes before the Synod in February 1972. Thus the log-jam on intercommunion which has for so long fouled up ecumenical relationships is now on the move (see above, pp. 495–503). Or at least partly so. The other half of the equation is that Anglicans should be able to receive communion in other churches. Here the tradition has been that the act is left to the individual's own discretion. But recently there has been some backing away from the liberal approach: a commission is now considering the question. Nevertheless this is a positive move – even if it has something of the character of too little and too late.

Secondly the Synod voted by an overwhelming majority that the Church of England should be in communion with the newly united churches of North India and Pakistan.

But when it came to voting on the Anglican/Methodist scheme (which had narrowly failed to gain the required 75 per cent majority two years before) matters were different. Motions which would have had the effect of putting the whole scheme into cold storage were defeated. A motion to refer the scheme to discussion by diocesan synods before bringing it back to the national synod was passed. But what was significant was the majority for this motion. The bishops passed it by 35 votes to 2. But in the clergy and laity houses the majorities were only about 60 per cent. This does not augur well for a vote of 75 per cent in favour of the Scheme when it is voted on on 3 May 1972. If the Scheme is rejected for a second time those who say that the Church of England is incapable of making up its mind will surely be seen to be right. The policy of the leaders of the C. of E. – and with it many years of work – wil be overturned and the unity position in England will be back at square one with a vengeance. And without doubt the reaction of a large number of lay people, both inside and outside the church, will be disgust and disillusion.

The final irony of the situation can fully be seen by comparing the synod majorities for intercommunion with North India and for continuing with the Anglican/Methodist Scheme. The one was overwhelming, the other a bare 60 per cent. Yet on the crucial point of the means of unifying the ministries of the uniting churches the two plans are similar. Indeed the English plan is an up-dating and presumably an improvement on the Indian (see above, pp. 367–71). The difference in the synod voting can, therefore, mean one of two things. Either those who voted for North India but against Anglican/Methodist felt that theology which would do for North India was not good enough for England, or they felt that unity was more urgent in India than in England.

At the 1968 Lambeth Conference for Anglican bishops the then Metropolitan of India, Archbishop Lakdasa del Mel, castigated his British brethren in a memorable speech. The burden of it was: 'You English will unite to the last Indian.' It looks as if he was right. The various schemes in the younger churches will probably move ahead, slowly maybe but probably also surely. What will happen in the British Isles – and when – is anybody's guess. And what will happen when the more radical schemes in the other 'western' churches – Australia, Canada, New Zealand and the United States – come to the vote, remains to be seen.

The last word must go to Rome. For when all is said and done there are more Roman Catholics in the world than Christians in all the other churches put together. Here the situation can be described but the future can hardly be divined. Rome's ecumenical attitude depends on the outcome of her own internal debate about the beliefs and practices of the church in the twentieth century. It is difficult to avoid the conclusion that probably the Pope and certainly the Curia are trying to stem the tide of liberalization and change. One example: in the summer of 1971 Rome released the draft of a *Lex ecclesiae fundamentalis*. This draft had been prepared in secrecy and it was proposed that it should be submitted to a hurried postal ballot of bishops. It was seen as 'a constitutional charter for the church' which would 'synthesize the essence of Vatican II's principal documents'. In fact there were many who felt that it put the clock back on Vatican II. Fr Laurentin, writing in the French paper *Figaro*, said that it took a 'preconciliar idea of the church as a pyramid of different powers with the pope at the top'. Professor Giuseppe Alberigo, lecturing in Rome, claimed that it showed 'a church conceived as one large diocese in which the pope

Epilogue

alone enjoys effective authority. No room is left, even at
the executive level, for local churches.' With reference to
the ideas of Vatican II he believed that it ignored the idea
of the church as a mystery and 'also the Council's other
precious rediscovery, that a hierarchy of truth exists'. In
short, commented the English *Tablet*, 'it is clearly evident
that such a fundamental law will be a very serious hindrance to the improvement of ecumenical relations'.[3]

The fate of the draft of this document is at the moment
uncertain; but the point is that it represents the strongly
entrenched conservative outlook of many of the people in
authority in Rome. Against this outlook there is much
open rebellion. In some places many of the 'liberals' are
leaving the church, while in others, such as Holland, it is
liberal policies which are being put into practice despite
the opposition of Rome. Meanwhile the theological debate
continues.

In 1971 the English translation of Professor Hans Küng's
book *Infallible?* was published. It appeared after the chapter in this book on the Roman Catholic position had been
written. But it seems that many of Küng's arguments about
infallibility and authority echo the points made there.
Küng points out that one of the main problems of up-
dating Roman Catholic teaching is that to do so is to
challenge the whole basis of the authority of former pronouncements. It seemed impossible to modify the teaching
on birth control because the prohibition of contraception
'had always, or at any rate for half a century before Vatican II, been taught unanimously by the ordinary teaching
office of the Pope and bishops; ... from the point of view
of the ordinary *magisterium* of the Pope and bishops, it
was therefore *de facto* an infallible moral truth, even
though it had not been defined as such'[4] (see above, p. 435).
Küng has various criticisms of the idea of infallibility. It
is in fact a fairly late medieval importation into the thinking of the church at a time when other 'triumphalist' ideas
were creeping in (see above, p. 425); it has come to be

equated with infallible propositions, which creates impossible logical situations (see above, p. 434); it must be recognized that all thought processes and the forms in which they are expressed are inevitably historically conditioned. In the end Küng seems to want to say little more than that the church's teaching is 'permanent': it has 'indefectibility or perpetuity, indestructibility and unperishability – in short a fundamental remaining in the truth in spite of all possible errors' (see above, p. 434). Christians believe that the church, because Christ has so promised, has 'remained in the truth' and will 'remain in the truth'.[5]

Küng's arguments are not likely to gain immediate and universal acceptance among Catholic theologians, let alone the more conservative ones.[6] But they open up an area of debate in which Catholics and non-Catholics alike can join. And, as has been seen so often in this book, this is *the* critical debate for the ecumenical movement. For the divisions of the church and the search for its unity turn fundamentally on the question of authority – the authority of the church and authority in the church. If this question could be solved, or some reasonable consensus reached, all others would fall into line. And it does seem that in Roman Catholic theology the tide is running in Küng's direction. Already Roman Catholics and Anglicans in the United States have reached agreement on eucharist and baptism (see above, p. 412); more recently the same consensus was found in 1971 between the R.C.C. and the W.C.C.; Roman Catholics and Lutherans found nothing to divide them on the controversial issue of justification and a surprising measure of agreement on the ministry. Now it seems possible that the lines are converging on authority, the most fundamental question of all.

The brutal fact has to be faced that much depends on how long the present pope holds office – and who is elected as his successor. But if it is true that the tide is flowing in one direction it cannot presumably be stemmed for ever.

Epilogue

If the dykes are really breached and the thought of Küng and people like him becomes generally accepted in the Roman Catholic church, then this could provide the new impetus which the ecumenical movement so badly needs. The movement towards organic union could gain fresh credibility – for organic union of all the churches including Rome is a very different agenda to that which had been discussed in the last fifty years.

In an exchange of open letters with Professor Küng after the *motu proprio* on mixed marriages the French liberal Catholic theologian, Yves Congar, coined a telling metaphor. It can be applied to the search for unity wherever the churches are engaged in it. It is certainly relevant to the Roman Catholic participation in the search, which could now be the clue to the whole matter.

> You think that evolution is not frank enough or fast enough. You already thought this during the [Vatican] Council. . . . You remember that I then pointed out to you the two ways of appreciating the same measure – half full or half empty. I believe in active patience and I see the half that is full : you the half that is still empty. This is always the difference between the reformist and the revolutionary.[7]

One of the lessons of this book is that the ecumenical movement, as it now stands, must be seen as 'the half that is full'. After centuries of division, antagonism and absolute rivalry, the churches *have* made great strides towards unity in the last fifty years and particularly since the war. In the perspective of history – which this book has been at pains to supply – there has been remarkable progress. The glass *is* half full. It is natural that the old leaders, who have seen and participated in this progress, should see the situation this way. For them 'active patience' is a reasonable policy indeed.

But is it, in fact, reasonable at the rate at which the world is changing? Is patience – even active patience – enough? If the world is really 'writing the agenda' for the churches, then the churches are hardly keeping up with the agenda. This is the feeling of those who wish to move forward faster. In his reply appealing for the support of the older liberal Catholic Hans Küng takes up the metaphor:

Long before me you were described as a revolutionary, because you were not satisfied with the half filled glass in our Church, when it would have been so easy to fill it to the top. I do not see this anyway as the difference between the revolutionary and the reformer. The revolutionary throws down the glass.... What we would have counted as progressive in 1965 is a disappointment in 1970. We no longer think in centuries.[8]

It is true that the churches have achieved more in unity in the last half century than in at least the last nine centuries of division before that. But can the churches any longer afford the luxury of this time scale? Must they not now be thinking in terms of decades rather than centuries? If they fail to do so the revolutionaries may fling away the glass of organic unity, and even of institutional religion. Or the world may simply discard it as meaningless and unworthy of the great truths it once seemed to contain.

References

1. The Ecumenical Movement: Causes and Attitudes

1. *The World Christian Handbook*, 1968/9 edition (World Dominion Press).
2. Bryan Wilson, *Religion in Secular Society* (Harmondsworth, 1969) pp. 15 f.
3. ibid.
4. Robert Currie, *Methodism Divided* (London, 1968), p. 92.
5. Quoted, ibid., pp. 187 f.
6. ibid., p. 273.
7. ibid., p. 111.
8. In *A History of the Ecumenical Movement, 1517–1948*, ed. Ruth Rouse and Stephen Neill (London, 1954), p. 362.
9. *Twentieth Century Theology in the Making*, Vol. III, *Ecumenicity and Renewal*, ed. Jaroslav Pelikan (English translation, London, 1970), p. 15.
10. *The Ecumenical Advance, A History of the Ecumenical Movement*, Vol. II, ed. Harold E. Fey (London, 1970), p. 316, note 1.
11. C. O. Buchanan, E. L. Mascall, J. I. Packer and the Bishop of Willesden, *Growing into Union* (London, 1970), pp. 103 f.
12. Stephen Neill, *The Church and Christian Union* (Oxford, 1968), p. 75.
13. ibid., p. 362.
14. *Anglican-Methodist Unity, The Scheme* (London, 1968), paras. 303 and 304.
15. Rouse and Neill, op. cit., p. 359.
16. *The Ecumenical Advance*, op. cit., p. 314.
17. Currie, op. cit., p. 109; compare Wilson, op. cit., p. 154.
18. Currie, op cit., p. 315.
19. Wilson, op. cit., p. 226.
20. Ian Henderson, *Power Without Glory* (London, 1967), pp. 8 and 9.
21. ibid., p. 162.
22. ibid., p. 173.
23. ibid., p. 38.
24. ibid., p. 102.
25. ibid., p. 95.
26. ibid., p. 12.

27. Quoted, Currie, op. cit., p. 201.

28. Barrie Hinksman, *Mission and Ministry, Ten Years' Ecumenical Work in Scunthorpe* (privately printed in Birmingham), p. 29.

29. Quoted, Ronald Jasper, *Arthur Cayley Headlam* (London, 1960), p. 277.

30. Quoted, Currie, op. cit., p. 196.

31. Walter J. Hollenweger in the *International Review of Mission*, Vol. LX, No. 238, April 1971, p. 232.

32. *Christian Unity, A Layman's Challenge and the Replies* (The Times, 1967), pp. 3–5 and 10–12.

33. ibid., p. 21.

34. Quoted, Currie, op. cit., p. 200.

35. *Agenda for the Churches, A Report on the People Next Door Programme*, ed. Kenneth Sansbury, Robert Latham and Pauline Webb (London, 1968), p. 22.

36. Rouse and Neill, op. cit., p. 495.

37. Neill, op. cit., p. 402.

38. Oliver Tomkins, *The Wholeness of the Church* (London, 1949), p. 11.

2. The Church United: The First Four Centuries

1. Sebastian Bullough, *Roman Catholicism* (Harmondsworth, 1963), p. 187.

2. For example Otto Karrer, *Peter and the Church* (English translation, London, 1963); and Hans Kung, *The Council and Reunion* (English translation, London, 1961), pp. 205 ff.

3. This point is made by B. H. Streeter, *The Primitive Church* (London, 1929), p. 81.

4. L. S. Thornton, *The Common Life in the Body of Christ* (3rd edn, London, 1950), p. 307.

5. For a typical example of this point of view see Geddes MacGregor, *Corpus Christi* (London, 1959), pp. 151 ff., where he strongly criticizes the idea that the church is the extension of the Incarnation.

6. Douglas Jones, *Instrument of Peace* (London, 1965), pp. 46, 51.

7. ibid., p. 49.

8. P. T. Forsyth, *Lectures on the Church and the Sacraments* (London, 1917), p. 40.

9. In *Ep. ad Ephes.*, Hom. xi, 5 (ed. Gaume, Paris, 1838, XI, 99–101).

10. This quotation is actually a collation of two separate quotations from St Augustine made by Isidore of Seville in the seventh century.

11. For a study of 'enthusiasm' as it has affected and divided the

References

church through the ages, see R. A. Knox, *Enthusiasm* (Oxford, 1950).

12. John Wesley, *Journal*, ed. N. Curnock (London, 1938), p. 256 n.

13. *On the Deity of the Son* (P.G. xlvi, 557b), quoted Timothy Ware, *The Orthodox Church* (Harmondsworth, 1964), pp. 43 f.

14. The passage of which this is a summary is quoted in full in S. L. Greenslade, *Schism in the Early Church* (London, 1964), pp. 15–16. This book is a useful further survey of the points discussed in this section of the chapter.

15. Eusebius, *Ecclesiastical History*, III, 39, 3 and 4 (ed. Lawlor and Oulton, 1927, p. 99).

16. Irenaeus, I, x, 2 (Ante-Nicene Christian Library, Edinburgh, 1868, Vol. I, p. 43).

17. Cyprian, *Epistle* LXIX, 3 (Ante-Nicene Christian Libary, Vol. VIII, p. 252).

18. Augustine, *Sermones de Scripturio Novi Testamenti*, CCLXXII.

19. Ignatius, *To the Smyrnaeans*, 8 (ed. J. B. Lightfoot, *The Apostolic Fathers*, London, 1926, p. 158).

20. H. Lietzmann, *The Beginnings of the Christian Church* (London, 1949), p. 248.

21. Clement, *To the Corinthians*, 44 (Lightfoot, op. cit., p. 76).

22. Irenaeus, III, 3–4. Quoted J. Stevenson, *A New Eusebius*, pp. 117 ff.

23. Cyprian, *Epistle* LI, 24 (Ante-Nicene Christian Library, Vol. VIII, p. 147).

24. Cyprian, *On the Unity of the Church*, 5 (ibid., p. 381).

25. ibid., p. 382.

26. For a brief summary of the Orthodox belief about episcopacy see Ware, op. cit., pp. 252–8. It is significant that Cyprian is the only writer of the ancient church quoted by Ware as typifying Orthodox teaching on the subject.

3. The Church Divided: The Last Fifteen Centuries

1. S. L. Greenslade, *Schism in the Early Church* (London, 1964), p. 66.

2. The phrase is that of Christopher Dawson, *The Making of Europe* (London, 1932), p. 114.

3. Figures from the *World Christian Handbook*, 1968 edition.

4. F. Dvornik in the *Cambridge Mediaeval History*, Vol. IV, part 1 (1966), 'Constantinople and Rome', p. 433.

5. ibid., pp. 435, 436.

6. ibid., p. 437.

References

7. ibid., p. 447.

8. ibid., p. 459.

9. ibid., p. 462.

10. Timothy Ware, *The Orthodox Church* (Harmondsworth, 1964), p. 67.

11. Quoted Ware, op. cit., p. 69.

12. S. Runciman, *The Eastern Schism* (Oxford, 1955), p. 101.

13. Quoted Ware, op. cit., p. 71.

14. ibid., p. 81.

15. ibid., p. 85.

16. Quoted in *Byzantium*, ed. Norman H. Baynes and H. St L. B. Moss (Oxford, 1953), p. 385.

17. *The Cambridge Mediaeval History*, Vol. IV, part 2, p. 375.

18. Quoted Baynes, op. cit., p. 390 f.

19. Paul Verghese in the *World Christian Handbook* (1968 ed. H. W. Croxall and K. Grubb), p. 390 f.

20. From the article on Innocent III in the *Oxford Dictionary of the Christian Church*, edited F. L. Cross.

21. The opening words of Owen Chadwick's *The Reformation* (Pelican History of the Church, Vol. 3), pp. 11 and 13.

22. ibid., p. 46.

23. ibid., p. 56.

24. ibid., p. 191.

25. ibid., p. 83.

26. R. N. Carew Hunt, *Calvin* (London, 1933), p. 259.

27. Chadwick, op. cit., p. 83.

28. Josef Rupert Geiselmann, a Roman Catholic contributor to *Christianity Divided* (Stagbooks, 1962), p. 48.

29. Chadwick, op. cit., pp. 266–7.

30. *The Writings of Robert Harrison and Robert Browne*, ed. Albert Peel and Leland H. Carlson (London, 1953), pp. 404 and 58.

31. George Fox, *Journal* (ed. N. Penney, 1901), p. 33.

32. The concluding words of an article, 'Presbyterianism in England', in the *Dictionary of English Church History*, ed. S. L. Ollard and Gordon Crosse (2nd edn, London, 1919).

33. Willard L. Sperry, *Religion in America* (Cambridge, 1945), p. 33.

34. This was Bishop A. C. Headlam of Gloucester, quoted Sperry, op. cit., p. 9.

35. Alec Vidler in an essay on 'The Appalling Religiousness of America' in *Essays in Liberality* (London, 1957), p. 174.

36. *Church and State through the Centuries*, ed. Sidney Z. Ehler and John B. Morrall (London, 1954), pp. 224 ff.

37. ibid., p. 225.

38. Sperry, op. cit., p. 71.

39. Timothy Ware, op. cit., pp. 87 ff.

40. Sperry, op. cit., p. 273.

41. Stephen Neill, *The History of Christian Missions* (Pelican History of the Church, Vol. 6), p. 459.

42. Sperry, op. cit., p. 76.

43. ibid., p. 103, summarizing Elmer T. Clark, *The Small Sects in America* (Nashville, Tennessee, 1937).

4. The Stirrings of Conscience

1. Quoted Owen Chadwick, *From Bossuet to Newman* (Cambridge, 1957), pp. 1 and 2.

2. W. K. Jordan, *The Development of Religious Toleration in England* (4 vols., London, 1932–40), Vol. I, p. 336. Jordan has a long summary of the thought of Acontius and is in general a very good work of reference on the development of more liberal thought.

3. Norman Sykes in *A History of the Ecumenical Movement, 1517–1948*, ed. Ruth Rouse and Stephen Neill (London, 1954), p. 134.

4. ibid., p. 136.

5. J. Bramhall, *Works* (Library of Anglo-Catholic Theology, Oxford, 1851), Vol. I, p. 199. The work from which this quotation comes is called, typically enough, *A Just Vindication of the Church of England*.

6. Hooker, *Of the Laws of Ecclesiastical Polity*, VII, v, 10; VII, iv, 4. For a discussion of Hooker's view of episcopacy see *The Historic Episcopate*, ed. K. M. Carey (London, 1954), pp. 70 ff.

7. Andrewes, *Opuscula* (L.A.C.T.), pp. 211 and 191.

8. Bramhall, *Works* (op. cit.), Vol. III, p. 518.

9. Historical Manuscripts Commission, Various Collections, I, 1901, p. 226. (From the Canterbury Cathedral Archives, Christ Church Letters, II, No. 172.)

10. Sykes, op. cit., p. 145.

5. The Modern Ecumenical Movement

1. Ruth Rouse, 'William Carey's "Pleasing Dream" ', in *International Review of Missions*, April 1949, pp. 181–92.

2. Ruth Rouse and Stephen Neill, editors, *A History of the Ecumenical Movement, 1517–1948* (London, 1954), p. 355.

3. Robert Currie, *Methodism Divided* (London, 1968), p. 200.

4. Rouse and Neill, op. cit., p. 233.

References

5. Owen Chadwick in *Anglican Initiatives in Christian Unity*, ed. E. G. W. Bill (London, 1967), p. 26.

6. Quoted Rouse and Neill, op. cit., pp. 264 f. The Preamble is from the Chicago document; the four points are given as modified from Chicago by the Lambeth Conference.

7. Hans-Ruedi Weber, *Asia and the Ecumenical Movement, 1895–1961* (London, 1966), p. 53.

8. ibid., p. 57. This book has two chapters on the importance of the W.S.C.F. and the Y.M.C.A. in the formation of ecumenical leadership in Asia (pp. 54–111).

9. Oliver Tomkins, *The Wholeness of the Church* (London, 1949), p. 11.

10. Quoted Rouse and Neill, op. cit., pp. 342 f. See Tissington Tatlow, *The Story of the Student Christian Movement* (London, 1933), pp. 389–412.

11. ibid., p. 343.

12. ibid., p. 355.

13. ibid., p. 406.

14. *World Missionary Conference, 1910, Official Report*, Section VIII, p. 83.

15. ibid., Section IX, p. 347.

16. Stephen Neill, *Men of Unity* (London, 1960), p. 85.

17. F. A. Iremonger, *William Temple* (London, 1948), p. 397.

18. Rouse and Neill, op cit., p. 554.

19. ibid., p. 575.

20. ibid., p. 416.

21. ibid., pp. 422 ff.

22. ibid., p. 433.

23. Ronald Jasper, *Arthur Cayley Headlam*, p. 277.

24. Rouse and Neill, op. cit., p. 426.

25. ibid., p. 434.

26. ibid., p. 683.

27. Ronald Jasper, op. cit., p. 279.

28. Rouse and Neill, op. cit., p. 447 f.

29. Iremonger, op. cit., p. 455.

30. Currie, op. cit., p. 259. This book devotes a whole chapter to the formation of the United Methodist Church (pp. 248–89).

31. Quotations from Currie, op. cit., pp. 273 and 289.

32. Rouse and Neill, op. cit., p. 457.

33. ibid., p. 470.

References

6. The World Council of Churches

1. Preamble to the Report on the Anglican–Presbyterian Conversations, quoted Norman Goodall, *The Ecumenical Movement* (2nd edn, London, 1964), p. 113.

2. *The World Council of Churches, Its Process of Formation* (Geneva, 1946), p. 75.

3. ibid., p. 56.

4. *The First Assembly of the World Council of Churches, Official Report* (1949), p. 9.

5. Quoted *The Ecumenical Advance: A History of the Ecumenical Movement*, Vol. II, ed. Harold E. Fey (London, 1970), p. 56.

6. For the evolution of this formula, see ibid., pp. 34 ff.

7. *The Amsterdam Report*, op. cit., pp. 127–8.

8. *The Report of the Fourth World Conference on Faith and Order* (Montreal, 1963), pp. 48 f.

9. Quoted, *The Ecumenical Advance*, op. cit., p. 31.

10. *Evanston to New Delhi, 1954–61* (Official Report to the Third Assembly of the World Council of Churches), p. 37.

11. ibid., p. 38.

12. ibid., p. 39.

13. *The Ecumenical Advance*, op. cit., p. 158.

14. *Evanston to New Delhi*, op. cit., p. 158.

15. *The Report of the Third World Conference on Faith and Order, Lund, 1952*, p. 34.

16. *Evanston to New Delhi*, op. cit., p. 52. These studies resulted in the publication of two important books: *Man in Rapid Social Change*, by Egbert de Vries (London, 1961) and *The Churches and Rapid Social Change*, by Paul Albrecht (London, 1961).

17. ibid., p. 73.

18. ibid., p. 80.

19. On this subject see Hans-Ruedi Weber, *Asia and the Ecumenical Movement, 1895–1961* (London, 1966).

20. H. L. Ellison in the periodical *Frontier*, Summer 1959, pp. 122–3.

21. *Evanston to New Delhi*, op. cit., p. 182.

22. Quoted Goodall, op. cit., p. 211.

23. ibid., pp. 38 f.

24. Quoted, Kenneth Slack, *Despatch from New Delhi* (London, 1962), p. 88.

25. Quoted, *The Ecumenical Advance*, op. cit., p. 188.

26. *New Delhi to Uppsala, 1961–1968* (Report of the Central Committee to the Fourth Assembly of the World Council of Churches), p. 54.

References

27. ibid., p. 54.

28. *The Fourth World Conference on Faith and Order*, ed. P. C. Rodger and L. Vischer (London, 1964), p. 36.

29. ibid., p. 26.

30. ibid., p. 39.

31. *New Delhi to Uppsala*, op. cit., p. 55.

32. *The Ecumenical Advance*, op. cit., p. 282.

33. Quoted by Dr Visser 't Hooft on 'The Mandate of the Ecumenical Movement' in *The Uppsala 1968 Report*, p. 315.

34. ibid., p. 20.

35. ibid., p. 19.

36. *New Delhi to Uppsala*, op. cit., p. 9.

37. *The Uppsala Report*, op. cit., p. xvii.

38. ibid., p. xvii.

39. ibid., p. 20.

40. *New Delhi to Uppsala*, op. cit., p. 161.

41. *The Fourth Assembly of the World Council of Churches* (Official Report), pp. 49, para. 20, and 62, para. 10.

42. *Central Committee, Minutes and Reports* (Canterbury, August 1969), pp. 126 f.

43. ibid., p. 277.

44. Press release from the W.C.C., 'Decisions of the Executive Committee of the W.C.C. Regarding the Special Fund of the Programme to Combat Racism', p. 3.

45. ibid., p. 5.

46. *The Uppsala Report*, op. cit., p. 15.

47. *New Delhi to Uppsala*, op. cit., p. 210.

48. *Report of the Structure Committee to the Central Committee*, October 1970, pp. 5 f.

49. ibid., p. 19.

50. ibid., p. 21.

51. From a commentary on *De Ecclesia* by Cardinal Bea, quoted in a speech by Fr Roberto Tucci, s.j., to the Uppsala Assembly, *Uppsala Report*, op. cit., p. 324.

52. ibid., p. 325.

53. *New Delhi to Uppsala*, op. cit., p. 12.

54. *The Uppsala Report*, op. cit., p. 325.

55. Thomas F. Stransky, 'Roman Catholic Membership in the World Council of Churches', in *The Ecumenical Review* (July 1968), p. 222.

56. Quoted Walter J. Hollenweger, 'Pentecostalism and the Third World', in *Dialog* (Minneapolis, Minnesota), Vol. 9, Spring 1970, p. 125.

57. ibid.

58. Quoted ibid., p. 126.

59. ibid.
60. Goodall, op. cit., p. 151.
61. *The Uppsala Report*, op. cit., p. 317.

7. Union Negotiations

1. Bengt Sundkler, *The Church of South India, The Movement towards Union, 1900–1947* (revised edn, London, 1965). Professor Sundkler is Professor of Church History and Missions at the University of Uppsala, Sweden.
2. Sundkler, op. cit., p. 101 (italics mine).
3. ibid., p. 28.
4. ibid., p. 26.
5. ibid., pp. 31 f.
6. ibid., p. 160.
7. ibid., p. 207.
8. ibid., p. 303. The quotation comes from a letter from Hollis to England.
9. ibid.
10. ibid., p. 141.
11. ibid., p. 213.
12. ibid., pp. 101 ff.
13. ibid., p. 117.
14. ibid., p. 118.
15. ibid., pp. 147 ff.
16. ibid., p. 163.
17. ibid., p. 269.
18. ibid., p. 229.
19. ibid., p. 240.
20. ibid., p. 294.
21. ibid., p. 174.
22. ibid., p. 216. See also Michael Hollis, *The Significance of South India* (London, 1966), pp. 38 f.
23. Sundkler, op. cit., p. 330.
24. F. A. Iremonger, *William Temple* (London, 1948), pp. 589–93.
25. These arguments were most clearly advanced – and with great learning – in *The Apostolic Ministry* (London, 1946), edited K. E. Kirk. But it is fair to say that the extreme position here taken up has not stood the test of time – even in the Anglo-Catholic party in the Church of England. The evidence, for all the learning mustered in *The Apostolic Ministry*, is not strong enough to support it.
26. The Report of the Commission was entitled *Renewal and Advance* (Madras, 1963).

References

27. Sundkler, op. cit., p. 346.

28. Hollis, op. cit., p. 65.

29. For a full list of the rules governing the relationship between the Church of England and the C.S.I. see, *The Lambeth Conference, 1968, Preparatory Information*, pp. 146 f.

30. Ruth Rouse and Stephen Neill, editors, *A History of the Ecumenical Movement, 1517–1948* (London, 1954), pp. 494 f.

31. Professor J. D. McCaughey, 'Church Union in Australia', in *Mid-Stream* (Council on Christian Unity, Indianapolis, U.S.A.), Vol. IV, no. 2, p. 21.

32. Quoted in 'Survey of Church Union Negotiations, 1965–1967', in *The Ecumenical Review*, Vol. XX, no. 3, July 1968, p. 270.

33. 'Survey of Church Union Negotiations, 1961–1963', ibid., Vol. XVI, no. 4, July 1964, p. 15.

34. Alan Wilkinson in an unpublished paper prepared for the 1968 Lambeth Conference, 'Review of Current Church Union Schemes', p. vii.

35. ibid., quoting the Anglo-Catholic theologian E. M. Mascall in an article in *Theology* for May 1966.

36. *Proposed Basis of Union* (Ghana Church Union Committee, 1963), p. 10.

37. *First Report of the New Zealand Joint Commission on Church Union* (September 1965), pp. 15 ff.

38. Quoted 'Survey of Church Union Negotiations, 1963–5', reprinted from *The Ecumenical Review*, Vol. XVIII, no. 3, July 1966, p. 35.

39. Norman Goodall, *The Ecumenical Movement* (2nd edn, London, 1964), p. 112.

40. Wilkinson, op. cit., p. iii.

41. ibid., p. 21.

42. ibid., p. 30.

43. Quoted 1968 'Survey', op. cit., pp. 263 f.

44. ibid., p. 289.

45. Wilkinson, op. cit., p. 5. This remark is made about the West Indian Anglican–Methodist scheme. The fact that this scheme is relatively recent in origin, but still bears a somewhat anachronistic stamp, bears out the remarks made above.

46. Quoted from an unpublished paper on 'Confessions of Faith in Church Union Negotiations' presented to the Limuru Faith and Order Conference on Church Union Negotiations by G. C. Oosthuizen, p. 8.

47. S. F. Bayne, *Ceylon, North India and Pakistan* (London, 1960), p. 186.

48. *Anglican–Methodist Unity, The Scheme* (1968), p. 10.

References

49. ibid., p. 18.
50. ibid., p. 33.
51. *A Plan of Union* (Princeton, New Jersey, 1970), pp. 9–11.
52. ibid., p. 31.
53. ibid., p. 45.
54. ibid., p. 70.
55. ibid., pp. 83 f.
56. ibid., p. 91.
57. ibid., Preface to the Ordinal.
58. Oosthuizen, op. cit., p. 32.
59. J. D. McCaughey, 'Church Union in Australia', in *Mid-Stream* (Council on Christian Unity, Indianapolis), Vol. IV, no. 2, p. 21.
60. *International Review of Mission*, Vol. LX, no. 238, April 1971. Article 'Latin America – An Ecumenical Bird's Eye View', by Victor Hayward, p. 163.
61. ibid., p. 173.
62. ibid., p. 176.
63. Quoted Wilkinson, op. cit., p. 13.
64. *Anglican–Methodist Unity*, op. cit., p. 34.
65. ibid., p. 172.
66. C. O. Buchanan, E. L. Mascall, J. I. Packer and the Bishop of Willesden, *Growing into Unity*, p. 158.
67. ibid., p. 127.
68. ibid., p. 77.
69. ibid., pp. 103–9.
70. ibid., p. 172.
71. *The Methodist Recorder*, xxviii, 24 July 1960.
72. James M. Gustafson in *Institutionalism and Church Unity*, ed. Nils Ehrenstrom and Walter G. Muelder (London, 1963), pp. 346 ff.
73. Mark Gibbard, *Unity is Not Enough* (London, 1965), p. 76.

8. The Roman Catholic Church and the Orthodox Churches

1. Xavier Rynne, *Letters from Vatican City* (London, 1963), p. 157.
2. Quoted *The Second Vatican Council*, ed. Bernard C. Pawley (London, 1967), p. 186.
3. ibid., p. 209.
4. Quoted ibid., pp. 45 ff.
5. *De Ecclesia, The Constitution on the Church of Vatican Council II*, ed. Edward H. Peters (London, 1965), p. 13.
6. Pawley, op. cit., pp. 56 f.
7. *De Ecclesia*, op. cit., p. 13.

References

8. Pawley, op. cit., p. 20.

9. *De Ecclesia*, op. cit., p. 12.

10. Quoted Pawley, op. cit., p. 187.

11. ibid.

12. Professor H. E. Root in Pawley, op. cit., p. 142.

13. From the full text of the Directory produced from the Vatican, Secretariat for Christian Unity, Information Service, 1967, no. 2, p. 7.

14. ibid., p. 10.

15. S.P.C.U. ibid., no. 8, September 1969, p. 4.

16. S.P.C.U. *Reports and Documentation*, p. 366.

17. ibid., p. 369.

18. ibid., p. 379.

19. S.P.C.U. Information Service, no. 1, p. 7.

20. Para. 19 of the Malta Report, quoted from an unreleased statement of the Joint Commission on Anglican–Roman-Catholic Relations in the United States (A.R.C.) Statement No. VII, December 1969, p. 11.

21. Joint Commission of the R.C.C. and the World Methodist Council, Progress Report, September 1969, p. 7.

22. *Reports and Documentation*, op. cit., p. 378.

23. *Recommendations for Diocesan Ecumenical Commissions* (Westminster, May 1968), p. 10.

24. ibid., p. 17.

25. The very significant text of these 'Guiding Principles' is printed in full, with a commentary from the R.C. side, in S.P.C.U. Information Service, no. 5, June 1968, pp. 12–20 and 22–5.

26. Owen Chadwick in *Anglican Initiatives in Christian Unity*, ed. E. G. W. Bill (London, 1967), p. 76.

27. S.P.C.U. Information Service, no. 4, March 1968, p. 17.

28. *The Tablet*, 2 May 1970, pp. 436 and 437.

29. ibid., 30 May 1970, pp. 515 f.

30. ibid., pp. 518 f.

31. Quoted J. C. Dickenson in *Infallibility in the Church*, ed. M. D. Goulder (London, 1969), p. 54.

32. R. W. Southern, *The Making of the Middle Ages* (London, 1953), pp. 142 f.

33. ibid., p. 136.

34. 'Rome and Renewal', in *New Directions*, Vol. I, no. 4, Winter 1969, p. 11.

35. Bernard Lambert, *Ecumenism* (English translation, London, 1967), p. 212.

36. ibid., pp. 247 ff.

37. ibid., p. 265.

38. ibid., p. 291.

References

39. ibid., p. 315.

40. ibid., pp. 495 f.

41. Harold E. Fey, *The Ecumenical Advance*, op. cit., pp. 420 f.

42. Maurice Villain in *Ecumenical Dialogue in Europe* (London, 1968), introduced by Patrick C. Rodger, p. 23. This study includes a full text of the theses.

43. *De Ecclesia*, op. cit., VIII, ch. 62.

44. A. M. Farrer in *Infallibility in the Church*, op. cit., p. 23.

45. Robert Murray, ibid., pp. 40 f.

46. Quoted in *The Tablet*, 7 March 1970.

47. Quoted, S.P.C.U. News Letter, 1967/3, pp. 12 f.

48. Timothy Ware, *The Orthodox Church*, op. cit., p. 315.

49. ibid., p. 318.

50. ibid.

51. These quotations are from an article on the modern Orthodox view of Economy by Francis J. Thomson in the *Journal of Theological Studies*, Vol. XVI, Part 2, October 1965, pp. 368–420. The article makes it clear that Orthodox theologians of the past century have not agreed on the meaning or working of Economy, but that for all that the idea itself exists in and is important to Orthodox theology.

52. *The Lambeth Conference of 1948* (S.P.C.K.), p. 70, n. i.

53. *Sobornost*, Series 6, no. 2, Winter 1971, p. 77.

54. Charles Malik in *The Witness of the Oriental Orthodox Churches* by Bishop Karikan Sarkissian (Beirut, Lebanon, 1968), p. 9.

55. ibid., p. 12.

9. The Grassroots: Inertia and Impatience

1. *I.D.O.C.* (*International Documentation of the Contemporary Church*), North American edition, 23 May 1970, pp. 67–81. 'The National Council of Churches and the Contemporary Ecumenical Movement', by Joseph V. Gallagher.

2. *Agenda for the Churches, A Report on the P.N.D. Programme* by Kenneth Sansbury, Robert Latham and Pauline Webb (1968), pp. 15 f.

3. ibid., pp. 12, 56, 57.

4. ibid., pp. 5, 54, 55.

5. ibid., pp. 22, 23, 60, 61, 25.

6. ibid., p. 25.

7. *Ecumenical Review*, Vol. XXII, no. 3, July 1970, p. 273.

8. *Intercommunion, A Scottish Episcopalian Approach* (1969), p. 37.

References

9. *Agenda for the Churches*, op. cit., p. 51.

10. Rita Mukerjee, 'The Church in the Ruhr of India', in *Changing Frontiers in the Mission of the Church*, ed. Barry Till (London, 1965), p. 30.

11. ibid., p. 31.

12. Sam Ijioma, 'New Dimensions of Christian Service in Port Harcourt', ibid., pp. 22 f.

13. *International Review of Mission*, Vol. LX, no. 238, April 1971, p. 165.

14. M. M. Thomas. 'The Christian Institute, Bangalore', Till, op. cit., pp. 64–6.

15. Betty Durham, 'Initiative, Planning and Co-operation in Literature', ibid., pp. 85 f.

16. Richard Holloway, 'The Gorbals Group – An Experiment in Service', ibid., p. 40.

17. ibid., p. 42.

18. Quoted, R. M. C. Jeffery, *Areas of Ecumenical Experiment* (British Council of Churches, 1968), p. 8.

19. ibid., p. 10.

20. R. M. C. Jeffery, *Ecumenical Experiments, A Handbook* (B.C.C., 1970), p. 39.

21. Jeffery, *Areas of Ecumenical Experiment*, op. cit., p. 10.

22. Jeffery, *Ecumenical Experiments*, op. cit., pp. 32 f.

23. ibid., p. 38.

24. ibid., p. 37.

25. *Unity Begins at Home*, Report of the Faith and Order Conference of the B.C.C. at Nottingham, 1964 (S.C.M.), p. 79.

26. Jeffery, *Ecumenical Experiments*, op. cit., p. 55.

27. Quoted ibid., p. 46.

28. ibid., p. 62.

29. D. H. R. Jones, *Planning for Mission in New Towns* (St George's House, Windsor Castle), para. 221.

30. ibid., para. 85.

31. ibid., para. 118.

32. ibid., para. 129.

33. ibid., para. 270.

34. Rudiger Reitz, *The Church in Experiment* (Abingdon Press, Nashville, 1969), p. 115.

35. Quoted, ibid., 67.

36. Quoted, *Ecumenical Experiments*, op. cit., p. 52.

37. Till, *Changing Frontiers*, op. cit., p. 41.

38. *Intercommunion Today* (Church Information Office, London, 1968), p. 114.

39. Article in *The Way*, April 1969, p. 115.

40. *Agenda for the Churches*, op. cit., p. 41 and pp. 31 f.

References

41. Quoted, *Intercommunion, A Scottish Episcopalian Approach*, op. cit., p. 33.

42. *The Lambeth Conference, 1968* (S.P.C.K.), Resolution 47, p. 42.

43. *Intercommunion, A Scottish Episcopalian Approach*, op. cit., p. 25.

44. *Lambeth Conference, 1968*, op. cit., p. 41.

45. *Christian Unity – A Layman's Challenge, and the Replies* (The Times, 1967), pp. 7–8.

46. Quoted in *Pentecost 1968: Intercommunion in Paris* by Claudette Marquet (A Monthly Letter about Evangelism, W.C.C./D.W.M.E., No. 5/6, May/June 1970), p. 2.

47. ibid., pp. 7–9.

48. The Archbishop of Canterbury in an address to a clergy conference, quoted *Ecumenical Experiments*, op. cit., p. 119.

49. *New Directions*, New Series, Vol. 1, no. 4, Winter 1969, pp. 5 f.

50. *Uppsala Report*, p. 12, para. 3.

51. Rudiger Reitz, 'The Underground Church in Germany' in *I.D.O.C.*, op. cit., p. 49.

52. ibid., p. 63.

53. *New Directions*, op. cit., p. 26.

54. ibid., p. 21.

55. *Observer*, 6 September 1970, p. 17.

56. Rudiger Reitz, Article in *I.D.O.C.*, op. cit., p. 46.

Epilogue

1. Faith and Order Commission, Louvain, August 1961.

2. Betty Thompson, 'State of the Union: American Protestantism and C.O.C.U.', *Frontier*, February 1971, p. 47.

3. *The Tablet*, Vol. 225, no. 6838, 26 June 1971, pp. 629 f.

4. Hans Küng, *Infallible?* (English translation, London, 1971), pp. 47 ff.

5. ibid., p. 153.

6. For a sympathetic but critical review of the book, see John Coventry, s.j., in *One in Christ*, 1971–4, pp. 349–57.

7. *The Tablet*, Vol. 224, no. 6791, 22 July 1970, p. 726.

8. ibid., Vol. 224, no. 6794, 15 August 1971, p. 782.

Suggestions for Further Reading

THE World Council of Churches is preparing a Bibliography of the Ecumenical Movement. It is said that it will run to three volumes and list some 270,000 printed works, leaving out the vast mass of duplicated material which is also important. The books suggested below are not a full, or even a partial bibliography. They represent an attempt to provide a genuine further reading list. Only books available in English have been included and on the whole recent books have been chosen except where a book is a 'classic' which cannot be neglected. The place of publication is London, unless otherwise specified.

General Books on the Ecumenical Movement

The standard work is the two-volume *History of the Ecumenical Movement,* Vol. I, ed. Ruth Rouse and Stephen Neill, 1517–1948 (1954), Vol. II, ed. Harold E. Fey, *The Ecumenical Advance, 1948–1968* (1970). Both these volumes, especially the second, suffer from the fact that they concentrate almost exclusively on the history of the World Council of Churches and its forerunners; the second makes no mention of current unity negotiations. The same is true of Norman Goodall, *The Ecumenical Movement* (2nd edn 1964). Other general books include: Bernard Lambert, *Ecumenism* (English tr. 1966); John Lawrence, *The Hard Facts of Unity* (1961); Eric Mascall, *The Recovery of Unity* (New York, 1958); Stephen Neill, *The Church and Christian Union* (1968); Leslie Newbigin, *The Household of God* (1964); George Tavard, *Two Centuries of Ecumenism* (English tr. New York, 1960); Oliver Tomkins, *A Time for Unity* (1964); W. A. Visser 't Hooft, *The Pressure of our Common Calling* (New York, 1959). A. C. Headlam, *The Doctrine of the Church and Christian Re-union* (1920), is a classic Anglican statement of the time. The essential documents up to 1957 will be found in G. K. A. Bell, ed., *Documents on*

Christian Unity (4 vols., 1920–57). For authoritative short articles on an immense variety of subjects and themes *The Oxford Dictionary of the Christian Church* (ed. F. L. Cross, revised edn 1963) is invaluable.

Chapter 1. The Ecumenical Movement: Causes and Attitudes

For statistical information on the churches, see successive editions of *The World Christian Handbook* (World Dominion Press). For the sociological approach to Christianity and to the ecumenical movement, see Bryan Wilson, *Sects and Society* (1961), *Religion in Secular Society* (1966) and *Religious Sects: A Sociological Study* (1970). For a historical follow-up to this approach: Robert Currie, *Methodism Divided: A Study in the Sociology of Ecumenicalism* (1968). For sociology from within the churches, see: M. Hill and David Martin, eds., *A Sociological Yearbook of Religion in Britain* (4 vols., 1968–71), and David Martin, *A Sociology of English Religion* (1967); also Kenneth Slack, *British Churches Today* (1970). For secularization and the churches' response to it, see in general the works of Dietrich Bonhoeffer, and Eberhard Bethge, *Dietrich Bonhoeffer* (English tr. 1970). See also: Harvey Cox, *The Secular City* (New York, 1965); Martin Jarrett-Kerr, *The Secular Promise* (1964); David Martin, *The Religious and the Secular* (1969); J. A. T. Robinson, *Honest to God* (1963); E. R. Wickam, *Church and People in an Industrial City* (1957). For responses to the ecumenical movement, see: *Christian Unity, A Layman's Challenge and the Replies* (The Times, 1967); Ian Henderson, *Power without Glory* (1967); Kenneth Sansbury, ed., and others, *Agenda for the Churches* (1968); and Oliver Tomkins, *The Wholeness of the Church* (1949).

Chapter 2. The Church United: The First Four Centuries

For the idea of the church in the New Testament, see: Hans Conzelmann, *An Outline of the Theology of the New Testament* (English tr. 1969); E. Käsemann, *The Testament of Jesus* (English tr. 1968), which makes a special study of John xvii; John Knox, *The Early Church and the Coming Great Church*

(1957); Emile Mersch, *The Whole Christ* (English tr. 1949); Paul Minear, *Images of the Church in the New Testament* (1961); Alan Richardson, *An Introduction to the Theology of the New Testament* (1958); E. Schlink, *The Coming Christ and the Coming Church* (English tr. 1968); B. H. Streeter, *The Primitive Church* (1929); L. S. Thornton, *The Common Life in the Body of Christ* (3rd edn 1950). For the general history of the early church, see: Henry Chadwick, *The Early Church* (Vol. I of the Pelican History of the Church, 1967), and Hans Lietzmann, *The Beginnings of the Christian Church, The Founding of the Church Universal, From Constantine to Julian, The Era of the Church Fathers* (English tr. 1937–51). Documents can be found in J. B. Lightfoot, *The Apostolic Fathers* (1st edn 1891 and many times reprinted); J. Stevenson, *A New Eusebius* (1957), and *Creeds, Councils and Controversies* (1966). Books which deal further with the subjects referred to include: on schism and its results: S. L. Greenslade, *Schism in the Early Church* (1964), and W. H. C. Frend, *Martyrdom and Persecution in the Early Church* (1965) and *The Donatist Church* (1952); on tradition and its development: H. E. W. Turner, *The Pattern of Christian Truth* (1954), and G. L. Prestige, *Father and Heretics* (1938), especially the introductory essay on tradition; on the ministry: H. B. Swete, ed., *Essays on the Early History of the Church and Ministry* (1918), especially the essay by C. H. Turner; W. Telfer, *The Office of a Bishop* (1962); and the essays on the New Testament and Early Church in K. M. Carey, ed., *The Historic Episcopate* (1954); on Cyprian: M. Benevot's annotated translation of Cyprian in *Ancient Christian Writers* (Vol. 25, 1957) and E. W. Benson, *Cyprian* (1897); on the creeds, J. N. D. Kelly, *Early Christian Creeds* (1950); on the rise of the papacy, T. G. Jalland, *The Church and the Papacy* (1944), and B. J. Kidd, *The Roman Primacy to A.D. 461* (1936).

Chapter 3. The Church Divided: The Last Fifteen Centuries

For the history and characteristics of the various churches see the Pelican religious series which includes Sebastian Bullough, *Roman Catholicism* (1963); Timothy Ware, *The Orthodox*

Church (1963); S. C. Neill, *Anglicanism* (1965); and Rupert E. Davies, *Methodism* (1963). For histories of the various stages of Christian division see: on the early schisms: K. Sarkissian, *The Council of Chalcedon and the Armenian Church* (1965); L. W. Brown, *The Indian Christians of St Thomas* (Cambridge, 1956); H. St L. B. Moss, *The Birth of the Middle Ages, 395–814* (1935); and Christopher Dawson, *The Making of Europe* (1932); on the Eastern Schism, see the articles referred to by F. Dvornik in the *Cambridge Mediaeval History*, Vol. IV, part I (1966); S. Runciman, *The Eastern Schism* (1955), *The Fall of Constantinople* (1965) and *The Great Church in Captivity* (1968); also Norman H. Baynes and H. St L. B. Moss, eds., *Byzantium* (1953): on the unity of the western medieval church, see W. Ullmann, *Mediaeval Papalism* (1949), and R. W. Southern, *Western Society and the Church in the Middle Ages* (Pelican History of the Church, Vol. 2, 1970). On the Reformation, two excellent introductory studies are Owen Chadwick, *The Reformation* (Pelican History of the Church, Vol. 3, 1968), and N. Sykes, *The Crisis of the Reformation* (2nd edn 1946). See also the first two volumes of the *New Cambridge Modern History*. On Luther, see R. Bainton, *Here I Stand* (1951); G. Rupp, *The Righteousness of God* (1953) and *Luther's Progress to the Diet of Worms* (1951); on Calvin, R. N. Carew Hunt, *Calvin* (1933), and J. T. McNeill, *The History and Character of Calvinism* (New York, 1954). For a modern ecumenical approach to divisive Reformation doctrines see Küng, Barth, Cullmann and others in *Christianity Divided* (1962). For the Reformation in England: A. G. Dickens, *The English Reformation* (1964); and for a moderate Roman Catholic analysis Philip Hughes, *The Reformation in England* (3 vols., 1954). For the churches which sprang from the English Reformation, see E. B. Castle, *Approach to Quakerism* (1961); H. Davies, *The English Free Churches* (2nd edn 1963); Harold Loukes, *The Quaker Contribution* (1965); E. A. Payne, *The Baptist Union* (1959); Eric Routley, *The Story of Congregationalism* (1961). For the Evangelical Awakening and the problem it presented to the Church of England, see Charles Smyth, *Simeon and Church Order* (Cambridge, 1940) and for the divisions of Methodism see Robert Currie, *Methodism Divided* (1968). For the history of the church in the seventeenth, eighteenth and nineteenth centuries, see the Pelican History of the Church, Vols. 4 and 5: G. R. Cragg, *The Church and the Age of Reason, 1648–1789* (revised edn 1970), and Alec R. Vidler, *The Church in an Age of Revolution* (revised edn 1971). For the churches in America: Willard L. Sperry, *Religion in America* (Cambridge, 1945); Emory S. Bucke, ed., *The History of American Methodism* (3 vols., New York, 1964); Douglas Horton, *The United Church of Christ* (New York, 1962); Robert G. Torbet, *A History of the Baptists* (Philadelphia, 1955). On the sects in America, see Elmer T. Clark, *The Small Sects in America* (Nashville, Tennessee, 1937). On Pentecostalism there is now a fairly substantial literature, but the definitive book will undoubtedly be Walter J. Hollenweger's forthcoming *The Pentecostals* (London, 1972). For the spreading of the divisions of the western churches, see the Pelican History of the Church, Vol. 6, Stephen Neill, *A History of Christian Missions* (1964).

Chapter 4. The Stirrings of Conscience

In general see the first four chapters of Rouse and Neill's *History*. For the growth of the idea of toleration, W. K. Jordan, *The Development of Religious Toleration in England* (3 vols., 1932–40). For the breakdown of the idea of uniformity and the move to toleration, Geoffrey F. Nuttall and Owen Chadwick, eds., *From Uniformity to Unity* (1962). For works on ecumenical pioneers: J. Minton Batten, *John Dury, Advocate of Christian Reunion* (Chicago, 1944), and Norman Sykes, *Daniel Ernst Jablonski and the Church of England* (1950). For the ecumenical stance of the Church of England: Norman Sykes, *The Church of England and Non-episcopal Churches in the Sixteenth and Seventeenth Centuries* (Theology Occasional Paper, No. 11, 1948) and *Old Priest and New Presbyter* (Cambridge, 1956), and Barry Till, essay in K. M. Carey, ed., *The Historic Episcopate* (1954).

Chapter 5. The Modern Ecumenical Movement

The period is covered at length in the remaining chapters of Rouse and Neill's *History*. For the general background of church history: Alec R. Vidler, *The Church in an Age of*

Revolution, and Owen Chadwick, *The Victorian Church* (2 vols., 1966 and 1970). For the ecumenical approach of the Oxford Movement, H. R. T. Brandreth, *The Oecumenical Ideals of the Oxford Movement* (1947), and for the general Anglican approach to other churches in this and other periods, E. G. W. Bill, ed., *Anglican Initiatives in Christian Unity* (1967). The various meetings of the International Missionary Council, Faith and Order and Life and Work all produced reports and in general started the voluminous publication programme which is associated with the work of the W.C.C. Typical, and very important at the time, were the *C.O.P.E.C. Commission Reports* (12 vols., 1924). Stephen Neill's *Men of Unity* (1960) is an excellent introduction to the ecumenical movement through short sketches of its leaders at this time and until the founding of the W.C.C. Other accounts can be gleaned from the following biographies: G. K. A. Bell, *Randall Davidson* (2nd edn 1938); Alexander C. Zabriskie, *Bishop Brent, Crusader for Christian Unity* (Philadelphia, 1948); Monica Sinclair, *William Paton* (1949) (see also William Paton, *Pathways to Christian Unity – A Free Church View* (1919)); Kathleen Bliss, *J. H. Oldham* (forthcoming); J. G. Lockhart, *Cosmo Gordon Lang* (1949); Ronald Jasper, *Arthur Cayley Headlam* (1960); F. A. Iremonger, *William Temple* (1948); N. Karlstrom, ed., *Nathan Söderblom* (Stockholm, 1931); Ronald Jasper, *George Bell, Bishop of Chichester* (1969). For plans for union during this period: Stephen Neill, *Towards a United Church, 1913–1947* (1947) and *Towards Church Union, 1937–1952* (1952); also J. R. Fleming, *The Story of Church Union in Scotland* (1929), and George C. Pigeon, *The United Church of Canada, The Story of Union* (Toronto, 1950). For the Old Catholic Churches, see C. B. Moss, *The Old Catholic Movement* (1948), and for the Philippine Independent Church, L. B. Whittemore, *Struggle for Freedom* (Greenwich, Conn., 1961). For the part played by Asians in the development of the ecumenical movement, Hans-Ruedi Weber, *Asia and the Ecumenical Movement, 1895–1961* (1966).

Chapter 6. The World Council of Churches

The literature produced by and about the W.C.C. is immense. For a full bibliography, see Harold E. Fey, ed., *The Ecumenical Advance, 1948–1968* (1960). This book is to all intents and purposes a history of the W.C.C. and some of its ancillary movements. Unfortunately it partakes to a marked degree of the character of much W.C.C. literature, that is it seems to be the W.C.C. talking to itself about itself. For this point, made with some force, see Paul Ramsey, *Who Speaks for the Church?* (Nashville, Tenn., 1967). For the developing process of ecumenical thought see successive numbers of the *Ecumenical Review* and of the *International Review of Missions* (both W.C.C., Geneva). The best running commentary on the growth and work of the Council is to be found in the reports of the various major conferences. Of these the most important are: W. A. Visser 't Hooft, ed., *The First Assembly of the World Council of Churches, 1948* (1949); *Man's Disorder and God's Design*, The Amsterdam Assembly Series (4 vols., New York, 1949); *The First Six Years, 1948–54* (The Report of the Central Committee to the Evanston Assembly, Geneva, 1954); *The Evanston Report, The Second Assembly of the W.C.C.* (Geneva, 1954); John Marsh, *The Significance of Evanston* (1954); *Evanston to New Delhi, 1954–61* (The Report of the Central Committee, Geneva, 1961); *The New Delhi Report, 1961* (1962); Kenneth Slack, *Despatch from New Delhi* (1962); *New Delhi to Uppsala, 1961–8* (Geneva, 1968); Norman Goodall, ed., *The Uppsala Report, 1968* (Geneva, 1968); Kenneth Slack, *Uppsala Report* (1968). On the Faith and Order movement: Oliver Tomkins, ed., *The Third World Conference on Faith and Order held at Lund ... 1952* (1953); Patrick Rodger and Lukas Vischer, eds., *The Fourth World Conference on Faith and Order, Montreal, 1963* (1964); Paul Minear, ed., *The Nature of the Unity We Seek* (St Louis, 1958). On the I.M.C.: Norman Goodall, ed., *Missions under the Cross. Addresses Delivered at ... Willingen ... 1952* (1953); Ronald Orchard, ed., *The Ghana Assembly of the I.M.C. ... 1958* (1958); Robert Latham, *God for All Men* (1964): Ronald Orchard, ed., *Witness in Six Continents, Records of the Meetings ... Held in Mexico City ... 1963* (1964). On inter-church aid: *Inter-Church*

Aid Year Books and Reports (Geneva, annually); *In the Service of Mankind. A Manual of Inter-Church Aid* (Geneva, 1963); Harold E. Fey, *Co-operation in Compassion. The Story of Church World Service* (New York, 1966). On 'Life and Work': *World Conference on Church and Society, Geneva ... 1966* (Geneva, 1967). Important books arising out of W.C.C. studies include: Paul Abrecht, *The Churches and Rapid Social Change* (1961); Egbert de Vries, *Man in Rapid Social Change* (1961); Colin W. Williams, *Where in the World?* (New York, 1963), and *What in the World?* (New York, 1964). For a W.C.C. comment on the African churches: Victor Hayward, ed., *African Independent Church Movements* (1963).

Chapter 7. Union Negotiations

For the Church of South India: Bengt Sundkler, *The Church of South India* (revised edn 1965): Mark Gibbard, *Unity is not Enough* (1965); Michael Hollis, *The Significance of South India* (1966) is a defence of – and plea for – the C.S.I. open-ended approach to union: as are Leslie Newbigin, *The Re-union of the Church, A Defence of the South India Scheme* (revised edn (1960), and *A South India Diary* (1951). The literature about various schemes currently being negotiated is not easy to come by – though see Robert Brown and David H. Scott, eds., *The Challenge to Reunion* (New York, 1963). In the nature of things it is subject to frequent changes and re-issues as the negotiations progress. It is best obtained by direct contact with the negotiating bodies. Various stages or statements of different schemes are referred to in the course of Chapter 7. There is a valuable series of studies of union negotiations – in progress, abortive or consummated – in Nils Ehrenstrom and Walter G. Muelder, eds., *Institutionalism and Church Unity* (1963). The title shows the general approach, which emphasizes the 'non-theological factors'. The W.C.C. produces a Survey every two years in the form of a Faith and Order Paper. These are as follows: *Survey of Church Union Negotiations* (Geneva, 1955), *1957–59* (Geneva, 1960), *1959–61* (Geneva, 1962), *1961–63* (Geneva, 1964), *1963–65* (Geneva, 1966), *1965–67* (Geneva, 1968), *1967–69* (Geneva, 1970). For the approach of the various churches to unity the following are representative: *Baptists and Unity*

(1967); C. O. Buchanan and others, *Growing into Union* (1970); William R. Estep, *Baptists and Christian Unity* (Nashville, 1967); Michael Hollis, *Mission, Unity and Truth: A Study of Confessional Families and the Churches in Asia* (1967); J. Marcellus Kik, *Ecumenism and the Evangelical* (Philadelphia, 1958); David Paton, *Anglicans and Unity* (1962); Erik Routley, *Congregationalists and Unity* (1962); Kenneth Sansbury, *Mission, Unity and Concord: Anglican Faith in Ecumenical Setting* (1967); *World Confessionalism and the Ecumenical Movement*, four articles in *Lutheran World*, January 1963.

Chapter 8. The Roman Catholic Church and the Orthodox Churches

On Vatican II: there is a large literature, both of diaries of the sessions and of texts and commentary on documents. The following are the most useful: Douglas Horton, *Vatican Diary. A Protestant Observes ... Vatican II* (4 vols,. Philadelphia, 1966); Hans Küng, *The Council and Reunion* (English tr. 1961), and *The Living Church: Reflections of the Second Vatican Council* (English tr. 1963); Bernard Pawley, ed., *The Second Vatican Council; Studies by Eight Anglican Observers* (1967); Xavier Rynne, *Letters from Vatican City* (4 vols., 1963–6); Edmund Schlink, *After the Council: The Meaning of Vatican II for Protestantism and the Ecumenical Dialogue* (English tr. Philadelphia, 1968); Christopher Butler, *The Theology of Vatican II* (1967); Bernard Leeming, *The Vatican Council and Christian Unity: A Commentary on the Decree on Ecumenism* (English tr. 1966); Cardinal Jaeger Lorenz, *A Stand on Ecumenism: The Council's Decree* (English tr. Dublin, 1965); Kevin McNamara, ed., *Vatican II: The Constitution on the Church* (1968); Edward H. Peters, ed., *De Ecclesia* (1967); Herbert Vorgrimler, ed., *Commentary on the Documents of Vatican II* (English tr. 3 vols., 1967–9). For up-to-date information about the various 'dialogues' and working parties in which the R.C.C. is involved and for other texts and documents the best source is the English edition of the *Information Service* produced by the Secretariat for Promoting Christian Unity (Via dell'Erba 1, Rome, Italy). On relations between the R.C.C. and the W.C.C. *The Ecumenical Advance* (op. cit., ed. Harold

E. Fey) has an excellent chapter by Lukas Vischer. For the
debate on 'liberal theology' within the R.C.C. which is essential
to the state of ecumenical relations between the R.C.C. and the
rest of Christendom, the following provide the best insights:
Gregory Baum, *The Quest for Christian Unity* (1963); Augustine, Cardinal Bea, *The Unity of Christians* (1963), *The Way
to Unity after the Council* (1967) and *Ecumenism in Focus*
(1969); Yves Congar, *Divided Christendom, A Catholic Study*
(English tr. 1939), and *Dialogue between Christians* (Dublin,
1966); Geoffrey Curtis, *Paul Couturier and Unity in Christ*
(1964); M. G. Goulder, ed., *Infallibility in the Church* (1968);
Hans Küng. *The Church* (1967) and *Infallible?* (English tr.
1971); Bernard Lambert, *Ecumenism: Theology and History*
(English tr. 1967); Bernard Leeming, *The Church and the
Churches* (1960); for a view from America, Samuel H. Miller
and G. Ernest Wright, eds., *Ecumenical Dialogue at Harvard*
(Cambridge, Mass., 1964); George Tavard, *The Church To-
morrow* (1965); Maurice Villain, *Unity; A History and Some
Reflections* (English tr. 1963), and *Ecumenical Dialogue in
Europe* (English tr. 1966); J. G. Willebrands, ed., *Problems
before Unity* (Baltimore, 1962). For Orthodoxy: Michael
Bordeaux, *Religious Ferment in Russia* (1968), and *Faith on
Trial in Russia* (1971); V. T. Istavridis, *Orthodoxy and Angli-
canism* (English tr. 1966); Vladimir Lossky, *The Mystical
Theology of the Eastern Church* (English tr. 1957); Maximos
IV Sayegh, ed., *The Eastern Churches and Catholic Unity*
(English tr. Edinburgh, 1963); Phillip Sherrard, *The Greek
East and Latin West* (1959); Methodios Souyas, *Orthodoxy,
Roman Catholicism and Anglicanism* (forthcoming, Oxford,
1972); Nikita Struve, *Christians in Contemporary Russia* (1966);
Timothy Ware, *The Orthodox Church* (Harmondsworth, 1963);
Nicolas Zernov, *Orthodox Encounter: The Christian East and
the Ecumenical Movement* (1961). A running Anglican–Ortho-
dox dialogue is maintained in the journal of the Fellowship
of St Alban and St Sergius, *Sobornost'* (52 Ladbroke Grove,
London, W11). For the Oriental Orthodox Churches:
Shenouda Hanna, *What are the Copts?* (Cairo, 1958); C-P.
Mathew and M. M. Thomas, *The Indian Churches of St
Thomas* (New Delhi, 1967); Bishop Karikan Sarkissian, *The
Witness of the Oriental Orthodox Churches* (Beirut, Lebanon,
1968).

Chapter 9. The Grassroots: Inertia and Impatience

On national councils of churches: K. Baago, *A History of the National Christian Council of India, 1914–1964* (Nagpur, 1965); Samuel McCrea Cavert, *American Churches in the Ecumenical Movement, 1900–1968* (New York, 1968); Forrest L. Knapp, *Church Co-operation: Deadend Street or Highway to Unity?* (New York, 1966); *Local Councils of Churches Today* (B.C.C., 1971); Ross W. Sanderson, *Church Co-operation in the United States* (Hartford, Conn., 1960); Kenneth Slack, *Growing Together Locally* (B.C.C., 1958); Enrique S. Sobrepena, *That They May Be One, A Brief Account of the United Church Movement in the Philippines* (Manila, 1964); *Unity Begins at Home, A Report from the First British Conference on Faith and Order, Nottingham, 1964* (1964). For ecumenical approaches to the mission of the church throughout the world: R. P. Beaver, *Ecumenical Beginnings in Protestant World Mission* (New York, 1962); Robert T. Handy, *We Witness Together; A History of Co-operative Home Missions* (New York, 1956); Stephen Neill, *The Unfinished Task* (1957); D. T. Niles, *Upon the Earth: the Mission of God and the Missionary Enterprise of the Churches* (1962); Ronald Orchard, *Out of Every Nation* (1959); Bengt Sundkler, *The World of Mission* (1965); Barry Till, *Changing Frontiers in the Mission of the Church* (1965). Many of the descriptions of local ecumenical experiment are in magazine articles or unpublished reports; the following will be found relevant: Trevor Beeson, ed., *Partnership in Ministry* (1964; this is a series of studies in team ministry); Barrie Hinksman, *Mission and Ministry* (unpublished, c/o the author, Birmingham, 1970); Fred Hoskins, *Servants of the Eternal Christ; Local Ecumenicity* (New York, 1962); R. M. C. Jeffery, *Areas of Ecumenical Experiment* (B.C.C., 1968), *Ecumenical Experiments: A Handbook* (B.C.C., 1971), and *Case Studies in Unity* (forthcoming, 1972); D. H. R. Jones, *Planning for Mission* (unpublished, obtainable from the author, The Pastoral Centre, High Street, Dawley, Telford, Shropshire); Bruce Kenrick, *Come Out the Wilderness* (1963; this is a modern Christian classic); Leslie Paul, *The Deployment and Payment of the Clergy* (1964; Church of England, but shows the appalling wastefulness and inefficiency of an unreformed and divided church); Rudiger Reitz, *The Church in Experiment* (Nashville, 1969); Kenneth Sansbury, ed., and others, *Agenda for the Churches* (1968). Radical reactions to the divisions, ineffectiveness and irrelevance of the contemporary churches are again largely to be found in magazine articles such as those quoted in the text. But see: P. R. Clifford, *Now is the Time* (1970); R. G. Jones and A. J. Wesson, *Towards a Radical Church* (1970); Stephen C. Rose, *The Grassroots Church: A Manifesto for Protestant Renewal* (New York, 1966); Helmut Thielicke, *The Trouble with the Church: A Call for Renewal* (New York, 1965); Gibson Winter, *The Suburban Captivity of the Churches* (New York, 1961). Out of this situation has also arisen the radical theological movement which has centred on what have come to be known as the 'Honest to God' and 'Death of God' debates.

Index

Index

Index

MORE ABOUT PENGUINS
AND PELICANS

Penguinews, which appears every month, contains details of all the new books issued by Penguins as they are published. From time to time it is supplemented by *Penguins in Print*, which is a complete list of all available books published by Penguins. (There are well over three thousand of these.)

A specimen copy of *Penguinews* will be sent to you free on request, and you can become a subscriber for the price of the postage. For a year's issues (including the complete lists) please send 30p if you live in the United Kingdom, or 60p if you live elsewhere. Just write to Dept EP, Penguin Books Ltd, Harmondsworth, Middlesex, enclosing a cheque or postal order, and your name will be added to the mailing list.

Note: *Penguinews* and *Penguins in Print* are not available in the U.S.A. or Canada

The Pelican Guide to Modern Theology

Theology today can mean anything from reverence for the living God to the proposition that God is dead. How has the 'science of thinking about God' reached this dilemma?

The Pelican Guide to Modern Theology, which is under the general editorship of Professor R. F. C. Hanson, discusses the outlook of modern Christian thinkers and their attitude to the work of past theologians. Its three volumes, which examine the very foundations of Christianity in such questions as 'What and how is God?', cover the philosophy of religion, historical theology, and the study of the Bible: they help to explain why, even in these secular days, some people find theology the most attractive, exacting, and satisfying intellectual pursuit of all.

Volume 1

SYSTEMATIC AND PHILOSOPHICAL THEOLOGY
William Nicholls

Volume 2

HISTORICAL THEOLOGY
J. Daniélou, A. H. Couratin and John Kent

Volume 3

BIBLICAL CRITICISM
Robert Davidson and A. R. C. Leaney

The Pelican History of the Church

1. THE EARLY CHURCH
Henry Chadwick

The story of the early Christian church from the death of
Christ to the Papacy of Gregory the Great. Professor Henry
Chadwick makes use of the latest research to explain the
astonishing expansion of Christianity throughout the Roman
Empire.

2. WESTERN SOCIETY AND THE CHURCH IN THE MIDDLE AGES
R. W. Southern

In the period between the eighth and the sixteenth centuries
the Church and State were more nearly one than ever before
or after. In this new book Professor Southern discusses how
this was achieved and what stresses it caused.

3. THE REFORMATION
Owen Chadwick

In this volume Professor Owen Chadwick deals with the forma-
tive work of Erasmus, Luther, Zwingli, Calvin, with the
special circumstances of the English Reformation, and with
the Counter-Reformation.

4. THE CHURCH AND THE AGE OF REASON
G. R. Cragg

This span in the history of the Christian church stretches from
the age of religious and civil strife before the middle of the
seventeenth century to the age of industrialism and repub-
licanism which followed the French Revolution.

5. THE CHURCH IN AN AGE OF REVOLUTION
Alec R. Vidler

'A most readable and provocative volume and a notable addition to this promising and distinguished series' – *Guardian*

6. A HISTORY OF CHRISTIAN MISSIONS
Stephen Neill

This volume of *The Pelican History of the Church* represents
the first attempt in English to provide a readable history of
the worldwide expansion of all the Christian denominations –
Roman Catholic, Orthodox, Anglican, and Protestant.